"COME, BLACKROBE"

De Smet and the Indian Tragedy

Peter John De Smet, as painted in 1864 by George C. Eichbaum. (Saint Louis University)

"COME, BLACKROBE"

*De Smet and the
Indian Tragedy*

By John J. Killoren, S.J.

University of Oklahoma Press
Norman and London

Published with the assistance of the National Endowment for the Humanities, a federal agency which supports the study of such fields as history, philosophy, literature, and language.

Library of Congress Cataloging-in-Publication Data

Killoren, John J.
    Come, Blackrobe : De Smet and the Indian tragedy / by John J. Killoren. — 1st ed.
        p.   cm.
    Includes bibliographical references (p. 403) and index.
    ISBN 0-8061-2615-9 (alk. paper)
    1. Indians of North America — West (U.S.) — Missions.   2. Indians of North America — Government relations.   3. Smet, Pierre-Jean de, 1801–1873.   4. Missionaries — West   (U.S.) — Biography.   5. Jesuits — West (U.S.) — Biography.   I. Title.
    E78.W5K55   1994
    978'.00497 — dc20   93-21108
                                                                      CIP

Text design by Cathy Carney Imboden.

2   3   4   5   6   7   8   9   10

To the Memory of
William and Julia Hadel
A Grateful Tribute

Contents

Illustrations

Maps

"The Trail of Father De Smet"

Interest in De Smet has been manifest throughout the twentieth century. As early as 1905, Hiram Chittenden and Alfred Richardson, functioning as editors, prepared a four-volume set of De Smet's letters. As recently as 1992 a doctoral dissertation at Washington State University reported on "Peter John De Smet, S.J.: Fundraiser and Promoter of Missions."

The varied activities of De Smet have served as subjects for theses, for example, at the University of Colorado in 1950 (on De Smet's services to the United States government); at Notre Dame University in 1933 (on literary aspects of De Smet's writings); and at St. Louis University in 1934 (on De Smet as ambassador to the Indians). Articles in historical journals have stressed other functions performed by De Smet: Merrill Mattes commented in 1949 on De Smet's contributions to western history as a cartographer; Reuben Thwaites, in 1904, and Larry Thompson, in 1985, called attention to De Smet's field experiences as a western explorer following the then-still-fresh footprints of Lewis and Clark.

In 1964 De Smet was the subject of a popular biography written by John Terrell, and in 1940, of a historical novel by Helene Magaret. Back at the start of the century, Eugene Laveille, a French Jesuit, reported De Smet's life in the hagiographic fashion of the period; an English translation of this pious presentation was published in 1915. Due to the exceptional interest in De Smet, the Chittenden-Richardson collection of Desmetiana was reprinted in 1969, and Laveille's edifying account was reissued in 1981.

Such continued interest, as an indication of De Smet's historical status, had been foretold by Chittenden. Following considerable research, Chittenden in 1902 had published *The American Fur Trade of the Far West* and, in the following year, *History of Early Steamboat Navigation on the Missouri*. It was as a consequence of his previous study of western history that Chittenden determined to serve as an editor for De Smet's letters. Regarding De Smet's notable connection with the pioneer history of the West, Chittenden predicted, "Explorers of this attractive field are constantly running across the trail of Father De Smet, which interlaces the whole Northwest from St. Louis to the Straits of Juan de Fuca. Wherever encountered, it is a tempting trail to follow, for it is marked in all its course by episodes romantic and interesting and frequently of weighty importance."

The interest has indeed continued. On the theme of De Smet and the Indians of the Rocky Mountains, a historical exhibition entitled "Sacred Encounters" opened in 1993 in Bozeman, Montana, with scheduled showings through 1995 in other locations. And throughout recent years the Chautauqua Lectures, as presented in various midwestern states, have featured portrayals of De Smet.

As noted, various scholars have found De Smet and his activities a tempting trail to follow. Their published articles, however, have dealt with distinct episodes of De Smet's full life; neither these separate reports, nor the conglomerate of such limited treatments, have resulted in any updated, consolidated, and integral study of De Smet. In format the historical novel presents cause for an interesting narrative, but that narrative may shift from its factual foundation to romantic fiction. Writers of biographies in the Victorian era generally shared the bias of the hagiographers: preoccupied with edifying their readers, the hero and saint makers simply presumed that their subjects always acted from the most noble motives. And in the more recent popular biographies, directed to a superficial reading, the author may fail to supply any documentary references to support the interpretations and conclusions presented.

The special Indian–De Smet relationship has been reported by some scholars, but few have noted its supreme importance. It was indeed a unique relationship: the ready unity between a religious-minded people and their spiritual leader. Initiated rather spontaneously by an invitation from one of the western tribes, this relationship permeated all aspects of life and transcended cultural differences. As a consequence of the relationship, De Smet was identified simply as "Blackrobe."

Furthermore, the Indian–De Smet relationship extended beyond the normal spans of time and space. As a revered consultant, De Smet was in close contact with two successive generations of Indian leaders. Also, De Smet was not restricted to being a Sioux Blackrobe; his role as spiritual leader was acknowledged by all the tribes he encountered on the central and northern plains and in the northern Rockies.

Even more important, De Smet so functioned during decades of drastic changes that transformed the West. In 1840, on his initial round-trip across their lands, De Smet moved amid peoples still enjoying the golden age of their Buffalo culture; on the Missouri headwaters, he had cause to dream of joining with tribal leaders in fashioning an independent "Indian Empire." Within a quarter century opposite conditions prevailed. By the 1860s the more knowledgeable Indian leaders shared De Smet's awareness that their native economy was collapsing. These Indians endorsed Blackrobe's grim assessment: without the buffalo their impoverishment was so absolute that they no longer held control of their future. The Arapaho, for example, might survive—but only with their dependence shifted to government programs; the surviving Arapaho could no longer be "Buffalo People."

Thus the De Smet story moves beyond the dimensions of an ordinary biography. Consequent to the unique identification forged by the Indian–De Smet relationship, this narrative assumes epic proportions. In the person of Blackrobe, De Smet's story represents a direct, firsthand report of the Indian tragedy. Furthermore, an in-depth report on De Smet points to an appreciative understanding: De Smet's varied experiences supply the context of two distinct cultures.

My primary purpose, therefore, is not to praise De Smet, nor to criticize De Smet's white associates—those responsible for implementation of the government's Indian policy on the Great Plains. Bernard DeVoto has reminded us that the exceptional Indian–De Smet relationship was an exchange of love. With a twofold sensitivity, then, this Blackrobe report points to a more complete evaluation of our lauded westward expansion. That expansion was not made in a vacuum. Tragically, the cultures were so diverse that they quickly proved to be incompatible.

JOHN J. KILLOREN, S.J.

St. Louis, Missouri

"COME, BLACKROBE"

De Smet and the Indian Tragedy

Where the Rivers Meet, De Smet Began (1823)

> We left home and country for the Indians; the Indians
> are in the West: to the West let us go.
> —Missouri Jesuits' statement of purpose, 1823

It was the thirty-first day of May of the year of our Lord, the one thousand eight hundred and twenty-third; of the independence of the United States, the forty-seventh; of the acquisition of the Louisiana Territory, the nineteenth; of the statehood of Missouri in the Union, the second; of the incorporation of the city of St. Louis, the first.

The western sky behind hillside St. Louis was rich with sunset colors as the young immigrant nicknamed "Samson" jumped from the ferryboat onto the natural levee. It was the close of Saturday, the close of a long and interrupted journey for Samson De Smet.

The last portion of that journey had consumed some fifty days. Early on the morning of April 11 the group of twelve Jesuits to which De Smet belonged had departed from White Marsh off the west coast of Chesapeake Bay. They had hiked westward along the National Pike from Frederickstown through Cumberland and across the Alleghenies to Wheeling. Then, with less physical effort, they had made the long float trip down the Ohio. Finally they had set out from Shawneetown, backpacking some 150 miles across the Illinois bottoms as they headed northwest to the east bank of the Mississippi, opposite St. Louis.

But prior to their sixteen-month stay at the Jesuit novitiate at White Marsh, there had been the long crossing of the Atlantic—for De Smet, only the first of nineteen Atlantic voyages to be made in his lifetime. Sailing on the brig *Columbia* out of Amsterdam, they had been forty days at sea. Actually their journey had begun on July 23, 1821, when they set out from the university town of Mechlin, Belgium, about one hundred miles south of Amsterdam.

Now all the delays, all the problems and toil of that travel, were forgotten. At the age of twenty-three, Peter John "Samson" De Smet had arrived finally at the new city he would for the next fifty full years fondly call "my beloved home."[1]

St. Louis was indeed a new city. Some sixty years had passed since

New Orleans fur trader Pierre Laclède-Liguest, with his young stepson Auguste Chouteau, had notched the trees "under the hill," marking the site for their new trading post. They had chosen a spot along a limestone bluff on the west bank of the Mississippi only a few miles south of "Where the Rivers Meet," the union of the Missouri with the Mississippi. However, St. Louis, as the city that developed from Laclede's post, was not incorporated until 1822. By the time of De Smet's arrival at the end of May 1823, the first elected mayor of St. Louis, Dr. William Carr Lane, had been in office for less than two months.

But De Smet quickly learned, to his surprise, that much about the St. Louis of 1823 was old—as old as the Old World he had left two years previously. Using in stilted fashion some of the English phrases he was still trying to master, De Smet addressed one of the boatmen working on the levee asking for directions to the St. Louis Cathedral. When the man with a shrug responded in French, De Smet shifted at once to that second language he had learned as a youth in Belgium (after his native Flemish). Within the next twenty-four hours De Smet would realize that the French were still the most influential group among St. Louis's population of six thousand and that the customs of the French were as well established there as their language.[2]

The final delays of the journey were experienced near the levee at the foot of Morgan Street. Father Charles Van Quickenborne, the leader of the Jesuit group, had to oversee the unloading of their spring wagon (packed with their bedrolls, other camping equipment, and religious supplies) from the ferry, and from a purse never heavy but now all too light he had to extract the coins to pay for their passage.[3]

The group walked westward from the landing at the foot of Morgan Street to the corner of rue Royal (Main Street), which paralleled the riverfront one block west. They decided to walk southward, down Main, for they had been told that by going nine blocks in that direction they would reach Market Street, the central east-west street of St. Louis.

From first impressions, De Smet must have realized that besides being both new and old, St. Louis represented still another unusual combination. In the past six months he had heard repeatedly that St. Louis was located at the end of the world, on the rim of civilization. Yet on this Saturday afternoon, to the young seminarian, this bustling river city must have seemed the busiest place in the world.

From all along the half mile of riverfront there came the sounds of activity—shouted commands, steam whistles, and bells—all swelling the din of the new steamboat traffic. Only five years previously the *General Pike,* six weeks out of Louisville, had become the first steamboat to tie up here at the foot of the long bluff on August 2, 1817, and within two months the *Constitution* had arrived as the first steamboat from New Orleans.[4]

De Smet must have been impressed by the new steamboats and their freight stockpiled along the levee. Later he would realize that what he heard and saw that afternoon along the riverfront was no mere renewal or expansion of the fur trade. What De Smet witnessed on his arrival in St. Louis was the birth of a new commerce, and much more. Starting in this summer of 1823, substantial changes were being made in the fur trade. Government supervision of the trade and its enforcement of an exclusive Indian country would quickly be reduced to mere tokenism. This was the start of a new era. The first large-scale invasion of the Great Plains was about to begin.

As the Jesuit group started south on Main Street, the first St. Louis structure they must have noticed was Major Biddle's Missouri Hotel, a new two-story building on the southeast corner of Main and Morgan streets. In all his later activities on the Great Plains, De Smet would have special cause to remember the wooden sign, emblazoned with an image of a buffalo, hanging over the hotel's doorway.

As a meeting place, the Missouri Hotel had become the political headquarters of the new state. The First General Assembly of Missouri had convened there on September 18, 1820; it was there on the following day that Alexander McNair had taken the oath of office as governor and William H. Ashley as lieutenant governor.[5]

As the Jesuits walked down Main Street followed by their wagon, they might have halted two blocks south of Morgan Street. Every newcomer of this period was impressed by Pierre Chouteau's mansion and its unusual setting. The office-storage building of Chouteau's fur trade operation was handily located on the river side of Main at the corner of Washington Street. At a higher elevation, on the west side of Main, Pierre Chouteau had duplicated his half brother Auguste's establishment just six blocks farther south.

The homes of the Chouteaus were thick-walled stone mansions two stories high with elaborate porticos. Each home, along with the service structures and grounds, occupied an entire block and was "enclosed by a solid stone wall two feet thick and ten feet high, with port-holes about every ten feet apart, through which to shoot Indians in case of attack."[6]

The Jesuit newcomers would have been relieved to know that the portholes never had been, or would be, utilized for their intended purpose. In this summer of 1823, as they had for many years, Indian delegations from the Great and Little Osage tribes would arrive here for their annual meetings with the Chouteaus.

The Native Americans, as De Smet would learn, were graciously received and entertained within the enclosures, where the temporary camp of tipis was set up. From here they paraded back and forth along Main Street between the grounds of Auguste and Pierre Chouteau. In 1823 the Chouteaus welcomed such visiting Indians with their already developed trade dependence and the annuities from their yielding of land titles as important customers. With notable personal benefits, the Chouteaus had for many years exercised their double role of official U.S. Indian agents for, as well as traders (by government appointment) to, the Osages. As secondary beneficiaries, the shopkeepers along Main Street readily put up with the idiosyncrasies of the Indian visitors. As early as 1823, Indians visiting St. Louis could purchase temporary tolerance with their furs or their annuity-based credit.

Noting such Indian presence in the city, the Jesuit newcomers might have believed that they had arrived at the frontier. As early as 1821, however, that line of demarcation had been pushed over two hundred miles westward. Only later would De Smet realize that the repeated policy in each newly established state had already been initiated. Even before the formal declaration of Missouri's statehood, its newly elected officials had demanded the removal of the Indian tribes. By 1825 these Osage Indians would no longer be residents of Missouri, and before the close of the 1830s there would be no Native American groups in the state.[7]

De Smet and his companions, continuing their walk southward, would have noticed another impressive building just to the southeast of Pierre Chouteau's enclosed mansion. On the east side of Main and south of Vine Street on a lot that extended down to the riverfront was the two-story home of General William Clark, in 1823 one of the finest buildings in St. Louis.

Certainly De Smet would have noticed the large building that adjoined Clark's home to the south. This addition was the official headquarters for Clark as the St. Louis superintendent of Indian affairs. It was the renowned council chamber, the special meeting place for all the delegations from the tribes located along the upper Mississippi and the Missouri. The council chamber, a large structure almost one hundred feet long and about thirty feet wide, served as a conference hall, and Clark had developed it as a museum, "the first in and of the West." The general had filled it with countless Indian artifacts, collected during his "Voyage of Discovery" from 1804 to 1806, and subsequent to his initial appointment as Indian agent in 1807. It was an unusual educational tool for the townspeople and the important visitors to early St. Louis.[8]

In this museum Clark received many visitors from the East and the West. Just a few days before De Smet's arrival in St. Louis, Paul Wilhelm, duke of Württemberg, had experienced the double functions of the hall. The duke had studied the displays intently, then sat in on a live show, witnessing a formal meeting of General Clark with the leaders of the Potawatomis and conferences with the Osage delegations.[9]

Indian delegations from the Upper Missouri and the Far Northwest were frequent visitors to the council chambers. For although St. Louis had been Chouteau Town to the Osages and the other tribes of the Lower Missouri, it was even more widely known among the many tribes of the Upper Missouri as the home of Red-Hair Chief, the Great Father, General William Clark.

Had Clark maintained a guest book of the many visitors to his council chambers, it might have recorded that the Jesuit group, as they walked down Main Street on that afternoon at the end of May 1823, respectfully halted at Clark's house. The Jesuit records fail to state they did so, nor is there any report of a conference with the Indian agent on the following day during the informal introduction of the Jesuit newcomers to the people of St. Louis. But it would have been strange indeed had they failed to meet at once with Clark.

For this group of Jesuits had come west on a project government-approved, even government-solicited and -funded. Just the previous May, to his complete surprise, Clark had been reappointed to the post of St. Louis superintendent of Indian affairs. In that capacity, Clark had received formal notification from Washington that this group of Jesuits was to start an Indian boarding school, St. Regis Seminary, at the farm of Bishop Louis William Du Bourg some fifteen miles west of St. Louis.

We know from Father Van Quickenborne's June report to Du Bourg that within ten days of the Jesuits' arrival he had a prolonged conference with Clark in the council chamber where he presented "a detailed scheme of Indian education that met with the General's special encouragement." In August 1823 Du Bourg commented that Clark received the Jesuits "with an interest both kind and active, and shows himself in an especial way their protector."[10]

Continuing to walk south, the Jesuits would have passed a large two-story building on the southwest corner of Main and Pine streets. This was Kibbey's Hotel, built in 1817. It was a meeting place comparable to the Missouri Hotel; the popular Washington Room at Kibbey's was the favorite gathering place of "the enterprising and enthusiastic Irish Group," the McKnights and the Bradys, among others. As they passed this building, the Jesuits might have heard the clicking of billiard balls on tables imported from France, a special pastime for the St. Louisans of the period.[11]

Farther down the block, De Smet and his associates passed the stone building that had been the impressive home of Charles Gratiot. Like a number of the early French, Gratiot had moved here in 1777 from the small settlement of Cahokia, east of the Mississippi. He had married Victoire Chouteau, the half sister of Auguste, and become a leading St. Louis merchant, investor, fur magnate, and land agent.

It had been Gratiot, not Auguste or Pierre Chouteau, who acted as the capable interpreter in the formal ceremonies of March 1804 marking the transfer of the Louisiana Territory to the United States. On his arrival in St. Louis in 1815, lawyer Thomas Hart Benton had been befriended by Gratiot. Benton was invited by the white-haired patrician to reside in Gratiot's home, where the rich and the powerful of the town stopped to call and the prominent Clark visited regularly. Gratiot and his associates evidently saw in Benton a potential agent for their manifold interests; the young man became "a promising addition to their circle." Benton made his home here until Gratiot's death following a paralytic stroke in April 1817.[12]

De Smet would learn that the Gratiots—with the Chouteaus, Bertholds, Cabannés, Sarpys, and Prattes—were among the coterie of French families who had long dominated affairs in St. Louis. Their little "junto" still exercised considerable power in 1823. However, the group's distinct ethnic cast had always been secondary to the more practical objective of material gain; their alliance had readily been broadened to include newly arrived American lawyers, businessmen, and land speculators.[13]

As the Jesuits reached Main and Chestnut, they could have seen on the southwest corner the first brick structure in St. Louis, erected in

1813. This two-story building had been the home of Manuel Lisa, who died there in 1820.

The hardworking Lisa had not made a host of friends. James Wilkinson, appointed as the first territorial governor in 1804, feared him; Meriwether Lewis, Wilkinson's successor as governor in 1808, despised him; and the French—especially Pierre Chouteau, who had competed against him in the fur trade—hated him. But Lisa had set an early and successful example, conducting in 1807 the first organized trading and trapping expedition to ascend the Missouri to the Rocky Mountains. His crew of sixty men included John Colter and other veterans of the Lewis and Clark expedition. And Lisa's workers had been armed with the important new trapper's tool—the metal beaver trap.

In 1809 Meriwether Lewis's brother Reuben and Lewis's partner Clark, along with the Chouteaus and others, hurried to join Lisa in forming the St. Louis Missouri Fur Company. Under Lisa they sent an expedition of over 150 men into the field.[14]

By 1823, with official barriers breaking down, four well-financed fur companies in St. Louis were imitating Lisa's early activities. From the St. Louis riverfront these companies had sent out over fifteen hundred men in the two months before De Smet's arrival.

Perhaps the Jesuits failed to notice the log building directly to the west of Lisa's brick structure. This building, on the south side of present Chestnut between Main and Second, had been taken over as the post office in 1822 with the returned Astorian Wilson Price Hunt as postmaster.[15] For some years, the Jesuits, like all St. Louisans, would be coming here to deposit their letters and pick up incoming mail, which might have been some six weeks in transit from the East Coast.

After walking a half block south of Lisa's former home, the Jesuits passed another brick structure, an office building on the northwest corner of Market and Main streets. Here was the office of the St. Louis Bank, relocated from its original quarters in a first-floor wing of Auguste Chouteau's mansion, on the south side of Market.

The first bank note issued here in 1817 had been good, very briefly, for a five-dollar exchange. More important for the history of the West was the engraved picture on this note: a trapped beaver. Soon De Smet would realize how significant this engraving was. The St. Louis Bank, not well organized, was short-lived; the St. Louis economy, however, would be based on the beaver until 1840. Even before 1823 St. Louis had become the marketplace for the beaver pelt, in international demand.[16]

De Smet and his fellow Jesuits had walked some nine blocks south from the ferry landing at the foot of Morgan Street. They had reached Market Street, the old rue Bonhomme. This had long been the trailhead, now the heart of St. Louis, to the West. That trail had already been pushed past Fort Osage, the government "factory" (trading post) that Clark had established in 1808 some three hundred miles up the Missouri. The trail had already reached past the booming Boonslick country, past the springs where Independence would be started in 1827, and beyond the mouth of the Kaw (the Kansas River). By way of this route, staying south of the Kaw and heading for the Cimarron Crossing of the Arkansas, a growing number of wagon trains were moving to and from Santa Fe. By its location and the early activities starting there St. Louis was destined to become the "Gateway City." As early as 1817 the *St. Louis Enquirer* had reported that "about 20 wagons per week for the past nine or ten weeks have passed through St. Charles—emigrants whose total number was supposed to amount to 12,000."[17]

From this corner of Market and Main, looking eastward to the river, the Jesuits could see the second ferry landing, the original Chouteau landing at the foot of Market Street. Stretching from the riverbank westward to Main and over the entire block from Market south to Walnut (Tower Street, the old rue de la Tour, leading to the stone tower on the crest of the hill at Fourth Street) was the public square, the center of all public life and group activities in St. Louis.

Toward the center of this square near the site of the original flagpole De Smet could see the pavilion-type structure that had been erected on September 1, 1812; sixty-four feet long by thirty feet wide, its partitioned stalls provided a market for trade in food and furs. The market was well located, for this was the center of St. Louis and would remain so for nearly a half century.

On this site the formal ceremonies marking the transfer of title to the Louisiana Territory from France to the United States had been conducted in 1804. Carlos Dehault Delassus, the Spanish lieutenant governor stationed in St. Louis, had cooperated fully in the transfer ceremonies directed by Captain Amos Stoddard representing the government of the United States. Delassus fulfilled Stoddard's request, sending out word to the Indian tribes in the vicinity: "You will be protected and sustained by your new father."

Standing next to Stoddard during all the ceremonies of transfer was Captain Meriwether Lewis, the personal representative of President Jefferson. As the leader of the great "Corps of Discovery" about to head up the Missouri, Lewis was understandably preoccupied with the final arrangements and securing necessary supplies. His men were all in camp, secluded some twelve miles north near the mouth of the Missouri River at Camp Dubois on the Illinois shore, his partner, William Clark, in command. The corps broke camp in the rain on Monday morning, May 14. Two and a half years later, they returned to the St. Louis riverfront.[18]

In July 1805, even before the return of Lewis and Clark, Lieutenant Zebulon Pike, a protégé of newly appointed Governor Wilkinson, had landed here with his family and a small detachment of soldiers from Kaskaskia. From here, in late July, Pike headed north for his exploratory expedition to the headwaters of the Mississippi. Again from here, just one year later, Pike was sent by Wilkinson on a second expedition, this time to the headwaters of the Arkansas.[19]

On March 8, 1808, returning from Washington where he had been acclaimed as a national hero, Meriwether Lewis had again disembarked at the riverfront. Along with the tribute he had received, Lewis had been appointed governor of Louisiana Territory. For the conscientious Lewis, eager to provide a second success story for his patron, Jefferson, this quickly proved to be a tragic, even fatal assignment.

The confused situation fashioned by Governor Wilkinson's strange dealings — the heavy problems presented by the much-divided power groups in St. Louis; the vast difference between remote Washington Indian policies and the realities of Indian treatment determined in St. Louis and affecting the entire territory; the combination of these and other difficulties — was too much for the overburdened Lewis. His important reports on the expedition to the Pacific Ocean were never completed. On September 4, 1809, only a year and a half later, Lewis would leave from here — a hero tarnished by the charges of new officials in Washington and a broken man, traveling to his unexplained death on the Natchez Trace on October 11.[20]

From this levee on October 21, 1810, the two barges and the keelboat of the first Astorian expedition began their journey up the Missouri. The return to this landing site was made a little before sunset on April 30, 1813, the entire population of St. Louis assembling on the riverbank to welcome the skin canoe of Robert Stuart and his returning Astorians.[21]

By 1819, this levee had grown in importance as the potential gateway to the Northwest. President James Monroe had given enthusiastic approval to Secretary of War John Calhoun's grandiose plans for the West. There would be a major scientific-military expedition to investigate and secure the Upper Missouri with the establishment of a permanent post at the mouth of the Yellowstone. The *Missouri Gazette* of April 21, 1819, predicted: "The Yellowstone Expedition will . . . encourage Western emigration; it will protect and encourage the fur trade which is now productive of such important benefits to the country, and which can be made much more productive."[22]

After an impressive but faulty start in 1819, the expeditionary forces were restructured by their leader, Major Stephen H. Long, in 1820. In this summer of 1823, Dr. Edwin James, botanist and geologist of Long's party, published the journal of the expedition made not to the Yellowstone but to the headwaters of the South Platte. James's report echoed Pike's critical description of the western plains, "the Great American Desert."[23]

But it was almost dark now, and the final steps of the Jesuits' journey had to be hastened. They turned away from the northwest corner of the city square. They made the steep climb up Market Street, north of the stone wall that secluded Auguste Chouteau's extensive grounds just to the west of the square. Upon reaching Second Street, rue de l'Église, they turned southward, following the wall.

Here De Smet and his companions walked past the old cemetery along the west side of Second Street. They would have noticed that there were no recent grave mounds or new crosses, for a city ordinance enacted earlier in 1823 had outlawed the practice of burial within the city limits. Finally, at the south end of the cemetery, the Jesuits halted. Standing at last before the facade of Bishop Louis William Du Bourg's new brick cathedral, they offered a silent prayer of thanksgiving.

The cathedral was a large building, especially large for St. Louis at the start of the 1820s. Perhaps the dark of the early evening concealed from the newcomers the sorry exterior lines and condition of the structure. Tomorrow they would be more edified by the interior decorations, all of which the bishop had solicited from benefactors during his recent tour of Europe.[24]

In the darkness the Jesuit newcomers knocked at the door of the two-story brick building adjoining the cathedral on the south. This was the episcopal residence in which was also located, as the Jesuits would quickly learn, St. Louis College, started by Du Bourg in 1820.

The rectory door was quickly opened by Father Francis Niel, president of the college and pastor of the cathedral. He welcomed the group in the name of Du Bourg, who had departed a few days earlier for New Orleans. The introductions of the members of the Jesuit group were made by Father Van Quickenborne, and to the new-comers Father Niel introduced Fathers Edmund Saulnier, Eugene Michaud, and Leo Deys, his assistants in the college and the religious activities of the cathedral.

Following supper, the comments and questions of the Jesuits must have been few; the exhausted De Smet and his companions would have excused themselves rather quickly. After thanking their hosts, they would have retired early, spreading their bedrolls in the small classrooms on the second floor. At least the extensive library donated by the bishop—over eight thousand volumes shelved around the walls of the classrooms—must have reminded the young Jesuits of the college atmosphere they had left at the *grand séminaire* of Mechlin.[25]

The next day, following the detailed instructions left by the bishop, they would all celebrate the feast of Corpus Christi. That Sunday morning, June 1, 1823, there was a prolonged ringing of the St. Louis bells. Their music was followed by the booming of the St. Louis cannon in the hilltop stone tower and the added fortifications hastily (and needlessly) erected to face the threats of the War of 1812. The St. Louis newspapers, the *Missouri Republican* and the *St. Louis Enquirer,* had already alerted some of the people of St. Louis regarding the newcomers, but at least 40 percent of the parishioners of the cathedral were unable to read. The official bell ringer of the city, walking through the various sections of town and ringing his bell to attract attention, would shout his brief newscast to interested citizens.

The Jesuits joined Father Niel and the other diocesan priests in vesting for the solemn services. In the richly decorated and crowded cathedral, the High Mass was sung in Latin, and the sermon and announcements were made in Father Niel's polished French. Then the entire congregation joined the celebrants in the traditional Corpus Christi procession, marching out of the cathedral, across the church grounds, and through the nearby streets.[26]

No names of the acolytes and the flower girls who participated in the ceremony are recorded, or of the parish members and non-Catholic guests who joined or watched the religious parade. But some of the Indian delegations, in their city regalia, must have been on hand, as well as a fairly complete "who's who" of regular St. Louis inhabitants.

Among the children would have been little Charles Pierre Chouteau and his cousin Edward. In 1828 they would be enrolled at the St. Regis Indian Seminary conducted by De Smet and his fellow Jesuits at Florissant. Among the acolytes and future students were the Cabanné boys, Francis, Julius, and Du Thil; John Julius, General Clark's youngest son; and young Howard Christy. Bryan Mullanphy, somewhat older, might have been the crossbearer at the head of the procession; he too would be enrolled at the Florissant school. And Bryan's young sister Mary, who would become the wife of General William S. Harney ten years later, may have been among the flower girls.[27]

That Sunday afternoon, following the services, would have been the time for the introduction of the newcomers to the people of St. Louis. At such a gathering the popular governor, Alexander McNair, who had defeated William Clark in the first elections held for the new state of Missouri some three years previously, would certainly have been present. And Mayor Lane, who would be reelected repeatedly, might well have officially welcomed the group. Clark had both official and family reasons to be present. In 1814 he had prevailed upon Bishop Flaget, visiting in St. Louis, to baptize three of his children.[28]

Perhaps later that afternoon there was time for sight-seeing around the city. The new home of Senator Benton, already known for its beautiful gardens, was only a block north of the cathedral. In the opposite direction, the home of William Ashley was an impressive two-story brick structure located just to the south of the recently erected Episcopal Christ Church. Neither Benton nor Ashley was present in St. Louis that day. De Smet would later become well acquainted with both leaders.

Retiring that night, De Smet might have offered a special prayer of gratitude that the preliminaries were finally over. Those preliminaries had been prolonged over seven hundred days, but now they were finished. Like his companions, De Smet had journeyed westward for something other than White Marsh, something different from conducting religious activities in St. Louis directed primarily to the spiritual benefit of non-Indians.

During their stay in the poverty-plagued Jesuit novitiate in Maryland, De Smet and his companions had been questioned about their uncertain future. Years later De Smet recorded their response: "We left home and country for the Indians; the Indians are in the West; to the West let us go." On the morrow, at long last, the group would head out to Florissant to a beginning of the Indian apostolate they had been assigned.[29]

That Indian school, a failure, would be terminated after some five years. A number of De Smet's fellow Jesuits would move to other Indian missionary endeavors in attempts to help the various tribes in their own, now more distant, territories. Other Jesuits would redirect their religious activities to seemingly more important apostolates, but De Smet's dedication to the Native Americans would continue for the next fifty years.[30]

Before the middle of the century De Smet would gain an international reputation. The exceptional experiences of his extensive travels in the wilderness would be widely publicized through his writings; he would be recognized as an outstanding authority on the Native Americans of the West and their vast territory. And that reputation would be solidly based. For through his direct contacts, his personality, and his unique role among the Indians, he would obtain a notable acceptance among the tribes. Through the third quarter of the century De Smet would become the most influential non-Indian among the tribes of the Great Plains.

Because of his reputation and persuasiveness, De Smet would be courted constantly by the power structure behind the mounting invasions of the West. His cooperation would be solicited by Washington politicians, St. Louis merchants involved in the new fur commerce, officials administering the government's Indian policy, and army officers.

De Smet would be more than a witness to, and a reporter of, the invasions of the Great Plains. Arriving in St. Louis in the summer of 1823, he had walked on stage for the opening scene of a grim tragedy that would be enacted within the next half century. In that tragedy he would be a major participant. His basic role would be that of "Blackrobe," a spiritual leader respected by the Native Americans; however, he would also serve those he called his "beloved Indians" as a dedicated activist in their cause. Further, he would serve his beloved adopted country as an intermediary with the Indians. Even before De Smet left the stage, the Indian problem would be all but resolved by the land-greedy whites. De Smet's story embraces that tragedy.

Part One

—

The Great Plains

—

The New Children
of the Great Father

Chapter One

The Jeffersonian
Conflict of Interests, 1775–1823

> It may be taken for a certainty that not a foot of land
> will be taken from the Indians without their consent.
> —Thomas Jefferson (1786)
> Commerce is the great engine by which we are to
> coerce them, and not war.
> —Thomas Jefferson (1808)

JEFFERSON'S PROPOSED INDIAN POLICY

The ascent from the Mississippi riverfront to the restored St. Louis Cathedral is still the steep climb that De Smet made for the first time in 1823. However, old Market Street has been eliminated, and one now moves westward up the grand center stairs of the memorial to western expansion. Here, in the center of the national park that stretches a quarter mile along the riverfront and westward to what was rue des Granges, the Third Street of old St. Louis, is the awesome Gateway Arch.

This impressive monument of steel and concrete, a sky-flung catenary curve reaching 630 feet upward from its north and south foundations, which are also 630 feet apart, is the gigantic symbol of what St. Louis had become in 1823. In that summer St. Louis was changed into the new capital of the developing "commerce of the West." The arch is the flamboyant historical symbol of the city that was to serve as the gateway to the fur-rich Great Plains and eastern slopes of the Rockies.

Throughout the next half century of expansion westward from the Mississippi, St. Louis would continue to be the Gateway City. By 1849 St. Louis was the entrance to the "great thoroughfares"—the passageways to and the supply corridors for—the two remote colonies then developing in the Northwest and the Southwest. The securing of the rapidly encircled Great Plains would be a consequent achievement. Appropriately, the St. Louis riverfront is the site of the great arch commemorative of that westward expansion.

Beneath the arch, in the foyer that opens onto the Museum of Westward Expansion, is Lloyd Lillie's bronze statue of Thomas Jefferson. As the nation's third president, Jefferson had directed the spread of the United States to the eastern bank of the Mississippi.

Having engineered the Louisiana Purchase, Jefferson initiated westward expansion across the Great Plains and Rocky Mountains to the shores of the Pacific Ocean. This entire complex—the Gateway Arch, the museum, and the national park setting—has been properly named the Jefferson National Expansion Memorial. The unique achievement realized by Jefferson was to double the size of his country.

There is irony, however, in Jefferson's statue being located here. For this was the Gateway City Jefferson never reached, the entrance to the West that he saw only through the eyes of Lewis and Clark, Zebulon Pike, and (not long before his death) Dr. Edwin James, chronicler of the Stephen Long expedition.

There is supreme irony in Jefferson's promise of 1786 regarding this vast territorial acquisition: "It may be taken for a certainty that not a foot of land will be taken from the Indians without their consent."[1] With an emphasis that Jefferson would have considered quite proper, this statement is prominently displayed immediately adjacent to his statue. More than a promise oft repeated, this was a policy principle that Jefferson boldly and proudly proclaimed through more than a quarter century of masterminding and personally directing western expansion.

Jefferson's formal political role had terminated in 1809 with the completion of his second presidential term. However, the influence of his thinking and the effective procedures initiated by his directives remained strong and active. Jefferson's ambitious dream for westward expansion far beyond the Mississippi and the Missouri would begin to be realized in the summer of 1823.

For the Indians of the Great Plains and the Rockies, that expansion would be implemented by an Indian policy based on principles and procedures compiled in the main by Jefferson and his associates. Westward expansion, by Jefferson's insistence, was to be a development beneficial for both Native Americans and the white newcomers, an achievement worthy of international praise and honor for the new nation with its adherence to the high principles so important to Jefferson.[2]

For the Indians, the "pursuit of happiness" would be directed by government initiative, albeit exercised in a paternalistic manner, for their assimilation with civilization. The government would provide both physical and nonmaterial enrichments for the tribes. At the same time, the voracious land hunger of the whites would be satisfied, richly and without stooping to such injustices as overpowering military campaigns. Jefferson assured Indian leaders that in line with the government's acknowledgment of full equality for Native Americans, the tribes would be free to realize all the advantages of complete acculturation: "We will never do an unjust act toward you. . . . In time you will be as we are: you will become one people with us; your blood will mix with ours: and will spread with ours over this great island."[3]

Jefferson believed that such total integration was both proper and feasible; that the Indians, with the experience of some contact, would desire to adopt the lifestyle of the whites; and that such acculturated Indians would be found acceptable by the whites. By way of compromise, Jefferson was willing to concede that some period of adjustment might be necessary, that this preparation required of the Indians might be a gradual process. Thus Jefferson came to regard Indian removal as a pragmatic program, though only a temporary one, a means of achieving his idealistic objectives — acculturation and full integration.

While concluding the Louisiana Purchase, President Jefferson considered an immediate use for the newly acquired territory: the Mississippi River might serve, temporarily at least, as the barrier against the Indians that the government had come to regard as necessary. In the fall of 1803 Jefferson sent Meriwether Lewis, his personal secretary, to the Mississippi frontier. Lewis was instructed to determine whether whites living west of the Mississippi might be persuaded to exchange their holdings for lands east of the river; the lands to the west might then become the new exclusively Indian country.

At the end of December 1803, Lewis reported to Jefferson that this plan for Louisiana might be realized "in the course of a few years provided the gouvernment of the U. States is justly liberal in it's donations." But Jefferson had already moved to his more immediate concern, the relocation of the eastern tribes quite independent of any removal of whites from the western bank of the Mississippi. Jefferson held that the justification for American expansion was the rich blessings of civilization. Initially, Jefferson ignored all realistic problems, in simplistic fashion declaring that American expansion would benefit not only the Americans but those from whom the land was taken.[4]

THE DEEPER MOTIVATION: *Necessities of the Times*
A federal Indian policy had been inaugurated by the Continental Congress in 1775. On July 12, 1787, Congress passed the Northwest

The St. Regis Indian School was located at Florissant, Missouri, a few miles west of where the Missouri and Mississippi rivers meet. The school program started in May 1824 with the enrollment of a few boys of the Sauk and Iowa tribes. (Sketch by J. B. Louis, S.J., in the Jesuit Missouri Province Archives)

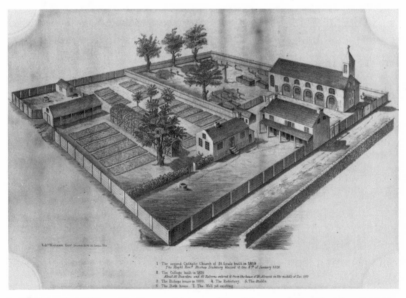

In 1818 Louis William Du Bourg, bishop of Louisiana and the Floridas, laid the cornerstone for the new church in St. Louis. The academy for boys was then built adjacent to it. (Lithograph by Jules Hutawa, Missouri Historical Society, St. Louis, neg. PB 435)

William Clark (1770–1838), as painted by Chester Harding. (Missouri Historical Society, neg. Por-C-26)

Thomas Hart Benton (1783–1858), as painted by Sarah Miriam Peale. (Missouri Historical Society, neg. Por-B-6)

During the first quarter century, the U.S. government's Indian policy in the West was directed by William Clark, the St. Louis superintendent of Indian affairs. Senator Benton's published account, Thirty Years' View . . . 1820–50, *reported on his prolonged exercise of power.*

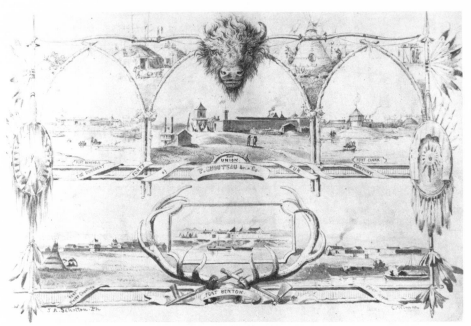

This representation of "The Different Forts of P. Chouteau Jr. & Co. Fur Company" was the work of the photographer John Scholten and the artist Carl Wimar. (Jesuit Missouri Province Archives)

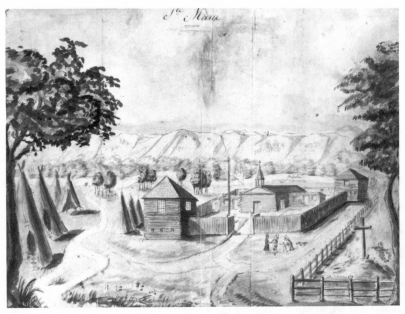

This initial St. Mary's Reduction, erected on the Bitterroot River in 1841, was founded by De Smet and Nicolas Point, who made this sketch. (Jesuit Missouri Province Archives)

As the guest of Brigham Young, De Smet visited in 1846 at the Winter Quarters of the Latter-day Saints near Council Bluffs. Pausing briefly on his voyage down the Missouri, De Smet attempted to respond to the requests of the Mormon leaders for information on the western territory. (Painting on canvas, by C. C. A. Christensen, in Museum of Fine Arts, Brigham Young University)

Medicine Snake Woman (Blackfoot) with her husband, Alexander Culbertson, and their son, Joe, about 1863. (Haynes Foundation Collection, Montana Historical Society, Helena)

Edwin Thompson Denig and his wife, Deer Little Woman (Assiniboine). (Smithsonian Institution, 24-a-2)

Fort Union, at the mouth of the Yellowstone, was a favorite resting place for De Smet during his travels in the wilderness. Before 1846 the Big House there was the home of his dear friends the Culbertsons; from 1846 through 1855 that main building housed the Denigs and their children.

Ordinance. The government specifically committed itself to an ongoing concern for legal safeguards to secure just treatment for the Indians: "The utmost good faith shall always be observed towards the Indians, their lands and property shall never be taken from them without their consent; and in their property, rights and liberty, they never shall be invaded or disturbed, unless in just and lawful wars authorised by Congress; but laws founded in justice and humanity shall from time to time be made, for preventing wrongs being done to them, and for preserving peace and friendship with them."[5]

The high principles expressed in such legislation gained Jefferson's ready endorsement, but for the majority of the members of Congress, utter pragmatism most likely served as the main motivating factor. The new nation faced innumerable difficulties, and peace was essential to provide untroubled development. Even though the legislation was expressed in positive, idealistic language, this was a stand necessarily taken for self-preservation. In view of the military power the combined tribes were presumed to be able to muster, the new nation was under strong pressure to treat Indian rights with full respect.[6]

Nonetheless, Congress had initially acted in a high-handed manner. In negotiating earlier Indian treaties consequent to the Revolutionary War, congressional representatives had insisted upon the right of conquest, demanding that the Indians cede lands desired by the victorious whites. But the tribes had refused to capitulate. The English, not their Indian allies, had admitted defeat. Congress abandoned its earlier claims and initial policy of open domination.[7]

The Ordinance of 1786 had appointed Henry Knox, secretary of war, to direct Indian policy and its implementation. From 1788 through 1793, Knox repeatedly warned the president and Congress that the Indian tribes must be able to rely on their treaties with the United States. In Knox's judgment, the treaty process was jeopardized not by the Indians but by congressional failure to enact implementary legislation. President Washington insisted that "to advance the happiness of the Indians and to attach them firmly to the United States . . . it seems necessary—That they should experience the benefits of an impartial dispensation of justice."[8]

Another basic consideration served to determine the government's Indian policy—finances. Historian Samuel Eliot Morison summarizes the realities facing the new government at the time of Washington's inauguration: "The American Confederation left nothing but a dozen clerks with their pay in arrears, an empty treasury, and a burden of debt. The American army consisted of 672 officers and men; the navy had ceased to exist. No successful leader of a revolution has been so naked before the world as Washington was in 1789. There were no taxes or requisitions coming in, and no machinery for collecting taxes." Knox realistically asserted that even if Congress decided to expel the Indians by force from the Wabash River region, "the finances of the United States would not at the present admit of the operation." The secretary recommended concern for humanitarian principles as an additional motivation. This official idealism was all the more attractive to Congress since it required no additional sacrifices. Proposing this double motivation, Knox effected a turnabout in congressional declarations of concern regarding the Native Americans and their rights.[9]

At the start of 1790, with the political leaders sharing to various degrees this twofold motivation regarding "the Indian relationship," Knox presented a key report to the president:

> It would reflect honor on the new Government, and be attended with happy effects, were a declarative law to be passed, that the Indian tribes possess the right of the soil of all lands within their limits; and that they were not to be divested thereof, but in consequence of open treaties made under the authority of the United States. . . . The independent nations and tribes of Indians ought to be considered as foreign nations, not as the subjects of any particular State.[10]

The three main points of Indian policy, a matter of congressional supervision and control, were thus enunciated. The Indian tribes were to be regarded as independent, sovereign nations. The rights of the Native Americans to their tribal homelands were to be honored. And the treaty system was declared the legal procedure by which Congress would direct any further acquisition of title to Indian lands. By means of this treaty system Congress would manage the relationships to be negotiated with the tribes.

That the First Congress in its second session accepted the principles proposed by Knox is evidenced by their enactment on July 22, 1790, in the initial Act to Regulate Trade and Intercourse with the Indian Tribes.[11] Washington's full acceptance of Knox's platform is indicated by his strong proclamation of August 26, 1790, demanding that the citizens of the United States observe the regulations of the treaties of Hopewell made in 1785 with the Cherokees and in 1786 with the Choctaws and the Chickasaws.[12] And Jefferson officially pointed out that the basic principles proposed by Knox were his own. In response to queries by President Washington to the members of his cabinet in 1793, Jefferson offered his complete agreement: "The Indians had the full, undivided and independent sovereignty as long as they choose to keep it, and that this might be forever."[13]

The first delineation of Indian country in a U.S. statute was not made until May 19, 1796, when Congress, following Washington's urging, passed the Intercourse Act, an enlarged version of the Acts to Regulate Trade and Intercourse, temporary and tentative legislation enacted in 1790 and 1793. As historian Francis Paul Prucha notes, the delineation of the Indian country "was meant to indicate with added clarity the government's intention to uphold the treaties." Again in 1799 Congress approved the 1796 act for another two years, and in 1802 it was reenacted as permanent legislation, the basic law governing relations with Indians until 1834. Yet Washington, ordering in 1796 that a line be drawn and forcefully maintained between the land of the United States and the territory of the Cherokee nation, predicted pessimistically: "I believe scarcely any thing short of a Chinese wall, or a line of troops, will restrain Land jobbers, and the encroachment of settlers upon the Indian territory."[14]

JEFFERSON: A Policy of "Coercion—by Commerce, Not War"
As early as 1791 Jefferson began to modify his stand for high principles. That summer, accompanied by James Madison, he made a visit to New York. These two members of the "Virginia Dynasty" described the purpose of their trip as botanical study, but while in the north they also exchanged political commitments with the Antifederalists. Morison notes the pragmatic consequences effected that summer: "Jefferson's 'botanical excursion' of 1791 began the substitution of expediency for idealism."[15] The adjustment of the working politician—cooperation through compromise—had been effected.

Although Morison attributes Jefferson's willingness to indulge in political compromises in general, Billington criticizes him as the pragmatic manipulator of Indian policy. In some sublimated manner Jefferson epitomized the insatiable land hunger that characterized his new countrymen, the emigrants from Europe. In Billington's judgment, Jefferson's "frontier background transcended his well-known humanitarianism." As patron of national expansion, Jefferson was eager to impress Europeans with an Indian policy of high idealism; however, in his implementation of that policy, Jefferson developed some of the pressure tactics that would be among the criticized features of the government's management of Indian affairs. Horsman offers a realistic explanation: "Jefferson soon discovered that as President he had to reconcile his ideals with the necessities of American interest."[16]

At the time of his election to the presidency in 1801, Jefferson believed he had the key to an effective, rapid, yet proper means to extinguish Indian title to their lands. His plan utilized a program Congress had already approved. Benjamin Franklin, in his practical wisdom, had recommended it as early as 1751, and with Washington's prodding, Congress had set it in action in 1796. This was the program of government-conducted Indian trading houses — "factories." With these establishments already functioning as an integral feature of federal Indian policy, in 1803 Jefferson added the enlargement needed for increased effectiveness and supervisory control.[17]

The factory system had already produced secondary benefits, and under Jefferson's plan those benefits were heightened. The government earned the goodwill of the Indians and at the same time eliminated unscrupulous private traders who continually fomented troubles between the Indians and whites. Moreover, the factory system was directed especially to its main objective, which Jefferson specified clearly in his famous confidential message to Congress of January 18, 1803.[18]

Jefferson noted that the Indians' opposition to further land sales had to be counteracted peaceably "to provide an extension of territory which the rapid increase of our numbers will call for." He proposed to encourage the Indians toward husbandry so that "the extensive forests necessary in the hunting life, will then become useless, & they will see advantage in exchanging them for the means of improving their farms." And to effect this change, Jefferson would exploit what he recognized as the growing tragic flaw of the Indians — their desire for manufactured goods. Jefferson proposed "to multiply trading houses among them, & place within their reach those things which will contribute more to their domestic comfort than the possession of extensive, but uncultivated wilds. Experience & reflection will develope to them the wisdom of exchanging what they can spare & we want, for what we can spare and they want."[19]

Jefferson realized, however, that Congress had to be very cost-conscious and therefore emphasized that the trade factories would be not only effective but economical:

> By establishing a commerce on terms which shall be
> advantageous to them and only not losing to us . . .

we may render ourselves so necessary to their comfort and prosperity that the protection of our citizens from their disorderly members will become their interest and their voluntary care. Instead, therefore, of an augmentation of military force proportioned to our extension of frontier, I propose a moderate enlargement of the capital employed in that commerce as a more effectual, economical, and humane instrument for preserving peace and good neighborhood with them.[20]

By that same procedure the mountain men would later betray the friendship extended by the Indians of the Great Plains. At the annual fur trade rendezvous on the Green River from 1824 through 1840, manufactured goods bartered for pelts would militate against the permanence of Indian independence.

Jefferson clearly anticipated and encouraged the Indians' increased desire for manufactured goods. In a letter of August 12, 1802, Jefferson conveyed to Secretary of War Henry Dearborn his eagerness "to extinguish the Indians' title to their lands."

The cheapest & most effectual instrument we can use for preserving the friendship of the Indians is the establishment of trading houses among them. If we could furnish goods enough to supply all their wants and sell these goods so cheap that no private trader could enter into competition with us . . . we should of course become objects of affection to them. There is perhaps no method more irresistible of obtaining lands from them than by letting them get in debt, which when too heavy to be paid, they are always willing to lop off by a cession of land.[21]

Six months later, on February 27, 1803, Jefferson wrote in a similar vein to William Harrison, governor of Indiana Territory and thus ex officio superintendent of Indian affairs for the tribes of that area. After stating his purpose of providing "a private and more extensive view of our policy respecting the Indians," Jefferson repeated his objective in pushing credit upon the Indians: "To promote this disposition [of the Indians] to exchange lands, which they have to spare & we want, for necessaries, which we have to spare & they want, we shall push our trading houses, and be glad to see the good & influential individuals among them run in debt, because we observe that when these debts get beyond what the individuals can pay, they become willing to lop th[em off] by a cession of lands."[22]

The factory system, as refashioned by Jefferson, would serve as the "effectual instrument" for acquiring Indian lands. In his eagerness to facilitate expansion, Jefferson had stooped to expediency. In the judgment of historian Bernard Sheehan, he had moved "over the edge of patriarchal manipulation and became outright deceptive." Jefferson understood that as they became dependent upon the manufactured goods, Native Americans would become increasingly subservient. Tribes thus pressured would enter into treaty negotiations and be manipulated thereby into further land cessions to accommodate the newcomers. At the close of 1804 Jefferson quite openly declared to Congress that the retention by the government of an exclusive commerce with the Indians west of the Mississippi was "a right indispensable to the policy of governing those Indians by commerce rather than by arms."[23]

Within a short time, however, Jefferson had abandoned his simplistic proposal of a government monopoly of the fur trade, though he continued to insist that the exchange be government-regulated. Jefferson's countrymen were as hungry for money as they were greedy for land, and the fur trade was about to become big business, the new commerce of the West that would affect the entire country.

Jefferson turned to the belief that with government trade factories established in key locations and agents supervising the better-controlled competition dominated by "large and respectable companies," the special objective of the trading program—gaining land titles from the tribes—would continue to be realized. In a letter to Lewis, Jefferson reported: "A powerful company is at length forming for taking up the Indian commerce on a large scale. . . . It will be under the direction of a most excellent man, a Mr. Astor mercht. of N. York, long engaged in the business & perfectly master of it. . . . Nothing but the exclusive possession of the Indian commerce can secure us their peace."[24]

Jefferson must have been impressed with the scope of John Jacob Astor's plan to build a chain of posts reaching from the Upper Missouri across the Rocky Mountains to a headquarters station at the mouth of the Columbia River. In fact, what Astor really wanted—and actually disclosed to state senator Clinton of New York, whose political backing Astor had sought—was a full monopoly of the fur trade. Although official monopoly status was never granted to Astor's company, its Western Department, conducted by Ramsay

Crooks, would become so strong that it exercised quasi-monopolistic powers on the Upper Missouri from 1826 to 1834.[25]

Jefferson's plan for domination, for gaining title to the lands of the western Indians, had been expressed in his directive of 1808 to Governor Lewis: "I have thought it best to communicate to yourself directly ideas in conformity with those I have expressed to him [General Henry Dearborn], and with the principles on which we have conducted Indian affairs. . . . Commerce is the great engine by which we are to coerce them, and not war."[26]

SENATOR BENTON:
"Throw Open the Fur Trade to Individual Enterprise"

The fur trade, as the ongoing basis of Indian-white contact, had been important from the start of the colonies. For the United States, that trade immediately became a major and direct concern, for a variety of reasons. There was the diplomatic motivation, lasting until about 1820: some government supervision of the trade seemed necessary to offset the feared military potential of the tribes and the possible influence of foreign agents among the Indians. However, after the War of 1812 and the ratification of the treaty with Spain in 1821, which transferred Florida to the United States, the tribes could no longer play American interests against those of Britain, France, or Spain. The national interests of the United States were no longer to be threatened by the Native Americans east of the Mississippi River.[27] Another consideration was financial. A growing trade relationship with the Indians would increase the manipulative powers of the government. Such magnified influence over the tribes would lead to a reduction in military expenditures, to lower defense costs, and this despite the ever-expanding frontier.

From the beginning, Congress had insisted that it properly held exclusive power regarding the management of Indian affairs. Some of the treaties had committed the government to providing the services of a trade factory. In addition to specific congressional legislation regulating trade and intercourse, the government in 1806 had established the post of superintendent of Indian trade, with the authorization for "carrying on a liberal trade with the several Indian nations, within the United States, or their territories."[28]

The basic cause for the problems that beset the factory system should be noted: as the two disparate cultures moved to heightened confrontation over the same territory, any attempt to apply the contradictory principles of Indian policy was predestined to result in confusion and failure. The Indians believed that they were to be treated in accord with the basic guarantee of peaceful coexistence. But the one freedom that the Jeffersonians failed to preserve for the Native Americans was self-determination on the most basic question: the Indian was no longer given the option to be Indian. As a consequence of a policy with no single purpose, there was no single objective in the handling of the Indian factories.

The defective supervision and operation of the government's program was widely and loudly criticized. Thomas L. McKenney, appointed superintendent of Indian trade in 1816, commented that it was "unjust in any one to rail against our Indian concerns or talk about their mismanagement. We who have to do with them know enough how slip-shod almost every thing is, but we know also it does not arise out of a lack of effort . . . but in a want of *a suitable system.*" But the unqualified director was only one cause of the problem. McKenney pointed out quite correctly that Congress was largely responsible for many of the inherent defects of the program. Without the required funding, the program was never of sufficient scope to plan and carry out the tremendous task that Jefferson had assigned. The governors of the western territories—Lewis Cass of Michigan, Thomas Posey of Indiana, Ninian Edwards of Illinois, and William Clark of Missouri—all joined in the chorus of criticisms directed in 1815 against "the inconveniences and evils" of the system.[29]

Another cause for the termination of the factory system was also the strongest and most effective. Even prior to December 3, 1821, the opening day of the Seventeenth Congress, the members were pressured into concentrating their attention on this specific matter by a powerful lobby group, perhaps the first of national scope and influence to descend on Washington. Certainly it was the first lobby whose committed agent and official spokesman held a congressional seat. For added power, that senator, "the First from the New West," was moving quickly to the chairmanship of the key committee, the Committee on Indian Affairs. With his penchant for oratorical flourishes loaded with classical allusions, Senator Thomas Hart Benton might well have described his personal interests and official activities by a comparison to the Trojan horse within the walls of Troy.[30]

In 1814, St. Louis merchant Charles Gratiot had written to Astor in New York that the situation of the Indian fur trade was both uncertain and unpredictable, "too precarious for anybody to hazard anything in it unless the factories were to be abolished."[31] Nonetheless, Astor appreciated the information, also reported by Gratiot, that the Chouteaus and the other fur traders in St. Louis were also looking forward to the termination of the government's factories.

From the start of 1819 Astor's hardworking lieutenant Ramsay Crooks made repeated visits to Washington to lobby against the factory system. In that year, Astor hired Benton, who worked as a lawyer and newspaper editor as well as a politican, to handle a lawsuit on behalf of a field operator of the American Fur Company against a U.S. Indian agent. By means of Benton's newspaper, the *St. Louis Enquirer*, the citizens of St. Louis presented to Congress in 1819 the "Missouri Scroll," a petition in which they asked for a variety of favors, including the abolition of the factories. Senator Benton's conflict of interests was all too obvious.[32]

By May 1821, Crooks's lobbyists for the American Fur Company had been joined in Washington by representatives of the St. Louis fur traders. Having carefully engineered a prolonged and massive campaign, Crooks had strong reason to expect the desired outcome. The act repealing the system was passed on May 6, 1822. Crooks's spokesman, Benton, later offered this summary of his labors: "I determined to bring the question before the Senate—did so—brought in a bill to abolish the factories, and throw open the fur trade to individual enterprise, and supported the bill with all the facts and reasons of which I was master. The bill was carried through both Houses, and became a law. . . . It cost me a strenuous exertion."[33]

In his presentation of the arguments gathered by Crooks, Benton presumed to speak in the name of the Indians and on their behalf. It seems strange that neither Benton, a congressional leader professedly concerned for the proper management of Indian affairs, nor McKenney, the defender of his Indian Office program, considered the possible introduction of immediate personal testimony by the Native Americans. The explanation cannot be the language problem; by means of interpreters, the Indians were supposed to be fully understanding participants in the land-cession treaties. The Indians were to be directly and notably affected by the congressional determination concerning the factories. Further, an Indian delegation representing five Missouri tribes connected with the factory at Fort Osage was visiting Washington during the debate; these were people from Benton's home territory with whom he obviously had direct contact. Benjamin O'Fallon, their agent—but not these Indian leaders—was called to testify. Indebted to Benton as his political patron,

O'Fallon offered only negative criticisms of the government's program. The Jeffersonians were of one mind in holding that they, rather than the Indians, had the qualified knowledge of what was good for the tribes. Invariably, what they called for also provided immediate or future benefits to the Jeffersonians.

In addition to the elimination of the factory system, the fur traders moved to gain their real but undeclared objective: the gradual reduction of government supervision of the fur trade and a lessened concern about the consequences of that new commerce upon the Indians. On the very day that it terminated the factory system Congress approved an amendment to the Intercourse Act of 1802, attempting to provide Indian agents with more precise supervisory powers over the fur trade in the areas of license control and exclusion of whiskey from trading operations.[34] Once again, however, this congressional declaration proved an empty show. The legislation was intended to safeguard Indian rights; however, to the extent that such regulations placed limitations on industrious traders, such restrictions were at best minimally enforced. "Within months," David Lavender points out, "traders everywhere knew that the 'severe' new law of 1822 was not going to be any more effective than its predecessor."[35]

By 1822, Congress—for various motives and by gradual modifications—had formulated an impressive Indian policy. The theory was laudable. The practice, through the middle half of the nineteenth century, would be so blatantly defective as to be severely criticized by De Smet and many of his contemporaries. Concern for Indian rights had guided the formation of policy; the implementation, at and beyond the Gateway City, amounted to mere tokenism.

ASHLEY'S REQUEST:
A License "To Hunt and Trap, and Trade"

The price of western expansion would be levied upon the Indians. Native Americans would be pressured into removal from the newly settled lands. Such a pattern was especially apparent in the actions of the members of the Missouri Territorial Assembly. At the close of 1820, they passed a resolution calling for Indian removal. By Lieutenant Governor Ashley's factual though unsympathetic report, "The subject had not a dissenting voice among the members." Early in 1822 Thomas Hart Benton and David Barton, as Missouri congressional delegates, notified Secretary of War Calhoun: "The undersigned have been called upon by the General Assembly of the State of

Missouri to apply to the General Government, and to solicit that the Indian title to all lands within the State may be extinguished—that in time to come no Indians may be removed into said State from other states—and that those which have heretofore been sent there by the General Government may be removed."[36]

By this time William Ashley had become a wealthy landowner, prominent for his military record and as a political figure in southeastern Missouri. Despite his official duties as lieutenant governor, Ashley was already making personal preparations for embarking upon the fur trade. As his new business partner, Ashley selected the experienced fur trader Andrew Henry. Along with Indian Superintendent William Clark and Reuben Lewis, brother of Governor Meriwether Lewis, Henry had been among the original incorporators of the Missouri Fur Company in 1809.[37]

The openly announced proposal of the Ashley-Henry Fur Company was to conduct a new type of operation in which actual trading with the Indians for furs would be only incidental. The "Ashley men" were employed specifically as hunters and trappers who would conduct a "fur gathering" program of their own. In Ashley's plan, the Indians were to have no active role. Their employment eliminated, the Native Americans were thereby stripped of their riches—the bartering power embodied in the game native to their lands. Hardly to be regarded as an unprincipled settler or ordinary frontiersman, Ashley boldly sought authorization from the federal government to conduct his self-serving program. Clearly, the project required authorization; the Ashley-Henry enterprise would be conducted well beyond the Missouri frontier in the supposedly exclusive Indian country.

Almost as if he were gathering evidence for a test case, Ashley made certain that his purpose was a matter of public knowledge, and he took steps to identify other prominent political and military figures of Missouri with his cause. Through February and March 1822, Ashley conducted an advertising campaign in the St. Louis newspapers—the *Missouri Gazette*; its successor, the *Missouri Republican*; and the *St. Louis Enquirer*—offering employment (of an unspecified nature) to "One Hundred enterprising Young Men" on the Upper Missouri. On April 13 the *St. Louis Enquirer*, reporting the departure of the Ashley-Henry party, also publicized its well-known purpose: "The object of this company is to trap and hunt— they are completely equipped, and number about 180 persons.— They will direct their course to the three forks of the Missouri, a region it is said, which contains a wealth in *Furs*, not surpassed by the mines of Peru."[38]

Thus, at the very beginning of 1822 Ashley went public in his efforts to obtain the necessary license. In January he approached General Henry Atkinson at Jefferson Barracks, south of St. Louis, requesting authorization to enter the Indian country beyond the Missouri. Atkinson informed Ashley that since no one in the area was then authorized to provide the license, application should be made to Secretary of War Calhoun.[39]

On January 25, however, Atkinson saw fit to notify Calhoun of Ashley's request, specifically reporting Ashley's announced purpose: "ascending the Missouri the ensuing spring, as high as the Yellow Stone to hunt and trap, and trade with the Indian Tribes." Atkinson expressed some reservations but concluded the letter with his personal endorsement of the project due to "the characters of the gentlemen who have the management of it."[40] Thus Ashley collected on his political debts, for in the previous June the lieutenant governor had joined with Governor McNair, Senator Benton, and other prominent Missourians in recommending to Calhoun that Atkinson be granted an increased military command.

Ashley was not content with the pressures placed upon Calhoun by his power position in Missouri or the qualified endorsement offered by Atkinson; the lieutenant governor also solicited support from the members of the Missouri congressional delegation, who forwarded "a recommendation and request" supporting his proposal to Calhoun. On March 9 Calhoun forwarded the Ashley-Henry licenses to Governor McNair, directing him to execute the formalities of bonding and signing.

Both in the Ashley-Henry licenses and his letter transmitting them to Governor McNair, Calhoun used the phrase "to trade with the Indians up the Missouri," making no reference to Ashley's proposal "to hunt and trap." Despite questions subsequently raised by agent O'Fallon regarding problems that might result from the announced activities and despite the advertisements Ashley placed in the St. Louis newspapers in January and February 1823, again seeking "One Hundred MEN, to ascend the Missouri river to the *Rocky Mountains*, there to be employed as Hunters," Ashley's request for a license renewal the following spring was granted readily without any indication of limitations or restrictions.[41]

By his preparatory activities in the spring of 1822, Ashley had clearly anticipated the congressional termination of the trade factory system. He also had gained practical advantages over most of the competition that would be operating from the St. Louis riverfront. Only one other firm had already renewed its license early in the spring of 1822. Recently reorganized following the death of Manuel Lisa in 1820, the Missouri Fur Company—directed mainly by Joshua Pilcher as the field supervisor in Council Bluffs and Thomas Hempstead as the St. Louis supervisor—had placed about 180 men on the Upper Missouri in the summer of 1821. In this year of developing competition, the firm would increase its force to about 300 men.[42]

The Columbia Fur Company did not receive its license until July 17, nor did the French Fur Company—Berthold, Pratte, Chouteau, and others—receive its license until two days later. These were granted by William Clark, who resumed the position of superintendent of Indian affairs in June 1822. Other firms were about to enter the competition. Jacob Astor's lieutenant Ramsay Crooks had already bought out the St. Louis supply firm of Stone, Bostwick and Company; the Western Department of the American Fur Company was about to be born. Within a few years, after first uniting with the Chouteau group and then absorbing the Columbia Fur operation, the American Fur Company would so dominate the Upper Missouri that the combined activities of all its competitors would be classified together as "the opposition."[43]

The objective of Senator Benton's campaign—"to open the fur trade to individual enterprise"—had been quickly achieved. Within four months of congressional rejection of the federal program, the *St. Louis Enquirer* printed the following report on "The Fur Trade": "Since the abolition of the United States' factories, a great activity has prevailed in the operation of this trade. Those formerly engaged in it have increased their capital and extended their enterprize, many new firms have engaged in it, and others are preparing to do so. It is computed that a thousand men, chiefly from this place, are now employed in this trade on the waters of the Missouri, and half that number on the Upper Mississippi."[44]

INDIAN SUPERINTENDENT CLARK:
"Jeffersonian Man on the Frontier"

In the spring of 1807, Lewis and Clark hoped to fashion a second success story for their political patron, President Thomas Jefferson. Lewis received the appointment as governor of the new territory of Louisiana; Clark was named agent for the Indians in the territory. Lewis died in 1809, and in 1813 Clark was appointed governor of

Missouri Territory—the change from "Louisiana" had been made the previous year. As a territorial governor, Clark became ex officio the superintendent of Indian affairs for the area under his jurisdiction. Thereafter, Clark was reappointed governor for successive three-year terms. However, the last of those, an appointment by President James Monroe on June 21, 1820, was cut short. In the first state elections, held on August 28, 1820, Clark, who had done little campaigning, was soundly defeated by his friend Alexander McNair, who took the oath of office as governor on September 19.[45]

In far-removed Washington there was a deeper appreciation of William Clark. Government officials held Clark in high esteem because of his effective handling of Indian affairs, an implementation in accord with the stated high principles and the unpublicized objectives of that Indian policy. Clark had been able to purchase peace along the frontier by presents far less costly than large-scale and long-term military involvements. Dealing with the tribal leaders in a gracious manner, acting as the local personification of the "Great Father," the president of the United States, Clark had gained great influence and exceptional power. He managed a mild yet effective domination, minimizing interracial violence despite the perennial frictions between the Indians and the westward-spreading settlers. In secretive fashion, by actions he confessed as deplorable but effective, Clark had reduced the danger of attacks by the more powerful and hostile tribes. The superintendent admitted privately that he had encouraged intertribal warfare by directing his agents Pierre Chouteau and Manuel Lisa to offer bribes of arms and supplies to certain Indian groups who had already been manipulated into subservience and dependence.

From his St. Louis headquarters, Clark had pursued an effective program aimed at gaining greater domination over the tribes. He sent delegations of Indian leaders to Washington to be impressed and intimidated with the evidence of the overwhelming power, material richness, strength, and numerical superiority of the whites. Moreover, Clark had served between 1815 and 1818 as head negotiator of some twenty-five treaties in which Native American groups of the Mississippi-Missouri area ceded extensive areas of land, and in directing these treaty cessions in the winning manner of Jefferson himself, he had manifested sympathy and humanitarian concern.[46]

Nonetheless, in October 1820, only a month after he left the governor's post, Clark was informed by Secretary of War Calhoun that his services connected with the Indian Office were to be terminated in June 1821. The congressional appropriation for the operation of the Indian Office had been drastically reduced, and Calhoun had decided to do without an Indian agent in the former St. Louis post. Clark was terminated.[47]

Almost exactly a year after Clark's dismissal Congress legislated the reappointment of a superintendent of Indian affairs in St. Louis. Benton and his associates had made it clear that St. Louis would be the center of the fur trade, and it was obvious that the Plains Indians would be especially affected by this developing commerce. Before the close of May 1822, Calhoun forwarded a letter of reappointment to Clark.[48]

Meanwhile, Indian agent O'Fallon returned to St. Louis from Washington on April 5, 1822. The published intentions of the Ashley-Henry party, which had set out two days earlier, must have been common talk on the St. Louis riverfront. Before proceeding to his post at Council Bluffs, O'Fallon determined that as the ranking official of the Indian Office in the area, he needed to call the matter to Calhoun's attention. Atkinson's earlier letter regarding Ashley's activities may have been disregarded by Calhoun as unfounded private gossip, but O'Fallon's letter of April 9 was a factual on-the-scene report of an Indian Office field official: "I understand that License has been granted to Mess Ashley & Henry to trade, trap, and hunt, on the upper Missouri—I have not seen it, but am in hopes that limits have been prescribed to their hunting and trapping on Indian lands, as nothing is better Calculated to alarm and disturb the harmony so happily existing between us and the Indians in the vicinity of the Council Bluffs."[49]

Officially notified now that Ashley's operational intentions had become widely known, Calhoun obviously could not avoid the issue. Washing his hands of the matter, Calhoun passed on to Clark the responsibility for initiating remedial action against Ashley's illegal invasion:

> The license which has been granted by this Department by order of the President to Genl. Ashley & Major Henry confers the privilege of trading with the Indians only, as the laws regulating trade and intercourse with the Indian tribes do not contain any authority to issue licenses for any other purpose. The privilege thus granted to them they are to exercise conformably to the laws and regulations that are or shall be made for the government of trade and inter-

course with the Indians, for the true and faithfull observance of which they have given bonds with sufficient security; consequently, it is presumed, they will do no act not authorized by such laws and regulations.[50]

Calhoun thus raised the moral issue connected with the obvious illegality, reminding Clark that for non-Indians to hunt or trap on Indian lands was unacceptable and in violation of the trade legislation enacted by Congress. Clark, however, simply ignored Calhoun's charge of illegality against Ashley's activities. Soothingly, the trusted Clark, experienced in his manipulative treatment of the Indians, informed his Washington superior that he anticipated no problems: "The License granted to Genl. Ashley and Majr. Henry I am inclined to believe will not produce any disturbance among the Indian tribes with whome we have much intercourse." Clark went on to assure Calhoun that "it will be the interest of those gentlemen to cultivate the friendship of the most distant tribes." In January of the following year, before issuing a renewal of Ashley's license, a renewal that would extend over five years, Clark piously informed Calhoun that the Ashley operation had already built its trading post, Fort Henry, on the Yellowstone River, yet as intended by Ashley and Henry, this structure was to serve as no more than a storage depot.[51]

With that facade established, Ashley had provided Clark with the important though only apparent justification for his authorized operation. Like his political patron, Clark's main concern was the appearance of a righteous policy. Imitating Jefferson's willingness to adjust to expediency, that is, to the pragmatic demands of the whites, Clark continued to move Indian policy to mere tokenism.

Clark's actions regarding Ashley's operations clearly contradicted the official stand he had taken regarding this matter some years earlier. In September 1808 Clark had informed Secretary of War Dearborn that "the maney abuses which has Crept into the habits of Indian Trade, and the unfair practices of the White hunters, hunting & takeing the fur, and killing the Deer & Elk for their Skins on the Indians hunting Lands has been a just cause of Complaint." Clark also had notified Dearborn that as Indian agent for Louisiana Territory, he had established regulations designed to eliminate such abuses: "In those regulations all traders are to reside with the *Ravelin* of the Fort out of which they are not to be promitted to trade, and to conform to the rules and regulations of the place—No hunter to hunt on the lands assigned for the Indians to hunt on."[52]

Despite his protests, however, such regulations were not followed by Clark himself. As early as the following year, Clark set a precedent for other offenders. In 1809, the expressed purpose of the Missouri Fur Company, of which Clark was a founding member and the St. Louis agent, was officially reported by Governor Lewis to Secretary of War Eustis as "to hunt and trade on the waters of the Misoury and Columbia Rivers." Clark doubly violated the Trade and Intercourse Act of 1802. Section 11 of that act prohibited any official authorized to grant trading licenses from having "any interest or concern in any trade with the Indians," and section 2 specifically outlawed entering the Indian country "to hunt, or in any wise destroy the game."[53]

The amended legislation of 1822 also emphasized the prohibition against introducing "ardent spirits" into Indian country. Under Superintendent Clark's supervision on the St. Louis levee, little corrective change was effected. Again, section 2 specified that the Indian agents were "to cause the stores and packages of goods of all traders to be searched." Under critical questioning by Washington superiors as late as 1831, Clark protested that because of his confidence in the good faith of the traders, "this delicate task was dispensed with." In the very next year, Clark allowed William Sublette to take 450 gallons of whiskey into the Indian country for the use of his "boatmen." Yet in that 1832 expedition Sublette hauled his goods overland; no boatmen were hired.[54]

In his official activities as superintendent of Indian affairs from 1824 to 1836, Clark succeeded in negotiating twelve more land-cession treaties with various tribes. Thus before his death in 1838 while still in office, Clark had fulfilled the official wish of the political leaders of Missouri; he had by these treaties effected the removal of all Indians from his state.[55]

In 1825, in one of his final letters to Jefferson, whom he had served for almost a quarter century, Clark penned a lamentation over the sorry conditions that had become the way of life for the impoverished Native Americans on the Missouri border. Regarding the tragic fate of "these unfortunate people," a fate in the fashioning of which he had played the key role, Clark wrote: "In my present situation of Superintendent of Indian Affairs, it would afford me Pleasure to be enabled to— —the conditions of these unfortunate people placed under my charge, Knowing as I do their retchedness and their rapid decline[.] It is to be lamented that the deplorable Situation of the Indians do not receive more of the human feelings of the nation."

In a superficial manner in his years of directing the implementation of Indian policy, Clark had publicly treated the Indians humanely. Yet even more than Ashley or Benton, Clark was, as his biographer Jerome O. Steffen designated him, the "Jeffersonian man on the frontier"; the paternalism he exercised had not necessarily been benign. For those who fashioned or applied Jefferson's Indian policy, in the final analysis, land was more important than the Native Americans.[56]

JUNE 1823: The Closing of the "Bloody Missouri"

Throughout the morning hours of June 1—it was a Sunday of celebration, of welcoming De Smet and the other Jesuit newcomers—most of the citizens of St. Louis were gathered in and about Du Bourg's cathedral on the crest of the bluff overlooking the St. Louis levee. William Clark must have been especially evident, for as superintendent of Indian affairs, he had been in on the bishop's planning for the new Indian school these teachers would conduct west of the city.

Perhaps the festivities on this June morning—the firing of the city's cannons and the prolonged ringing of the cathedral bells—reminded Clark of another celebration that had been held along the riverfront earlier in the spring. The public ceremonies on March 10 had marked the beginning of the second annual Ashley expedition. A group of musicians hired by Ashley had serenaded the spectators while the two keelboats, loaded with some seventy hunters and trappers and their cargo, headed out from the bank "with sails up and colors flying."[57]

On this June morning Ashley was ordering the anchoring of those keelboats near the Arikara villages about 150 miles north of Council Bluffs. On the morrow, Ashley's men would be fired upon and routed by belligerent Indians. And on that June morning Clark had no way of knowing that disaster had already overtaken two other parties of St. Louis–based fur companies.

Throughout July, expresses from the Upper Missouri disclosed to Superintendent Clark all the sorry details of widespread Indian violence against the fur traders. Before the close of May, Henry's men had been attacked near the mouth of the Yellowstone by a group of Blackfoot warriors and had suffered four immediate fatalities. A few days earlier, farther upstream, seven field workers of the Missouri Fur Company had been killed in an attack by another Blackfoot war party. By mid-1823, the upper river had become the "Bloody

Missouri." As a fur traders' highway, it had been closed. At the urging of agent O'Fallon, Colonel Leavenworth would conduct a military campaign against the Arikaras; of questionable success, that operation failed to guarantee an immediate opening of the Missouri River to commerce.[58]

At the end of August, from their retreat encampment near the confluence of the Missouri and White rivers, Ashley and Henry determined to change their field of operation. Led by Henry, the hunters and trappers headed westward across the heart of the Great Plains. It would be the first of many crossings and recrossings. Men like Thomas Fitzpatrick and Jedediah Smith would discover and repeatedly use the ancient tribal highway, the Great Platte River Road. De Smet would at midcentury report the Indian name: "The Great Medicine Road of the white nation." Along the rivers of western Wyoming—the Green, the Wind, and the Snake—the Ashley men, working year-round as beaver hunters on both slopes of the continental divide, would become the original mountain men.[59]

After his initial crossing of the Great Plains, De Smet would participate in the mountain men's final rendezvous in 1840; it was the end of the beginning, the concluding act of the initial invasion of this Indian country. De Smet would repeat that journey the following year, but this time, along with his fellow missionaries, as a member of the first emigrant wagon train headed for the Pacific. Pausing on the banks of the Green, the travelers would mark this 1841 crossing as the beginning of the end—the beginning of the settlers' invasion of the Great Plains, the beginning of the dispossession of the native tribes.

Chapter Two
The End of the Beginning—1840 (1823–40)

> Come, we are done with this life in the mountains—
> done with wading in beaver-dams, and freezing or
> starving alternately—done with Indian trading and
> Indian fighting. The fur trade is dead in the Rocky
> Mountains, and it is no place for us now, if ever it was.
> —Mountain man "Doc" Newell
> to Joe Meek (1840)

THE WINTER COUNT: An Annual Report, 1823–40

The "winter count" was a Plains Indian chronological record painted on a buffalo hide, a calendar so named because during the halt of winter the annual addition of a new pictograph on the hide would commemorate a notable tribal event of the previous moons.

This chapter serves as a similar chronology, listing the more influential happenings of the years from 1823 to 1840. During this period St. Louis would become the commercial capital of the West, serving the entire drainage of the Missouri River. The fur trade rendezvous, generally held in midsummer along the Green River in Wyoming, would become the focal point of the beaver trappers' major invasion of Indian country. De Smet and his fellow Missouri Jesuits, sharing the pressures of the other frontiersmen, would make pragmatic adjustments in their apostolic activities. It was a special period of beginnings, one that combined orderly developments and abrupt changes.

1824   The party of Ashley men headed by Jed Smith crossed South Pass and made a successful hunt at the head of Green River. Thomas Fitzpatrick's group returned across the central plains. Henry's group returned from the Wind River country by the northern route, losing men and furs to hostile Indians along the Yellowstone and the Missouri. Arriving at St. Louis, Henry retired from the fur trade. With a new license from Clark to trade with the Snake Indians west of the Rocky Mountains, Ashley set out for Fort Atkinson.[1]

The pioneer Jesuits had gathered the previous year at the village of St. Ferdinand in the Florissant Valley northwest of St. Louis. St. Rose Philippine Duchesne and the Sisters of the Sacred Heart, who had recently established their missionary program at Florissant, came to the aid of the Jesuits, their generosity continuing long after the Jesuits had constructed their buildings on the farm purchased by Bishop Du Bourg. As De Smet and his six fellow novices completed their probationary period, they pronounced their Jesuit vows on October 1 and immediately began their studies of philosophy and theology. For the young Jesuits, these must have been busy days. In addition to their studies and the labor of construction, they acted as teachers and supervisors. On May 11, when two young Sauk boys arrived, the St. Regis Indian Seminary started its program. These initial students were joined during the following month by three sons of Iowa chiefs. The preliminary phase of Bishop Du Bourg's 1823 proposal had been implemented.[2]

1825 Ashley had determined upon Henry's Fork on the Green as "The place of randavoze for all our parties on or before the 10th July next." Over 120 trappers participated in this initial rendezvous. With Jed Smith as his new partner, Ashley took supply orders for the following year, then returned to St. Louis by the northern route while some twenty-five lodges of his trappers set up winter camps in the mountains. Joined by Robert Campbell, Smith set out from St. Louis at the close of October; seventy trappers accompanied the supply caravan, along with 160 horses and mules. Because of the weather, the party had to winter along the Platte River near Grand Island.[3]

This year the number of Indian students at St. Regis increased to eight. According to Father Van Quickenborne, the students' demonstration of learned skills at the start of the year caused Superintendent Clark and a visiting delegation of Iowa chiefs to be "highly satisfied." The Sisters of the Sacred Heart at St. Ferdinand accepted six Indian girls for their school program; however, their request for the necessary and anticipated government financial support was denied on the grounds of lack of funds.[4]

1826 Ashley departed St. Louis on March 18 and reached the Smith-Campbell party on April 1 at Grand Island. From there they moved westward on what would become the Oregon Trail: up the North Platte, the Sweetwater, then across South Pass to the Green. Ashley announced that the rendezvous would be held at Cache Valley on the Bear River in June. After supplying over a hundred trappers, Ashley sold out to Jed Smith, David Jackson, and William Sublette;

however, he contracted to supply merchandize for the following summer if notified by March 1. While other trappers wintered in what would become Yellowstone Park, Jed Smith with fifteen trappers set off for an overland journey to California.[5]

In reply to a report on the Indian school sent by Father Van Quickenborne, Indian superintendent Thomas McKenney forwarded from Washington a statement by the secretary of war approving the Jesuits' program of Indian education.[6]

On the advice of Indian superintendent William Clark, General Atkinson selected the Mississippi River Bluffs just south of St. Louis as the site for a new military post, Jefferson Barracks.[7]

1827   After a very difficult winter journey to St. Louis to order the Ashley supplies, William Sublette obtained a license from Clark for trading operations at three western locations. The Ashley expedition departed St. Louis on March 30 with equipment that included a carriage-mounted four-pound cannon, the first wheeled vehicle to cross South Pass. At the rendezvous, held at Bear Lake in Mexican Territory, the cannon was fired to celebrate the arrival of Jed Smith, who had been given up as lost. After the rendezvous, the caravan returned, hauling seven thousand pounds of beaver pelts.[8]

Following his summer visit to St. Regis, Father Dzierozynski, Maryland superior of the Jesuits, reported: "The Indian school . . . makes excellent progress alike in morals, letters and manual labor in the fields. . . . The boys number only thirteen, but the house cannot accommodate any more. . . . St. Ignatius Day was celebrated with a solemn high mass and panegyric in St. Ferdinand's church, some of the Indian boys singing with Ours in the choir."[9]

Joseph Rosati, successor to Du Bourg as bishop of the newly founded diocese of St. Louis, took up residence in March. The western boundary of Rosati's jurisdiction reached to the continental divide. De Smet was among the group of four young Jesuits ordained by Rosati at St. Ferdinand's Church in Florissant on September 23; two of their fellow Jesuits had been ordained the previous year.[10]

In the Indian country on the west bank of the Missouri about twenty-five miles north of the mouth of the Kaw (Kansas) River, Fort Leavenworth replaced the now abandoned Fort Atkinson (opposite Council Bluffs) as the military outpost of the West. In the Far Northwest, agreement was reached between the United States and Britain to renew the joint Anglo-American occupation of the Oregon country, according to the 1818 treaty.[11]

1828   Between 1826 and 1828 Astor's American Fur Company absorbed a number of competitive firms: Pratte and Chouteau, the Columbia Fur Company, William Henry Vanderburgh and Joseph Robidoux. Under Etienne Provost the American Fur Company pushed a group of trappers into Crow country.[12]

On June 29 Bishop Rosati ordained Francis Regis Loisel, the first St. Louisan elevated to the priesthood. Francis was related to many of the Creole families of the community. The fur trade activities of his father, Regis Loisel, supposedly predated the departure of Lewis and Clark for the Upper Missouri. In answer to Bishop Rosati's appeal, four Sisters of Charity of Emmitsburg, Maryland, arrived in St. Louis to conduct Mullanphy Hospital, the first hospital west of the Mississippi. In 1831 three additional sisters arrived to conduct the first orphanage in the West. As early as 1825 four white boys had enrolled at St. Regis. Since the St. Louis College had closed in 1827, some eight white boys, including Charles Pierre Chouteau, became students at Florissant; in 1829 an additional eight, including Julius Clark, were enrolled.[13]

1829   William Sublette supplied a small rendezvous in July on the Popo Agie River, and Fitzpatrick supplied another in August at Pierre's Hole. At year's end, Sublette made another difficult winter journey to St. Louis.[14]

Father Saulnier offered the funeral mass for Auguste Chouteau, who as a lad had assisted Pierre Laclede in founding the original post at St. Louis. As expressed in the 1823 concordat with Bishop Du Bourg, the Jesuits' purpose in coming to St. Louis was twofold: to care for the Indian missions to be established along the Missouri and for the white population of the region. With conditions unsatisfactory at Florissant the Jesuits closed St. Regis and opened St. Louis College; some ten boarders and thirty day students, all non-Indians, were enrolled. Along with other St. Louis contributors De Smet pledged his inheritance toward construction costs. Neither Rosati nor the Jesuit superior regarded the new college as a new and distinct apostolate; they saw it as supporting the Jesuit apostolate to the Indians. In 1824 the bishop had stated to Jesuit authorities in Rome: "A college at St. Louis could be of great help to the establishment at St. Ferdinand [Florissant] for the Indian agents reside there, and there, also, are held the councils of deputies from the various Indian nations."[15]

1830   Having again received a trading license from Clark, William Sublette put together a supply train of twelve wagons and some eighty men. After the rendezvous, in mid-July at the junction of the Popo Agie and Wind rivers, the trapper leadership was reorganized as the Rocky Mountain Fur Company. The return of the fur train to St. Louis caused a great stir. On October 29 the new leaders informed Secretary of War John Eaton that their easy journey westward proved "the facility of communicating overland with the Pacific ocean." The entire eastern half of the Oregon Trail, the road of the emigrants, had already been opened.[16]

Father Van Quickenborne notified Secretary of War Eaton that he had closed St. Regis Seminary. Having become convinced that "the youth of the aborigines stand in need of as much perhaps more assistance after they have left the school than when they actually enjoy[ed] its advantages," Van Quickenborne indicated that he hoped to implement a different program. Meanwhile De Smet, an English teacher at the Jesuits' St. Louis College, had been appointed treasurer. From the very start De Smet was concerned over the grave financial situation and realized that fund-raising would be necessary.[17]

1831   The supply caravan from St. Louis took an unusual route, its initial stop for trading purposes at Santa Fe. The renowned Jed Smith was killed on the Cimarron. Fitzpatrick rescued and adopted a stray Arapaho lad, who was given the new name "Friday." William H. Ashley, former leader of the mountain men, became their congressional spokesman. Elected to the House of Representatives, Ashley pushed the interests of the Rocky Mountain Fur Company against Astor's consolidated firm, the American Fur Company. Astor put two groups of trappers on the Great Plains. Andrew Drips, along with his partner, Lucien Fontenelle, returned to St. Louis for supplies; it was supposedly with this party that the initial Flathead delegation traveled to St. Louis to request that missionaries be sent to their people.[18]

Having arrived in St. Louis the previous summer, George Catlin began his famous Indian paintings while a house guest of William Clark. Later De Smet would tell the tragic story of "Pigeon's Egg Head," the young Assiniboine leader whose portraits, before and after his trip to Washington, were painted by Catlin.[19]

With the other priests of the area De Smet joined in laying the cornerstone of Rosati's "new" (today the restored "old") St. Louis cathedral. Rosati reported at year's end on the unusual purpose of the

Flathead visitors—to request that a Catholic priest be sent to them. Two of these four Indians, having manifested signs of some Catholic background during their final illness, were baptized and buried from the cathedral.[20]

1832   William Sublette was granted a two-year trading license, listing some thirty-nine employees. He also obtained a permit from Clark to carry 450 gallons of whiskey "for the special use of his boatmen"—his assistants in crossing the Great Plains. The expedition of eighty-five men and three hundred head of stock, including cattle and sheep, was joined by the Nathaniel Wyeth party and a few days later another group of trappers. The rendezvous, which took place at Pierre's Hole, was one of the largest ever held. After the rendezvous, a band of Blackfeet attacked some of the trappers but was driven off. Fitzpatrick and his workers supplied Sublette and Campbell with 11,246 pounds of beaver pelts for the return caravan. Washington Irving, who met the returning party in western Missouri, reported that they "looked like banditti returning with plunder."[21]

Following her maiden voyage in the previous summer, the American Fur Company's steamboat *Yellowstone* became the first steamboat to reach Fort Union at the mouth of the Yellowstone. The period of steamboat traffic on the Upper Missouri had begun.[22]

1833   Sublette and Campbell were licensed by Superintendent Clark to trade for a year and a half at thirty-three locations in the Indian country; in addition to the mountain trade, they erected a northern trading post, Fort William, two miles below the mouth of the Yellowstone. Assisted by 45 men, Campbell directed the supply caravan of 120 pack mules to the Green River for the rendezvous held near Bonneville's "Fort Nonsense." William Drummond Stewart, along with Edmund T. Christy and Dr. Benjamin Harrison, were among the first visitors at the rendezvous. Fontenelle and Drips brought in supplies for the trappers of the American Fur Company; Bonneville's outfit also arrived, as did Wyeth on his return journey from Oregon. The Rocky Mountain Fur Company had 55 trappers; the American Fur Company, 160 men. In addition to all these company trappers, by 1833 there may have been as many as several hundred free trappers, individuals who worked alone.[23]

Maximilian, prince of Wied-Neuwied, and his artist companion Karl Bodmer departed from the St. Louis levee on the *Yellowstone* for an extended tour of the Upper Missouri. Before their return the following year, Bodmer would have completed many of his famous Indian paintings.[24]

Asiatic cholera broke out again in St. Louis, as it had the previous year. De Smet noted that "out of a population of some six thousand about two hundred individuals succumbed within three-four weeks," although everyone connected with the Jesuit school was spared. As the first president of St. Louis University, Jesuit Father Verhaegen reported that by the spring of 1834 some 150 boarders would be enrolled. The U.S. Catholic bishops at the Second Provincial Council of Baltimore recommended that Indian missions be assigned to the Jesuits. This assignment was decreed by Pope Gregory XVI in the following year, and the responsibility was formally accepted by Jesuit Superior Roothaan in Rome.[25]

Having interviewed Superintendent Clark the previous year, William Walker prepared an account of the religious appeal of the Flathead delegation that began the Oregon missionary movement. To Walker's report, published in the *Christian Advocate and Journal*, G. P. Disoway added: "Let the Church awake from her slumbers and go forth to the salvation of these wandering sons of our native forests."[26]

On September 23 De Smet was naturalized as a citizen of the United States; by his signature he declared his name to be "Peter John De Smet." A few days later he was sent back to Europe to raise "men and means" for the Jesuit apostolates in Missouri. There were also personal health reasons for the trip. Verhaegen begged the Jesuit authorities in Rome, even if De Smet's health was not fully restored, to "be so good as to send him back after some time to the Mission."[27]

1834   Among the members of the supply expedition led by Nathaniel Wyeth to the rendezvous on Ham's Fork of the Green were five Oregon-bound Methodist missionaries with Jason Lee as their leader. Sublette's supply caravan left a crew of twelve men at the mouth of the Laramie to complete the construction of Fort William, the trading post that was to develop into the famous Fort Laramie. This was the last rendezvous for the Rocky Mountain Fur Company; reorganized as Fontenelle, Fitzpatrick and Company, it became the final merger of the field-experienced mountain men with the experts of the Chouteau-Astor combination, men skilled in marketing. The Wyeth group left the rendezvous for Snake River where they built Fort Hall at the mouth of the Portneuf; from there the missionaries were guided to Oregon. Fitzpatrick, with a crew of fifty-seven, directed the return of the fur caravan to Council Bluffs; from there

Etienne Provost supervised the shipment of over 5,300 beaver pelts to St. Louis.[28]

Non-Catholics as well as Catholics participated in the dedication ceremonies of Bishop Rosati's new cathedral overlooking the St. Louis levee. In late October De Smet informed Verhaegen of his departure from Antwerp with both men and means. However, taken sick in the North Sea, De Smet disembarked at Deal on the English coast while the new men and the solicited supplies continued on to New York and St. Louis. De Smet returned to Belgium hoping to regain his health.[29]

The House Committee on Indian Affairs introduced on May 20 bills to organize the Indian department, to establish new trade and intercourse rules, and to organize a government in the western Indian territory for native and transplanted tribes. Although the committee argued for passage of all three bills, Congress saw fit to enact only the first two. Critics have pointed out that without effective organization in the West, there was little hope that Indian rights would be protected or that the new intercourse act would be enforced any better than its predecessors. Nonetheless, this legislation was historic, for the Indian country was defined: "All that part of the United States west of the Mississippi, and not within the states of Missouri and Louisiana, or the Territory of Arkansas."[30]

1835   The rendezvous this summer was on the Green, the first conducted by the American Fur Company. Fontenelle had led a supply caravan of sixty men and two hundred horses to Fort Laramie. The party included two missionaries, Dr. Marcus Whitman and Rev. Samuel Parker. With Fitzpatrick as guide, the caravan reached the Green on August 12; by Whitman's estimate over two thousand Indians were present for the rendezvous. William Stewart, having wintered at Fort Vancouver, was also present. Informed by Stewart of some of the practical needs of establishing a mission in Oregon, Dr. Whitman sent Parker ahead while he returned east to fill those needs. Parker was escorted by Jim Bridger to the Flathead territory, and from there he continued his journey to Oregon. Fontenelle hauled back to St. Louis some 120 packs of beaver pelts and 80 bundles of buffalo robes. This proved to be the first year that buffalo robes sold better in St. Louis than beaver pelts. Fitzpatrick remained at Fort Laramie to trade with the Indians and was joined there by David D. Mitchell, who had been trading on the Upper Missouri.[31]

Sick and discouraged, De Smet requested and obtained release from membership in the Jesuit order on May 8. Joined to the diocese of Ghent, De Smet served as a chaplain in religious institutions in Dendermonde, his native town; however, he continued his solicitations of manpower and financial support for the Missouri Jesuits.[32]

The second delegation from the Flatheads arrived in St. Louis, again seeking the assignment of a "Blackrobe" from the Jesuits. This time the Flatheads sent Old Ignace, the Iroquois who had first told them about Catholicism, accompanied by his two small sons, who were baptized in the chapel of St. Louis University. The only answer to Ignace's request was a vague promise that a priest would be sent if possible. However, all available Jesuit manpower, including Van Quickenborne, was committed to establishing an Indian mission among the Kickapoos north of Fort Leavenworth.[33]

1836   Fitzpatrick returned to St. Louis in the spring. He managed to get financial backing from Chouteau, who obtained a trade license from Clark for the partnership of Fitzpatrick, Sublette, Bridger, and Drips. William Sublette and Robert Campbell determined to remain in St. Louis as merchants. William Drummond Stewart returned for another western tour, accompanied by four assistants and two wagons loaded with special supplies. Dr. and Mrs. Whitman, Rev. and Mrs. Henry Spalding and their assistant William H. Gray, and two young Nez Perce boys Dr. Whitman had brought the previous year all prepared to depart from St. Louis, Spalding having received there official authorization to establish a mission in the Indian country. Narcissa Whitman and Elisabeth Spalding, though devout Protestants, visited Rosati's cathedral for a few moments of prayer. However, since the bishop was conducting High Mass, with all its incensations and other formalities of Romish ritual and regalia, the ladies were distracted and antagonized. They declared later that "witnessing their heartless forms and ceremonies, induced us soon to leave, rejoicing that we have never been left to embrace such delusions." Yet in the Northwest the same Catholic emphasis on external rituals would prove a special attraction to Native Americans.[34]

Fitzpatrick and his staff departed from Council Bluffs with the supply caravan; seventy men directed twenty mule carts, along with a herd of some four hundred horses and mules. Heading westward along the north bank of the Platte, the company established the route that in 1847 would become the Mormon Trail. Several reasons made this rendezvous particularly significant. For the first time in its fifteen-year history white women were present. Osborne Russell noted that Mrs. Whitman and Mrs. Spaulding were "the first white women ever seen by these Indians and the first that had ever penetrated into these wild and rocky regions." Moreover, it was the first time an Indian agent attended the rendezvous. Joshua Pilcher, who had been appointed subagent "for a portion of the Sioux high up the Missouri," was far from his post at Fort Lookout, but he was not present as an agent of the Indian Office. Dr. Whitman reported that Major Pilcher acted "as agent of Pratt, Choteau & co., in whose behalf he bought out the 'mountain partners,' so that the whole [fur] business now belongs to them." After the rendezvous the missionary party was conducted to Fort Hall by Drips and Hudson's Bay lieutenants.[35]

The board of trustees of St. Louis University formally declared its indebtedness to De Smet for his activities in soliciting support; his name was placed at the head of the register of contributors. In addition to new candidates for the Jesuits and funds for their programs, De Smet had forwarded educational equipment and some fifty paintings by European artists.[36]

Heading a group of four Jesuits, Van Quickenborne left St. Louis to begin the mission among the Kickapoo Indians on the west bank of the Missouri. They planned to establish a "reduction" modeled after the Jesuit pattern for Indian missions in the Western Hemisphere developed two centuries earlier in Paraguay. As early as 1830 Van Quickenborne had discussed this plan with President Andrew Jackson, intending to establish such a reduction among the Osages. Aided by Father Christian Hoecken's knowledge of the Kickapoo language, an Indian school supported in part by a government subsidy was now begun, continuing until the mission was terminated in 1840.[37]

1837   Stewart again prepared to join the caravan heading to the rendezvous. He readied three supply wagons and was accompanied by Alfred Jacob Miller, a young artist who would paint the western scene, especially rendezvous activities. Fitzpatrick's caravan of some forty-five men and twenty mule-drawn carts arrived at Horse Creek in mid-July. After the rendezvous Fontenelle and Bridger led seventy-five trappers to a winter camp on the Powder River.

This year the American Fur Company steamboat *St. Peters* spread smallpox among the Indian tribes of the Upper Missouri. The epidemic all but destroyed the Mandans and spread quickly among the Blackfeet, traditional foes of the fur trappers.[38]

In 1836 Washington Irving published *Astoria,* followed the next year by *Adventures of Captain Bonneville, or Scenes Beyond The Rocky Mountains of the Far West*; together, these books offered the first published reports on the fur trade in the West and were widely read. The third Flathead delegation, headed once more by Old Ignace, departed from the rendezvous with William Gray. On their way to St. Louis, however, the entire delegation was killed by a party of Sioux at Ash Hollow. Joseph N. Nicollet, a French scientist in U.S. government service, visited St. Louis; at the cathedral on November 25 he witnessed the baptism by Bishop Rosati of William Drummond Stewart, recently returned from the rendezvous.[39]

Assured of readmittance to the Jesuits, De Smet, along with four new candidates, set out from France, arriving in St. Louis on November 27. He immediately joined the group of novices in their probationary period at Florissant.[40]

1838   With some forty-five men Andrew Drips directed the American Fur Company supply caravan of eighteen carts and two hundred horses and mules. Joined by Fontenelle at Fort Laramie, they headed to the rendezvous at the junction of the Popo Agie and Wind rivers. Stewart was there again, this year with five guests, including two sons of William Clark. Four new missionary couples and their three assistants were also present. Francis Ermantinger from Fort Hall, along with other Hudson's Bay trappers, escorted the missionaries westward.[41]

On July 5 Congress created the Corps of Topographical Engineers, which was to play a decisive role in the exploration and development of the West. Historian William Goetzmann characterizes the corps as "a central institution of Manifest Destiny." Among its first and most famous members was Lieutenant John C. Frémont, whose initial assignment was to assist Nicollet in scientific expeditions west of the upper Mississippi.[42]

At the request of the Potawatomi Indians Van Quickenborne and Verhaegen negotiated with the Indian Office to open a mission at Council Bluffs. Joining two other Jesuits as a last-minute replacement, De Smet, having pronounced his Jesuit vows, departed the St. Louis riverfront on the steamboat *Howard*. The signing of De Smet's passport, still a legal requirement for entering Indian country, was one of Clark's final official acts as superintendent of Indian affairs; he died on September 1.[43]

At St. Joseph's Mission in Council Bluffs De Smet began an

activity that would continue throughout his life—raising funds for the Indian missions by correspondence. Appreciating the widespread interest in the unknown West, De Smet became an observant reporter. All the essentials for effective fund-raising were present—a special cause, an extreme financial dependence, and mounting social pressures. By means of his letters, addressed primarily to relatives and friends, he developed a wide audience in Europe and the Western Hemisphere.[44]

1839   A greatly reduced supply caravan—only four two-wheeled carts—left Independence in mid-April for the rendezvous on the Green. Dr. F. A. Wislizenus, a German physician from St. Louis, headed a party of four other visitors, and there was a missionary group composed of two couples and three assistants. By now the beaver had been hunted almost to extinction, and the beaver trade was already in decline. At the gathering on the Green it was rumored that the rendezvous was about to be terminated, that the company might not outfit any more trapping brigades.[45]

De Smet's letters from the Potawatomi mission realistically reported achievements and failures. These reports marked the beginning of a lifelong crusade against the "abominable traffickers" of the whiskey trade. As late as 1870 De Smet was to characterize these early bootleggers as the "tools of hell."[46] At the end of April De Smet boarded the American Fur Company steamboat for a brief voyage to southeastern Dakota. Among the passengers were the former mountain man Etienne Provost, Lieutenant Frémont, and Joseph N. Nicollet. At the mouth of the Vermillion De Smet disembarked for a self-appointed task: the attempt to conduct a peace conference to eliminate intertribal disputes.

De Smet's adventuresome spirit, unselfish concern, and sensitivity certainly contributed to his success; so did his acceptance by the Indians, based largely on his ability and willingness to adjust to "the Indian way." He instinctively respected tribal protocol and readily participated in Native American rituals. With a patience that was more than tolerance he accommodated himself to prolonged oratory and lengthy preliminary feasting. By affectionate good grace, good manners, and good fortune, De Smet seems not to have experienced a detectable degree of cultural shock. In all his years of accepting Indian hospitality De Smet apparently never had to feign a happy and relaxed identification with his hosts.

De Smet was effective in his peacemaking attempts at Camp

Vermillion, and the concluding ceremonies of the calumet dance were performed in his honor. A second important success followed: determining to make his return to Council Bluffs as a real outdoorsman, De Smet passed the physical endurance test. After three days of floating downriver in a dugout canoe, sleeping at night in a buffalo robe on a sandbar, and enjoying the evening soup "made with the muddy water of the Missouri," De Smet returned to St. Joseph's Mission as a camping enthusiast. Beyond simple endurance he had enjoyed the physically demanding life of the wilderness country.[47]

In these two all-important respects De Smet could feel himself qualified to work among Native Americans. Thus in the late summer of 1839 he was prepared to respond to the invitation extended by the fourth Flathead delegation. De Smet reported:

> On the 18th of last September two Catholic Iroquois came to visit us. They had been for twenty-three years among the nation called the Flatheads and Pierced Noses [Nez Percés], about a thousand Flemish leagues from where we are. . . . By their instructions and examples they have given all that nation a great desire to have themselves baptized. . . . The sole object of these good Iroquois was to obtain a priest to come and finish what they had so happily commenced. We gave them letters of recommendation for our Reverend Superior at St. Louis.

Arriving in St. Louis, the two members of this delegation made a strong impression on Bishop Rosati and Father Verhaegen. Both petitioned Rome for volunteers to answer the Indians' request. Rosati reported administering the sacrament of confirmation to both Indians, and Verhaegen offered his promise that two priests would journey to that distant region in the spring to live for a time among the Flatheads. One of the delegates, Verhaegen noted, left at once to carry the glad tidings to his people; the other (Young Ignace) would stay on through the winter to travel westward with the Jesuit priests.[48]

1840—DE SMET'S TRIAL JOURNEY TO THE FLATHEADS

Through the winter Doc Newell, Joe Meek, William Doughty, and a reduced number of other trappers continued their activities in the mountains, wondering if a supply caravan would arrive in the spring for a final rendezvous.[49]

Since additional goods were needed for St. Joseph's Mission, De Smet left Council Bluffs on February 13 for a difficult two-week trip by horseback to St. Louis. There Verhaegen informed him of a new assignment. De Smet's earnest wish had been granted: he was to head west in the spring as the requested Blackrobe of the Flatheads. He would be replaced at Council Bluffs by Father Christian Hoecken.

Once more De Smet was a last-minute choice. Because the circumstances seemed to favor the establishment of reductions in the highly successful Paraguayan style, there was no lack of volunteers in St. Louis or in Rome. At the close of the previous year Verhaegen had directed two younger Jesuits to complete their theological studies to be ready for ordination at an advanced date, after which they would be sent to the Rocky Mountains. However, in a letter to De Smet's family in Belgium, Verhaegen explained why he finally selected his former classmate De Smet: "He manifested such eagerness and ardent zeal for the work; he possessed, moreover, such remarkable qualities, that it was hardly possible for us to make another choice. His prudence and ability assured the successful termination of his journey."[50]

In the early spring Jim Bridger and Henry Fraeb left St. Louis to join Moses Harris and the mountain supply caravan, traveling by steamer to Independence. Either during the voyage or through the previous days of preparation along the St. Louis levee De Smet came to know Jim Bridger; a lasting relationship of affection and respect developed between them.

To the surprise of the Jesuit authorities in Rome, De Smet set out without a Jesuit companion. Verhaegen provided the highly realistic explanation: the additional thousand dollars needed to meet the expenses of a second Jesuit could not be raised. Besides, De Smet's purpose was exploratory, to evaluate the prospects for a permanent mission in the Rocky Mountains.

According to his many fellow travelers over the years to come, De Smet was a congenial and interesting companion, but whether on the Missouri or crossing the Plains and Rockies, he would never cease to be a priest. As Major General David S. Stanley noted of him in 1868, when among the Indians, De Smet "always wears the cassock and crucifix." Arriving in Westport, De Smet baptized the two children of Andrew Drips, who was to command the annual caravan that De Smet would join on his trip to the Flatheads. De Smet purchased the equipment and horses needed for his escort, Young Ignace, and for himself.[51]

On April 30 some forty people left the trailhead at Westport in the caravan led by Drips. Besides De Smet's carts, there were the two wagons of three other missionary families—Mr. and Mrs. Harvey Clark, Mr. and Mrs. Alvin Smith, and Mr. and Mrs. P. Littlejohn. Two other wagons transported the five children and supplies of Joel P. Walker and his wife, the first declared emigrants for Oregon. Crossing the Indian frontier, the train headed westward along the recently established Oregon Trail. In the heart of the buffalo country they forded the South Fork of the Platte and arrived on June 4 at Fort Laramie, where De Smet was feasted in the nearby Cheyenne camp. After moving up the North Platte to Red Butte, the caravan headed cross-country to the Sweetwater near Independence Rock, a landmark henceforth known by the name De Smet gave it: "the great register of the desert." Snowbanks lined the trail as they rode over the gentle South Pass on June 23. After seven more days they reached Green River at the mouth of Horse Creek.[52]

Of this rendezvous Doc Newell reported: "Mr. Drips, Fraeb, and Bridger, from St. Louis with goods; but times were certainly hard—no beaver, and everything dull." As a newcomer, De Smet was more impressed, noting that "Indians of different nations and the trappers had assembled at the rendezvous in great numbers for the sake of the trade."[53]

De Smet and Young Ignace, moreover, had a special reason to rejoice. Some thirty Shoshone tribal leaders held a feast in De Smet's honor at which the old chief welcomed the Blackrobe with these words: "All our country is open to you." Soon the long-anticipated meeting with the Flatheads became a reality: a delegation of ten men rode into camp to welcome and escort De Smet to their home territory. "Our meeting was not that of strangers," De Smet reported, "but of friends." Later De Smet wrote:

> On Sunday, the 5th of July, I had the consolation of celebrating the holy sacrifice of mass *sub dio*. The altar was placed on an elevation, and surrounded with boughs and garlands of flowers; I addressed the congregation in French and in English, and spoke also by an interpreter to the Flatheads and Snake Indians. It was a spectacle truly moving for the heart of a missionary, to behold an assembly composed of so many different nations, who all assisted at our holy mysteries with great satisfaction. The Canadians sang hymns in French and Latin, and the Indians in their native tongue. It was truly a Catholic worship.[54]

Some of the French trappers present may have belonged to the party headed by Francis Ermantinger, whose brigade had come to the rendezvous after depositing supplies at Fort Hall. After the rendezvous Newell guided the missionaries and the Walker family to the Hudson's Bay post; from there other trappers took them to the Whitman mission at Waiilatpu.[55] Although it has been suggested that Bridger accompanied him, De Smet's accounts of the trip do not mention Bridger. The knowledge De Smet displayed—the identification of the continental divide between the almost adjacent headwaters of the Missouri and Snake rivers—may have been learned from Bridger in earlier conversations. De Smet's narratives of this trip mention only "ten brave Canadians," one of whom, Jean-Baptiste de Velder, would be De Smet's devoted companion and guide all the way back to Westport.[56]

Leaving the rendezvous, De Smet and his party headed northward up the Green, then descended westward along the Gros Ventre River into Jackson Hole. After bull-boating across the Snake, they crossed the southern pass of the Teton Range to Pierre's Hole. Almost directly west of the Three Tetons they were welcomed at a camp of more than 150 lodges of Flatheads and Pend d'Oreilles. Big Face, the old chief, expressed the gratitude of his people: "Black Robe, welcome to my nation."[57]

Slowly the large encampment moved north into the homeland of the Flatheads. Crossing the divide by way of Red Rock Pass on July 24, they halted to offer a mass of thanksgiving: "The altar was made of willows; my blanket made an altar cloth, and all the lodge was adorned with images and wild flowers; the Indians . . . took assiduous part with the greatest modesty, attention and devotion, and since various nations were among them, they chanted the praises of God in the Flathead, Nez Percé and Iroquois languages. The Canadians, my Fleming [de Velder] and I sang chants in French, English and Latin."[58]

Their journey continued down the Big Hole–Jefferson drainage to the Three Forks of the Missouri, one of the Flatheads' favorite hunting grounds for winter food supplies. There some four hundred horsemen started out on a buffalo hunt, De Smet's first. "In three hours," he proudly noted later, "they had killed more than 500."[59]

After a stay of less than two months De Smet realized it was time to depart. He had baptized nearly six hundred Flatheads during this initial visit and fulfilled the purpose of his journey. From all he had seen these were the people and their secluded homeland the place to establish the planned reduction. De Smet's decision, announced in the mountains, was one that the Jesuits in St. Louis would eagerly accept; and that decision offered an important consolation to his hosts — "a formal promise of a prompt return in the following spring, and of a reinforcement of several missionaries." The farewell speech offered by Big Face must have pleased De Smet, and he must have appreciated how deeply it would impress those who read his reports:

> Black-robe, may the Great Spirit accompany you in your long and dangerous journey. We will offer vows evening and morning that you may arrive safe among your brothers at St. Louis. We will continue to offer vows until you return to your children of the mountains. When the snows disappear from the valleys, after the winter, when the grass begins to be green again, our hearts, so sad at present, will begin to rejoice. As the grass grows higher, our joy will become greater; but when the flowers appear, we will set out to come and meet you. Farewell.[60]

Accompanied by de Velder and an escort of Flatheads, De Smet departed August 27 on a route that would take them past the forts of the American Fur Company on the Yellowstone and the Upper Missouri. For his general knowledge, as well as his personal sense of adventure, De Smet wanted as much direct information as he could gain on this vast country. They rode up the Gallatin, then headed eastward over Bozeman Pass to the Yellowstone River. Before reaching Fort Cass at the mouth of the Big Horn, they were greeted by a large party of Crows. There De Smet dismissed the Flathead delegation on September 13 and continued northeast along the banks of the Yellowstone. At the junction of the Missouri they visited Fort Union, where De Smet "regenerated sundry half-breed children in the holy waters of baptism."[61]

Leaving on September 23, they rode south for ten days, passed the Mandan villages, and were ferried in bull boats across the Missouri by a large group of Gros Ventres (Hidatsas), Arikaras, and Mandans. Some ten miles farther south they arrived at Fort Clark. After a brief rest they continued south, heading for Fort Pierre. Suddenly they were confronted by a large party of Blackfoot Sioux, impressed by the strange figure of a man wearing a black robe whose name was announced as "The Man Who Talks to the Great Spirit." Seated on an outspread buffalo robe, De Smet was carried into the camp and welcomed with a feast. Following their meeting, the Sioux supplied De Smet and de Velder with a party of guides as they continued on their journey.

Arriving at Fort Pierre, De Smet and de Velder remained for several days. On October 17 they departed for Fort Vermillion where De Smet renewed his acquaintance of the previous year with the Yankton Sioux. The prolonged ride had so exhausted their horses that they left Fort Vermillion on November 14 in a dugout canoe, arriving ten days later at St. Joseph's Mission. The night they landed at Council Bluffs river traffic was closed for the season by the heavy ice flow.[62]

Though De Smet's report to his fellow Jesuit missionaries at Council Bluffs was hopeful, theirs was not. Problems relating to the liquor traffic had dispersed the Potawatomis. De Smet and his companion departed Council Bluffs on December 14; by the following August St. Joseph's Mission was closed.[63]

Father Nicolas Point, already assigned to the missionary venture being considered for 1841, arrived at Westport on November 1 to prepare for the coming trip and serve as temporary chaplain for the growing frontier post. On December 22 the travelers arrived at Father Point's. Pausing only briefly, De Smet gratefully bid farewell to de Velder and left the following day by stage from Independence. Returning to St. Louis, De Smet completed his first great circle of western travel. On New Year's Eve, the weary Blackrobe was welcomed home by his Jesuit brethren at St. Louis University.[64]

Historians often comment on the simultaneous but unrelated endings in 1840 of the demand for and supply of beaver pelts. Silk had replaced beaver felt for top hats in the style centers of the world; the resulting drop in demand for beaver pelts made trapping unprofitable. Moreover, in the mountain meadows that were the headwaters of the great watercourses east and west, the supply of beavers had already been all but exhausted by fifteen years of overtrapping.[65]

In its rush westward and brief but frantic activity along the western border of the Great Plains, the fur business would now be changed. The trappers' repeated incursions had already disturbed the lifestyle of the Native Americans, but that growing disturbance was only the end of the beginning. The annual rendezvous would shortly give way to the permanent trading post, and commerce would escalate from beaver pelts to buffalo robes until the buffalo and the Indians' way of life were gone from the Great Plains.

Few historians, however, comment on what the western tribes had lost as early as 1840 through these early invasions of their country by the beaver hunters. As Billington reported, these invaders prepared more than the trails across the Great Plains and the passageways through the Rockies. They accomplished in the West the very objective to which Jefferson had directed the operation of the eastern trade factories: "They had deprived the red men of self-sufficiency by accustoming them to white men's goods."[66] Following their peaceful acceptance by the Indians, the mountain men betrayed their hosts. Enticed by the loaded wagons of supply caravans, the Indians developed a thirst for ardent spirits and manufactured goods.

In addition to losing their independence, by 1840 the Indians of the Great Plains had lost their privacy. Following the initial invasions of the fur trappers, there would no longer be an exclusive Indian country. President Washington had feared that something as distinct as "a Chinese wall" would be required to protect the rights of the Indians. By 1834 those rights were so violated that government investigators, calling for some remedy, suggested "a neutral strip of land five miles wide between the lands of the two races, on which all settlement would be prohibited." Congressional leaders, however, like the people they represented, proved to have little unselfish concern for the Indians.[67]

Chapter Three
1841 — The Beginning of the End (1841–50)

> Andrew Drips at last took to the Flatheads the right
> kind of missionary. He was the famous Jesuit Pierre-
> Jean de Smet; he did not ask much of the Flatheads
> except that they should assign his supernaturals a
> more powerful medicine than their own, and beyond
> that he loved them.
> —Bernard DeVoto, *Across the Wide Missouri*

THE REDUCTION PROGRAM:
To Form a Native Christian Empire

The year 1841 began with both good and bad news for De Smet. In a
very human fashion De Smet enjoyed the good, briefly. Then, using
his personal talents for salesmanship, he quickly remedied the bad
news.

The Jesuits' hope for a successful apostolate among the Native
Americans had been deeply shaken. Their initial project, St. Regis
Indian School at Florissant, had proved an unproductive and short-
lived exercise in assimilation. Even the slight missionary training
these young Jesuits had received pointed to different objectives and
procedures than those that had been implemented by Bishop Du
Bourg. They had studied briefly the philosophy and the practices of
the seventeenth- and eighteenth-century Jesuits who worked with the
Guarani and other native tribes of Paraguay, their textbook Luigi
Muratori's *A Relation of the Reductions of Paraguay*. Furthermore, at
the close of 1829 Jesuit Superior Roothaan in Rome directed them
"to ascertain and follow as far as possible the methods employed of
old by our Fathers in Paraguay," noting simplistically that such
methods had proven "most successful."[1]

This reminder of the independent *reducciones*, the Native Christian Empire developed by the Jesuits among these South Americans,
was a call to use the traditional Jesuit missionary approach, a
philosophy that French Jesuits had later used with the Iroquois,
Hurons, and other tribes in New France. De Smet, after dealing with
two transplanted Iroquois in 1839, would testify to its lasting results.
The traditional Jesuit presentation actually predated both New France
and Paraguay and had been used on other continents.

Historically, such an approach was not original. As Jesuit historian Robert Burns points out, it represented a "patristic tradition," a repetition and application of the freedom Saint Paul had established at the very start of his presentation of Christ's message to the non-Jews. Peter, James, and other leaders had agreed in Jerusalem that Paul's converts, the new "Christians" of Corinth, should not be obligated to observe strictly Judaic practices and rituals. At the close of the sixteenth century the Jesuit missionary Matteo Ricci had requested that Rome recognize Chinese converts as distinctly Chinese, not European, Christians. In India at the opening of the seventeenth century, Jesuit Roberto de Nobili had called for similar religious universality in seeking ecclesiastical approbation of the Malabar Rites for the natives of that peninsula.[2]

Based upon the premise that native tribal cultures were to be left largely intact and thus to serve as the context for new expressions of Christianity, the Jesuit missionaries of Missouri were directed by their Roman superior to follow the principle of accommodation. The gospel message was to be adjusted as far as possible to the particular culture and tribal heritage of those Native Americans who would request the missionaries' help. The difficulty that the Missouri Jesuit leadership had failed at first to appreciate was the demoralized state of the "border tribes." Stripped for the most part of their homelands and their traditional lifestyles, these groups were bands of people so lost in impoverishment and rejection that they awaited only disappearance through gradual acculturation or extermination.

St. Regis Indian School had not been the only Jesuit Indian apostolate to fail. By the close of the 1830s the reports coming to the Jesuit residence at St. Louis University from the Kickapoo mission north of Fort Leavenworth and from the Potawatomi mission farther up the Missouri were sadly negative. The moral fiber of these tribal remnants had already been seriously weakened by enforced dependence and the contaminating vices of frontier contact. Realism was demanded: for these Indian groups already all but destroyed, the missionary philosophy of accommodation was not applicable.[3]

Some sparks of hope had been kept alive through the 1830s by the repeated delegations of a tribal confederacy with homelands secluded in the remote northern Rockies and their repeated request for missionaries. Following the fourth request in 1839, Catholic authorities in St. Louis petitioned Rome for added volunteers to serve in this field. Widely read in the Jesuit communities in Rome, the strong appeals by Bishop Rosati and Father Verhaegen produced results.

The young Jesuit Father Gregory Mengarini, well qualified by his aptitude for languages and music, arrived in St. Louis near the close of 1840. Another volunteer, Father Nicolas Point, was given a preparatory assignment as chaplain at Westport on the Missouri frontier. Meanwhile, Verhaegen awaited De Smet's return from his preliminary journey of exploration and reconnaissance. The commitment to a full-scale permanent mission was dependent upon De Smet's assessment of the situation. As Verhaegen declared, "We shall be guided entirely by the report that he gives."[4]

A more positive report by a more enthusiastic individual could not have been given. In relating his personal experiences and his seemingly well-founded convictions, De Smet moved beyond an unqualified recommendation. Jubilantly De Smet insisted that the Jesuits' dream of a mission modeled on the eighteenth-century reduction plan in Paraguay would now be entirely feasible and among the Flatheads would prove even more fruitful than in its original application.[5]

De Smet's Jesuit audience reacted with equal enthusiasm; their hopes and simplistic expectations skyrocketed. But the response from the superior was not all that the eager De Smet had expected. Verhaegen pointed out that he could not realistically fulfill all of De Smet's requests. There was bad news as well as good.

The good news: De Smet, by Verhaegen's unsolicited appointment, would direct the project. Further, Verhaegen, as requested, would assign six Jesuits: three priests and, as the manpower item of highest practical importance, three Jesuit brothers. Further, Verhaegen and De Smet both regarded the artisan skills of these "temporal coadjutors," a uniquely pragmatic treasure of Jesuit organization (composed of priests and brothers), as utterly essential for any implementation of the reduction plan.[6]

The bad news: De Smet's budget requests could not be met. Since the previous spring the Jesuit superior had been acting as a temporary substitute for Bishop Rosati. The St. Louis prelate had been forced to attempt to answer the serious financial needs of his diocese by making a fund-raising tour of Europe. Verhaegen told De Smet that the Jesuits' financial situation was almost as serious.[7]

In a letter to the *Catholic Herald* some months later De Smet reported his initial reaction: "The thought that the undertaking would have been given up, that I would not be able to redeem my promise to the poor Indians, pierced my very heart."[8]

De Smet's instant reaction, however, was that of the strongly dedicated. Refusing to accept postponement for lack of material and means, he offered to solicit funds from other sources. In what was to become his main activity for the rest of his life, the task of the missionary fund-raiser, De Smet made his beginning at the start of 1841. From this time on he missed few opportunities for publicizing his cause or expressing his gratitude.

Facing a late March deadline, De Smet conducted a twofold campaign. He wrote multiple copies of an appeal letter addressed to potential benefactors in the East. On February 8 he left St. Louis by steamboat for a series of personal solicitations in and about New Orleans.[9]

On this begging tour De Smet took the opportunity to raise funds not only for the Rocky Mountain mission but also for a mission school in eastern Kansas for Indian girls. A few days after returning from his 1840 journey De Smet had met with Mother Duchesne, who from the mid-1820s shared with the Jesuits a special concern for educating Indian children. In New Orleans De Smet met with Mother Duchesne's superior and presented their joint request: that the Sisters of the Sacred Heart open an Indian girls' school in conjunction with the Jesuits' Potawatomi mission at Sugar Creek in Kansas. In addition to his arguments De Smet announced some initial funding— $500 he had solicited from Catholics in the South. Before the close of 1841 Mother Duchesne, assisted by three other Sisters of the Sacred Heart, opened the Sugar Creek school.[10]

It was a grateful De Smet who returned to St. Louis "with $1,100 in cash and six boxes full of various and most useful articles." It was a happy De Smet who eagerly opened a stack of reply mail in his office at St. Louis University. The largest donation had been sent by Francis P. Kenrick, coadjutor bishop of Philadelphia.[11]

One envelope, however, contained bad news, and again the bad news was serious. De Smet had counted on his band of missionaries being escorted to the mountains by "an exploring expedition belonging to the United States," which, he had been informed, would be led by his friend Joseph Nicollet. But Nicollet, busy in Washington completing his map of the Mississippi Valley, wrote De Smet on March 12, reporting sadly: "I cannot get away this season."[12]

Once more it looked like an indefinite postponement. From Charles Chouteau, his former student at St. Regis, De Smet had already learned that no caravan of American Fur Company hunters would be heading west that spring. The annual rendezvous in western Wyoming had been terminated.

The following eight days must have been marked by frantic

activity as De Smet addressed himself to solving yet another major problem. On April 24 Father Mengarini reported the good news in a brief farewell note to Rome: "The caravan has been found and today . . . we are setting out for Westport where we shall find Father Point and thence proceed to the Rocky Mountains."[13]

THOMAS FITZPATRICK, THE FIRST WAGONMASTER

"Caravan" was an exaggeration. Actually the services of a guide who would captain their expedition had been secured. Presumably De Smet's search had been directed to the St. Louis riverfront where amid the steamboats tied up along the levee and the warehouses of the fur traders he located Thomas Fitzpatrick, a fur trader both qualified and willing to provide the needed leadership. Fitzpatrick became closely associated with De Smet.

The Jesuit party boarded the new steamboat *Oceana* shortly before it departed St. Louis on April 24. The voyage to Westport took seven days since low water slowed traffic on the Missouri that time of year. Before disembarking, De Smet, as quartermaster, must have reviewed his checklist. Additional manpower, along with carts and animals, provisions and supplies, for a four-month journey through the wilderness—all would have to be obtained at the staging post of Westport. In addition, basic essentials were needed to construct and equip the planned reduction village. During their nine-day stay in Westport, housed in "an abandoned little cabin," De Smet found no time for writing. By the evening of May 9 the party was prepared, and their supplies had been loaded. Point, designated party diarist by De Smet, recorded that they left Westport on May 10.[14]

After a few days travel De Smet's party reached the south bank of the Kaw River near present Topeka. Here they met two men who had ferried some of their baggage up the river; they were also assisted in making their crossing by White Feather, the well-known chief of the Kansa Indians. On May 18 they were joined at the Soldier Creek campground by the various units of the Bidwell-Bartleson party. This collection of emigrants heading for California included at least five women and perhaps some ten children among its sixty-nine members whose baggage and supplies were loaded into thirteen wagons.

Point recorded that at an important camp meeting held that night Fitzpatrick's leadership was accepted by all. The next morning Fitzpatrick, riding horseback, led the caravan in a northwest direction toward the Platte River. Within a few days six more travelers joined the expedition. On May 27, the final addition, Rev. Joseph Williams, a Protestant minister on his way to Oregon, rode into camp.[15]

Both De Smet and Point expressed praise for Bidwell, Bartleson, Williams, and the rest of their associates on the trail, despite their theological differences. In his published journal Williams characterized De Smet as "extremely kind to me. . . . He appeared to be a very fine man." Bidwell wrote: "He was a genial gentleman, of fine presence, and one of the saintliest men I have ever known, and I cannot wonder that the Indians were made to believe him divinely protected. He was a man of great kindness and great affability under all circumstances."

De Smet and Point shared a spirit of Christian competition that by later ecumenical attitudes might be regarded as the deplorable religious prejudices of the period. When the groups separated after their last shared campground, Point commented: "We had lived together for three months amidst the same perils and were as of one fatherland. Farewells were sad. Many prejudices had disappeared during the journey. But, since most of them seemed firmly attached to error, there seemed little hope that we should see each other in the true fatherland."[16]

Point gave this description of the normal movements and camp procedures of the expedition: "Each day the captain gave the signal to rise and to depart, ordered the march and the stops, chose the spot in which to camp, and maintained discipline. Whenever possible, camp was pitched on the wooded bank of some river. . . . From the moment when the camp retired until the break of day, all the travelers, including the priests, stood watch according to roster, in order to guard against a surprise attack."[17]

As the caravan moved westward along the Platte and the Sweetwater and then by way of South Pass to the Green, it recorded a number of firsts. It was the first well-recorded expedition moving along the now established Oregon Trail. In addition to Point and De Smet, Bidwell and Williams and others in the party would later publish journals of this trip. These journals record the first emigrant casualty, an accidental death by gunshot, to occur on the trail. Two weddings were also recorded, probably the first on the Plains for whites.[18]

Along the trail the Jesuits had conducted religious services in the privacy of their tent. At the encampment on the Green, however, De Smet celebrated a public mass, a first-anniversary celebration of the mass that he had offered on July 5 the previous year with the trappers and Indians who had attended the final rendezvous. This year there were only the vanguard of the Flatheads and a party of French Canadians returning from California, but, Point reported, "all who were Catholic assisted most piously."[19]

Perhaps there at the Green, alive with memories of the annual rendezvous, Fitzpatrick fully appreciated his new position. His days of freedom as a mountain man were over. He now faced the responsibilities of the hired wagonmaster and guide. Although this 1841 caravan might halt briefly at the campfires of Fraeb and Bridger or any of the other active remnant of Fitzpatrick's former associates, it would not be returning to St. Louis with furs. The wagons Fitzpatrick now directed were heading permanently westward, over the mountains of Wyoming to their western destinations.

The permanent and growing invasion of the land hunters had begun, and that of the gold hunters would quickly follow. Within five years the first wave of that invasion carried over ten thousand emigrants across the Green. Just nine years later, in the short travel season of 1850 alone, the invasion would increase to an estimated total of fifty-five thousand emigrants.[20]

The final shared campsite of the 1841 expedition was at Soda Springs on the northernmost bend of the Bear River. Half of the Bidwell party had now become discouraged. Lacking an experienced guide, only thirty-two members were still determined to attempt a direct route to California. The other thirty-two preferred to accompany the Jesuit party to Fort Hall; from there they would head down the Snake and Columbia rivers to Oregon.

On August 15 Fitzpatrick led the reduced caravan into Fort Hall. At this Hudson's Bay post both groups obtained provisions for their continuing journeys. For the Jesuits there was also a warm welcome from a group of Flatheads. During their three-day stop De Smet spent one day writing letters. Besides a progress report to Verhaegen, he wrote Father Blanchet and Doctor John McLoughlin, governor of the Hudson's Bay Company, letters that Francis Ermantinger would hand-deliver as he conducted the remaining emigrants to Fort Vancouver. As one of the Hudson's Bay officials at Fort Hall, Ermantinger proved helpful and generous to De Smet and his companions; further, he promised to recommend their project to McLoughlin.[21]

Guided by the Flatheads, the De Smet party left Fort Hall on August 18. Moving northward past the headwaters of Henry's Fork, they crossed the continental divide once more and continued northwest to the Beaver Head, a tributary of the Jefferson. On September 1 De Smet wrote a report from "Beaver Head, Camp of the Big Face," describing at length his joyful reunion with Chief Big Face (Paul) and the Flathead people. This encampment, however, was only the summer camp of a nomadic people; Chief Paul and his council had already selected two possible sites for such a permanent village as De Smet had proposed the previous year. Since it was already fall, the missionaries and the Indian leaders were anxious to settle on a specific location. As the large group once again crossed the continental divide, this time westward down to Hell Gate, they came to the Bitterroot, "the river of the Flatheads." The Flatheads informed De Smet that they were following the 1805 trail of the Blackrobe's special heroes, Lewis and Clark.[22]

De Smet declared later that on September 24, after moving southward up the Bitterroot valley, they had arrived at the site chosen for the main mission. Point recorded in his diary: "This large valley, protected against the Blackfeet on the south by a chain of mountains, was sheltered from the rigors of the north by another chain of mountains on whose slopes grew forests, so necessary as a source of construction materials. . . . Everyone thought we would be able to find nothing better anywhere else. It was there that we pitched our tents, intending to lay the foundations for our future reduction, which we began by erecting a large cross."[23]

ST. MARY'S ON THE BITTERROOT: The First Reduction

De Smet had immediately gained a widespread acceptance by the Flatheads during his reconnaissance expedition of 1840. With his outgoing personality, broad interests, and ready adaptability, he had answered the Indians' desire for a Blackrobe. Following his return to St. Louis, he had single-handedly overcome heavy odds to get his new project under way. At Westport he had properly outfitted his party for a journey from the frontier that had taken over one-third of a year. There had been near tragedies on the trail, but his forces had arrived safely. Now, welcomed by the Indians, the Jesuit missionaries were marshaled in this remote area of the Bitterroot. Certainly De Smet had reason to rejoice, convinced as he was that this site would long be secluded from the contaminating pressures of white expansion.

Based upon the remoteness of the location and the positive disposition of the Indians, De Smet dreamed of developing colonies like those of Paraguay throughout the area. In these well-organized and at least quasi-independent reductions the Native Americans would be able to adapt to new ways while retaining sufficient roots in their own culture. With their culture respected but modified, they could grow in dignity and health, religiously oriented as they already were, into individuals prepared for the world that was changing about them. All this was noted by De Smet in his initial reports:

> Still more the good dispositions manifested by the Indians, will appear very proper motives to inspire us with fresh courage, and with the hope of establishing here, on a small scale, the order and regularity which once distinguished our missions in Paraguay. This hope is not founded on imagination, for whilst I am writing these lines, I hear the joyful voices of carpenters, re-echoing to the blows of the smith's anvil, and I see them engaged in raising the house of prayer.[24]

The enthusiastic De Smet went further. He predicted that the reductions here would be even more successful than the original missionary centers: "From what has hitherto been said, we may draw this conclusion, that the nation of the Flatheads appear to be a chosen people—'the elect of God,' that it would be easy to make this tribe a model for other tribes,—the seed of 200,000 Christians, who would be as fervent as were the converted Indians of Paraguay. . . . They have no tribute to pay but that of prayer."[25]

Seemingly, De Smet's optimism could not be faulted. The cooperative disposition and long-tested interest of the Flatheads, together with a happily secluded location, were apparently all that could be desired. De Smet also had the ready cooperation of an unselfish and dedicated group of coworkers. Based on progress to the end of December, a still enthusiastic De Smet filed a glowing report:

> All goes to prove what I have advanced in my preceding letters. . . .
>
> We enclosed the field destined to become God's portion of the settlement. We started the buildings intended to be hereafter dependencies of the farm, but serving temporarily for a church and residence, on account of the approach of winter, and our wish to unite the whole colony. These works were indispensable, and were carried on with such spirit that in the space of a month the new buildings could shelter from 400 to 500 souls.[26]

De Smet also acknowledged the very important services of two interpreters—Gabriel Prudhomme, "of mixed blood, but an adopted child of the [Flathead] nation," and Charles, who was in the employ of Governor McLoughlin of the Hudson's Bay Company. As a notable linguist, which De Smet was not, Mengarini began at once to develop a Flathead grammar. It had been determined from the very beginning that the official language of St. Mary's Reduction would be Flathead. Further, as a talented musician, Mengarini added the organ, tambourine, piccolo, accordion, flute, clarinet, and cymbals to the traditional Indian drums and whistles.[27]

Before the close of 1841, therefore, the foundation of St. Mary's — the first reduction — had been established. This, however, was only the beginning of De Smet's dream. Before 1841 had ended, that dream had expanded into the concept of a vast empire spreading from the Rocky Mountains across the Great Plains:

> Three Indians, belonging to the tribe called Coeur d'Alènes, having been informed of our arrival among the Flatheads, have just come to entreat us to have pity on them. . . . The Flatheads and the Coeur d'Alènes, it is true, are not numerous tribes, but they are surrounded by many others who evince the best dispositions.
>
> The Pend d'Oreilles are very numerous, and live at a distance of four or five days' journey from our present establishment; the chief [Walking Bear] who governed them last year and who has been baptized and called Peter, is a true apostle. . . . Next to these are found the Spokans, who would soon follow the example of the neighboring tribes; then the Nez Percés . . . the Snakes, the Crows and the Bannocks whose chief we have seen. Last year I visited the Cheyennes, whom I twice met on the banks of the Platte; the numerous nation of the Sioux, and the three allied tribes called Mandans, Aricaras and Minnetarees, who all have given me so many proofs of respect and friendship; the Omahas, with whom I have had so many conferences on the subject of religion, and many others who seem inclined to embrace the truth.[28]

For a dream of such tremendous scope the laborers were few indeed. That scarcity of coworkers, however, would be only one of the major practical difficulties that De Smet had to face. Throughout the next few years as director of the reduction program, De Smet was called upon to exercise the leadership roles of both optimistic planner and realistic producer. Within that period, despite the prolonged time spent in project-connected travel, De Smet's personal efforts would increase the number of laborers from six to twenty-three and raise an additional $35,000 for the implementation of this project. De Smet's naive anticipation that additional manpower would guarantee "a great harvest," however, was mistaken. Despite repeated attempts, his reduction project proved an impossible dream—in whole, even in part.

It is not known whether De Smet's August letter to McLoughlin from Fort Hall specifically requested immediate provisions for the mission. If so, no delivery to St. Mary's had been made by late October. By then De Smet had developed an objective besides that of obtaining needed supplies: he was eager to contact the Pend d'Oreilles on Clark's Fork.[29]

So on October 28 De Smet set out for Fort Colville, the Hudson's Bay post located near Kettle Falls on the Columbia, accompanied by ten Flatheads and a caravan of seventeen horses. Their round trip took forty-two days, repeatedly interrupted by De Smet's visits to camps of the Kalispels and Pend d'Oreilles along the trail. On December 8 they arrived back at St. Mary's. De Smet later reported that he had contacted over 2,000 Indians, baptized 190 individuals, and discovered a fine location for another mission.[30]

Most of December at St. Mary's Reduction, and especially the first Christmas, was devoted to special religious ceremonies. Amid his music lessons and composing his grammar of Flathead, Mengarini joined Point, who had already completed a number of paintings, in offering religious instructions in the Indian camp. On the final day of 1841 De Smet reported:

> Twenty-four marriages . . . had been celebrated during my absence, and 202 adults, with little boys and girls from eight to fourteen years of age, had been baptized. There were still thirty-four couples, who awaited my return to receive the sacraments of baptism and marriage, or to renew their marriage vows.
>
> . . . I commenced giving three instructions daily, besides the catechism, which was taught by the other Fathers. They profited so well that, with the grace of God, 115 Flatheads, with three chiefs at their head, thirty Nez Percés with their chief, and the Blackfoot chief and his family, presented themselves at the baptismal font on Christmas day.[31]

Even before the special religious ceremonies that spring, De Smet had set out on another journey. The mission needed further provisions and clothing, and De Smet wanted to confer with the Canadian missionaries Fathers Blanchet and Demers regarding mission planning. Late in 1841 De Smet had received a letter from Blanchet strongly recommending that the main base of the Jesuits' mission operation be set up in the area of Fort Vancouver. A meeting with McLoughlin was also needed, for reasons both material and spiritual. The Hudson's Bay posts provided the only supply bases in the territory; moreover, McLoughlin had strongly seconded Blanchet's recommendation regarding the location of mission headquarters. De Smet's early departure may also have been precipitated by cabin fever due to the cramped winter quarters. By this time he had become addicted to travel, and any journey seemingly appealed to his sense of adventure.

With his interpreter, Charles, and three other companions, De Smet left St. Mary's on April 13 for Fort Vancouver. By May the party had reached their first objective, Fort Colville, where they encountered rivers flooded by an early runoff, causing a month-long delay. De Smet spent his days visiting nearby camps of the Kalispels, Kutenais, Coeur d'Alenes, Spokanes, and Shuyelpis. On May 30 the De Smet party began their voyage down the Columbia aboard Peter Ogden's newly constructed Hudson's Bay Company barge.

On the second day, however, the expedition suffered a serious tragedy. De Smet had just disembarked to walk along a stretch of the bank when the barge, upon returning into the swift current, capsized and sank in an extended rapid. Horrified yet unable to help, De Smet watched as five boatmen drowned. Charles, the interpreter, was one of three survivors.[32]

Exercising greater caution with the remaining barges, the group descended the rest of the Columbia without incident. Only brief stops were made at the Hudson's Bay posts Forts Okinagan and Walla Walla. Later De Smet reported that following his arrival at Fort Vancouver, he met with Fathers Blanchet and Demers and Governor McLoughlin:

> [The priests] are laboring in these regions for the same object that we are trying to accomplish in the Rocky Mountains. . . . They assured me that immense good might be done in the extensive regions that border on the Pacific, if a greater number of missionaries, with means at their command, were stationed in these regions. . . .

The Governor of the honorable Company of Hudson Bay, Dr. McLoughlin, advised me to do everything in my power to gratify the wishes of the Canadian missionaries. His principal reason is, that if Catholicity was rapidly planted in these tracts where civilization begins to dawn, it would be more quickly introduced thence into the interior.[33]

During his sojourn at Fort Vancouver De Smet made a brief trip with Demers, heading south up the Willamette River to visit the first Catholic post in the Pacific Northwest, Blanchet's St. Paul Mission. De Smet would return to this site in 1844 to begin construction of St. Francis Xavier Mission, a new headquarters for the reduction program intended to serve as the training site for future missionaries.

Following more discussions with Blanchet, De Smet and his host must have realized that the plans they were developing would require De Smet's immediate return to St. Louis. They must have agreed that even with Verhaegen's approval in St. Louis, De Smet would need to travel to Europe to solicit the greatly increased supplies and recruits that would be required. They also agreed on a new proposal regarding ecclesiastical jurisdiction. Together they would request the pope to assign a new bishop for this American-British territory west of the Rockies.[34]

De Smet began his return trip on June 30, again a guest on the Ogden barge as far as Fort Walla Walla. Heading east from there, De Smet arrived at St. Mary's on July 27. However, he stayed only two days. Father Point had already departed with the buffalo hunters for the tribal summer hunting grounds to the southwest. De Smet determined to visit them briefly before continuing his return journey to St. Louis. In early August De Smet joined the hunting encampment, which soon left Three Forks and moved up the Madison River. On August 15, the feast of the Assumption, De Smet reported: "I offered up the sacrifice of the mass in a noble plain, watered by one of the three streams that form the head waters of the Missouri, to thank God for all the blessings he had bestowed on us during this last year."[35] De Smet recounted a number of those blessings with high satisfaction in a letter written at Madison Forks. With the cooperation of the Flatheads, the reduction at St. Mary's seemed well established; Father Mengarini and Brothers Claessens and Specht would remain there to continue serving the Flatheads and Pend d'Oreilles. In November Father Point and Brother Huet would begin another foundation for the Coeur d'Alenes; this Reduction of the

Sacred Heart, originally located at the north end of Lake Coeur d'Alene, was soon moved to the St. Joseph River a short distance southeast of the beautiful lake.

More manpower and more supplies, De Smet reported, would be needed to answer their immediate needs; indeed, even more would be required to respond to the other requests for foundations that De Smet was receiving. De Smet supported these requests with some impressive religious statistics, including over 1,600 baptisms as evidence of religious fruitfulness at St. Mary's. In relating such instant success, De Smet professed high hopes for the project's future.[36]

Bidding farewell to Father Point and his beloved Flatheads, De Smet headed eastward, accompanied by some twelve Indian companions. After a few days of travel they were welcomed into a large encampment of the Crow tribe along the Yellowstone. Assisted by his Flathead companions, De Smet conducted a religious seminar for the Crows, using rituals already adapted to the Flathead language and customs. His message proved highly acceptable; on his departure he promised to send the Blackrobes the Crows had requested.

From August 25 through September 10 De Smet and four companions made the long horseback ride down the banks of the Yellowstone. Game was plentiful, and the party slept under the stars. After riding into Fort Union, the American Fur Company trading post at the confluence of the Yellowstone and the Missouri, they rested for three days. Since their horses had been too heavily used, De Smet determined to head down "the impetuous waters of the Missouri in a skiff," accompanied by his Flathead companions Ignatius and Gabriel. Later De Smet reported on this final leg of his 1842 travels:

> On the third day of our descent, to our great surprise and joy, we heard the puffing of a steamboat. . . . Four gentlemen from New York, proprietors of the boat, invited me to enter and remain on board. . . . On entering the boat I was an object of great curiosity — my black gown, my missionary cross, my long hair, attracted attention. I had thousands of questions to answer and many long stories to relate about my journey. . . .
>
> On the last Sunday of October, at twelve o'clock, I was kneeling at the foot of St. Mary's Altar, in the [St. Louis] Cathedral, offering up my thanksgiving to God. . . . From the beginning of April I had traveled 5,000 miles.[37]

GATHERING "MEN AND MEANS"
TO GUARANTEE THE "GREAT HARVEST"

That Sunday afternoon in late October 1842 was marked by high excitement and rejoicing in the Jesuit quarters of St. Louis University. De Smet's success story, told and retold, must have thrilled and inspired his religious brethren. The unique Jesuit mission program of the reductions had been reestablished. After initial failure among the Border tribes the Paraguay plan had been reinitiated in the secluded Rocky Mountains, and within a brief period it had already proved more fruitful than anticipated.

Perhaps no Jesuit was more pleased with De Smet's optimistic report than Verhaegen. Certainly De Smet's request for additional manpower and funding placed a great burden on Verhaegen, for at the close of 1842 this Jesuit superior faced more serious problems in personnel and finances than he had at the start of 1841. As he commented in a report to Rome, "Everywhere, but especially in the colleges, there are complaints of lack of [Jesuit] personnel." Yet by the start of 1843 Verhaegen had assigned three additional Missouri Jesuits to labor with De Smet at the reduction in the Rockies. But Verhaegen could provide no funding; in fact, with the total contracted debt of the Missouri Jesuits amounting to $45,000, he was considering applying to European sources for a loan. Thus Verhaegen supplied De Smet with additional motivation for a European trip. Along with soliciting "men and means" for the reduction program, De Smet was commissioned by Verhaegen to arrange a loan of $10,000 to fund the other apostolates of the Missouri Jesuits.[38]

His European trip determined, De Smet was extremely busy through the opening months of 1843. His preliminary task was to raise funds to send the newly assigned Jesuits to the reductions. Again, his fund-raising campaign would be conducted on a double front; this time, however, he would try another publicity tactic. Hoping for a larger audience than that of his appeal letter in early 1841, De Smet published his reports as *Letters and Sketches, with a Narrative of a Year's Residence among the Indian Tribes of the Rocky Mountains.* Printed at once in Philadelphia, this English-language edition was quickly followed by translations into French, Dutch, German, and Italian. A program of individual appeals, made in conjunction with personal public appearances, was also arranged. On a whirlwind tour, De Smet hurried through New Orleans, Boston, Louisville, Cincinnati, Pittsburgh, Baltimore, Philadelphia, Washington, and New York.

De Smet returned to St. Louis for a very brief stay. On April 25 he boarded the steamboat *John Auld* with his newly assigned Rocky Mountain missionaries—Fathers De Vos and Adrian Hoecken and Brother Peter McGean.

Both the *John Auld* and the *Omega*, the other steamboat scheduled to head up the Missouri that day, were crowded. In addition to westward-heading emigrants, William Drummond Stewart was leading a large group of his friends for an extended outing on the Green River. Having developed an acquaintanceship with Stewart during their eight-day voyage, De Smet and the other Jesuits had lunch on May 10 in Stewart's Camp William, one mile beyond the Westport trailhead. It may have been in or about Westport that De Smet encountered Frémont and Fitzpatrick, who was serving as a guide for the Second Expedition of Exploration. It seems there was also a meeting with Dr. Marcus Whitman, who reported that "De Smet has gone back in order to go to Europe and bring others [priests] by ship."[39]

This trip up the Missouri provided De Smet the opportunity to meet old friends and make new acquaintants. At a stop for firewood De Smet joined the Stewart party visiting passengers on the *Omega*; all seemed anxious to meet and listen to the renowned artist John James Audubon, who was on board. It was also aboard the *Omega* that De Smet renewed his acquaintance with Etienne Provost, whom he had met at Council Bluffs in 1839. De Smet's most significant meeting, however, was with Captain Joseph La Barge, the pilot of the *Omega*. Across the next quarter century a close friendship developed between these two men through De Smet's frequent voyages on the Missouri.[40]

With the $5,000 he had gathered, De Smet outfitted his party in Westport and purchased additional supplies for the reductions.[41] Having prepared his new missionaries for their journey and turned them over to their guide, Solomon Sublette (a brother of the more famous William Sublette), De Smet returned to St. Louis.[42] After a brief stay he set out for New York and on June 7 began his fourth crossing of the Atlantic. As always, De Smet the traveler made friends among his companions, including Bishop John Hughes of New York and the bishop's friend Thurlow Weed. De Smet's fundraising began even before his arrival in Europe. Weed reported: "We have been delighted during the passage with his [De Smet's] recital of Indian habits, customs, wars, worship, etc. . . . My travelling companions have made a donation to the good Father for the benefit of his Indians."[43]

After a voyage of twenty-one days De Smet landed in Ireland. By the end of July he was in Brussels where his address to the students of St. Michael's College was but one of his fund-raising activities. His publicity campaign had been effective; his book had gained him celebrity status as an authority on Native Americans. However, before concentrating on solicitations for his Indian missions, De Smet arranged for the loan for St. Louis University. This matter concluded, he left Belgium early in August for appearances in Lille, Paris, Chalons, Lyons, and Marseilles.[44]

Upon his arrival in Rome De Smet presented glowing reports to the Jesuit superior, John Roothaan, who had become especially supportive of De Smet's reapplication of the reduction program. Their meeting was an exchange of good news. Roothaan reported on the recent group of Jesuit volunteers he had assigned to the project. The appeal letters of Rosati and Verhaegen, followed by De Smet's detailed reports of 1840, had proven effective: by March 20 four Jesuits, three priests and a brother, sailed from Havre for New Orleans. Roothaan also arranged a personal interview for De Smet with Pope Gregory XVI to discuss De Smet and Blanchet's petition for the appointment of a bishop for the Oregon country. Not only did Roothaan support the petition; he also endorsed De Smet's urgent request that the position be assigned to Blanchet rather than himself.[45] De Smet vividly presented the cause of the Native Americans and extended to the Holy Father the special invitation made by Chief Victor of the Flatheads: "If the Great Chief of the Christians is in danger, send him a message from me. We will build him a lodge in the middle of our camp; we will hunt game that he may be fed; and we will be his guards to protect him from the enemy."[46]

After stops at Lyons, Avignon, and Paris De Smet worked his way back to Holland and Belgium, having now in his company five more Jesuit recruits for the reductions. On November 10 in Belgium he won the commitment of six religious, sisters of Notre Dame de Namur, to implement the proposal he had made with Blanchet to found a school for Indian girls on the Willamette.

By December De Smet had gathered his recruits and purchased supplies at Antwerp. At that port he located Captain S. J. Moller, whose two-masted brig *Infatigable* was scheduled to depart immediately for Valparaiso. De Smet contracted for an extension of the voyage to proceed up the Pacific coast to Astoria and up the Columbia to Fort Vancouver. This voyage, De Smet's fifth on the Atlantic, was a lengthy diagonal crossing; the vessel rounded Cape

Horn on March 20. After extended stops at Valparaiso (April 13–May 1) and Lima (May 11–27) the *Infatigable* reached Fort Vancouver on August 5. The eight-month voyage finally concluded when De Smet and his new missionaries reached Blanchet's St. Paul Mission on the upper Willamette River on August 18.[47]

De Smet remained at St. Paul's until October 3. By that time the nearby site of the new Jesuit missionary headquarters, St. Francis Xavier, had been selected, and construction of the two-story log building was under way. The sisters, for whom De Smet had conducted English classes during their prolonged sea voyage, opened their boarding school for Indian girls. De Smet later learned that at this time the four Jesuit missionaries dispatched by Roothaan in March 1843 had finally arrived at St. Mary's Reduction. Fathers Joset, Zerbinatti, and Soderini and Brother Magri had enjoyed the services of Young Ignace, who served as their guide from the Green River. Before the close of October Father De Vos came down from St. Mary's to take charge of St. Francis Xavier. De Smet had escorted De Vos, along with Father Adrian Hoecken and Brother McGean, to Westport in March 1843. The five missionaries who accompanied De Smet from Antwerp—Fathers Nobili, Accolti, Ravalli, and Vercruysse, along with Brother Huysbrecht—were given a variety of assignments. Schoenberg reports that "they studied English while they built their house and barns. They also spent part of their time in apostolic work."[48]

Moving up the Columbia from Fort Vancouver, De Smet and Mengarini directed the transporting of the newly acquired supplies and equipment to the reductions. Mengarini returned to St. Mary's. De Smet directed the supply caravan to Sacred Heart, then to the site selected for the new establishment—the Reduction of St. Ignatius among the Kalispels (Pend d'Oreilles). Mountain snows forced De Smet to remain with Father Hoecken in the winter camp of the Kalispels.

The Christmas season of 1844, unlike that of the previous year confined aboard the port-bound *Infatigable*, was a time not only of deep religious rejoicing for De Smet but also of personal satisfaction in the remarkable achievements for his beloved Indians. That Christmas and the following few months may well have been the happiest period of his entire life and the brief golden age of his reduction project.

DE SMET'S PUBLISHED REPORTS OF EARLY 1845:
The Golden Age
One report De Smet composed at the start of 1845 seems especially notable, particularly for its positive emphasis and as an example of

De Smet's writing style, which combined narration and description so well. Further, it intimately discloses De Smet the individual, the warm human being marked by his basic religious orientation and his outgoing personality, one who enjoyed the complementary satisfactions of the missionary-outdoorsman:

> I shall always remember with pleasure the winter of 1844–5, which I had the happiness of spending among these good Indians. The place for wintering was well chosen, picturesque, agreeable, and convenient. The camp was placed near a beautiful waterfall. . . .
>
> The great festival of Christmas, the day on which the little band [comprising 124 adults] was to be added to the number of the true children of God, will never be effaced from the memory of our good Indians. The manner in which we celebrated midnight mass may give you an idea of our festival. The signal for rising, which was to be given a few minutes before midnight, was the firing of a pistol, announcing to the Indians that the house of prayer would soon be open. This was followed by a general discharge of guns in honor of the birth of the Infant Savior, and 300 voices rose spontaneously from the midst of the forest, and entoned in the language of the Pend d'Oreilles the beautiful canticle: *"Du Dieu puissant tout annonce la gloire."* — "The Almighty's glory all things proclaim." In a moment a multitude of adorers were seen wending their way to the humble temple of the Lord—resembling indeed the manger in which the Messiah was born. . . .
>
> Of what was our little church of the wilderness constructed? . . . Of posts fresh cut in the woods, covered over with mats and bark; these were its only materials. . . . The altar was neatly decorated, bespangled with stars of various brightness, and covered with a profusion of ribbons—things exceedingly attractive to the eye of an Indian. At midnight I celebrated a solemn mass and the Indians sang several canticles suitable to the occasion. That peace announced in the first verse of the angelic hymn—the *Gloria*—"Peace on earth to men of good will," was, I venture to say, literally fulfilled to the Indians of the

forest. A grand banquet, according to Indian custom, followed the first mass. . . . The union, the contentment, the joy and charity, which pervaded the whole assembly, might well be compared to the *agapé* of the primitive Christians.

. . . Permit me to repeat here that I should be delighted could I but communicate to the zealous and fervent those pleasurable feelings—that overflowing of the heart, which one experiences on such occasions. Here, indeed, the Indian missionary enjoys his greatest consolations; here he obtains his strength, his courage, his zeal to labor to bring men to the knowledge of the true God, in spite of the poverty, the privations of every description, and the dangers with which he has to contend.

With information gathered later, De Smet included a synopsis of similar celebrations at the other reductions he had established in the mountains:

Fathers Mengarini and Zerbinati . . . [with the four coadjutor brothers at St. Mary's] had the consolation to see the whole tribe of the Flatheads, among whom they had been laboring, approach the holy table on this day. . . . Fathers Point and Joset [at the Sacred Heart Reduction] had also the consolation of admitting for the first time nearly the entire tribe of the Coeur d'Alènes, on this auspicious day, to the holy communion. . . . The Christmas of 1844 was, therefore, a great and glorious day in the Rocky Mountains.[49]

By the spring of 1845 De Smet had worked his way through the lasting snow fields of the mountains to the Reduction of St. Mary's. He was more than thrilled to join his Flathead people in the celebration of his return: "The solemn feast of Easter, all the Flatheads at St. Mary's devoutly approached the most blessed sacrament during my mass; and about 300 Pend d'Oreilles (the greater number adults) belonging to the station of St. Francis Borgia [a satellite mission of St. Mary's], presented themselves at the baptismal font. Five chiefs were among their number."[50]

Leaving St. Mary's Reduction, De Smet stopped at the new establishment of St. Ignatius. The site selected by the Kalispel leaders and Father Hoecken seemed well chosen. With a list of provisions and equipment needed for this new reduction, De Smet departed for Fort Vancouver. On his return in July De Smet brought back the skilled Jesuit carpenter Brother McGean and two hired workmen, along with eleven packhorses hauling plows, spades, scythes, pickaxes, and carpenter's tools.

De Smet's report on the beginning of this reduction was all positive; he was thrilled with both the spiritual and material achievements. Fourteen log houses and a large barn were being erected; the timbers had already been prepared for an impressive church structure; a substantial fence enclosed some three hundred grain-planted acres; and the reduction's livestock included thirty head of cattle as well as hogs and domestic fowl.

On the feast of the Ascension Father Hoecken baptized more than a hundred adults. De Smet figured that more than four hundred Kalispels, including adults and children, had now been baptized. Moreover, he had received requests for similar foundations from the neighboring tribes, and two new satellite stations had already been started—St. Paul's for the Skoylepi and St. Peter's for the Okinagans.[51]

After going by horseback to Fort Walla Walla, De Smet headed westward to embark on the Columbia. Moving speedily with the current, he covered the five hundred miles to Fort Vancouver in five days. At Vancouver De Smet received more encouraging reports. Father Nobili had spent his first eight months as a missionary learning the Indian language; with that and other practical preparations, he was now ready to help De Smet extend the program even further. Before his departure on December 5 bishop-elect Blanchet had left a letter requesting De Smet to send some of his coworkers into New Caledonia to introduce the reduction program in that area.[52]

The episcopal appointment Blanchet received on November 4, 1844, was further cause for De Smet's optimism. With Blanchet as the ecclesiastical authority directing the religious activities of the Catholics in the area, De Smet was more than relieved not to have been assigned himself. He now anticipated that Blanchet's appointment would finally resolve what was basically a twofold communication problem. De Smet had made the initial moves toward solving that problem during his 1843 visit to Europe. He had sought more than men and means and had requested more than the episcopacy for Oregon and for Blanchet. He had pressured Roothaan to appoint Father John Elet, his friend since seminary days in Belgium, to head the reduction program.

Religious superiors, De Smet had learned, might properly be interested in and solicitous for the Indian apostolate of the far west, but restricted to residences in St. Louis, Quebec, or Rome, they operated under serious handicaps. There they were subject to repeated pressures and higher-volume demands for nearer apostolates. Moreover, without direct knowledge of the unique situation of the remote reductions, they could not exercise sufficient awareness of other cultures or the problems of the missionaries serving in varied circumstances. Certainly they could not readily sense the urgency of De Smet's requests for immediate and gigantic commitments, nor could they envision the impending dislocations of the Indians resulting from the mounting invasions of the Indian country. True to the cause to which he had been assigned, De Smet noted that such remote authorities could not effectively guide affairs in a terra incognita.

De Smet rejoiced, then, in anticipation that Blanchet and Elet would provide knowledgeable leadership combined with special concern for the Indians. Further, with Blanchet as the ecclesiastical authority and Elet as the local director of the Jesuit program, De Smet believed he had eliminated the second grave communication problem — prolonged and frustrating delays in the exchange of letters with distant authorities.

De Smet was highly impatient with the primitive and uncertain mail of the period. Regarding proposals he saw as requiring immediate implementation, or the rethinking and adoption of possible alternatives, the lengthy delays in gaining approval from St. Louis or Rome were intolerable. Yet such procedures were among the vowed-obedience demands placed upon De Smet and his religious coworkers. Among the grim realities of life in Oregon in the 1840s was a two-year delay for an exchange of letters and the uncertainty of delivery. With both Blanchet and Elet as local, quasi-independent Catholic and religious authorities, dependence on such unsatisfactory communication procedures would be greatly reduced.[53]

Setting off from Fort Vancouver with Nobili, De Smet made the sixty-mile journey up the Willamette in a Chinook canoe. The first reports De Smet received, at the Jesuit missionary headquarters and at the Falls, were added causes for rejoicing. The residence of St. Francis Xavier had been completed to serve as a seminary to prepare young Jesuits for mission work. Definite progress had also been made by the new missionaries from Europe. Ravalli, skilled in medicine, had rendered valuable service to settlers in the area. De Vos, with his ability to speak English, had been providing spiritual care for the increasing number, now over four thousand, of American Catholics. At Blanchet's request Vercruysse had directed spiritual activities for the outlying Canadians; a new church structure was about to be erected for them. At the Falls, De Smet received more good news. Demers was preparing to construct a brick cathedral. The convent school, conducted by the sisters of Notre Dame for the Indian girls, had increased enrollment to some fifty boarders. Blanchet had obtained two additional diocesan priests from Quebec: Father Langlois was developing a parish among the Catholics at Cowlitz; Father Bolduc was directing the newly established Bishop's College, a school with an enrollment of "forty young men, chiefly half-breeds."[54]

De Smet realized that for his expanding reduction project a great amount of supplies, additional manpower, and items of equipment would be necessary. However, with his well-proven talent for gaining publicity, soliciting recruits, and raising funds, that problem now seemed more manageable. With his efforts since 1838 De Smet had developed the special interest of a goodly number of benefactors, not all of them foreign. In his report of positive achievements and blessings De Smet noted the goodwill of many individuals who staffed the various posts of the Hudson's Bay Company. Late in June De Smet headed eastward, leading a packtrain of supplies for the reduction at St. Ignatius. Having delivered all the materials to Hoecken, De Smet rode on for another two days to Fort Colville, resting there at the end of July.

Successful so far, De Smet now devoted himself to an attempt to solve one of the major problems remaining. The incursions of the hostile Blackfeet had become a continuous threat to St. Mary's Reduction. Already near the headwaters of the Columbia, De Smet now proposed an arduous journey that would provide the ultimate test of the spiritual leadership he had been accorded by all the tribes he had contacted. He proposed to present the Blackfeet within their main encampment the Great Spirit's message of peace. Begun in early August, De Smet's journey called for crossing the continental divide and riding far eastward along the Athabasca and Saskatchewan rivers. It was a difficult journey, especially because it extended through the winter of 1845–46. Moreover, it was a fruitless journey, for he failed to contact the Blackfeet leaders and wasted almost a year in the attempt. For De Smet, it was an ill-chosen journey; representing more than a personal failure, it provided further cause for the mounting criticisms directed against him.[55]

THE UNREPORTED FAILURES: "The Dream Is Ended"

De Smet's reports were deliberate publicity releases. His widely publicized letters, designed to gain support for his reduction project, emphasized specific positive achievements. Travel-related difficulties and other problems that might impressively suggest the dedication demanded of the missionaries were graphically related. The really negative factors, however, were not recounted. Yet by the middle of 1845 such problems were increasing in number and intensity.

It was late May 1846 before De Smet, utterly frustrated in his attempt to contact the Blackfeet in Alberta, returned to Fort Colville. Graciously treated at this post, De Smet continued to sing the praises of the Hudson's Bay Company. His personal charm, along with his influence upon the neighboring tribes, still merited him special personal treatment. But for De Smet the fund-raiser the important benefit of a 50 percent discount in the purchase of mission supplies had been discontinued; hereafter the reductions would be charged regular market rates. Moreover, with the influx of Americans in Oregon, the company had determined to reduce its operations south of Puget Sound; a number of the posts, including those at Walla Walla, Boise, and Hall, would be closed.[56]

By early June De Smet had worked his way down to Vancouver. There, as throughout the Willamette area, the situation was strained by the threat of war. For almost a year the eighteen-gun British sloop of war *Modeste* had remained at anchor in the Columbia opposite the fort. It was a strange display of force considering other British attempts to effect peaceful relations. Even before De Smet arrived at Vancouver, however, the Oregon Boundary Treaty had been presented by Lord Aberdeen to President Polk; by June 15 the 49th parallel had been determined as the boundary line from "The Stony Mountains" westward through the middle of the Strait of Juan de Fuca. De Smet offered a brief comment: "The poor Indians of Oregon, who alone have a right to the country, are not consulted."[57]

Departing Fort Vancouver in late June, De Smet headed up the Willamette. What he found throughout the valley was additional churches, but they were churches to provide for the religious needs of the growing numbers of emigrants. The U.S. Congress, delayed by the debate over the extension of slavery, did not formally establish the Oregon Territory until August 13, 1848. Yet as early as mid-1845 a new wave of over three thousand settlers reached the Oregon end of the trail. Here was another major problem for De Smet: competition was increasing for the religious services of the Jesuits he had gathered for his reduction program.[58]

In the remote wilderness De Smet had no conflicting interests. Since there were no chaplains at the mountain posts or, later, at the forts along the Upper Missouri, he readily offered his religious services as requested, happily serving Indians and mixed bloods, Americans and French Canadians, civilians and military personnel. Taking only a few hours or days at these posts, these activities did not negate De Smet's primary dedication to the Native Americans. As "The Man Who Talks to the Great Spirit," De Smet exercised a universal priesthood.[59]

As the first superior of the Oregon Jesuits' reduction program, De Smet had faced, but had not solved, a growing problem, one that developed into a serious dilemma for his successors. Since all of Oregon was missionary territory for both newcomers and natives, how exclusively should the limited Jesuit personnel be assigned to the reduction program? Facing that dilemma amid the pressures both spiritual and material of their day, both of De Smet's successors, Joset (1846–49) and Accolti (1850–54), would make compromises for which both would be as strongly criticized by Roothaan as De Smet was in the late 1840s.

In theory it was simply a matter of priorities. The Catholic authorities in the United States, with the approval of Rome and the acceptance of the Roman Jesuit superior, had officially assigned to the Jesuits missionary activities for Native Americans. For this group of Jesuit missionaries there was a specific task, following De Smet's strong recommendation of 1840, to conduct in the Rocky Mountains, primarily among the Flatheads, a renewal of the reduction missionary program of Paraguay using the traditional Jesuit missionary approach.

From his headquarters in Rome Roothaan accorded the matter this simplistic interpretation. As Jesuit superior, he enthusiastically endorsed De Smet's reduction proposal as in line with his earlier directives. Further, De Smet's positive reports following his 1840 preliminary expedition had offered a marked contrast to the previous missionary failures of these Jesuits along the Lower Missouri. Following the glowing reports De Smet had presented during his 1843 visit to Rome, Roothaan had good cause to anticipate a successful program. With very limited awareness of the Oregon context, from which the operations of these Jesuit missionaries could not be excluded, Roothaan expected highly concentrated efforts by all these volunteers to their specified assignment.[60]

The conflict of services had disturbed De Smet from his initial meeting with Blanchet in the spring of 1842. Even before heading down the Columbia, De Smet had received requests from various Indian tribes for additional reductions. At Fort Vancouver, however, he had faced the call to assign his Jesuit workers to activities only indirectly related to the reduction program. Blanchet, whose cooperation was so important for De Smet's plans, had strongly emphasized the importance of meeting the religious needs of the white newcomers to the Willamette area. McLoughlin, whose strongly voiced convictions also could not be disregarded since he directed both the policy and the posts of the Hudson's Bay Company, had favored Blanchet's proposal.

McLoughlin was unaware of the basic philosophy of the reduction program. Also, Blanchet may not have known that seclusion from the white colonists in Paraguay had been an essential element in the development of the original Jesuit reductions. The message that De Smet was hearing from both these established and experienced leaders was that Oregon Territory was not, and could not be, Paraguay—that since the natives could not be secluded from the Oregon newcomers, the good example of white Catholics was the best means to encourage the development of the Indians. For a number of reasons and under various pressures, De Smet had compromised the program from the very start. He had allowed himself to be persuaded by Blanchet as early as 1842 to make the Willamette the center of his operations.

In late June 1846 De Smet reached the Jesuit headquarters of St. Francis Xavier near St. Paul. For De Smet, the new but almost empty building was more than just another problem. He could recall his high hopes in the summer of 1844 for the development of this anticipated "nursery" for Jesuit personnel to staff the reductions. Now the unused structure had become a symbol of a broken program. Within two months Roothaan would order St. Francis Xavier to be closed as "an economic burden and useless for the purposes intended."[61]

Before leaving St. Francis Xavier for his return journey down the Willamette, De Smet must have reviewed his manpower situation. The strategy he had so strongly pursued in 1843 had backfired. De Smet had not obtained Elet as his chosen successor to head the reduction program. In the light of his triumphal 1843 European tour, De Smet's strong requests might have seemed appropriate. Missouri superior Father Van de Velde informed Roothaan that his Jesuits faced such an economic crisis, had become so debt-ridden, that they might have to sell their property and leave Missouri. Van de Velde insisted that Elet could not be spared.

Neither was De Smet's power structure any longer what he had hoped and worked for. Although he had gathered in Oregon a number of Jesuit recruits, in few cases was he able to locate them among the mountain tribes. As early as 1845 De Vos had been sent to serve the growing white community at Oregon City. Working out of St. Francis Xavier, Vercruysse was assigned in 1845 to the Canadians at Grand Prairie. Accolti, like his other European companions, had been busy learning English; in addition, however, rather than studying an Indian language, he had set himself to learn Spanish, intending to work among the Spaniards and Mexicans who were coming up from California.[62]

Fathers Joset and Zerbinatti had reached St. Mary's in the fall of 1844. Their companion on the trail, Father Soderini, did not arrive until later. In less than a year Zerbinatti's services were lost; on September 15 he drowned in the Bitterroot. Soderini's contribution had been even less; on July 15, 1845, De Smet wrote McLoughlin that he had sent the young Italian Jesuit back to Rome. Point had helped De Smet to establish the first two reductions, but as early as 1843 Point had departed angrily from the Coeur d'Alene reduction. After a personality clash with De Smet in April 1845, Point had forwarded to Rome his petition for withdrawal from the reduction program. Point spent the winter of 1846–47 at Fort Lewis awaiting his reassignment.[63]

It is easy for the historian to list the specific weaknesses and personality defects of De Smet and his group of coworkers; the records they left are extensive. No formal screening or testing procedures had been used to check the volunteers' preparedness and specific qualifications for such demanding missionary roles. As historian John Fahey concludes: "The discomforts of mission life were debilitating." The Jesuits' reports are sometimes preoccupied with petty, negative details. Their reports often express frank critical judgments. Vercruysse was characterized as brusque and irritable; Point, intractable, moody, and easily disheartened; Joset, impractical and impetuous; De Smet, too eager to please the Indians with lavish personal promises.

The reporter, however, eager to pass along such gossipy details, might not have evaluated his sources very carefully. The disclosures indicate that these men, like many other mortals who have endured similar circumstances, suffered from cabin fever. Moreover, with the possible exception of De Smet, each of these missionaries suffered some degree of cultural shock. Demanding and difficult though they may have been at times with each other, such defects are minor considering their attempt to give of themselves for unworldly motives under circumstances that frequently became extremely trying. Nobili, like De Vos, burned out after only two years; Mengarini, his health shattered, lasted only eight years.

Food, by primitive mountain standards, was plentiful only at St. Mary's. At the other reductions actual hunger frequently accompanied a most restricted diet. There was the deadliness of utter monotony, the heavy loneliness of extended isolation, the frustrating problem of unsatisfactory communication—all combined with the basic challenge of accommodating themselves to an alien culture. Then there were, always too repeatedly, the rigors of difficult travel. Joset reported that the missionaries averaged three months of the year in the saddle, and it is fairly certain that not one of these Jesuits, the romantic De Smet excepted, enjoyed the physical demands of the trail.[64]

In the context of these wilderness realities the exceptional De Smet related to his coworkers poorly as a superior. In many areas his sensitivities were not identical with theirs. His was a personal, distinctive satisfaction in the adventures and physical demands of outdoor life. In natural appetite and interest De Smet was related, as none of the others were, to the exploring mountain men. His coworkers knew only the monotony of prolonged on-site assignments in a foreign land. For the mobile De Smet, there were always the pleasures connected with new scenes, the thrills and challenges of discovering new trails.

Most of all, for De Smet alone there was a special recognition, a distinctive gratitude and respect. The Indian people, even though they were daily served by other missionaries, recognized De Smet in a unique fashion as *the* Blackrobe. In the judgment of the Indians, only De Smet could do no wrong. De Smet alone was free from the constant pressure of repeatedly proving his dedication. Only De Smet, universally and almost spontaneously, was granted hero status. As Schoenberg notes:

> Hoecken, Joset, Huet, Magri, and other Jesuits lived
> among the Indians, learned their language and gained
> their respect, even their love. But all these lacked the
> mystique that De Smet conveyed to almost all Indians

everywhere, including non-Christians. De Smet had never lived with Indians for any length of time, though he traveled often with them. He had never learned their language. But they were bound to him, and he to them, by bonds that could never be explained. . . . His love and loyalty . . . showed through his aging, peasant-like face.[65]

DE SMET'S DEPARTURE FROM THE REDUCTIONS

It was a somber De Smet who headed north down the Willamette at the close of June 1846. With the depletion of his Jesuit manpower, still more volunteers would have to be recruited. The return of Bishop Blanchet from Rome was anticipated for mid-1847, and De Smet expected that the dedicated Blanchet would have solicited the services of a number of Jesuits. Realistically, however, De Smet knew that he could not count on all of them. They turned out to be six in number to be assigned exclusively to the reduction program.

By the time De Smet arrived at the supply base, Fort Vancouver, he had determined upon a return trip to St. Louis; there he would present once more the necessity of increasing the number of missionaries. It was not an easy decision. Instead of the hero's reception he had previously received, De Smet realized, he would now have critics to face and pointed questions to answer. He was aware that his prestige and standing among the religious leadership in Rome and St. Louis had been weakened.

Regarding personal criticism, De Smet would ever remain highly sensitive. He enjoyed the acceptance and the esteem of popularity; further, he feared, with good reason, that his cause had become identified with himself. Through his own personal efforts he had sold the proposal of the reductions program. It was he who had directed the initiation of the project and had exercised primary responsibility for five busy years. With personal criticisms, De Smet saw the potential danger of a lessening Jesuit dedication to the entire Indian apostolate.

Such worries, however, were temporarily set aside at Fort Vancouver. De Smet occupied himself with obtaining supplies for the reductions. At the beginning of July he headed up the Columbia. Eight days later he started overland from Fort Walla Walla with a string of mules and horses; this would prove to be his final trip to supply his reductions.[66]

It was a preoccupied De Smet who rode eastward a day's journey — he reported a distance of about sixteen miles — along the Walla Walla

River. The caravan then headed northward; after five days of travel that included fordings of the Snake and Spokane rivers, he arrived at St. Ignatius Reduction. De Smet was still preoccupied when in the context of his meetings with Father Adrian Hoecken he composed a late July report on his journey from the original Fort Walla Walla.

One must wonder why De Smet made no mention of the Whitman Mission, a prominent development located only a short distance from the fort and almost adjacent to the heavily traveled Oregon Trail. Further, one must wonder why the sensitive and concerned De Smet, generally alert to Indian-white relationships, failed to mention the disturbed state of the Cayuse Indians along the trail. By the summer of 1846 the Cayuse had become provoked by the sorry consequences of the heavy traffic through their territory; with sickness introduced by emigrant trains the following summer, tribal members would be seriously stricken by measles and dysentery. The massacre of a dozen people at the Whitman Mission at the close of November 1847 would mark the opening of the Cayuse War. Quickly, as Burns reports, there were serious repercussions throughout the interior of Oregon.[67]

On July 26, having exchanged farewells with Hoecken, De Smet set out to move the assigned supplies to Sacred Heart and St. Mary's. He was received at Sacred Heart Reduction by Fathers Joset and Point and Brothers Magri and Lyons. Having gained their approval for his proposed trip to St. Louis, De Smet appointed Joset as acting superior of the reductions. Roothaan's letter of the previous August appointing Joset (rather than Elet) as De Smet's replacement had not yet been received. Point, still awaiting Roothaan's response to his petition for reassignment, accompanied De Smet to St. Mary's Reduction, then went on to Fort Lewis.

De Smet's supply train reached its terminus at St. Mary's on August 8. With understandable pride De Smet recorded the growth of this reduction. A sawmill had been constructed, twelve frame houses built, and a new larger church was about to be erected. A flourmill had been developed, which ground ten to twelve bushels per day. The stock at the reduction's farm had increased in number and variety. An irrigation system had been contrived; there were abundant crops of wheat, oats, and potatoes.[68]

After a brief rest De Smet pushed on, for the main body of the Flatheads had already set out on their fall buffalo hunt, moving to their favorite hunting camp in the Three Forks area of southwestern Montana. By early September, accompanied by Point, De Smet joined the encampment of the hunters.

Still eager to extend his influence to the Blackfeet, De Smet continued northeast past the headwaters of the Musselshell River. There, on September 14, the Blackfeet and their allies arrived, presenting a calumet to the Flatheads in token of peace. The next day De Smet arranged an impressive religious ceremony. With a congregation of some two thousand Flatheads, Nez Percés, Piegans, Bloods, Blackfeet, and Gros Ventres, using his interpreters Gabriel and Charles, De Smet offered an open-air mass, praying that all might be joined in the bonds of peace. By September 24 De Smet and Point had ridden into Fort Lewis on the Upper Missouri. During his visit there, De Smet began a close and lasting relationship with the Culbertsons. Point agreed to remain at the post through the winter as chaplain for the Blackfeet camped in the area.[69]

With a few companions, De Smet left Fort Lewis on September 28 to begin an adventurous voyage of over two thousand miles down the Missouri. Moving rapidly with the current, they reached Fort Union on October 11, Fort Berthold on the nineteenth. At the end of October they landed at Fort Pierre. On November 5 De Smet visited Fort Bouis, the following day Fort Lookout, and on the thirteenth Fort Vermillion. These outposts of the fur trade operation had multiplied since De Smet had made his initial voyage upriver from St. Joseph's Mission at Council Bluffs in 1839.

At Fort Pierre De Smet met a small party of the Sioux tribe; well accepted, he baptized fifty of their little children. Outside Fort Lookout he was again received into a Sioux encampment. In council there with about thirty tribal leaders De Smet asked if he would be welcome to remain in their midst to speak of the Great Spirit. It was the beginning of a special relationship that was to last until the end of his life. In all his subsequent travels across the Great Plains De Smet would repeatedly be thrilled by the special reception extended him by the Sioux people. With lasting pride De Smet would remember the welcome addressed to him by the Sioux chieftain on November 6, 1846: "Blackrobe, come and set up your lodge with ours; my heart tells me you will be listened to."

Having resumed his voyage down the Missouri, De Smet approached Council Bluffs. He put ashore on the west bank of the river at "a temporary establishment of the Mormons." There he met with "their President, Mr. Young, an affable and very polite gentleman." Although invited to remain at the Mormon winter quarters for a few days, De Smet felt the need to hurry downstream. He stopped on November 23, however, to pay a brief visit to the new pastor, Father

Scanlan, in the new town of St. Joseph. On the twenty-eighth he disembarked at Westport. With ice running in the river, De Smet hastened across Missouri for an early December arrival in St. Louis.[70]

THE TERMINATION OF THE REDUCTION PROGRAM

Two and a half years had passed since De Smet had last walked the levee at St. Louis, but he had not been forgotten. At the close of 1846 his popularity had increased, even among his peers. He was counted now among the frontiersmen and fur traders who headquartered in St. Louis. Like the other frontier achievers, he had become almost a folk hero. With his exceptional knowledge of the topography of the Far West and his unique connection with the western tribes, De Smet had become one of the most outstanding citizens of St. Louis.

Early in 1847, perhaps capitalizing on his popular reputation, De Smet was assigned to another European trip, again to solicit men and means for the apostolates of the Missouri Jesuits. This time De Smet used another promotional technique: letters of recommendation solicited from ecclesiastical and political leaders. De Smet departed St. Louis in April, traveling with Father John Elet, who was to participate in Jesuit meetings in Rome. A year later, in April 1848, De Smet and Elet left Liverpool to return to the United States. Among their six recruits were Fathers Miége, Ponziglione, and Charles Elet, John's brother. The group arrived in St. Louis at the end of May. In June one of the first reports sent to Rome by Father Elet, then serving as superior of the Missouri Jesuits, announced that because of their late arrival in St. Louis, De Smet's departure for Blackfoot country would have to be delayed until the following year. De Smet was therefore able to spend the following four months on an extended, though not too successful, visit to the Sioux.[71]

Among his Jesuit brethren De Smet's activities did not meet with universal approval. Criticism from some, though limited, was directed against his activism. Negative judgments concerning his ongoing travels and popular writings were sent from St. Louis to Rome. Some of the Oregon missionaries found fault with his management of mission funds and his rapid expansion of the reduction program.

Reporting to Van de Velde, the Missouri Jesuit superior, De Smet was informed of Roothaan's new edict: De Smet's direct participation in the reduction program had been terminated. Roothaan eventually became so frustrated with the failure of the reduction program that until his death on May 8, 1853, he would hold De Smet responsible for its defeat. That from the program's failure De Smet should rise in international popularity Roothaan found difficult to accept.[72]

Perhaps De Smet exemplified for Roothaan that special fault the Roman superior noted repeatedly in the Missouri Jesuits. From 1830, when they first became a distinct group operating directly under Roman supervision, each successive Jesuit superior in St. Louis was reprimanded by Roothaan for attempting too much too quickly. De Smet's exuberance, his eagerness to attempt the expansion requested by the Indian tribes, was characteristic of the Missouri Jesuit pattern that Roothaan deplored. The pace of western growth, the rapidly developing opportunities, perhaps not to be repeated, and the newcomers' call for religious services in and about St. Louis and other midwestern cities and throughout Oregon Territory were difficult for the Jesuit superior in Rome to appreciate. There was also Roothaan's abiding anxiety that "the classical and scholastic formation [of the Missouri Jesuits] was being neglected" because of the "incessant pressure of a superabundance of apostolic labours."[73]

Roothaan was further disturbed by news from St. Mary's Reduction contained in Ravalli's report of June 28, 1847. Ravalli complained that the Flatheads manifested a changed and deplorably negative attitude, which he attributed directly and totally to De Smet: "From his first arrival in the Mountains he had beguiled them with promises and hopes of a village, animals, plows, etc. . . . We are expecting other distressing things to occur very soon by reason of the lavish promises which Father De Smet scattered about him everywhere in his journey, and which neither he nor others will be able to keep." That same complaint about De Smet, "the generosity of his gifts, promises, etc.," had been forwarded to Roothaan by Point.[74]

De Smet's promises to the Indians certainly had been lavish, but they had not been empty. Within a few years he had worked minor miracles in founding the reductions. By his own efforts and through the generous support of the benefactors whose interest he had developed, he had been able to deliver stock and equipment and to supervise the construction of the basic structures of the reductions. Other individuals with fewer talents, less developed skills, imagination, or initiative, might not have been so effective. Not every missionary could be expected to duplicate De Smet's outgoing personality; few, indeed, would prove as dedicated or effective at fund-raising.

With accusations against De Smet mounting, Roothaan was further disturbed by the report from Elet, whom he had appointed recently as superior of the Missouri Jesuits. Elet informed him that he had singled out De Smet for two key posts. As Elet's official assistant, De Smet would help in directing the Missouri Jesuits; as treasurer, he would supervise all the financial operations. Roothaan responded at once with letters to Elet and De Smet, in Garraghan's phrase, "deprecating the appointment."

The response from St. Louis must have surprised Roothaan. Elet plainly informed the Roman superior that the extravagance alleged against De Smet was unfounded and that De Smet was showing himself the most efficient custodian of temporalities the Missouri Jesuits had ever known. Further, Elet specifically pointed to De Smet's experience and success in public relations: "He has single-handed done more for the reputation of the Society in the United States than all the rest in the two provinces. He is all powerful with the Bishops."

Initially Roothaan may have been inclined to attribute such high praise to Elet's close personal friendship with De Smet. Early in 1852, however, Elet's successor presented the same report. On August 25, 1851, Roothaan had assigned Father William S. Murphy to replace the dying Elet. After seven months of close association with De Smet in St. Louis, Murphy reported:

> I am satisfied with him in every respect, and in money matters I don't see what the vice-province would do without him.
>
> He is faithful, so it seems to me, in his exercises of piety and ready to obey in all things. It appears it has been reported to your Paternity that his book has done harm here in America. I confess this amazes me. I should have said just the opposite according to what I have read and heard.[75]

At about the same time Roothaan received the delayed and final report on St. Mary's Reduction. Ravalli's letter of April 5, 1851, presented the grim details of its closure following the Flatheads' rejection and departure. Facing what they considered a potential repetition of the Whitman tragedy, the Jesuits had withdrawn.[76]

Although he had long fought against accepting the evidence, Roothaan began to realize the impossibility of the dream he had shared with De Smet. In a letter to De Smet of April 15, 1852, Roothaan made it clear that despite their differences, he had come to

share De Smet's realistic evaluation. The Roman superior enumerated some of the basic reasons that militated against success:

> It seems that the idea of renewing the miracles of
> Paraguay amid those mountains was a Utopia. In the
> first place, we could not hope for the means which our
> Fathers received from the Crowns of Spain and Portu-
> gal. Then, it was impossible to keep the whites at a
> distance; then, too, the nature of the land is quite
> different and one cannot hope to wean the bulk of the
> savages from their nomadic life during a great part of
> the year. . . . I declare, my dear Father, I don't see
> how one can have any success at all.[77]

Despite Roothaan's lament, the overwhelming demands for manpower and funding, demands both he and De Smet had worked so
vigorously to meet, had never been the basic problem. De Smet and
the other religious authorities had been far too simplistic in their
belief that such investments in Oregon would guarantee the same
results achieved centuries before in Paraguay. It was obvious now, to
De Smet at least, that there was neither time nor place—there never
had been—for the program. Nor was there the potential for the
cultural blending that was the basic premise of the reduction. The
missionaries had done much to accommodate their message to the
culture of the Flatheads, but they were destined to fail in their
attempt gradually to modify that culture. To combine the Indians'
manner of living with the philosophy of the reductions or the lifestyle
the white invaders were rapidly imposing upon all the residents of
Oregon proved impossible.

In his historical assessment, Chittenden suggested that had the
Indians been able to retain their hunting way of life, the missionaries
could have accomplished their conversion to the Christian religion
without seriously interfering with their native customs.[78] However,
the buffalo culture was not adjustable to the agrarian life about which
the permanent village, the heart of the reduction, was structured.
With the migrating herds as the wandering center of all Indian life,
the buffalo was the source of food, clothing, lodging, and utensils.
The proposed gradual transformation to farming simply could not
answer all those basic needs.

Further, it was impossible to seclude the Flatheads from the
Blackfeet and the Bannocks or from their increasingly fierce competition over the buffalo. The same herds, though depleted in number
and confined to smaller locations, were the life source for all these

tribes. Moreover, it was utterly impossible to keep the Flatheads isolated from the corrupting influences of the white invaders. The Bitterroot Valley, considered so happily secluded by De Smet in 1841, had been thoroughly and lastingly breached in the mid-1840s.

Finally, it was impossible to achieve in one generation in Oregon what had only gradually flowered in the more spaced and lengthy efforts in Paraguay. In their eagerness both De Smet and Roothaan had paid little attention to the initial difficulties experienced earlier in South America. Nor could they have foreseen the startling rapidity of the Oregon invasion or the pressures caused by its sheer magnitude. Only with hindsight did DeVoto recognize that "there was no time at all."[79]

The Jesuit missionaries continued to serve at various sites after the termination of the reduction program, but their missionary activities were now based on a different philosophy. Burns states: "The effort changed into something of a race to elevate these people to a position of minimum parity with the aggressive Whites." The dream of "a living reorientation rather than a brutal end and beginning" had been shattered. Of necessity, mission methodology at the Jesuit institutions also changed. As a later form of colonial evangelizing, these missions operated in general as a pressured combination of "Christianizing and civilizing." For the tribes of the Rocky Mountains as well as those of the Great Plains, the sole alternative to extinction increasingly became some degree of acculturation.[80]

Thereafter Catholic missionary work among the tribes was less concerned with social justice. Indian rights would seldom be stressed, and native customs were usually discouraged. Christ's teachings were still presented, but the salvation promised through Christ became identified with civilized life. The First Great Commandment was given priority while the Second Great Commandment was relegated to the need for preparatory and remedial activities intended to transform the Indians into white Christians.[81]

Summing up De Smet's work with the Indian missions in the Northwest, historian Wilcomb E. Washburn comments: "The job was too big; the obstacles too great."[82] Nevertheless, in the traditions and legends treasured by the Indians De Smet had answered their request with all the loving dedication they had anticipated. His reduction program had attempted to present Christ's message to them as Indians.

Part Two

—

The Immediate Problem

—

The Necessary Thoroughfares

Chapter Four

Mounting Confrontations
on the Great Plains (1840–50)

> The shifting frontier and the changing policy pre-
> saged what was evident almost from the beginning:
> the "permanent Indian frontier" was doomed to fail-
> ure. . . . By 1850, the Indian country was not outside
> the United States; it was right in the middle, a barrier
> that had to be removed.
>   —James C. Olson, *History of Nebraska*

THE BUFFALO CULTURE OF THE PLAINS INDIANS

Even before the close of the eighteenth century the Indian tribes of
the Great Plains were enjoying the golden age of their buffalo culture.
This last period of material richness, this flowering of a unique
lifestyle, lasted through 1840. Shortly thereafter tremendous
changes across the Great Plains violently terminated that golden age.
Although Commissioner David Mitchell announced to the assembled
tribes in September, 1851, "Your condition is now changed," those
changes were so complete and so abrupt, so utterly beyond the
comprehension of the Native Americans, that the entire buffalo
culture quickly became only the memories of Indian legends. With
no time for the Indians to adjust, all the realities upon which their
way of life had been founded were eliminated.

Flamboyantly riding into the nineteenth century—for horse acquisition by then had provided mobility for all the Plains tribes—was
the stereotyped figure of the Native American of the West. He was
the proud hunter on horseback with feathered headdress, moccasins,
and breechcloth whose portable home and total lifestyle were entirely centered on the buffalo. The Plains Indians modeled their tribal
ways on the comings and goings of the buffalo herds.[1]

The country of the nomadic peoples of the High Plains was
identified, like their tribal existence, with the ranges of the buffalo
herds. Along both sides of the present Canadian border were the
tribes of the Blackfeet Confederacy. About the Yellowstone and its
tributaries were the Crow people. In the more secluded high country
of the Northwest were the various Salish groups, including the
Flatheads. Moving in but recently from the prairies east of the

Missouri were the powerful Lakota, the Teton or Western Sioux. Roaming the central regions of the Great Plains were the Arapahos and the Cheyennes. Along the eastern slopes of the Rocky Mountains were the Shoshone people.

Down in the Arkansas River country were the Kiowas, and below the Arkansas were the Comanches and Plains Apaches, the dominant tribes of the southernmost plains. Along the Missouri River lived the earth-lodge tribes, peoples who grew corn in their permanent villages but seasonally lived in tipis and hunted buffalo on the plains as a mainstay of their lives. Along the middle reaches of the Missouri were the Mandans and Hidatsas; downriver, the Arikaras and Pawnees (related tribes, speaking Caddoan languages), the Dheigha Siouans (Omahas, Poncas, Kansas, Osages and Quapaws) and the Chiwere Siouans (Iowas, Otoes, and Missourias).

The Plains Indians lived in notable and readily defended freedom—personal, band, and tribal—with a rich natural abundance and a highly treasured independence. In fact, they lived with only one specific dependence, a dependence not only of each tribal individual but the entire Indian society—the intimate and total connection with the buffalo to provide all the commodities of prime importance. De Smet enumerated the uses of the buffalo:

> I have often spoken of the bisons, improperly called buffaloes, without mentioning the great use which the Indians make of this interesting animal. They supply almost all the necessaries of life. Their skins form lodges or dwellings, and serve as clothing, litters, bridles, and saddle coverings, vessels to hold water, boats to cross lakes and rivers; with the hair, the Indians make their cordage; with the sinews, bowstrings and thread for clothes, as well as glue; the shoulder-blade is spade and pickaxe. The bison is their daily bread, their chief food.[2]

But the Plains Indians did more than hunt the buffalo as the rich provider of all life's basic needs. They revered and respected the buffalo as the gift of the Great Spirit, for they regarded the buffalo as the bountiful blessing providently offered by God. In the Indians' judgment, the comings and goings of the tremendous herds were directed by Father Above, a sign of his pleased concern when the buffalo were made available, their absence connected with his displeasure. Such a dependence the religious-minded Indians could frankly acknowledge. It was a dependence that did not disturb the

Indians' self-security; rather, it fostered their self-reliance and ingenuity.

And the number of buffalo, the extent of the great herds, was
legion. The early white explorers in the West consistently commented with amazement upon the numbers of buffalo. As late as 1840
the great animal was still commonly believed to be in never-ending
supply. Even after the mounting pressures on the herds caused by
emigrants forging the transcontinental roads during the 1840s, the
number of buffalo on the Great Plains has been conservatively
estimated at thirty million.[3]

Only upon studied reflection can one now appreciate the extent of
the buffalo's influence upon these Native Americans and the Indians'
multiple uses of the buffalo. The broad assessment by Tom McHugh
in his study of the buffalo is no exaggeration: the by-products of the
buffalo, "an endless list, founded on the essentials of meat and
hides," included "a series of luxury items of almost unbelievable
variety. The total array made the buffalo a tribal department store,
builder's emporium, furniture mart, drugstore, and supermarket
rolled into one—a splendidly stocked commissary for the needs of
life."[4]

Specialized technology was the key to preserving buffalo meat.
Dehydrating the meat to make jerky began with a skilled process of
cutting the meat into thin strips, which were then dried by sun and
wind or by fire. This process reduced the weight to about one-sixth
that of the fresh meat. Then, to reduce the bulk, the jerky was
pounded until pulverized and packed into rawhide containers, sealed
by pouring in liquid fat. Protected from air and moisture, pemmican
could be stored for years.[5]

As clothing, buffalo hide literally enwrapped the lives of the
Plains Indians. Infants were swaddled in the supersoft skin of the
unborn calves; the thick robes from mature bulls were used as
winding sheets for the corpses of departed elders. The dressing of
hides—almost always an occupation for the women, following the
male role as hunter-provider—was a developed skill. The skins
intended for clothing, as distinct from those prepared for tipi covers
and liners and blankets or robes, received the final treatment of
smoking over a smoldering fire. Such treatment produced a garment
that would dry soft and pliant after the wetting by rain or snow.

From experience Indians learned of the variations in the quality of
buffalo hides depending on the animal's sex and age and very
important, the season of the year in which the hunt was made. The

toughened rawhide of the old bull's neck could be made into a warrior's shield effective against arrows; the heavy-haired winter hides of the animals during the cold season made the best insulating blankets and robes.

Depending on the size of an individual tipi, ten to twenty hides would be sewn together to form a wind- and rainproof covering. With additional skin liners stretched inside the tipi walls lashed to the tipi poles, the portable buffalo-hide home of the Plains Indians would not be equaled by army canvas or modern nylon tents. When a tipi cover was replaced after several seasons of use, the smoke-impregnated hide at the top would be cut up and sewn into durable moccasins.

The diverse uses of hide and hair were only a portion of buffalo by-products. The list of utensils fashioned from other portions of the animal is long and varied. Such objects might be practical containers and implements-instruments or such artistic items as brushes, ornaments, and ceremonial decorations and symbols. Drums and drumsticks, for example, were made for the music of dances and ceremonials. Even the sun-dried dung of the buffalo ("chips") provided fuel that burned hotter than charcoal, longer than wood, with almost no smoke. Pulverized buffalo chips made a highly absorbent and delicate powder that was poured into a baby's cradleboard to provide a disposable diaper and protect against skin irritation. Every part of the buffalo was utilized to the full, seemingly answering completely all the needs of Indian life.

And yet the relationship of the Native Americans with the buffalo was much more than the sum of these material uses. That relationship was, among other things, the basic source of community, the uniting force of a tribe.

The communal buffalo hunts, the outstanding events of the entire year, were a sharing in the key tribal activity. All members of the tribe took part, each with specific functions assigned: the scouts and hunters, the women who butchered the carcasses, and all other tribal members who cooperated in processing the buffalo for food and equipment.

Further, there was an essential connection between the buffalo harvest and the Sun Dance. As their most sacred religious ceremony, the Sun Dance marked the professed dependence of the Plains tribes upon Father Above. Held before the highly important late summer hunts, the Sun Dance was both a preparatory and a sacrificial action. Thoroughly related to the buffalo, the religious ceremony publicly proclaimed the petition and the thanksgiving of a deeply religious people.

CIRCULAR TO INDIAN AGENTS, TRADERS, &C.

Office Superintendent Indian Affairs, }

ST. LOUIS, APRIL 4th, 1851. }

To the Indian Traders and others, on the Upper Missouri, Arkansas and Platte Rivers:

GENTLEMEN:

Congress has authorized the President of the United States to hold a Treaty with all the Prairie Tribes of Indians residing South of the Missouri River. and North of Texas. The objects of the Government are just and humane, and intended entirely for the benefit and future welfare of the Indians. Should the Treaty be productive of all the good we anticipate, it will tend greatly to promote the safety and interests of the Traders, as well as the Indians themselves. It is, therefore, confidently hoped and expected that you will all unite and use your best exertions to aid in assembling the Indians at Fort Larimie. on the first of September, 1851, at which time and place I will meet them, for the purpose of making such a Treaty as will, it is hoped, be greatly to their advantage for the time to come. You are authorized to assure the Indians that they will be amply compensated for all the depredations of which they complain, on account of the destruction of game, timber, &c., by the passing of white men through their country. You can also say to them, that after the ratification of the contemplated Treaty, each Tribe will receive an annual present, in goods, from their Great Father—the amount to be made contingent upon their faithful observance of their treaty stipulations. A suitable quantity of provisions will be provided.

You can also state to them, that they can assemble at the time and place designated, and remain there during the necessary time for holding the Treaty, with the most perfect safety—as a large military force will be on the ground, for the purpose of keeping order and preserving friendly relations.

The different tribes are authorized to come *en masse*, with all their women and children; or to send delegations, composed of men alone : the former, however, would be much preferred, as the presence of the women and children would be an additional guarantee for the good conduct of the parties present. It is hoped, among other beneficial arrangements, (intended for the permanent good of the Indians,) that we will be enabled to divide and subdivide the country into various geographical districts, in a manner entirely satisfactory to the parties concerned. This, if accomplished, will go far towards extinguishing the bloody wars which have raged from time immemorable—producing such a horrible waste of human life, and innocent blood. The many objects so fondly hoped to be accomplished are, however, too numerous to be stated or commented upon in this brief Circular; they will *all* be fully explained around " our council fires."

As this undertaking will involve some expense, and great labors, a fair compensation will be allowed in proportion to the services rendered. This is intended to apply to the Indian Traders, Interpreters, &c.—not to any officers of the Government, their compensations having been fixed by law.

Very respectfully, your obedient servant,

D. D. MITCHELL, *Sup't Indian Affairs.*

This is the initial publication of this document. Seemingly, Mitchell did not file a copy with the Indian Office, and the reports of the period carry no reference to this flier—"the Circular That Changed the West." Recently a few copies were discovered in De Smet Papers. (Jesuit Missouri Province Archives)

David D. Mitchell (1806–61) (Missouri Historical Society, neg. Por-M-33)

Robert Campbell (1804–79) (from Scharf's *History of St. Louis*)

St. Louis Superintendent of Indian Affairs Mitchell and his assistant, Agent Thomas Fitzpatrick, conducted the 1851 Fort Laramie treaty negotiations with "the Indian tribes of the prairies." After competitive bidding against Pierre Chouteau, Jr., Robert Campbell's firm received the government contract to supply the specified list of goods for the Indians.

Thomas Fitzpatrick (1799–
1854)

Margaret Poisal Fitzpatrick
(1832–72)

*Margaret Fitzpatrick, wife of
Thomas, was the daughter of
Snake Woman (the sister of
Arapaho chief Left Hand)
and of John Poisal, a French-
Canadian trapper who
served as the Arapaho interpreter in 1851 (listed as
Pizelle). Margaret also attended the conference at
Horse Creek; on September
12, 1851, she participated
there in the baptism by De
Smet of her son, Andrew Jackson. (Photographs in Colorado Historical Society)*

William Claessens (1811–91), pictured here, was trained as a blacksmith. He joined Gregory Mengarini (a musician and a linguist) and Nicolas Point (skilled as an artist) among the Jesuits who participated with De Smet in the founding of St. Mary's Reduction in 1841. (Oregon Province Jesuit Archives, Gonzaga University Special Collection)

Adrian Hoecken (1815–97), *left*, shown here with De Smet, began St. Ignatius Mission north of Lake Pend d'Oreille in 1844, as directed by De Smet. Ten years later Hoecken cooperated with Chief Alexander in moving the Kalispel–Pend d'Oreille mission with the tribe to the current site in western Montana. (Jesuit Missouri Province Archives)

De Smet identified this picture in the Linton Album as taken at St. Louis before the extended tour of eastern cities led by Agent Fitzpatrick. This group of "Rapahos and Sheyennes" made up half the tribal delegates assigned at Horse Creek in 1851. (Jesuit Missouri Province Archives)

Among the Indian leaders of the Northwest was, *above left*, Aeneas (or Young Ignace), who extended the Flatheads' 1839 invitation to De Smet at Council Bluffs and in the following year accompanied Blackrobe on his initial journey to the Northwest. Red Feather (Michael or Insula), *above right*, became De Smet's special friend, and after the friendly rendezvous, this Flathead chief became the adopted brother of both Robert Campbell and Thomas Fitzpatrick. (Sketches made by Gustavus Sohon in 1854, in the Smithsonian Institution, 37-416G and 37-416A)

De Smet returned to the high country in the fall of 1858. In the following spring he escorted this group of tribal leaders to Fort Vancouver for a conference with General William S. Harney: *front row, left to right,* Victor (Kalispel), Alexander (Pend d'Oreille), Red Feather (Flathead), Andrew (Coeur d'Alene); *standing,* Ennis (Skoyelpi), Bonaventure (Skizoumish), De Smet, and Francis (Flathead). (Linton Album, Jesuit Missouri Province Archives)

No wonder, then, that throughout the entire year the buffalo was the center of tribal social life. The animal was the subject of countless recitals by the camp's storytellers and the central figure of fairy tales spoken by grandparents. Buffalo were the objects of games fashioned by children and the dreams of adults. Buffalo were imitated and involved in the prayers of the people in public dance and private orations to the Great Spirit. The buffalo dominated all aspects of Plains Indian culture, forming the center of their religious rituals. Indeed, the Plains Indian culture was the buffalo culture.

How all-pervasive was this buffalo culture among the Plains Indians? How deeply was it treasured? Over a century has passed since that unique lifestyle was terminated completely. At least five generations of Native Americans have so lived only in their precious legends. And still the loss of that buffalo culture remains a personal and tragic deprivation. In his history of the Western Indian tribes, Dee Brown suggests that "the poverty, the hopelessness, and the squalor" that have all too frequently characterized reservation life, even to the present, are the consequences and manifestations of a more basic loss—the poverty of spirit that followed the extermination of the buffalo.[6]

THE EXTENDED MILITARY ARM OF THE UNITED STATES

Historians point out that the Compromise of 1850 was connected with two major wars. Subsequent to the Mexican War, the Compromise determined the status of slavery throughout the extensive areas thereby acquired. Regarding the War of Secession, seemingly so inevitable, the Compromise postponed that rebellion for another decade.[7]

The Compromise of 1850 also had much to do with a third major military conflict, one that was becoming highly probable at the time. As Congress was temporarily freed from its preoccupation with the power question of the extension of slavery, attention could be turned to the mounting tension on the Great Plains. The troubled relationship there had become a serious threat to any development of the colonies recently established on the Pacific coast. Serving as the necessary links with the new western territories, the great thoroughfares passed through Indian country. The use of these corridors resulted in confrontations.

However, the threat of a third major military conflict, one initiated by the Indians, was stillborn. In a power move that was an effective application of the ancient Roman technique *divide et impera*, the procedure for absorbing new territory, congressionally appointed commissioners by means of diplomacy seized permanent control of the Great Plains. Unwittingly the Indians capitulated during the 1851 treaty council at Fort Laramie.

Moreover, even prior to midcentury Congress had created by an ongoing display of military might a basic change on the Great Plains. Following his initial expedition in 1842, Lieutenant John C. Frémont had called for the erection of a permanent military post, recommending the area of the Fort Laramie trading post as the most suitable location.[8]

Frémont's second exploratory journeys in 1843 and 1844, for which Fitzpatrick served as guide, were initiated and subsequently publicized by his father-in-law, the determined expansionist Senator Thomas Hart Benton. Further, President James Polk was pledged to unrestricted expansion; Polk sought exclusive title to Oregon, official annexation of Texas, and acquisition of California. Polk shared with Benton the desire to encourage the settlement of the West. Their top priority was that the passageway for this migration be safeguarded and secured. In his first annual message to Congress on December 2, 1845, Polk recommended that "a suitable number of stockades and block house forts be erected along the usual route between our frontier settlement on the Missouri and the Rocky Mountains, and that an adequate force of mounted riflemen be raised to guard and protect them on their journey." On May 19, 1846, congressional authorization of the Oregon Trail Act granted the requested legislation.[9]

Fitzpatrick returned to Washington in late November 1846 to present firsthand reports of the success of General Kearny's Army of the West at Santa Fe and Frémont's initial activities in California. Moving at once to the desks of the Indian Office (the headquarters of the commissioner of Indian affairs was still located within the War Department), Fitzpatrick received a commission as Indian agent, a political appointment that had been arranged by Frémont's highly influential father-in-law.[10]

In April Senator Benton had proposed the creation of a new Indian agency for the Upper Arkansas and Platte under the supervision of the St. Louis superintendency, recommending that Fitzpatrick be assigned to the post. In his initial report at the start of 1847, agent Fitzpatrick immediately offered a strong endorsement of Frémont's proposal regarding the best means of securing the passageways:

> My opinion is, that a post at, or in the vicinity of
> Laramie is much wanted. It would be nearly in the

center of the buffaloe range, where all the most
formidable Indian tribes are fast approaching and near
where there will eventually (as the game decreases) be
a great struggle for the ascendancy. 300 mounted men
at that post would be necessary. . . .

Another post at or near Fort Hall with a force of 100
or 150 men, would be advisable, not more on account
of the protection it would afford travelers than to have
it as a place for resting and recruiting men and
animals, for the further prosecution of the journey to
and from the Pacific. The next and last of that line I
would place as near as practicable to the mouth of
Columbia River, where it would serve many purposes
not necessary to relate.[11]

On May 10, 1849, Lieutenant Colonel William Loring led a
regiment of mounted riflemen out of Fort Leavenworth westward on
the Oregon Trail. He positioned two companies at each of three new
forts—Kearney, Laramie, and Cantonment Loring (outside Fort
Hall). By October, when Loring garrisoned the final four companies
of his regiment at Fort Vancouver, the one-armed colonel had
extended the government's powerful military supervision across the
length of the trail.[12]

The post on the south bank of the North Platte River, just
downstream from its confluence with the Laramie River, had been
erected by William Sublette in 1834 to supply his beaver hunters in
the Rockies. Within a few years, however, control of both these
trappers and this supply post was taken over by the powerful
American Fur Company. On June 26, 1849, Major Winslow Sanderson, the first commanding officer of the new military post, purchased the buildings from the American Fur Company for $4,000,
and the post was thereafter officially called Fort Laramie.[13]

Westward from Fort Leavenworth on the Missouri, by way of Fort
Kearney (actually the second Fort Kearney, "the post at Grand
Island") and Fort Laramie across the breadth of the Great Plains, the
Frémont-Fitzpatrick proposal for the abiding presence of military
might had been implemented. Further, these forts spaced along the
passageway were more than military barracks and permanent displays of the government's potential for punitive actions. In addition
to safeguarding the emigrants, the forts served that secondary and
practical function Fitzpatrick had suggested. On October 16, 1849,
the St. Louis newspaper *Missouri Republican* published this regard-

ing Fort Laramie: "Nearly all the parties remain here a few days to reset wagon tires, exchange and purchase cattle, mail letters for the states, and replenish their supply of provisions from the commissary, who is permitted 'to sell to those actually in want.' "[14]

Such military stations, therefore, in line with government planning, provided both passive and active encouragement and support for the continuing invasions of the emigrants. The history of the West marks 1849 as the year the California argonauts first swarmed westward in high numbers over the Oregon Trail.[15] Of even greater significance for the future of the tribes of the area was the power play that had been made within the seven operational months of 1849. The initial move to territorial domination was complete; in precautionary fashion the military arm of the United States had been extended across the Great Plains.

FITZPATRICK'S MOTIVATION: To Secure Unmolested Passage
As early as 1846 Thomas H. Harvey, St. Louis superintendent of Indian affairs, heard complaints from Indian tribes on the Plains that the whites were "wantonly destroying the buffalo." Harvey alerted Washington officials, recommending "a general council inducing the Indians into treaties of peace and friendship":

> I would again call the attention of the Department to the necessity of buying out a road or roads to the mountains, and paying the Indians through whose country they might pass, such compensation as the government might deem proper. . . . A trifling compensation for this right of way would be calculated to secure their friendship towards the whites while passing through their country. . . .
>
> When the buffalo becomes scarce, the stock and persons of the emigrants will hardly be safe . . . especially when they [the Indians] look upon the emigrants as the cause of the scarcity of their source of subsistence.[16]

At the close of 1847 Harvey repeated his recommendation to hold a general council of the Plains tribes. Again the superintendent called attention to the twofold motivation—concern for the whites and the Indians. However, in his report of October 29 Harvey had manifested a new attitude toward the Indians and a changed policy:

> The many acts of violence that have been committed on the plains by what are called the "wild Indians,"

call loudly for some more energetic system than any
yet put in practice in relation to Indians. The application of our humane system to these people is entirely
insufficient to restrain them; we must deal with men
as we find them, not as we would have them to be.
Many acts of the most flagrant character committed
by the Sioux within the last few years yet remain
unpunished. . . . In fine, they [the Indians] must be
made to feel the power of the government.[17]

Rather quickly Harvey had adopted the philosophy, was even using
the terminology, of his newly appointed assistant, Thomas Fitzpatrick. Through the next two years Harvey attached his personal
endorsement as he forwarded Fitzpatrick's reports to the Indian
Office. At the close of 1847 Harvey notified Washington officials, "I
cannot too strongly recommend the views advanced by Agent Fitzpatrick."[18]

Fitzpatrick declared a preliminary punitive program conducted by
the Indian Office to prove the "ability and willingness to punish
insult and injury" to be all-important. Moreover, he initially questioned Harvey's high hopes that a general council would produce
lasting peaceful relations. Pointing to "the treachery, cunning and
great inferiority of the Indian compared to the white man," Fitzpatrick declared that he could make a treaty at any time with any tribe
"if I happened to have sufficient merchandise on hand to make
presents." He hastened to add, however, that the Indians could not be
counted on to abide by the stipulations of the treaty "for one single
moment longer than a favourable opportunity offers for its violation."[19]

It had been Fitzpatrick, more than any of his associates among the
mountain men, who had fashioned the Oregon Trail. It had been
Fitzpatrick, the outstanding guide from Westport, who had conducted the first wagon trains—including that of the Whitmans as
well as De Smet's missionaries—up the Platte River and over South
Pass. Now it would be Fitzpatrick with his special status as Indian
agent who would secure the overland road to Oregon and California.
In accord with his frontier sense of priorities, Fitzpatrick repeatedly
insisted that all the emigrants wanted was "a free and unmolested
passage through to their destination"; he also openly declared that
"they ought to have it, cost what it may."[20]

Regarding the Plains Indians, their new agent quite frankly stated
his pessimistic view: "I consider them a doomed race, who must

fulfill their destiny." Writing from Bent's Fort on the Arkansas in 1847 Fitzpatrick began his official criticisms of the Indian character:

> I will further remark that I fear the real character of the Indian can never be ascertained because it is altogether unnatural for a Christian man to comprehend how so much depravity, wickedness and folly can possibly belong to human beings.
>
> It has always appeared to me that great error exists in the public mind, in regard to the relations between the white man and the Indian, inasmuch as whatever atrocities have ever been committed by the Indians are invariably attributed to the rascality and swindling operations of the white man. . . .
>
> I am aware that great violations of justice have been committed on both sides; but the Indians of whom I now speak, (the wild tribes of the prairie,) have always kept far ahead of the white man in the perpetration of rascality; and I believe it is only in order to keep pace, and hold his own with the Indian, that the white man is often obliged to resort to many mean practices.[21]

At Benton's instigation Fitzpatrick was summoned in 1848 to Washington to make further presentations in interviews with Commissioner Medill. In his oral and written reports Fitzpatrick called for a military solution to the mounting threats against travelers on the transcontinental thoroughfares. The agent repeated his call for strong punitive measures: "These Indians are not at all aware of our capacity or power to chastise them, & never will believe it until they have proof of the fact." "Severe chastisement," he suggested, would "be the means of putting a stop to the frequent robberies and murders in that country."[22]

Having returned to St. Louis, Fitzpatrick continued to call attention to the troubled lot of the emigrants. Before his October departure for his agency Fitzpatrick composed his annual report for 1848. He declared specifically that he would continue to speak out on this issue "until the government puts forth such measures as will give protection to the citizens of the United States passing and repassing through that wild region."[23] By focusing attention on the plight of the endangered white emigrants, Fitzpatrick acted as the voice for the new crusade. His arguments presented to the Indian Office the simple fact: the Manifest Destiny of the United States demanded the Oregon Trail as a secured passageway.

In August 1849, exactly one year after his previous visit, Fitzpatrick returned to Washington. Mindful of his previous inability to dictate a military policy to government leaders, Fitzpatrick was now endorsing a proposal recommended by Superintendent Mitchell, who had returned to the St. Louis post as Harvey's replacement in April 1849. Mitchell refined and amplified Harvey's suggestion for a conciliatory treaty council with the tribes.[24]

By August 1849, then, the Indian Office had been presented with options, even though these were limited to the simple choice between army domination or diplomatic negotiations.

Even before Fitzpatrick departed Washington, Orlando Brown, Medill's replacement as commissioner of Indian affairs, had determined to take action. Returning to the St. Louis office, Fitzpatrick brought a letter from Commissioner Brown instructing the St. Louis superintendent and his agent for the Great Plains to proceed with their plans for a treaty conference. Mitchell and Fitzpatrick were appointed commissioners to conduct that conference and were given a subsidy of $5,000 to purchase presents to be used in the negotiations. Furthermore, they were authorized following the treaty council to bring a delegation of tribal leaders to Washington to impress them with the power and greatness of the United States.[25]

Despite the grim situation in St. Louis in August 1849—perhaps precisely because of the cholera epidemic and their anticipation that the Forty-Niners would be spreading the disease and other problems along the overland roads—Mitchell and Fitzpatrick decided to act at once. Fitzpatrick was to set out immediately to announce the good news: the Great Father would provide compensation to the tribes of the Great Plains for their losses.

Mitchell was already planning to include in the treaty council "all the wandering tribes that inhabit the plains of the Arkansas, the Platte, and the Missouri." As for the site, after further consideration Bent's Fort on the Arkansas was regarded as too far south. Fort Laramie, only recently purchased by the army, was still being secured and developed; supplies were still being hauled out from Fort Leavenworth. Still another consideration was the time factor: by the time of Fitzpatrick's arrival on the Plains, the tribes would already be absorbed in their highly important fall buffalo harvest.

At the close of August 1849 Superintendent Mitchell informed the Indian Office of Fitzpatrick's departure and his purpose—to notify the tribes to assemble at Fort Kearney about July 1, 1850. Mitchell also reported that he had instructed Fitzpatrick to hurry to Fort

Leavenworth where he would be able to join the command of Colonel John Munroe heading for New Mexico; the troops would serve as an escort for Fitzpatrick and the Indian presents he was transporting.[26]

However, Fitzpatrick arrived at Fort Leavenworth too late. In a bitter letter written from Westport on September 8 he informed Mitchell that "the very generous and judicious plans of the Department had been smashed." Expressing his anger, Fitzpatrick blamed military officials for a lack of cooperation: "Col. Monroe had left Fort Leavenworth for Santa Fe five days previous to my arrival. Yet if the transportation expected had been furnished immediately I could have overtaken Col. Monroe before reaching the Arkansas River. . . . I am of the opinion that since the separation of the Indian Bureau from the War Department, that Department has not the same disposition to accommodate as heretofore."[27]

Even more determined after this initial failure, Mitchell informed Commissioner Brown of enlarged plans for the treaty council. In reply the commissioner directed Mitchell to submit an estimate of the cost of his proposal to be presented to Congress. On October 26, 1849, Mitchell requested a $200,000 appropriation; he also called for military participation of some ten companies. At the close of November Commissioner Brown endorsed the proposal in his annual report. Promised the support of Missouri senator David Atchison and Stephen Douglas, chairman of the Senate Committee on Territories, the Indian Office anticipated prompt action by Congress. In spring 1850 Mitchell headed to Washington to assist in preparing the legislation. Fitzpatrick carried on a different campaign, spreading among the tribes of his agency the Great Father's plan and promise to enter into a treaty of peace and friendship with all the tribes.[28]

On June 27 the *Missouri Republican* informed its readers that Fitzpatrick had returned to St. Louis the previous day. In Mitchell's office Fitzpatrick learned that the official approbation of their treaty proposal had been delayed. Under Atchison's sponsorship Senate Bill 157 had passed on April 30; however, with Congress still preoccupied with the slavery issue, obtaining the attention and approbation of the House in the immediate future seemed unlikely.[29]

For Mitchell and Fitzpatrick the only course of action was to file early and impressive reports for the current year and to hope that the newly appointed commissioner of Indian affairs, Luke Lea, would do the same. Mitchell's report would emphasize the time factor, the urgency that "the *just* and *humane* objects contemplated be carried out during the summer of 1851." Fitzpatrick highlighted the basic

issue: "At once, and without further delay, to have some understanding with them in regard to the right of way through their country; and
whatever our and their rights may be, let us and them know it, that we
may have some data on which to base future proceedings."

In the conclusion of his report Fitzpatrick supplied additional
motivation for congressional approval. To considerations of both
good economy and justice Fitzpatrick added the serious threat of an
expensive war:

> Through these districts all the great leading thorough-
> fares pass; and the immense emigration travelling
> through that country for the past two years has deso-
> lated and impoverished that country to an enormous
> extent. . . . For my own part, I am satisfied it would
> be economical, and good policy, for the government at
> this time to extend even a little show of justice to the
> Indians of that country, and to avoid a hostile collision
> if possible; because, if we may judge from the diffi-
> culties, disasters, and expenditures occurring in New
> Mexico, in endeavoring to guard against a few miser-
> able, unarmed wretches, what then will be the conse-
> quences should twenty thousand well armed, well
> mounted, and the most warlike and expert in war of
> any Indians on the continent, turn out in hostile array
> against all American travellers through their country?[30]

On November 27, 1850, Commissioner Lea presented his annual
report, together with those of Mitchell and Fitzpatrick. By then
congressional preoccupation with the slavery issue had ended: the
Great Compromise had been enacted into legislation. On September
30 the 31st Congress concluded its first session. The Mitchell-
Fitzpatrick treaty proposal remained unfinished business.

THE MISSOURI TRAILHEADS: *Multiplied and Contaminated*

De Smet had been scheduled to depart St. Louis in the early summer
of 1849. Serving as an assistant to the newly appointed Missouri
Jesuit superior, Father John Elet, De Smet joined in planning a
supervisory tour of the Jesuit Indian missions located among some of
the border tribes west of the Missouri frontier. Their departure,
however, was long delayed. In the late spring and then throughout the
summer months, two major catastrophes struck St. Louis.

The first was the Great Fire, which broke out on the St. Louis
riverfront on the evening of May 17. The second was a cholera

epidemic. In various letters composed from the start of May through late August, De Smet's comments provide an ongoing report on the serious situation:

> MAY 4th—Cholera is raging around us. Five persons died of it yesterday, in our parish alone. . . . MAY 14th—Cholera continues raging here, people dying off very fast. . . . MAY 19th—The conflagration is the greatest calamity that ever befell St. Louis. . . . MAY 22nd—We have had a dreadful calamity, such a scene of desolation no man here has ever witnessed. About five hundred houses are lying in ruins and are still smoking. MAY 25th—The cholera continues, and deaths are very numerous. Nearly five hundred houses burned, and twenty-three steamboats—a loss of about 3 millions of dollars. Thousands are ruined, and a great check and gloom rests over the city. . . .
>
> JUNE 3rd—Your Reverence must have read about the St. Louis conflagration. The whole college, Fathers and Brothers and Scholastics, were at work all night. I was the first of ours at the Archbishop's; fire was falling as thick as a heavy snow. I carried on my back the whole contents of the Archbishop's safe. . . . The Cathedral, the Archbishop's house, the orphan asylum, all escaped after all. . . . JUNE 15th—The cholera is now most awful; hundreds of new cases occur daily. . . . JUNE 28th—The cholera is dreadfully ravaging St. Louis; thousands have died of it already, within these fifty days past. It appears still on the increase; hundreds of families are leaving the city. . . .
>
> JULY 12th—All business is dead here. A great many of your acquaintances are gone; old Pierre Chouteau, among others you know. . . . JULY 17th—Cholera is continuing its havoc in the city; ten Nuns have died of the sickness. But the number of citizens is diminishing much daily; the population is supposed to have lowered from 65 thousand to 30 thousand. . . .
>
> AUG. 20th—Since my last letter St. Louis has suffered severely by fire and sickness. More than one-tenth have died within five months. AUG. 22nd—St. Louis is gradually recovering. The health of the city is as usual, and business is briskly setting in.[31]

Reportedly introduced by the steamboat traffic, there had been isolated cases of cholera in St. Louis in the final months of 1848; as De Smet noted, however, the spread of the disease did not occur until the late spring of 1849. Early that year there was the notable growth of St. Louis as the primary easternmost gateway for the gold seekers. Steamboat traffic to the levee at St. Louis had greatly increased; from New Orleans, from the Ohio and Illinois rivers, and from the Upper Mississippi there were 2,546 steamboat arrivals in 1849.[32]

Also in 1849 at the St. Louis levee there were some 350 arrivals of steamboats operating on the Missouri River. The number of steamboats committed especially to traffic on the Missouri had increased to fifty-eight. After unloading their cargoes of fur on the St. Louis riverfront, these steamers returned upriver jammed with emigrants heading for the various trailheads spread between Kansas City and Council Bluffs. The greater number of emigrants had departed St. Louis before the spread of the disease; however, they arrived in areas where cholera already had become a grave danger. Moreover, since many of the wagon trains departed that spring with infected individuals in their company, cholera was spread rapidly from the banks of the Missouri along the entire eastern half of the Oregon Trail.

By the close of August 1849 the sickness had so abated in the St. Louis area that Elet and De Smet were able to set off on their delayed journey, ascending the Missouri to Westport. Heading out from the original trailhead there, they became quickly aware of the extent to which cholera had spread westward. As they rode along the Independence Road, the emigrants' initial passageway from the mouth of the Kansas River to the Great Plains, they noted that almost every campground had been "converted into a burial ground." The two Jesuits could bear testimony to the grim pronouncement of Dr. T. McCollum, another westward traveler of 1849: "The road from Independence to Fort Laramie is a graveyard."[33]

As early as April the emigrant-crowded Kansas-Westport-Independence area had become alarmed. Between April 25 and April 30 over twenty people had died of cholera. Heading westward on the St. Joseph Road to Fort Kearney, Dr. B. B. Brown reported that cholera was "sweeping over the [wagon] trains on this road with fearful mortality." By mid-May the St. Joseph newspaper the *Gazette* announced that six recent cases of cholera there had "terminated fatally," also that at Fort Leavenworth across the river, with twenty-five deaths occurring on one day, business had been suspended at the military post. The steamboat *Mary,* heading up the Missouri with still more Mormons traveling to their staging grounds at Omaha, was not permitted by the citizens of St. Joseph to tie up at the levee; forty-seven of the passengers had already died of cholera. By May 16 when the *Mary* finally arrived at Council Bluffs, fifty-eight deaths from cholera had occurred on board since the boat's departure from St. Louis.[34]

Within a few years an area of over two hundred miles from the mouth of the Kansas northward to the mouth of the Platte—the entire west bank of the Missouri—had been transformed into what might be regarded as a single prolonged and scattered trailhead. The ferry crossings of the Missouri had multiplied; at least twelve crossing sites were being used day and night north of St. Joseph. The staging areas or encampments were spread out in all directions from the five towns that served as sources for the purchasing of livestock, transportation equipment, and provisions. And in the late spring of 1849 the transient population in every section of this extended trailhead had become rife with cholera.

As the lands of the border tribes along the west bank had been invaded by the cluttered encampments, the Indians were rapidly stricken by the disease. De Smet and Elet learned that even before the close of May cholera deaths had occurred among the Miamis, Shawnees, Delawares, and Wyandottes. On May 25 the St. Joseph *Gazette* reported that a large number of cholera deaths had occurred among the Iowa and the Kickapoos. Staying overnight at the Ottawa Baptist Mission on September 24, De Smet and Elet were informed that thirty Sauk and Fox men had died of cholera in addition to women and children; also, about one hundred Kansa and many Osages, Otoes, and Pawnees. Reaching the Jesuit St. Mary's Mission on the Kaw in late September, De Smet learned that by late June the surviving Potawatomis had fled from the neighborhood of the Oregon Trail; the mission school had been closed for fear of the disease. Later in the year Indian agent John Barrow reported that over 1,200 Pawnees, nearly one-fourth of the tribe, had died of cholera in the summer of 1849.[35]

Captain Howard Stansbury, surveying a new route to Salt Lake, came up the Platte River in July and found individuals dead and dying in almost every Sioux camp he encountered. Accompanying Fitzpatrick, William Bent came to Westport from his fort on the Arkansas, reporting they had counted six to ten deaths at each of the emigrants' encampments on the trail. Returning to his fort in early August, Bent learned of the tragedy that had struck his Cheyenne people: within weeks the cholera epidemic had wiped out half the Southern Cheyennes.[36]

Historian Margaret Coel offers this summary of the cholera deaths and related sufferings endured by the Plains Indians following the emigrant invasion of 1849: "In addition to the trail of buffalo carcasses and devastated grazing lands, the goldseekers also left diseases to which the Plains Indians had little immunity. Cholera spread through the tribes during the spring and summer of 1849, and hundreds of men, women and children died in agony."[37]

The situation reported by Coel referred to conditions south of the Platte. Regarding the sufferings experienced by the Sioux on the northern Plains, historian Robert Trennert presents this summary: "Buffalo and other game had all but disappeared from the Platte valley, and although the Oglala and Brulé could still find animals to the north and west, the border tribes were in a precarious situation. . . . By the middle of the year [1850] death and devastation was rampant throughout the vast Sioux lands from Minnesota to the Platte."[38]

COMMISSIONER LEA'S REPORT:
A Christian Takeover of Barbarian Lands

De Smet had visited the growing settlement of Westport on eight occasions in the 1840s. He had first entered Fort Leavenworth in 1838; over the next ten years he had observed the growth of that command post of the Army of the West, with its roads off the west bank of the Missouri heading northwest to the Platte and southwest to the Santa Fe Trail. He had visited Joseph Robidoux in 1838; returning there in late November 1846, he had found the area about the Robidoux trading post transformed into the new city of St. Joseph, with 350 houses, two churches, a city hall, and a jail. Stopping for another visit in 1848, he learned that the river town had become almost as popular as Kansas City in serving as a staging area for the departing emigrants.[39]

Heading upriver in 1838, De Smet had stopped at the post of Pawnee agent John Dougherty below the mouth of the Platte; in 1846 on his downriver voyage he had again visited there. Above the Platte he had visited the various trading posts—Sarpy's, Cabanné's, and "the ancient post" originally established by Manuel Lisa. North of these trading centers during his stay in the area from 1838 to 1839 he had rummaged amid the ruins of Fort Atkinson, and in 1846 he had visited Brigham Young at the Mormons' "winter quarters." De Smet was therefore well aware of the great changes imposed on the Indian groups concentrated throughout this area, both the natives and the recently transplanted tribes.

De Smet had lived among the exiled Potawatomis at Council Bluffs. After 1849 he would remain in contact with the tribe, relocated between the Oregon Trail and the Santa Fe Road in eastern Kansas. He also had firsthand knowledge of the pressures on the Osages and Miamis, now situated west of the Missouri frontier in the area of Fort Scott. He had visited with the Yankton and the Santee Sioux north of Council Bluffs, and in 1848 he had spent a month among the Poncas, encamped west of the Missouri near the mouth of the Floyd. During his journeys in the 1840s he had visited with other border tribes: Iowas, Omahas, Otoes, Kickapoos, Sauks, and Foxes. North of the Kansas River he had contacted the Kansa, Pawnees, Delawares, and Shawnees. On the basis of direct knowledge De Smet reported at the close of the 1840s:

> Formerly the Iowas, the Omahas and the Otoes sub-
> sisted principally on the product of their buffalo
> hunts; at present they are reduced to the most pitiful
> condition, having nothing for food but a small quan-
> tity of deer, birds and roots. . . .
>
> The Pawnees and the Omahas are in a state of
> nearly absolute destitution.[40]

De Smet's firsthand knowledge was not restricted to these tribes. Having made three trips on the Upper Missouri, by 1849 he had visited among the Blackfeet, Crows, Mandans, Assiniboines, and Arikaras. From 1840 through 1846 he had worked among the mountain tribes of the northern Rockies. By means of his extensive travels throughout this period he had become aware of the condition of the tribes along the western slope. Not only the Bitterroot Valley, he realized, but the entire northwestern territory was being invaded.

Further, by references contained in his letters, De Smet indicated his awareness of conditions along the southern and southwestern borders of the Plains. He realized that during the decade of the 1840s the new territories of the expanding United States had completed the encirclement of the final Indian country, the Great Plains. In addition to that encirclement, the central portion of the Plains had been split in two by the invasion corridor of the Oregon Trail. Moreover, De Smet anticipated that this passageway would shortly be used for a mounting invasion:

> Already, even (in 1851), it is perceptible that the
> whites look with a covetous eye on the fertile lands of

the Delawares, Potawatomies, Shawnees, and others
on our frontiers, and project the organization of a new
Territory—Nebraska. The great openings offered to
emigration by the definitive arrangement of the Oregon Question, as well as the acquisition of New
Mexico, California and Utah, have alone, thus far,
hindered any efforts for extinguishing the Indian titles
or rights to the lands situated immediately west of the
State of Missouri, and those situated on the south side
of the river Missouri.[41]

De Smet realized that the Indians' buffalo culture was ending, and
in abrupt fashion, that the entire way of life for the Indians of the
Great Plains was under mounting attack. The slaughter of the buffalo
had begun in the 1830s; through the 1840s the demand for meat and
hides had multiplied. The diminishing herds, retreating from the
hunting pressures along the Missouri and the Platte, had become
concentrated in the areas of the more remote tribes. The tribes in
turn, still dependent on the buffalo for their needs, were being forced
into violent competition to survive. It was a sorry theme, a grim
conviction, to which De Smet returned again and again in his letters
of the period. To some of his benefactors in Europe De Smet wrote on
June 10, 1849:

> The facts . . . reveal clearly the melancholy future
> which at no very remote epoch awaits these nations, if
> efficient means are not employed for preventing the
> woes with which they are threatened. . . .
>
> The buffalo is disappearing and diminishing each
> successive year on the prairies of the upper Missou-
> ri. . . . The area of land that these animals frequent is
> becoming more and more circumscribed. . . .
>
> Thence arise the incursions which the Sioux make
> into the territories of the Aricaras, the Mandans, the
> Minnetarees, the Crows and the Assiniboins; thence
> also the mutual invasions of the Crows and the Black-
> feet in their respective hunts. . . . In the plains, war
> and famine lend their aid; on the frontier of civiliza-
> tion, liquors, vices and maladies carry them off by
> thousands.[42]

By midcentury, then, and with solid evidence, De Smet was
uneasy about the Indians' future. In 1848 he expressed his fears to
Thomas Harvey, St. Louis superintendent of Indian affairs, urging

action by the national government "to save the tribes from extermination." It was as a prominent citizen of St. Louis enjoying an established reputation for his knowledge of the Indians that De Smet entered the political arena. He found cause to become an activist as early as midcentury in his exceptional knowledge of the overall conditions among the various tribes. In historian Robert Trennert's judgment, "Father Pierre De Smet expresses more than anyone else at this time a sincere concern for the fate of the people of the plains." De Smet already realized that the future of the West, and consequently of the Indians, was passing from Indian control; changes made by the whites along the trails would expand across the entire Great Plains. Supposedly in charge of Indian affairs, Congress had so far endorsed only actions initiated by the fur traders and the emigrants. Throughout the second quarter of the century Indian policy as administered by the Indian Office had been manipulated to serve the interests of the western fur traders.[43]

By 1847 the volume of emigrants crossing the Indian country by the Oregon Trail led Commissioner Medill to propose a new removal program. In his 1848 annual report Medill set forth the new thinking of the Indian Office. The Western tribes would be gathered in two secluded colonies located to the north and south of a great belt of land extending from the western boundary of Missouri to the Pacific coast: "An ample outlet of about six geographical degrees will be opened for our population that may incline to pass or expand in that direction; and thus prevent our colonized tribes from being injuriously pressed upon, if not swept away."[44]

At the same time Medill called for important reforms in the manner of making treaty payments intended to protect the tribes ceding land to the government from the greed of the traders. Medill pushed these reforms through Congress as additions to the 1847 trade and intercourse legislation. But in short order the new law was restricted to mere paper reform. Medill was dismissed from office; Luke Lea, his successor, quickly rejected any implementation of Medill's reforms. Moreover, in negotiating the 1851 treaties with the Minnesota Sioux, Lea revealed his total allegiance to the interests of the traders. The procedures in which Lea indulged presented a sorry example of all the deplorable tactics and questionable actions for which the treaty process in general is so seriously faulted.[45]

All too often appointments to national and local posts in the Indian Office were controlled by powerful politicians committed to supporting the interests of the St. Louis–based fur traders. Clark's successor to the post of St. Louis superintendent, Joshua Pilcher, received his appointment on the recommendation of Senator Benton, but one example of Benton's placement of pro-trader personnel in a branch of the government service that was supposed to protect the rights of the Indian tribes. It was also an example of the overall power of the traders in directing Indian policy. Still another serious problem resulted from the midcentury development of political patronage as the basis for appointments to positions in the government service. In the Indian Office the spoils system resulted in lack of continuity in policy and personnel. The tribes were voiceless, remote and se-cluded; the administrators and staff of the Indian Office were their only connection to the government. Neglect of duty owing to an agent's lack of qualifications or motivation might escape remedial action.

By midcentury the diminishing of the buffalo herds and the violations of the Indians' exclusive right to occupy the Great Plains were only two negative factors affecting the western tribes. With altered policy and less than qualified personnel, the Indian Office itself had been developed by Congress into an effective tool for achieving Manifest Destiny at the cost of racial justice. At the close of 1852 Commissioner of Indian Affairs Lea made the following pronouncement in his annual report:

> Among the errors that abound respecting our Indian relations, there is one so injurious to our national reputation that it should not be disregarded. The opinion is extensively entertained that our whole course of conduct towards the red men of this country has been marked by injustice and inhumanity. An enlightened consideration of the subject will lead to a different conclusion.
>
> When civilization and barbarism are brought in such relation that they cannot coexist together, it is right that the superiority of the former should be asserted and the latter compelled to give way. It is, therefore, no matter of regret or reproach that so large a portion of our territory has been wrested from its aboriginal inhabitants and made the happy abodes of an enlightened and Christian people. . . . Much of the injury of which the red men and his friends complain has been the inevitable consequence of his own perverse and vicious nature.[46]

These statements express the serious prejudices of the day. Such self-justifications may have been expected from land-hungry frontiersmen or equally greedy politicians in the sale of their services to the fur traders. But derogatory declarations would not be expected from the top official assigned by the Great Father to safeguard the rights of Native Americans. Commissioner Lea, in the introductory remarks to his annual report for 1852, had justified the Christian takeover of the lands of the barbarians.

Clearly the need for De Smet's services as an activist was not restricted to the frontier. Repeatedly across the years De Smet would contradict Fitzpatrick's general conclusion that the Indians "always kept far ahead of the white man in the perpetration of rascality." In De Smet's judgment based on a lifetime of direct contact even more extensive than that of his associate Fitzpatrick, the cause of racial animosity was the misconduct of whites. "Nine times out of ten," De Smet repeated, "the provocations come from . . . the scum of civilization, who bring to them [the Indians] the lowest and grossest vices, and none of the virtues, of civilized men." De Smet's abiding judgment was a condemnation of his fellow citizens: "If the poor and unfortunate inhabitants of the Indian Territory were treated with more justice and good faith, they would cause little trouble."[47]

Chapter Five

The Move to Paternalistic Control (1846–50)

Considering the massive threat to their romantic way
of life posed by the migration, with its attendent evils
of whiskey, cholera, and the wasteful destruction of
buffalo, it is somewhat puzzling that the Sioux stayed
tolerant and law-abiding as long as they did.
—Merrill Mattes, *The Great Platte River Road*

THE CIRCULAR THAT WON THE WEST

The members of the 31st Congress began their second session on
December 2, 1850. On February 27, 1851, the Deficiency Appropriations Act was passed, addressing many of the business items
backlogged during the lengthy fashioning of the Compromise of
1850. The act contained an appropriation of $100,000, a total of less
than half the requested amount, "for Expenses of holding treaties
with the wild tribes of the prairie, and for bringing delegates on to the
seat of government."[1]

Mitchell hurriedly returned to his St. Louis office; with Fitzpatrick, he arrived at some basic decisions. On March 22 Mitchell
informed the commissioner that the date and place for the council
had been determined: September 1, Fort Laramie. Mitchell also
reported to Lea, as he had to Brown, that he and Fitzpatrick were
counting upon a military presence of some ten companies.[2]

Mitchell's assignment would remain unofficial until the commissioner's formal letter of appointment on May 26. In the meantime
Mitchell boldly attempted to make the other necessary arrangements. On April 1 he contacted the St. Louis firms R & W Campbell
and the American Fur Company regarding presents and annuity
goods to be distributed at the council. Providing samples and a
listing of items, Mitchell invited bids for Indian goods in the amount
of $60,000. Later Robert Campbell informed Lea that his company's
bid, the lowest by $1,600, had been officially accepted.[3]

With such details seemingly settled, Mitchell concentrated on his
main concern: to ensure the participation of the many tribes located
throughout the Great Plains. In 1849 Mitchell had glibly predicted
that "the necessary notices could be given without difficulty or
expense, through means of the government officers and Indian

traders." Further, Mitchell had presumed that the printing cost of a number of copies of such a notification, a circular, would be slight and that the circular would be readily distributed by "the Indian Traders and others, on the Upper Missouri, Arkansas and Platte Rivers."[4] However, Mitchell now realized that to be effective, his call for tribal participation would have to be a skillful exercise in salesmanship to the traders as well as the Indian leaders. In marked contrast to the utilitarian arguments he had presented in Washington, Mitchell's single-page circular dealt with promises.

To the traders the circular offered the assurance that the treaty conference would promote their "safety and interests." To gain the traders' active cooperation, Mitchell promised "fair compensation" for bringing tribal delegations to the council grounds and performing, if capable, as the all-important "good interpreters." For satisfactory communications, Mitchell's dependence upon such individuals should be noted; besides their linquistic competence, the interpreters had to be men "in whom mutual confidence could be reposed."[5]

For the tribes the circular emphasized that the whole project of the council was "intended entirely for the benefit and future welfare of the Indians." The original objective—for many Indians, the solitary purpose—of the gathering was stressed: the Indians "will be amply compensated for all the depredations of which they complain." In addition, "after the ratification of the contemplated Treaty, each Tribe will receive an annual present, in goods, from their Great Father."

Mitchell was well aware of the bitter enmity among some of the tribes resulting from the mounting competition for buffalo. His circular offered assurance of "the most perfect safety—as a large military force will be on the ground, for the purpose of keeping order and preserving friendly relations." As "an additional guarantee for the good conduct of the parties present," the tribes were encouraged to come "*en masse,* with all their women and children." Mitchell appreciated that Indian war parties did not travel about with their families. Mindful also of the traditional Indian practice of hospitality the circular promised that "a suitable quantity of provisions will be provided." In conclusion the circular guaranteed that other beneficial arrangements "intended for the permanent good of the Indians" would be made by the council: "The many objects so fondly hoped to be accomplished are, however, too numerous to be stated or commented upon in this brief Circular; they will *all* be fully explained around 'our council fires.' "[6]

Mitchell's circular was dated April 4. The superintendent immediately began the distribution of copies among the traders departing from the St. Louis riverfront. Fitzpatrick set out on April 22. After passing out copies to the traders at Westport, he headed west on the Santa Fe Trail. Mitchell could count upon Fitzpatrick, as Indian agent for the Upper Platte and Arkansas, to alert the tribes of the southern and central sections of the Great Plains.

In the northern section, however, Mitchell faced a problem in distributing the circulars. He had been informed by Secretary of Interior Thomas Ewing on March 29, 1849, that John Wilson, the Upper Missouri agent, was being transferred to a new post at Salt Lake. With no official of the Indian Office to distribute his circular and to encourage tribal participation across the northern half of the Great Plains, Mitchell had to turn to substitutes. The St. Louis superintendent determined to capitalize on his relationships with two interested individuals, both men of notable influence with the Native Americans of the area.[7]

As director of the fur trade operation of the American Fur Company on the Upper Missouri, Alexander Culbertson had headquarters at Fort Union near the mouth of the Yellowstone, a post that Mitchell had held. From there Culbertson would be able to spread the message of the circular among the Crows, Blackfeet, and other tribes of the Upper Missouri. Mitchell could presume that Culbertson would cooperate, for Culbertson has served in the early 1830s as an assistant to Mitchell at the remote post of Fort Mackenzie.[8]

In addition, Mitchell wrote to De Smet on April 19. Knowing that the Jesuit would soon start for the Upper Missouri country, Mitchell asked for his help in distributing the circular and encouraging tribal participation. Mitchell asked more: "Should your other engagements permit I shall be rejoiced to see you at Fort Laramie. Any sketches that you can take and the outlines of maps of this prairie and mountain country will be of great importance and would be highly appreciated by the Government, as will any information with regard to the habits, history or other interesting matters appertaining to the upper Indians."[9]

With his proposal now being publicized by Fitzpatrick, Culbertson, and De Smet as well as the traders, Mitchell had realistic hopes that "the largest Indian meeting ever held" would be assembled at the Fort Laramie council. One major worry for Mitchell was the response of April 7 from Secretary of War Charles M. Conrad. Showing little appreciation of the scope of Mitchell's project, the

War Department expressed regrets that "it is entirely out of the power of this department to comply with the demand," since it would require withdrawing troops "from service much more important." Mitchell was dismayed. Now expecting fifteen thousand Indians, "tribes that have never met except on the battlefield," Mitchell pointed out that "the party acting as umpire and peacemaker should have at least one thousand men on the ground."[10]

Finally on May 26 Lea informed Mitchell that he and Fitzpatrick had been designated as "the officers of this department to carry the objects of the appropriation into effect." Lea summarized the objectives:

> A paramount object will be to define, by treaty stipulations what is and will be reciprocal obligations.
> . . . For the unrestricted right of way through the country, and for the other advantages enjoyed and the injuries committed by the emigrants, the Indians consider themselves entitled to a reasonable compensation, and have for some time been led to expect it by promises made. . . . Justice and good policy, therefore, alike require that such compensation be made.

Lea's letter continued with an insistence on the control technique that Mitchell had previously expressed. "Embodied in the treaty" should be the understanding that annual distribution to the cooperating tribes would be contingent "upon their good conduct," an evaluation to be made by the government. Thus through treaty the government moved toward control of the Great Plains. Lea also noted that fixed boundaries, as determined among the tribes, should mark off their home territories, areas in which each tribe would be responsible for maintaining the peace. Finally the commissioner reminded Mitchell that the appropriation was also intended to cover the postcouncil expenses of escorting a delegation from the tribes to Washington. Determinations on the number of delegates and the schedule were to be made by Mitchell and Fitzpatrick.[11]

DE SMET'S 1851 "JOURNEY TO THE GREAT DESERT"

About to note his fiftieth birthday, De Smet offered this portrait of himself at the close of 1850. Writing to a favorite niece, Silvie, who had recently been married, De Smet displayed that humor that was an abiding trait of his personality:

> You must be careful to give him [your husband] a
> faithful description of your uncle, so that if I should

happen in on him in your absence, he would recognize me without ever having seen me. Uncle Pierre, tell him, is a man of medium size, with grey hair, tending to white. The centre of his wide face (a foot, or near it), is occupied by a nose with which a Greek or a Roman would not find much fault. Its nearest neighbor is a mouth of ordinary size, which hardly ever opens save to laugh or to make others laugh. It makes people love the Good Lord in that manner. The rest resembles a man of fifty years, who weighs 210 pounds. If ever you build a new house, give the door of my chamber six inches extra width, because I don't like to be bothered in getting into a room. Joking aside, a thousand compliments to my dear nephew, your husband.[12]

In 1849 the American Catholic hierarchy met in their Seventh Provincial Council in Baltimore. In their previous meeting in 1842 the bishops had requested Rome to set up an ecclesiastical authority for the Rocky Mountains; now Pope Pius IX was petitioned to assign a vicar-apostolic for the Great Plains. Reporting to Jesuit headquarters in Rome, the Missouri Jesuit superior, John Elet, stated: "The Bishops in council have resolved to propose one of our Fathers to the Holy See as a future vicar-apostolic. Father De Smet was proposed, but I answered that he would not suit. The Archbishop of St. Louis [Kenrick] then spoke to me of Father Miége, and I answered that he would suit, but that I thought it my duty to refrain from pronouncing for or against the measure."[13]

John B. Miége received episcopal consecration in the College Church in St. Louis on March 25, 1851. Anticipating Miége's appointment at the start of 1851, De Smet saw himself working as an assistant to the missionary bishop. As late as March 8 De Smet informed a friend that Miége would leave for his mission — St. Mary's on the Kansas River — in May and that De Smet expected to accompany him to introduce him to the Indians up the Missouri.[14]

However, Superintendent Mitchell's request of mid-April changed De Smet's plans. Government officials for the first time had officially solicited De Smet's help. Believing each of the extravagant promises expressed in Mitchell's circular, De Smet was inspired by the policy of concerned interest now manifested by the government. Seemingly a new day had dawned in the official treatment of Native Americans. As a novice activist, De Smet hastened to obtain Jesuit approval for his participation in the council.

De Smet was fortunate that the Missouri Jesuit superior at the time happened to be his longtime friend Father John Elet, who readily approved the project and assigned a companion to accompany De Smet. Moreover, Elet excused himself from implementing a last-minute directive from Jesuit headquarters in Rome that would have canceled De Smet's participation. In a letter of May 15 De Smet stated that he would be leaving "about the end of the present month on the steamer of the American Fur Company bound for the Yellow-stone . . . to attend a general meeting of Indians which is to take place at Fort Laramie."[15]

The American Fur Company's steamboat *St. Ange*, captained by De Smet's friend Joseph La Barge, did not pull away from the St. Louis levee until June 7. Father Christian Hoecken, S.J., brother of the Adrian Hoecken who had worked with De Smet as director of St. Ignatius Reduction among the Kalispels, had been assigned as De Smet's companion. De Smet could not have asked for a more qualified helper. Christian Hoecken had worked for over a dozen years among the Potawatomis and other border tribes; he exhibited the happy combination of De Smet's concern and adaptability and was an accomplished linguist.

Senator Benton had requested that his twenty-year-old son Randolph travel in De Smet's company, but those plans, although approved by De Smet, had not materialized. There were also on board about one hundred passengers, most employees of the American Fur Company. In that number was the young Swiss artist Rudolph Friederich Kurz, heading upriver for a year of service in the fur trade at Fort Berthold. Kurz was one of the few passengers who boarded the *St. Ange* at the St. Joseph levee. Kurz would be one of the few artists to sketch De Smet.[16]

The *St. Ange*, with a deck length of 180 feet, had been put into service on the Missouri in 1849. In April, on the boat's initial run to Independence, Captain La Barge had reported one death on board from cholera. After his return to St. Louis at the close of 1851 De Smet reported on the tragedy that quickly developed aboard the steamboat following their June departure:

> Six days had hardly elapsed from our departure, when
> the boat resembled a floating hospital. We were 500
> miles from St. Louis when the cholera broke out in the
> steamer. On the tenth a clerk of the American Fur
> Company, vigorous and in the prime of manhood, was
> suddenly seized with all the symptoms of cholera, and

expired after a few hours' illness. The following days
several others were attacked with the same malady,
and in a short time thirteen fell victims to the epidemic.

A bilious attack confined me to my bed nearly ten
days. Good Father Hoecken devoted himself to the
sick night and day, with a zeal at once heroic and
indefatigable. . . .

[On the night of June 18, I found Father Hoecken]
ill, and even in extremity. . . . Dr. Evans, a physician
of great experience and of remarkable charity, endeav-
ored to relieve him, and watched by him, but his cares
and remedies proved fruitless. . . .

I shall always remember with deep gratitude the
solicitude evinced by the passengers in his [Father
Hoecken's] dying moments. My resolution not to leave
the body of the pious missionary in the desert was
unanimously approved. A decent coffin, very thick,
and tarred within, was prepared to receive his mortal
remains: a temporary grave was dug in a beautiful
forest . . . and the burial was performed with all the
ceremonies of the Church.

De Smet noted five additional fatalities from cholera aboard the *St.
Ange*. Later he gratefully reported that Captain La Barge kindly
halted on the return voyage to transport Hoecken's coffin downriver
for reburial in the Jesuit cemetery at Florissant.

De Smet's activities, and his journals, became more positive. As
the steamer ascended the Missouri, "the epidemic gradually disappeared." De Smet reflected on "the beauties of the wilderness" and
his special concern, "the future of these interesting solitudes—
above all, of their poor, despised inhabitants":

But then, what will become of the Indians, who have
already come from afar to abide in this land? What
will become of the aborigines, who have possessed it
from time immemorial? This is indeed a thorny question, awakening gloomy ideas in the observer's mind,
if he has followed the encroaching policy of the
[United] States in regard to the Indian. . . .

At last we reached the Great Bend, where the boat
came to land opposite a camp of Yanktons, a powerful
tribe of the Sioux nation. . . . The Indians gave us

the sad tidings of the ravages which the smallpox was then causing. . . . At my request the captain put me ashore, and two hours after I was among the sick. I baptized all the little children who had not yet been fortunate enough to receive that sacrament. I spent the night with them, giving them all the consolation in my power.

On the 14th of July, the steamboat *St. Ange* reached our destination, Fort Union. This post is situated at 48° North latitude. I had then to make all my preparations for my long journey on land. Yet, withal, I found time to instruct and baptize twenty-nine little children, between Fort Union and Fort William, which are only three miles apart. I said mass daily at the fort, and gave an instruction.[17]

Culbertson had already received his copies of Mitchell's circular. Through the rest of July the major continued with De Smet to encourage Indian leadership to participate in the planned council. Accompanying a group of some thirty delegates—Assiniboines, Hidatsas, and Crows—Culbertson and De Smet rode out from Fort Union on July 31. They had been promised that an even larger Crow delegation would be escorted by the trader Robert Meldrum; however, both they and Meldrum would fail to cause participation by tribal representatives of the Blackfeet.

"THE GREAT MEDICINE ROAD OF THE WHITES"
With two wagons and two carts the party rode in a southwesterly direction along the Yellowstone. After a layover of six days at Fort Alexander, Culbertson's auxiliary trading post near the mouth of the Rosebud, they crossed the Yellowstone and headed south. Theirs was the first wagon crossing of a country that a quarter century later would be the site of the final violent convulsions of an Indian society already destroyed.[18]

As superintendent of the American Fur Company posts on the Missouri and Yellowstone, Culbertson's long experience in the fur trade had centered on that territory. In 1848, in charge of the Western and Upper Missouri departments, which included Fort Laramie, Culbertson had traveled up the Platte, but he had not gone west of Fort Laramie. The travels of the Indian leaders had been restricted to their homelands in the Upper Missouri country. When the party topped the ridge in central Wyoming whose northern slope heads the

Powder River drainage northward to join the Missouri by way of the Yellowstone and whose southern slope turns the North Platte River on its eastern journey across the breadth of the Great Plains to its downstream meeting with the Missouri, De Smet alone was on familiar ground. Only he recognized the Red Buttes, that distinctive Oregon Trail landmark off the southeastern bank of the North Platte.

Yet even De Smet must have been astonished by what the party discovered as they rode down to the Platte. It had been ten years since he had last crossed the river here at Bessemer Bend. From the Red Buttes, as the party could clearly see, the trail angled off to the southwest, a fifty mile cross-country trek to Independence Rock near the junction of the Sweetwater with the North Platte. Later De Smet reported:

> The 2d day of September, 1851, we found ourselves on the Great Route to Oregon, over which, like successive ocean surges, the caravans, composed of thousands of emigrants from every country and clime, have passed. . . .

> Our Indian companions, who had never seen but the narrow hunting-paths by which they transport themselves and their lodges, were filled with admiration on seeing this noble highway, which is as smooth as a barn floor swept by the winds, and not a blade of grass can shoot on it on account of the continual passing. They conceived a high idea of the countless White Nation, as they express it. They fancied that all had gone over that road, and that an immense void must exist in the land of the rising sun. Their countenances testified evident incredulity when I told them that their exit was in nowise perceived in the lands of the whites. They styled the route the Great Medicine Road of the Whites.[19]

With De Smet leading, the party rode eastward along the Oregon Trail. In early September the trail was empty, few of the emigrant caravans venturing westward from Fort Laramie after the end of July. The party progressed slowly, however; the Indians' interest called for an inspection of the many campsites along the trail, all strewn with debris. During the months of June and July about ten thousand emigrants had made some five consecutive night camps — and possibly additional Sabbath layovers — in this stretch of the trail between Red Buttes and the mouth of the Laramie River. De Smet commented:

> They [the Indians] visited and examined in detail all
> the forsaken camping-grounds on the way; they brought
> a great variety of objects to me to have their use and
> signification explained; they filled their pouches with
> knives, forks, spoons, basins, coffee-pots and other
> cooking articles, axes, hammers, etc. . . .
>   The countless fragments of conveyences, the heaps
> of provisions, tools of every kind, and other objects
> with which the emigrants must have provided them-
> selves at great expense.

Obviously some of these abandoned items had been but recently
discarded; other scattered debris had been covered by the snows of
one or more winters. In the June-July period of 1850 over 50,000
travelers had followed in the ruts made by the wagons and carts of
some 30,000 Forty-Niners. Since De Smet's first westward journey
in 1840 some 100,000 emigrants had passed along this trail.

Other items along the trail aroused the Indians' curiosity. There
were, as De Smet noted, "the bleached bones of domestic animals
disseminated profusely" along the route. There were also mounds,
each "marked with a narrow strip of board or stone," with rudely
carved inscriptions. Cholera may have stopped before Fort Laramie
because of that post's location at an elevated altitude, but the death
count from other sicknesses and accidents continued throughout the
emigrants' passage.[20]

Riding eastward along the Oregon Trail, De Smet and his companions must have become well aware of two notable changes from the
conditions they had previously experienced on their journey. From
the Yellowstone southward they had wandered with difficulties and
uncertainty through an unmarked wilderness. Their battered wagons, moreover, testified to the endless problems of trailless travel.
Once on the Oregon Trail, however, they found a ready passageway;
furthermore, no guides were needed. By the late 1840s guides
experienced in locating the trail for emigrants had been supplanted:
guidebooks offering information about conditions to be anticipated
along the trail had become popular. By midcentury the leadership
function of those directing the various groups' westward movement
was that of the authoritarian wagon master.[21]

In 1851, therefore, De Smet and his companions were never in
danger of losing their way because of an undefined trail. They were,
however, in real danger, their supply wagons now empty, of being
forced to ride on with little nourishment. The game that had been so

numerous about the Yellowstone, the Rosebud, the Tongue, and the Powder rivers, game that had been plentiful along the entire Platte drainage as late as 1840, was now eliminated from Bessemer Bend to the Missouri. The natives of the territory had been forced to evacuate a corridor that could no longer support life.

For the invaders, game was only a supplement to the provisions hauled in their wagons or their herds of sheep and cattle. The emigrants, who did not share the Indians' complete dependence upon the land and its natural resources, were only slightly inconvenienced that by midcentury a sterile belt of land had been fashioned across the heart of the Indian country. For the Native Americans, however, a serious change had occurred.[22]

De Smet's prediction, as repeated in the reports of St. Louis superintendent Harvey to the Indian Office, was now becoming the sorry reality: "The Platte valley was fast becoming an uninhabitable area for the Indians."[23]

INITIAL FAILURES: If Anything Can Possibly Go Wrong . . .

For Commissioner Mitchell—the superintendent's title as he conducted the negotiations during the Fort Laramie treaty council—it had been a short and relaxing voyage. Along with his companions, Mitchell had boarded the steamboat *Cataract* on the St. Louis riverfront on July 24; on the twenty-ninth they had arrived at Kansas Landing (Kansas City); dry weather had contributed to a pleasant trip.

Also, the early reports—only later would they learn that these were far too optimistic—had indicated that cholera had disappeared from the overland trails. Moreover, Mitchell was pleased with his two companions: B. Gratz Brown had proved to be a capable and devoted secretary, and predictably, A. B. Chambers, as senior editor of the St. Louis newspaper *Missouri Republican*, would gain important publicity and frontier support for Mitchell's efforts to negotiate a treaty. Chambers's purpose was to accompany the commission to send back reports on the council and its achievements.[24]

Interest in the Fort Laramie council had become widespread. Robert Campbell, the trader contracted to provide Indian goods, arrived in Kansas City on August 6. One of Campbell's fellow passengers on the steamboat *Saranak* from St. Louis was another reporter, George W. Kendall of the New Orleans *Picayune*. Kendall also planned to cover the council for his newspaper. But for a number of camp followers the council was regarded as serving more selfish interests than newsgathering. Historian Robert Trennert notes: "The council also offered incentives for white speculators. Merchants, freighters, traders, and general hangers-on all prepared to get in on the bounty." Campbell, in his personal carriage, set out at once on the Oregon Trail, leading Kendall's party. Although some days behind Mitchell's party, they hoped to catch up with them.[25]

It is not known whether Campbell united with Mitchell before reaching Fort Laramie. It is to be presumed, however, that when the meeting took place, it was a stormy encounter. When Mitchell arrived at the frontier at the end of July, he had expected a report that the slow-moving supply wagons were already well on their way across the plains. To his utter dismay Mitchell learned that the wagons had not been loaded. After venting his anger, on August 3 Mitchell set out with his party for Fort Leavenworth; there he was further upset to discover that his military escort, Troop B of the First Dragoons, had already departed. Early on the following morning Mitchell and his party headed west from the fort. Chambers filed the following report under the heading "Snake Creek, in the Pawnee Country" on August 11: "Here we are, eighteen miles beyond the Blue. . . . This morning, after a ride of about 18 miles, we came up to the encampment of Major Chilton, in command of the Dragoons. . . . The wagon trains are all behind, and it is now certain that they cannot arrive at Laramie by the time expected. This will be a great disappointment to Col. Mitchell, and a heavy loss to the contractors, who are under bonds to deliver them by the 1st of September."[26]

Mitchell led his party into Fort Laramie on Saturday morning, August 30. It had been, as Chambers noted, "a dull and monotonous trip." After a brief stop at Fort Kearney they had continued up the Platte, expecting to kill buffalo to supplement their food supply, but they had not succeeded in killing the single cow they spotted. Such a scarcity of game was already a major worry for Mitchell with his expectation of countless guests to be provisioned during the council. Chambers reported their experiences as the party drew near the fort:

> As we approached Fort Laramie, we found many
> Indians encamped on the Plains. The various bands of
> the Sioux, the Arapahoes, and a portion of the Chey-
> ennes, came in before the time designated, and had
> become tired of waiting. . . . It is amusing to hear the
> extravagant ideas which the Indians have formed of
> the mission. Madam Rumor has just as much to do out

here in this wild county as in the States, and she has not been idle. Our escort and company have been magnified into thousands; instead of an escort of only thirty-three men, we were reported as coming with 1,500 troops, and all other things in proportion.

Our train, with Major Chilton's company of dragoons, moved up and encamped on the Laramie, about four miles above the Fort. Col. Mitchell and myself remained in the fort until after dark, when we went out to our camp. On Sunday morning Col. Mitchell and myself visited the encampment of Maj. Fitzpatrick, the associate Commissioner in this negotiation. The Major's camp is about a mile and a half above ours, on the Laramie.[27]

It was the end of August. For the two commissioners meeting in their long-delayed conference it must have seemed the end of all their hopes and plans. The reports they exchanged presented so many problems that both Mitchell and Fitzpatrick, as realists, must have strongly considered canceling the treaty council on the eve of its scheduled opening. Facing five major difficulties, they might well have concluded that with everything gone wrong, they could hardly anticipate a successful conference.

First there was the military failure. The report published by Chambers must have echoed the bitter criticisms expressed by both Mitchell and Fitzpatrick: "The Government has not acted judiciously in the military escort, and much of the effect that ought to have been given to the treaty will be lost. . . . Here we are to have all, or at least a majority, of the wild tribes of Indians assembled, to be talked to, and, if possible impressed with the necessity of keeping peace among themselves, and refraining from depredations on the neighboring tribes and the emigrants."[28]

Mitchell reported to Fitzpatrick that his repeated demands had been refused by the War Department. Although the commissioners had repeatedly insisted on the need for a force of one thousand men, a total of fewer than three hundred had been assigned. Mitchell and Fitzpatrick's unpublicized objective—gaining mastery of the Indians by military intimidation—would not be possible. Further, the important promise proclaimed in Mitchell's circular—"a large military force on the ground, for the most perfect safety"—had not been kept. The anticipation of violence had already spread among the tribal encampments. Indeed the commissioners realized that such fears were well founded. On their way to the council the large Shoshone delegation had been attacked by a Cheyenne war party.[29]

With an insufficient police force, the commissioners were worried about maintaining peace. This serious situation, however, was only one of their major problems. The second failure, unsatisfactory tribal representation, was reported by Fitzpatrick. Having arrived on June 1 at his new post, Fort Sumner on the Arkansas, Fitzpatrick had immediately sent out runners to notify tribal leaders that their agent had a message of very great importance from their Great Father. To the assembled "Camanches, Kiawas, Apaches, Arripahoes, and Cheyennes," Fitzpatrick had explained that "their great father had it in contemplation to . . . make restitution for any damages or injury which they were liable to, or might suffer hereafter from American citizens travelling through their country." However, when he announced that the council would be held at Fort Laramie on September 1, only the Cheyennes and Arapahos agreed to attend. The other tribes insisted that such business must be conducted on the Arkansas in their own country.[30]

Further, it was an attendance failure that would be repeated by the tribes from the northern Plains. A double delegation from the Crow would appear; the powerful Blackfeet, however, estimated by Mitchell to have almost as many warriors as the Sioux, would not participate. "The lateness of the season and the great distance" were the excuses presented by Culbertson for the nonattendance of the Blackfeet.[31]

Ironically, the one tribe whose participation was not desired by Mitchell was heavily represented. As superintendent at St. Louis, Mitchell's responsibilities extended to the tribes of the Great Plains; the invitation of his circular excluded none, but it was intended for the many tribes of the Missouri, the Platte, and the Arkansas. Working with a reduced appropriation, Mitchell regarded the mountain tribe of the Shoshones, under the recently established Utah Agency, as outside his jurisdiction. The Shoshone delegation would be welcome guests at the council, but despite the promises of the circular, they would not even be recompensed for their travel expenses.[32]

A third serious problem of growing concern to the commissioners was the outbreak of cholera. Mitchell informed Fitzpatrick of the tragedy that had taken place on the *St. Ange.* An express from Fort Pierre brought the report that the cholera deaths aboard that steamboat had not been isolated cases. From June through August cholera spread through the towns on the Missouri River and through the

Indian country. Mitchell and Fitzpatrick were not alarmed about an outbreak of cholera among their council participants; since Fort Laramie was located at a higher altitude, it had a reputation for being safe. However, both commissioners must have feared the possible negative repercussions if the delegates, on returning to their homelands, found their tribes ravaged by the white man's disease. If the cholera conditions of 1849 were repeated in late 1851 across the Great Plains, any peace commitments made in council by the Indians would be seriously jeopardized.[33]

Chambers's reports repeatedly noted a fourth major problem that seriously complicated matters for the commissioners:

> In this expedition, Col. Mitchell has been put to perplexing and annoying vexations by the delay of the trains which are bringing up the provisions and presents for the Indians. When we arrived in Kansas, we expected that the wagons, twenty-seven in number, were at least six or seven days in advance of us, but much to our disappointment, they were not even started, nor all loaded. As this transportation was all at the risk of the Contractors, the Superintendent had no control over their movements. . . .
>
> Owing to these circumstances, Col. M[itchell] had to make temporary provision for meeting the Indians on the Monday following our arrival. It is a standing rule with the Indians, that whenever they meet, especially upon occasions of this character, they must have presents of some kind or other. Generally, they expect tobacco to smoke, provisions to eat, and at times, other presents.[34]

Obviously Chambers, as a novice in dealing with Indians, was only repeating the frustrations voiced by Mitchell and Fitzpatrick over Campbell's failure to deliver the presents, provisions, and annuity goods as scheduled. Both the commissioners had been much concerned about presenting the government's image as Great Father, benign and generous. Both appreciated the Indian tradition of hospitality, and in accord with that long-established practice they had planned an introductory feast and a preliminary distribution of presents to gain ready cooperation from the council participants.

Fresh from the trail, Mitchell must have shared with Fitzpatrick the gloomy prediction that the arrival of the wagon train could not be realistically anticipated before September 20. Following the exceptional rains of late summer, the Kendall party, having at last arrived at Fort Kearney on August 30, reported: "We have finally reached this military post . . . at least ten days behind our time. For a week after leaving . . . the Kansas, we were daily visited by drenching showers, swelling the small streams, cutting up the roads, and rendering our progress almost impossible. . . . The long train of wagons containing Indian presents is still behind, and can hardly reach Laramie before the 20th of September."[35]

Moreover, Campbell's supply failure, especially as extended over such a long period, pointed up the commissioners' fifth and most urgent problem. Fitzpatrick had been camped on the Laramie River above the fort since July 25. Well aware of the prevailing conditions throughout the area, he must have hurriedly informed Mitchell of the problems of the site. It had been easy for the commissioners, making their plans in St. Louis during the previous March, to project that the council participants would be able to live off the land. By the close of August, however, and even before convening the council, the game supply in the general area of the fort had been depleted; also, nature's supply of forage for the countless horses and mules of the Indian encampments had been exhausted. For the commissioners responsible for over a thousand lodges without provisions, the situation at Fort Laramie presented a serious crisis.

Before ending their private meeting on August 30, the commissioners reached three decisions. First, the council time would have to be extended; it was unthinkable that the conference should be terminated without the distribution of goods among the tribal delegations. Second, whatever supplies might be held in the sutler's post at Fort Laramie would have to be commandeered immediately by Mitchell. Third, with provisions and other necessities so insufficient, some other site for the council would have to be chosen at once.

PREPARATORY MEETING WITH TRIBAL LEADERS
On Monday morning, having made his arrangements with the sutler's store, Mitchell presided over a preliminary meeting with tribal leaders. Chambers reported this initial gathering:

> On September 1st, according to arrangement, Major Chilton's company of dragoons, a portion of the infantry and one of the rifle companies, marched up and formed in the vicinity of Col. Mitchell's tent. Soon after, the chiefs and braves of the various bands commenced coming in. They were all mounted, and as

they rode at full speed, they made quite an imposing appearance. The Brules came in, each man carrying a green bush to shield him from the sun; a native illustration of 'Birnam wood coming to Dunsinane.' . . .

Tobacco was handed round to all the chiefs and braves in Council, and then we had a general smoke. This custom seems to be observed in the same manner by all. The principal chief fills his redstone pipe full of tobacco and kinnekinick, and after lifting it east, west, north and south, and up to the Great Spirit, takes a smoke himself, and it is passed around for all others to smoke. All of one tribe or band, and their friends, when present, smoke from the same pipe. . . .

This ceremony over, Col. Mitchell having instructed the interpreters to interpret truly what he said, addressed the Indians as follows:

"I have been sent here by your Great Father and as his representative, I shake you all by the hand. Your Great Father has appointed Major White Hair Fitzpatrick with me to making this treaty; you will respect him as such. The officers of the army are here; they are prepared to protect you, and will do it, and they will punish any one who does wrong. . . . The only object today is to ask you among yourselves to fix upon a place for an encampment. I will not suggest a place, but if a place is selected below the Fort, we will sooner meet the train which has the goods and provisions for you. I leave it to you to select the place. . . . I have some beef which I will distribute to the various tribes to eat; this and some tobacco and vermillion is about all I will be able to give you until the train comes up. . . . I leave you to consult among yourselves, and when you have agreed upon a place, let me know."

After a prolonged debate among the Indians, the recommendation of Terra Blue, a chief of the Brulé Sioux, was agreed upon. The mouth of Horse Creek was selected — a site on the Platte some thirty-six miles below the fort. In a notably diplomatic fashion, Mitchell had solved his most urgent problem. Chambers concluded his report for September 2: "Tomorrow will be taken up in making preparations for breaking up our encampment and moving, on the 4th, to Horse Creek, which we will reach on the 5th. Here all the Indians will be assembled by the 7th or 8th; and if the trains with the provisions and presents for the Indians were up, we would be able to get through in a week or so. But the train is many days behind, and we expect to be detained for some time."[36]

Chapter Six
Initial Great Smoke:
The First Fort Laramie Treaty (1851)

We are but the agents or representatives of your Great
Father at Washington, and what we propose is merely
what he desires you should do for your own happiness.
We do not want your land, horses, robes, nor anything
you have; but we come to advise with you, and to
make a treaty with you for your own good.
— D.D. Mitchell, opening speech
to chiefs, September 8, 1851

MOVE OF THE COUNCIL ENCAMPMENT
TO HORSE CREEK

The selection of Horse Creek as the new encampment site was a great
help to the troubled commissioners. The fresh location for the gathering
offered some solution to the provision needs of the participants and
their stock. Further, the commissioners had gained almost ten days; the
council opening would be postponed for a week, and for the supply train
two additional days of trail travel up the Platte had been eliminated.

The move down the Platte was reported in considerable detail by
editor Chambers, whose field reports were printed in his St. Louis
newspaper. After traveling with the army units on the first day,
Chambers and his associate Brown joined up with "a large party of
Cheyennes." Chambers penned a description of the Indians' unusual
means of moving camp:

> The lodges are moved by means of what are here
> called "Prairie Buggies." These consist of their lodge
> poles, one end of which is fastened on each side of the
> horse's neck, and the other end dragging on the
> ground. On these poles they put their lodges, camp
> equipage, children, and sometimes their dogs. Some
> have a kind of rude wicker work which they fasten to
> the lodge poles, forming something like a canopy —
> over this they throw a dressed skin, and form a neat
> and cool shelter for themselves and children.[1]

As the Cheyennes and their reporter companions journeyed eastward
along the Platte bottoms, they encountered factual evidence of the need

for a treaty council—a Mormon train of some twenty-nine wagons "laden principally with merchandise, and the effects of a number of men, women, and children" heading toward Salt Lake City.[2]

The reestablishment of the tribal camps occupied most of the weekend. The tribes were scattered about in distinct designated locations along both banks of the Platte and Horse Creek. The sites were assigned by the commissioners; they designated the triangular area southeast of the junction of Horse Creek with the Platte as the council grounds.

Their lodges once more set up, various delegations reported at Mitchell's tent headquarters throughout Saturday the sixth. By means of these visitors and their interpreters, the commissioner was able to send two announcements throughout the encampments. The following day, Sunday, was declared "the White Man's Medicine Day," and for that reason the commissioners "would not hold Council, or transact any business." On Monday morning, however, "at the firing of the cannon," the council would convene.[3]

SEPTEMBER 7: Arrival of Trader Campbell and the Blackrobe

Chambers reported that through the day "the Sioux and Cheyenne women erected in the centre of the encampment a kind of ampitheatre," an arbor composed of tipi cover and poles, to serve as a stage for the commissioners, interpreters, and other dignitaries. Chambers's special assignment was to hoist the stars and stripes in front of Colonel Mitchell's tent.

That day Mitchell composed his optimistic report to Commissioner Lea: "I am now in the midst of the Plains Indians and commenced this morning to talk over business matters. A very friendly feeling seems to prevail, and I have great hopes that all the advantages contemplated by the treaty will be accomplished."[4] Mitchell would not send another report to the Indian Office until October 25, a few days after his troubled return trip to St. Louis.

About sunset on Sunday an unusual prairie buggy—a carriage, not a travois—came to a halt before Mitchell's tent. Some of the older Indians—those Arapahos who had attended the rendezvous in the 1830s or the Cheyennes who had traded at old Fort Laramie—might have recognized the driver as Indian trader Robert Campbell. The other newcomer, his distinctive garb evident as he stepped down from the carriage, was immediately identified. The report spread at once through the Indian camps that the Blackrobe, Father De Smet, had arrived. Later De Smet reported:

After eight days' journey along the Platte [eastward on the Oregon Trail, from Red Buttes], we arrived at Fort Laramie, without the least trouble or accident. The commander of the fort informed us that the Great Council was to take place at the mouth of Horse river, in a vast plain situated nearly thirty-five miles lower down on the Platte. The next day I accepted the polite invitation of the respected Colonel [Robert] Campbell, and took a seat in his carriage. We arrived at the plain of the intended council about sunset. There the superintendent, Colonel Mitchell, received me with warm friendship and cordiality, insisting that I should become his guest during the whole time of the council. . . .

I had also the pleasure of renewing acquaintance with my good Friend, Major Fitz Patrick.[5]

SEPTEMBER 8:
Mitchell's Introductory Statement of Treaty Objectives

No accurate count was made of the Indians assembled at Horse Creek. Reflecting the estimates of the commissioners and traders, Chambers reported the total figure as "exceeding ten thousand," and De Smet's narratives only repeat that estimate. Mitchell would state later: "The number of Indians present was variously estimated as from eight to twelve thousand."[6]

No photographer or artist was on hand to record this gathering— an Indian assembly unmatched in tribal scope and number. However, Chambers's reports gave an impressive picture of the opening ceremonies:

Every one, whites and Indians, seemed to look for the morning, and every body was early afloat. From dawn until 9 o'clock, when the cannon was fired and the flag hoisted, as a signal for the Council to assemble, parties of Indians were coming in from every direction. . . .

When the cannon had given forth its thunder, the whole plains seemed to be covered with the moving masses of chiefs, warriors, men, women, and children; some on horse-back, some on foot. . . . Until the signal was given for the Council to assemble, the masses had remained at a distance from the temporary arbor prepared for the occasion. But when the whole

body commenced moving to the common centre, a
sight was presented of most thrilling interest. Each
nation approached with its own peculiar song or
demonstration, and such a combination of rude, wild
and fantastic manners and dresses, never was previously witnessed. It is not probable that an opportunity
will again be presented of seeing so many tribes
assembled together displaying all the peculiarities of
features, dress, equipments, and horses.[7]

As Chambers noted, only the principal headmen of the Indian
groups were assembled in the council circle. The council grounds
resembled an incomplete circle; like the lodge opening, the area
directly to the east was left open. Around the remainder "sheds had
been erected with lodge poles and lodge skins," and these served the
tribal leaders located to the north, west, and south.

Far reaching in the rear of the Indian Chiefs and
Braves, stood the attentive members of their respective tribes. For quietness, decorum and general good
behavior, on such occasions, the Indians might be
made models for more civilized society. Although
they were pressed together, every thing was as quiet as
in church. . . .

It is an undoubted fact that the bearing, character,
manners, courage, habits and nearly all leading char-
acteristics of the Indians of the plains and mountains,
strongly contrast with that of the more easterly Indians—say from the Pawnees to our State line. The
former are proud, manly and high toned sons of the
wilds—the latter are dirty, beggarly and cowardly
compared with the former. The latter have had more to
do with the whites, have learnt many of their vices and
few of their virtues. What contamination may do with
the former remains to be seen.[8]

The commissioners moved immediately to a position of dignity
and recognized authority; they were seated under an arbor located in
the center of the council grounds. Seated about Mitchell and Fitzpatrick were Chambers and Brown, serving as the council secretaries,
the army officers and Utah Indian agents, De Smet, Campbell, and a
number of interpreters.

To this group came a late and highly impressive addition. Chambers reported that during the opening ceremonies of the council the

wife of Lieutenant Washington L. Elliott of the mounted rifles approached the arbor, was received by the commissioners, and was prominently seated. Chambers also pointed out that with diplomatic skill Mitchell capitalized on this highly unusual presence: "Mrs. E[lliott] was the only white lady in the encampment, and her presence created an agreeable sensation throughout the assemblage. Col. Mitchell, on receiving her, remarked to the Indians, 'That in her presence the white men gave them evidence of their peaceful intentions, and thus confidence in their power to punish any wrongs. Her presence, too, was also an evidence of the confidence that was reposed in their honesty and good intentions.' "9

Appreciative of the Indian tradition, Mitchell also turned the introductory ceremony—the shared smoking of the peace pipe—to his diplomatic gain. Through the interpreters the commissioner announced to the assembled tribes:

> I am sent here to transact important business with you. Before commencing that I propose to smoke all around with you. The ceremony of smoking I regard as an important and solemn one, and I believe you all so regard it. When white men meet to transact business, and they desire to test their truth and sincerity, they lay their hands on the Bible, the Book of the Great Spirit—their Great Medicine—and take an oath. When the red man intends to tell the truth, and faithfully fulfill his promises, he takes an oath by Smoking to the Great Spirit. The Great Spirit sees it all and knows it. Now, I do not wish any Indian to smoke with me that has any deceit or lies in his heart—or has two hearts—or whose ears are not bored to hear what his Great Father at Washington has to propose, and perform whatever is agreed upon. All such will let the pipe pass. I don't want them to touch it.10

Such an auspicious opening of the council immediately established Mitchell's leadership and control. With frequent pauses so that the interpreters might communicate his statements to their respective tribal audiences, the commissioner formally introduced himself and his purpose:

> I am glad we have all smoked together like brethren, and I trust we have all spoken the truth, without any lies in our hearts. Your Great Father at Washington has sent me and my white-haired brother (Major Fitzpat-

rick) to make peaceful arrangements with you for your benefit. We are but the agents or representatives of your Great Father at Washington, and what we propose is merely what he desires you should do for your own happiness. We do not come to you as traders; we have nothing to sell you, and do not want to buy anything from you. We do not want your lands, horses, robes, nor anything you have; but we come to advise with you, and make a treaty with you for your own good.

In his general statement of the proposed objectives of the council Mitchell developed, as he had in his circular, the mythical image of the benign Great Father, concerned for the good of the Indian. Mitchell enumerated the government's demands not as requiring major Indian concessions but as promising lasting benefits to the Indians.

Certainly there would be just compensation for the losses caused by the emigrants' passages through the Indian country: "The ears of your Great Father are always open to the complaints of his Red Children." However, the Great Father "expects and will exert the right of free passage for his White Children over the roads running through your countries, and restitution for any injuries they may receive from you or your people" during such travels. To eliminate any connected problems caused by either whites or Indians, the Great Father's "right to establish military posts, and such other posts as he may deem necessary," should be expressly acknowledged by the Indians.

"In order that justice may be done each nation," the Indian country would be divided into districts assigned to the various tribes. This proposed division, however, was "not intended to take any of your lands away from you, or to destroy your rights to hunt, or fish, or pass over the country, as heretofore." Rather, with the assigned tribe responsible for any depredations in its designated though not exclusively held area, the Great Father would thus be able to achieve his sole objective—"to punish the guilty and reward the good," the enforcement power to effect a peaceful coexistence.

All the advantages of peace to be achieved through the insistence and powers of the Great Father would thus be enjoyed among all the tribes of the Great Plains. Consequent to the general acceptance of these proposals there would be "no occasion for war parties going into the country of another nation." Further, it was the Great Father's resolve "to drive the bad white men out from amongst you."

As a sign of tribal unity and to provide a representative authority figure, each tribe was requested to select a "Chief of the whole nation." This chief would be acknowledged by the Great Father as his representative; he would be a chief respected and revered, for the Great Father would "support and sustain him . . . so long as he acts properly."

Among the tribes agreeing to these proposals, the Great Father would distribute an annual annuity of $50,000 for the next fifty years. It would be an annuity presented not "in money, so that white men may cheat you out of it"; rather, the payment would be in practical, suitable goods and provisions. And these goods, Mitchell promised, would be "faithfully delivered." The Great Father, however, reserved the right to condition this annual payment on good conduct during the preceding year, as judged by the Great Father. Implicitly but definitely, Mitchell was pointing to government control over the tribes.

Finally, each tribe was urged to select some outstanding leaders who would return as the guests of the commissioners to Washington. By personal contact with the Great Father these Indian delegates might verify that the council proposals were the sincere wishes of a benignly paternalistic government. Returning to their homes in the spring, these Indian leaders would then provide a firsthand report on "the strength, power and numbers of the white men."[11]

The commissioner ended his speech with an explanation for his failure to provide rations for the participants. Promising that there was "a large train of ox wagons on the way, containing a large amount of presents and provisions" that would arrive in a few days, Mitchell urged the tribes to hold councils among themselves, to "think, talk and smoke over" the proposals. Commissioner Fitzpatrick immediately offered a brief endorsement of Mitchell's proposals and recommendations. Fitzpatrick repeated the suggestion that the Indian leaders "mingle with each other" and talk the matter over so that "you understand the subject properly." Fitzpatrick assured the Indian leaders that he and Mitchell would be available if there were any uncertainties.

The immediate reactions of some of the Indian leaders were reported by Chambers. Three chiefs, representing the Sioux, Arikaras, and Shoshones, offered brief positive statements indicating their trust in the Great Father. It was obvious from the start that the assembled Indians had been influenced by Mitchell's repeated declarations of the Great Father's benign concern.[12]

During the subsequent days of the council there were debates on some of the details; some questioning and reluctance to endorse specific items would be manifested, especially by the powerful Sioux. De Smet noted that the terms of the treaty had in fact been set in advance by the government, and he commented following Mitchell's opening speech that "the object of the assembly was the acceptance by them of the treaty, such as it had been prepared beforehand."[13]

The specific treaty directives formulated by the Indian Office were indeed presented by Commissioner Mitchell. Admittedly, these demands would continue, rather than resolve, the problems caused by whites passing through the Indian country. Only the official status of these emigrants would be changed from invaders to authorized travelers. However, with diplomatic skill, Mitchell emphasized seemingly acceptable solutions to these problems. The designated tribal territories, along with the forts and posts to be erected on Indian lands, would protect the rights of the native groups attending the council as well as the transient aliens. Furthermore, the promises Mitchell spoke for the Great Father would guarantee compensatory benefits for cooperative tribes.

With what degree of good faith Mitchell promised such justice and peace to the assembled Indians cannot be determined. Shortly after declaring that "we do not want your lands," the commissioner insisted upon the "right of free passage"—a land use that would prove destructive of the Indians' way of life, as he would later openly admit. Obviously Mitchell's declarations of the Great Father's benevolence were at best pronounced exaggerations; he was well aware of the minimal interest in Congress concerning tribal rights on the remote Plains. Yet the Indians accepted the treaty promises on the strength of Mitchell's portrayal of a benignly paternalistic government.

Regarding subsequent failures of the government to act according to the promises he had been authorized to make, Mitchell cannot be held responsible. Yet Mitchell knew before the council opened that much more than the treaty concessions would be demanded of these Indians. During his enumeration of the council objectives Mitchell had paused to offer a historic warning. It was only apart from the context of all the ready promises made by Mitchell that the Indians could have appreciated the threat and grave warning he offered: "Your condition is now changed from what it formerly was. In times past you had plenty of buffalo and game to subsist upon. . . . Now, since the settling of the districts West of you by the white men, your condition is changed, and your Great Father desires you will consider and prepare for the changes that await you."[14]

How successful the interpreters were in conveying this warning might well be questioned. Securing supply corridors across Indian country was only the initial objective of the council. The change awaiting the Indians as a result of the Fort Laramie treaty was great indeed. The Great Smoke had to deal with their enforced change to another lifestyle. The change would lead to their dispossession of the entire Great Plains.

SEPTEMBER 8–9: Intertribal Visiting and Deliberations

The commissioners had scheduled no general council meeting; rather, the time had been consigned to private tribal discussions of the government's proposals as presented by Mitchell. Chambers reported: "In the morning Col. Mitchell and myself went to the Sioux villages, across the Platte, to visit some of the Chiefs, at their invitation. On arriving, we found them in council among themselves, on the subject of the treaty, and we would not interrupt them."[15]

Mitchell and Fitzpatrick had encouraged intertribal visiting to foster more friendly relations. Attending many of these gatherings, the editor of the *Missouri Republican* was able to describe various Indian habits and customs.

On the afternoon of the eighth, accompanied by De Smet and Brown, Chambers witnessed two ceremonies: a "scalp peace" between the Cheyennes and the Shoshones, and the ritual of piercing the ears of Indian children. Chambers also noted the Monday-evening arrival at the Horse Creek encampment of Culberston and the party of tribal delegates from the area around Fort Union.[16]

On the afternoon of the ninth the Cheyennes put on a double display for Chambers and his associates: an enactment of military maneuvers by their young braves and public "counting *coups*," the latter a ritualistic reenactment by warriors of their notable accomplishments.

Closing his report for this day, Chambers noted one important council item, an action by which the Cheyennes manifested their readiness to accept the commissioners' proposals: "This evening they [the Cheyennes] presented to Col. Mitchell two men who had been selected to form a part of the delegation to go east—Little Chief and Rides-on-the-Clouds. The Colonel made them some presents, and they went on a visit to the other villages."

SEPTEMBER 10:

Indians' Anticipation of Promised Compensation

The commissioners, anxiously awaiting the arrival of Campbell's supply train, must have welcomed any delay in the conducting of council negotiations. Such a delay occurred on Wednesday morning, as reported by Chambers:

> The cannon was fired this morning, and the flag raised for the assembling of the Council, at 9 o'clock. About that hour, it was announced that the Crows were coming in, conducted by Mr. [Robert] Meldrum, their Interpreter. Col. Mitchell and party went out and met them beyond our encampment. . . . Their coming was expected, and had called out the Indians from all the surrounding villages. The whole plain seemed alive with the moving mass of red skins. Amidst it all, the Crows seemed not the least disturbed or alarmed. Col. Mitchell met them; the Chiefs dismounted, made a short speech in reply to the Colonel, smoked all round, and then he assigned them a camp ground near his own, and invited the Chiefs and principal men to attend the Council that morning.

Even after the Crow leaders were seated in the council circle, there were additional delays. The preliminary smoking ceremony had to be repeated and the newcomers informed of the government's proposals. Then the commissioner, noting that all the propositions had been presented and explained, asked the Indian leaders to express the reactions of their tribes.

Representing one group of the Sioux, the most numerous tribe participating in the council, Chief Terra Blue of the Brulés offered this report to Commissioner Mitchell in the presence of the assembly:

> Father, you and the whites have a great deal of sense, and you and our Grand Father have put yourselves to a great deal of trouble to come out here to see us. But we are all glad in our hearts that you have come. We know you want to do us good, to make us be at peace with each other and the whites, and we want to be at peace. I and my band, the Brule's, have heard all you have said, and we have talked together about it. Some things you propose are very well, but in some things we don't agree with you. We are a large band, and we claim half of all the country; but, we don't care about

that, for we can hunt anywhere. But we have decided
differently from you, Father, about this Chief for the
nation. We want a Chief for each band.

Chambers's reports contain no comment on the reaction of the
commissioners to the initial speech by this Sioux leader or the
subsequent statements by representatives of the Cheyennes and
Arapahos.[17] Mitchell and Fitzpatrick, however, must have been
highly pleased. Their major proposals, at least by implication, had
been accepted, and a positive tone of trustful cooperation with the
Great Father in a concern for peace had been manifested by all the
participants.

Later Mitchell would take steps to resolve the problem advanced
by the Sioux of selecting a single chief to represent their numerous
nation. On this occasion the commissioner informed the Sioux that
even with their larger number, they must unite, that their relatives the
Santee Sioux would be selling their lands and seeking homes with
them across the Missouri, and that all the Sioux should form one
nation.[18] According to Chambers's report, Mitchell, the civilian,
offered advice to the Sioux that no military leader would repeat: "He
explained to them that, divided as they were, they were weak and
defenseless. If you take one lodge pole you can easily break it, but if
you take all the poles of a lodge together, it is very hard to break
them. So, if your bands unite and all become one nation, it will be
hard to break you."

Regarding the second complaint expressed by Terra Blue — "We
are a poor people, and want very much to see the presents" —
Mitchell would continue to have no answer for ten more days. At this
assembly, following Terra Blue, several other Sioux leaders voiced
the same complaint, in Chambers's words: "They were all very poor,
very hungry, and hoped the goods would soon be here."

Chambers reported on these "begging speeches" with some impatience and very little understanding. De Smet declared later that
during the council various camps were indeed short of provisions.
Further, in their announcements prior to the council, Mitchell and
Fitzpatrick had stressed that the participants would be amply compensated for their previous complaints. The reception of such compensation, not the opportunity to hear new proposals, had been the
primary if not exclusive motivation for many of the Indian leaders
now in attendance.

Other speeches were made by various Indians, and the council
meeting was extended "until a late hour." Before the closing of the

session, however, the commissioners marked further gains. "The Cheyennes and Arappahoes, having selected a chief for their respective nations, they brought them up, and they were received and recognized as such by the Commissioners. On receiving them, Col. Mitchell caused the names to be announced to all the other tribes, and at the same time informed them that henceforth the Government would regard them as the Chiefs of those nations, and they must be so received, respected and obeyed by all others."

SEPTEMBER 11: Introduction of Big Robber, Crow Chief

At the opening of this session leaders from various branches of the Sioux expressed their problem: each of the bands wanted the nation's chief to be named from their own membership. The commissioners, however, took a firm stand. Mitchell, having insisted once more that there must be a single chief as the choice of the entire nation, "advised them to consult further, and smoke together, and see if they could not agree."[19]

It was then the Crows' turn to address the commissioners and the assembled tribes. Chambers was obviously impressed:

> *Big Robber,* a Crow chief, very elegantly dressed—as fine a specimen of a man, large, well developed and symmetrical, with as intelligent a face as I ever saw— was introduced. He made the most sensible speech I heard from the Indians. He said:
>
> ["]Father, the Crows are a small nation, and those that are with me here have been selected to come and see you, and do whatever is most for the good of the Crow people. We live a great way off, many days travel from here, and we have but little to do with the whites, but are willing to be at peace with them. As to making peace with the other Indian nations here, I have but little to say. . . . But, Father, if you desire us to make peace with them, we are willing to do it, for we think it would be for the good of all to be at peace and have no more war. I am but a young man—our old men are at home. We listen to our old men; they told us to come here to see what we could do for the good of our people, and they told us that what we did they would abide by, and sustain it, both with the whites and Indians. Father, I have not two hearts; what I promise I expect to perform, and my people will sustain me. . . .

["]Father, I want all the red men here to see me and
understand what I have told you—that, if hereafter, it
is performed, they may know who it was that promised; and if it is not fulfilled, that they may laugh at the
Crows and the man who spoke. The sun, moon and
earth are all witnesses of the truth I have spoken, and
that all I have promised will be fulfilled."[20]

Before this session of the council ended, Mitchell announced that
the agenda for the following day would be defining the territories of
the tribes and suggested a preliminary meeting of tribal leaders. The
commissioner asked each tribe to appoint a five-member committee
to meet with him the next morning.

SEPTEMBER 12–13: "Divide et Impera"

For the commissioners and their tribal committees, this proved a
lengthy and difficult day. The "attempt to designate on the map the
territory of each of the nations" demanded a geographical knowledge
of the vast area from the Arkansas on the south to the Missouri on the
north, from the Rocky Mountains on the west far eastward across the
Great Plains. Also necessary was at least a general awareness of the
traditional homeland territories of the tribes.

Mitchell had some direct knowledge of the Upper Missouri country; of the Southwest, Fitzpatrick was better informed. Further, the
commissioners were assisted by two exceptionally knowledgeable
individuals, De Smet and Jim Bridger. Chambers's report expressed
high praise for both:

> In this effort, the Commissioners had the assistance of
> the Rev. Father De Smidt, who has probably a more
> perfect knowledge of the topography of the country,
> than any one now living. To an enlarged and compre-
> hensive, as well as learned mind, he combines great
> aptitude and facility of knowing and understanding a
> country. He has travelled in nearly every direction
> from the Western boundary of Missouri to the Pacific.
> All that he has seen, and everything that he has been
> able to gather, either from the Indians, traders or
> trappers, as to the course or character of rivers, ranges
> of mountains, and extent of plains, their peculiar
> formation—in a word, everything pertaining to the
> topography of the country—he has carefully collected
> and embodied in a great number of small maps,

which, combined, contain a greater amount of correct information than can be found anywhere else. He has very thoroughly explored the Eastern and Western slopes of the Rocky Mountains, as far South as the line of Oregon; and we hazard nothing in saying that there is no man living so extensively and correctly informed as to the geography of the headwaters of the Mississippi [Missouri], the Yellow Stone, and the Columbia Rivers, and their tributaries and lakes, and the mountains from whence they rise, or through which they pass, and how they interlock and pass each other. He has accumulated this mass of information, in part, from his own observations. He has spent many years amongst the roving Indian tribes, traversing their country many hundreds of miles, even far beyond the Northern boundary of the United States. He has gathered from those whom he has met and conversed with, and he is enabled now to correct many of the gross errors which are to be found on all the maps now published.

Obviously, Mitchell, Fitzpatrick, Campbell, and others had informed Chambers of De Smet's reputation and unique background. And from these same sources the reporter must have learned about the legendary Jim Bridger:

In addition, the Commissioners had the assistance of Mr. James Bridger, the owner and founder of Bridger's Fort, in the mountains. This man is a perfect original. He is a Kentuckian by birth, but has been in the Indian country since he was sixteen years of age. He was with Gen. Ashley in his early trapping expeditions, and afterwards with various companies, and finally, roamed over the country on his own hook, in the capacity of trapper, hunter, trader, or Indian fighter, as the emergency demanded. He has traversed the mountains East and West, and from the Northern boundary of the United States to the Gila river.

Even with such help the territorial division required a prolonged session. Chambers noted that there was "much consultation, particularly of the Indians among themselves." Before nightfall, however, this planning group had fashioned specific proposals for dividing the Indian country into geographical districts.

The council convened, the commissioners might have expected some objections to their proposals. Again the Sioux, this time the Oglala band, strongly complained that their assigned area was less than proper. Speeches by The Snake, The Brave Bear, and Black Hawk insisted on their right by traditional usage to hunt south of the Platte, in the country that had been assigned jointly to the Cheyennes and the Arapahos.

A few days later Chambers offered a generally optimistic summary of the first week of the council. In an account headed "Progress of the Treaty" he explained the basic problem faced by the Sioux:

> So far we have had no difficulty in coming to a full understanding with all of the Indians, except the Sioux. They have advanced many objections to the stipulations of the treaty; but they are so split up into small bands, and the bands residing on the Platte are so much more numerously represented than those on the Missouri, that there is a great deal of jealousy and opposition from this quarter. Then there are the conflicting views and interests of traders and others to be encountered, and many obstacles are presented to the formation of a satisfactory Treaty.[21]

The Sioux objection was apparently resolved by Mitchell's repeated caveat: the territory to be assigned to a tribe would not be held exclusively by that tribe, for "so long as they remained at peace," the tribes might go into one another's territories for hunting and other reasons.

SEPTEMBER 14: The Mass of the Council

De Smet recorded this second Sunday of September as the Feast of the Exaltation of the Holy Cross. It was a special day for his public function as a Blackrobe. Chambers reported:

> To-day a novel and interesting sight was witnessed on the Plains. In the Half-Breeds' camp, a large lodge had been thrown open, that is, it had been extended so as to form a semi-circle, and on either side other lodge skins had been extended until the area was sufficiently large to accommodate a number of people. At the upper end, a sanctuary had been erected; and in this temporary chapel, the Rev. Father De Smidt said Mass, according to the forms of the Catholic Church. The attendance was respectable.

Father De Smidt, attired in the robes of his office, and before saying Mass, addressed the crowd, in French, explaining the meaning and purposes of the forms and ceremonies used by the Catholics, in this part of their worship, and urging upon his audience the necessity of improving in their conduct, and of embracing religion. The lecture, for it may more properly be so called than a sermon, was beautifully delivered, forcible in language and thought, and appropriate to the occasion. Father De Smidt is highly esteemed by all the Interpreters, Traders, Half-Breeds, and the Indians, and is the medium of great benefit to them. He is peculiarly mild and amiable in his manner. He wins all men, even the wild Indian, by the kindness of his disposition, and the respect and esteem of all the purity and uprightness of his life. As a Missionary, he is in every respect well suited to his vocation. The Indians regard him as a Great Medicine man, and always treat him with marked respect and kindness. During yesterday and today, I understand that he has baptized about twenty-five Half-Breed children and two hundred Indian children.[22]

It was a busy time for De Smet; serving as Mitchell's cartographer was only one of his secondary functions. De Smet reported:

During the two weeks that I passed in the plain of the Great Council, I paid frequent visits to the different tribes and bands of savages, accompanied by one or more of the interpreters. These last were extremely obliging in devoting themselves to my aid in announcing the gospel. The Indians listened eagerly to my instructions.

239 children of the Ogallalas (the first of their tribe) were regenerated in the holy waters of baptism. . . . Among the Arapahos, I baptized 305 little ones; among the Cheyennes, 253; among the Brules and Osage Sioux, 280; in the camp of Painted Bear, fifty-six. The number of the half-bloods that I baptized in the plain of the Great Council on the river Platte is sixty-one. In the different forts on the Missouri, I baptized, during the months of June and July last, 392 children. Total number of baptisms, 1,586.[23]

It was at the treaty council, as De Smet noted later, that the appreciative Sioux honored their Blackrobe by bestowing upon him a new Indian name: "The name by which they called me is Watankanga Waokia, which signified literally, 'The Man Who Shows His Love for the Great Spirit.' "[24]

SEPTEMBER 15: Selection of Sioux Leader—Frightening Bear

Chambers provided no explanation for the late opening of the council on this Monday: "The firing of the cannon and the hoisting of the flag, called the Indians together about eleven o'clock."[25] Addressing the assembly, the commissioner asked the Indian leaders if all the proposals had been understood and found acceptable. A few inquiries, minor difficulties, and doubts were voiced. Seemingly, Mitchell's explanations of these points was "satisfactory to all."

The one major problem was once more advanced by the Sioux. In speeches by Terra Blue, Old Smoke, and other tribal leaders representing the ten bands of the Sioux at the council, the commissioners were notified that the Sioux nation "could not agree in the selection of a chief." Noting that the commissioner's proposal for a solution would be "The First Election Among Indians," Chambers reported:

> After the speeches were through, Col. Mitchell informed them that, as they could not agree among themselves, he would select one [head chief] himself; that he would require them to signify their approbation or disapprobation of the man selected; and if they did not like the man proposed, he would select another. . . .
>
> All things being ready, the Colonel proceeded to select his man for Chief. No one present, save himself and colleague, knew on whom the choice would fall, but it so turned out that the man he had selected was . . . the Fright[e]ning Bear. . . . He is a man of between thirty and forty years of age, and as fine a formed person as was to be found among the Indians. He is connected with a large and powerful family, running into several of the bands, and although no chief, he is a brave of the highest reputation. Among the whites, and nearly all of them knew him, he bears an unspotted reputation for honesty, courage and good behavior. His face indicates intelligence, firmness and kindness, and his eyes are clear and piercing. . . . In

form and manner, I certainly did not meet with his
superior, if there was any one equal to him, among all
the Indians assembled.

Clearly, Chambers was impressed by the Indian Mitchell had
nominated. The reporter went to some lengths to note "the sensitive-
ness and native modesty of the man"; further, he recorded the initial
speech of Frightening Bear rejecting the tribute of nomination.

Commissioner Mitchell, however, assured Frightening Bear and
all the other Sioux representatives that his selection had been made
for good cause—"the character he bore among the whites and
Indians, for honesty, intelligence and courage." Noting again the
demand that there be only one principal chief, Mitchell promised that
if the Sioux nation selected this man, "his Great Father would sustain
him in his office." Chambers also reported the consequent acceptance speech by the commissioner's nominee:

> Father, I am not afraid to die, but to be chief of all the
> Dahcotahs, I must be a Big Chief. If I am to be chief I
> must be a Big Chief, or in a few moons I will be
> sleeping (dead) on the prairies. I have a squaw and
> papooses that I do not wish to leave. If I am not a
> powerful chief, my opponents will be on my trail all
> the time. I do not fear them. I have to sleep (die) on the
> prairies some time, and it don't concern me what time
> it comes. If you, Father, and our Great Father, require
> that I shall be their chief, I will take this office. I will
> try to do right to the whites, and hope they will do so
> to my people. . . . The Great Spirit, the sun and
> moon, and the earth, knows the truth of what I speak.

The outcome of Mitchell's bold intervention remained in question
for over an hour. The commissioner had placed in the hand of each
Sioux leader a short stick. The candidate was to be placed in the
middle of the council circle, and if the voters were willing to accept
and sustain him as chief, they were to present their sticks to him.
Extended consultations were made among the representative voters
and their bands. Finally one of the voters, a chief of the Yankton
Sioux, approached Frightening Bear and gave him his stick. Another
followed; then all the voters moved forward, so that the election was
unanimous. In the reactions of Frightening Bear Chambers continued to find cause for praising this Indian:

> We had a strong and marked evidence of native and
> untutored dignity. Not one of the band to which Mah-

toe-wah-yu-whey [Frightening Bear] belonged, voted until all the others had given in theirs, and he himself threw away the stick which had been given him before he was selected. . . . One of the old Chiefs harangued the bands, and especially the young men, telling them to open their eyes and look upon the man who was hereafter to be the Chief of the nation. . . . Hereafter, this Chief was to be the voice of their Great Father.

SEPTEMBER 17: The Formal Signings of the Treaty

Chambers published no report of council activities conducted on the sixteenth. It might be presumed that Chambers and Brown, supervised by both commissioners, spent the day writing out the final copy of the treaty's preamble and eight articles. On the seventeenth Chambers reported:

> This morning, the usual signals summoned the Council together. The officers of the United States army, and other gentlemen on the ground, had been invited to attend, as witnesses of the consummation of the Treaty. As far as possible, they did so. . . . But the Chiefs, Braves and old men turned out in more than their usual numbers. They appeared in council with all the gravity and dignity that ought to characterize such an occasion.
>
> When the Council was opened, Col. Mitchell explained the purpose of the assemblage to be the signing of the treaty, as it had been prepared in conformity to previous agreement. He then read it to them, sentence by sentence, and caused it to be fully explained by the different Interpreters. At the instance of some of the Chiefs, portions of it were read several times, for their better understanding. Every effort was made, and successfully too, to give them the full and just import of each article.[26]

The first to sign were the commissioners, Mitchell and Fitzpatrick. Then, representing the eight participating tribes of the Great Plains, twenty-one Indian chiefs put their mark on the official papers. Finally, the fifteen witnesses to the chiefs' signings wrote their names: Chambers and Brown, five officers of the army, six interpreters, and the two traders, Campbell and Edmund F. Chouteau.[27]

Chambers's report continues: "The ceremony of signing being over, several of the old Chiefs harangued their tribes, especially the young men present, impressing upon them the necessity of being awake and attentive to what had been agreed upon with their Great Father. That they must now perform what they had promised—be at peace with the whites, and not molest them in passing through the country, and keep peace with each other. The Council now broke up."

SEPTEMBER 18–20:
New Proposal—Formation of a Half-breed Territory

The ceremony of the formal signing having taken place, the commissioners had completed the official agenda of the council. Mitchell remained "exceedingly annoyed" by the failure of Campbell's supply train to arrive at the council ground. He might well have been temporarily perplexed how to keep the Indians together until he could complete the long-delayed distribution of the presents and annuities.

Mitchell, therefore, must have welcomed an item of new business presented to the assembly. In his report for September 20 Chambers stated:

> Day before yesterday, the Chiefs and principal men of the tribes were assembled, and a proposition was submitted—not by the commissioners, but as coming from the parties most interested, the traders, Interpreters and others having Indian wives, and half breed Children—that a portion of country should be set apart for the future use of the Half Breeds. . . . whereon farms might be made, schools and churches erected by the parents, and their children brought up in some knowledge of the advantages and usefulness of civilized life.

In such a proposition both Mitchell and Fitzpatrick would obviously have had personal interest. Mitchell, moreover, in his subsequent recommendations of this proposal to the Indian Office, noted that during the council he had "talked this matter over frequently with the half-breeds and Indians; both parties were delighted with the plan."[28]

With special interest, De Smet reported the introduction of "another treaty in favor of the half-breeds and the whites residing in the country."[29] Chambers reported that the proposition was well received by all the assembly. In fact, he did more. Manifesting an exceptional sensitivity, a laudable appreciation of the human emotions and racial attitudes involved, Chambers called the proposition to the attention of his St. Louis readers by an article in the *Missouri Republican* of November 30, 1851. Along with the actual statement of the submitted proposition, Chambers offered a dignified lamentation over the racial prejudices of both cultures:

> This application on the part of the parents of the Half Breed children, has many strong claims to consideration. They are, in many respects, estranged from civilized society. The white man who has taken a squaw for a wife, however honestly and virtuously they may have lived, (and in this many of them will compare advantageously with some who claim to be civilized) is, with his wife, for ever debarred admission into society. He has shut himself out, and must reap the consequences which his own course has entailed upon him. Yet, toward the offspring of this alliance, the affections are as warm, and we believe we could with truth say as devoted, as can be found any where in civilized life. The man who has given himself up to the attractions of the wild life of the plains—who has formed matrimonial alliances, and abandoned his native land for the exciting and enthusiastic life of the hunter or trader—still looks back, at times, with pleasure and regret, to the early scenes of his youth, and he looks forward with transporting hope to see his children forsake the life of suffering and poverty which marks the savage state. The predominance of this native goodness and just parental spirit is manifest among the major part of the Traders, Hunters, and others who have matrimonial alliances in the Indian country. Many of them are as attached to their squaws by an affection as strong and enduring as can be found in the best circles of refined society—*all* seem to have more than ordinary regard for the future of their children.[30]

Mitchell later reported that discussion of the proposition was tabled following some intense expressions of sentiments. A specific site (the Denver area) was widely recommended; however, since this area was located in the designated Cheyenne and Arapaho country, these tribes presented numerous objections. The commissioners themselves, though deeply interested, "did not think it came within the scope" of the instructions they had received regarding a basic treaty. Moreover, after the disappointment of prolonged waiting word had suddenly been spread among the participants that the long-delayed supply train was about to arrive. Chambers noted the pleased reaction: "This evening [September 20], the Train having the Indian presents arrived and formed a *corral,* much to the joy and delight of every one. It was amusing to see how this item of news spread through the Indian Villages, and how soon a crowd of men, squaws and children, could collect. It was late in the evening when the train came up, but notwithstanding, they were surrounded until a very late hour in the night."[31]

With an optimism based upon the promises of the Great Father, De Smet offered his narrative of and comments on the conclusion of the Great Council:

> The wagons containing the presents destined by the Government to the Indians, reached here on the 20th of September. The safe arrival of this convoy was an occasion of general joy. Many were in absolute destitution. The next day the wagons were unloaded and the presents suitably arranged. . . .
>
> Colonel Mitchell employed the Indians as his agents in distributing the presents to the various bands. The arrangements were characterized by benevolence and justice. The conduct of this vast multitude was calm and respectful. Not the slightest index of impatience or of jealousy was observed during the distribution. . . .
>
> The happy results of this council, are, no doubt, owing to the prudent measures of the commissioners of the Government, and more especially to their conciliatory manners in all their intercourse and transactions with the Indians. The council will doubtless produce the good effects they have a right to expect. It will be the commencement of a new era for the Indians—an era of peace. In future, peaceable citizens may cross the desert unmolested, and the Indian will have little to dread from the bad white man, for justice will be rendered to him.[32]

"THE CAPTAINS AND THE KINGS DEPART"

News in addition to the arrival of the wagons spread rapidly through the hungry encampments. "They had heard the good news," De Smet reported, "that the bison were numerous on the South Fork of the Platte, three days' march from the plain." The bands of hungry Indians were not the only groups to make a hurried departure from Horse Creek. The dragoons, led by Major Chilton and accompanied by Colonel Cooper, set off in advance of Mitchell's party. After a brief stop at Fort Leavenworth the arrival of this military detachment in St. Louis was announced in the *Missouri Republican* on October 17. Under Captain Duncan and Lieutenant Elliott, the mounted riflemen rode down the trail as a military escort for the commissioners and their associates.[33]

From De Smet's journal of the return trip it is evident that trading posts in addition to the converted post of Fort Laramie had been established in the Indian country before the council agreements. De Smet noted, "On the 24th, before sunrise, we set out in good and numerous company. I visited, in my way, two trading-houses, in order to baptize five half-blood children." De Smet also experienced a real surprise along the trail—a meeting with Prince Paul of Württemberg, "accompanied only by a Prussian officer, on their way to enjoy a hunt in the Wind River Mountains."[34]

Following a stop at Fort Kearney the company parted. The military units headed east, escorting Mitchell and most of his associates by the Table Creek route to Nebraska City on the Missouri. De Smet reported that Major Fitzpatrick, surely with De Smet's urging, "preferred taking the southern route, in order to give our friends, the Indian deputies, an opportunity of witnessing the progress that the tribes are capable of making in agriculture and the mechanic arts." Twelve envoys had been deputized by the tribes to meet the Great Father and experience directly the lifestyle of the whites in their main cities. De Smet believed the learning process might best begin with a two-day visit to St. Mary's Mission, where the envoys could identify with other Indians. De Smet reported:

> We reached St. Mary's, among the Potawatomies, on the 11th of October. Bishop Miège and the other Fathers of the Mission received us with great cordiality and kindness.
>
> To give the Indian deputies a relish for labor by the tasting of the various products of farming, a quantity of vegetables and fruits were set before them. Po-

tatoes, carrots, turnips, squashes, parsnips, melons, with apples and peaches, graced the board, and our forest friends did them most ample honor.

The day after was Sunday, and all attended high mass. The church was well filled. The choir, composed of half-bloods and Indians, sang admirably the Gloria, the Credo and several hymns. The Reverend Father Gailland delivered a sermon in Potawatomi, which lasted over three-quarters of an hour. . . . We found the mission in a flourishing state; the two schools are well attended; a community of nuns of the Sacred Heart have conciliated the affection of the women and girls of the nation, and are working among them with the greatest success.[35]

With continued good weather, the journey from St. Mary's to Westport took only three days. While waiting there for passage on a Missouri River steamboat, Fitzpatrick arranged for his group to stay at the Union Hotel. On the eighteenth, boarding the steamboat *Clara,* they were reunited with Colonel Mitchell and his party. De Smet reported on the reactions of the Indian delegation to their new experiences:

Our Indian deputies had never seen a village or settlement of whites except what they had seen at Fort Laramie and at Fort Kearney; they knew nothing of the manner in which houses are constructed, hence they were in constant admiration; and when for the first time they saw a steamboat their wonder was at its height, although they appeared to entertain a certain fear as they stepped on board. A considerable time elapsed before they became accustomed to the noise arising from the escape of steam, and the bustle that took place at the ringing of bells, etc. They call the boat a "fire canoe," and were transported with delight at the sight of another boat ascending with a small boat behind, which they called a "papoose," or little child. When their apprehensions of danger had subsided, their curiosity augmented; they took the liveliest interest in whatever they saw for the first time. They were in grand costume and seated themselves on the promenade deck; as the boat approached the several towns and villages in her progress, they hailed each with shouts and songs.

On the 22nd of October we reached St. Louis. A few days after all the members of the Indian deputation were invited to a banquet given in our university. They were highly pleased at the reception given them by the Reverend Father Provincial, and overjoyed at the encouraging hope that he gave them of having Black-gowns among them.[36]

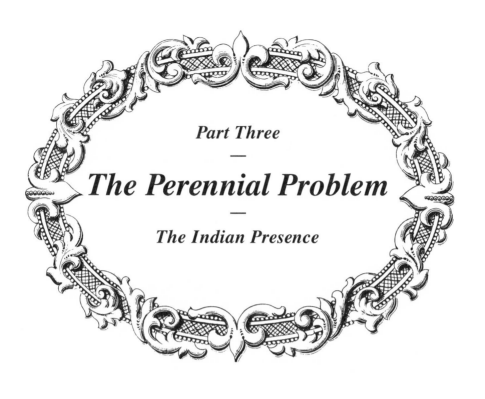

Part Three

—

The Perennial Problem

—

The Indian Presence

Chapter Seven

The Attempt at
Peaceful Coexistence (1852–59)

The promise of Fort Laramie soon faded. The treaty
notwithstanding, conditions on the central plains de-
teriorated steadily during the 1850s for the Southern
Arapahos and Cheyennes. Immigrant trains, surveying parties, and troops continued to plow through the
land, slaughtering game, dispersing buffalo herds,
and cutting through the ranges of grass. The continuing devastation threw the tribes into panic and confusion. Poverty and hunger were now their constant
companions.

—Margaret Coel,
Chief Left Hand, Southern Arapaho

THE REPORTS OF SUPERINTENDENT MITCHELL

For Mitchell and Fitzpatrick as for De Smet, the return to St. Louis
did not mark the conclusion of their treaty-related activities. Mitchell
had to write his reports to the Indian Office. Fitzpatrick was again to
act as a guide, but this time in a reversed function: he would be
escorting the tribal delegates on their tour of Washington and other
eastern cities. De Smet, having returned to his bookkeeping office in
the Jesuit Residence at St. Louis University, for another two weeks
would attend to matters other than the financial records of his fellow
Jesuits: at Mitchell's request he was busily engaged in drawing a large
map of the Indian country east of the Rocky Mountains for the use of
the government.

While waiting for De Smet to complete the map, Mitchell composed his 1851 annual report on the general situation in the Central
(St. Louis) Superintendency. Mitchell made a loose distinction
regarding the Indian nations of the West: the "border tribes" and the
"Prairie and Mountain tribes" (with whom the Fort Laramie treaty
had just been concluded). To advance the Indians in civilization and
promote intermixture with whites, he proposed "the laying off of
Nebraska Territory." To each head of an Indian family Mitchell
would assign a section of land so that tribal individuals would be
pressured to adapt an agrarian lifestyle. Those who survived the

process of intermixture and amalgamation would be granted citizenship.

Mitchell's proposal thus pointed Indian policy to the assimilation of both the Indians and the Indian country. His proposal would obviously eliminate one of the basic tenets Indian policy had been founded on—the assurance of a distinct "Indian country." Mitchell boasted that his plan would "give to the United States *all* the agricultural lands south of the Missouri river that are considered exclusively Indian territory." Under Mitchell the administration of Indian policy played a major role in westward expansion.[1]

It was not until November 10 that De Smet presented the finished map to Mitchell. The superintendent must have been pleased as he unrolled the large sheet of heavy paper, fifty-four inches in width and thirty-six inches in height. De Smet's map covered the area from 36 degrees north latitude northward beyond the Canadian border at the 49th parallel. Mitchell had asked that the headwaters of the Columbia as well as the Platte and the Missouri be traced out. Starting (on the right) to the east of the 91 degrees longitude west, the map treated the area westward to a point slightly beyond the 119th. In addition to the overprinted territorial boundaries as of 1851, De Smet had heavily indicated the commissioners' achievement—the territorial boundaries of the Indian tribes as designated in the treaty. Transmitting the official treaty papers to Commissioner Lea, Mitchell wrote: "The accompanying map, upon which these national boundaries are clearly marked and defined, was made in the presence of the Indians, and fully approved and sanctioned by all. As a map of reference, it will be of great service to department."[2]

De Smet apparently still believed that his map would contribute to the Indians' enjoyment of "a period of peace and justice," that within these designated boundaries the tribes would live in peaceful coexistence as guaranteed by the promises spoken for the Great Father. However, Mitchell emphasized quite another consequence of the treaty: he proudly noted the government's power move making the division and domination of the tribes. As Mitchell informed his superiors, one important benefit would be the elimination of quarrels between the tribes and harmful repercussions for white emigrants.[3]

Listing the key objectives that had been obtained by the treaty, Mitchell especially noted that the right "to establish roads, military and other posts, throughout the Indian country" had been "acknowledged and granted, on the part of the Indians, to the United States." The legal justification for the transcontinental roads had been established. Furthermore, the compensation for problems that had been caused the tribes by previous use of those passageways had now been offered and accepted: restitution had supposedly been made.

However, in Mitchell's listing of the most important provisions of the treaty there was an omission, one that the Indian leaders would have considered a serious failure. He neglected to point out the key promise made to the tribes: "Your Great Father desires to drive the bad white man out from amongst you." This commitment, stated in Article 3 of the treaty, was the formal profession of a reciprocal obligation on the part of the government: "In consideration of the rights and privileges acknowledged . . . the United States bind themselves to protect the aforesaid Indian nations against the commission of all depredations by the people of the said United States."[4]

Mitchell's report, however, did point out the other basic promise that had been made to the tribal leaders — a $50,000 annuity for fifty years. Mitchell hastened to express the reasons for this stipulation: "Fifty thousand dollars for a limited period of years is a small amount to be distributed among at least fifty thousand Indians, especially when we consider that we have taken, or are rapidly taking away from them all means of support, by what may be considered a partial occupancy of their soil."

Mitchell was therefore well aware that the anticipated roads and military posts would cause the impoverishment of the Native Americans. With good cause he had warned the tribal leaders assembled at Horse Creek: "Your condition is now changed." Facing that change, one already being experienced by midcentury in certain areas of the Great Plains, Mitchell presented two arguments to Congress for an official acceptance of his proposed annuity. Again, as throughout the history of Indian policy, a concern for justice or humanity to the Indians was openly acknowledged. However, such moral principles were again presented as secondary to financial considerations and the material advantages that would accrue to the United States.

> On the score of economy, to say nothing of justice or humanity, I believe that amount will be well expended. In the opinions of the best informed persons . . . it will, in all probability, save the country from the ruinous and useless expenses of a war against the prairie tribes, which would cost many millions. . . . Fifty years it was thought would be time sufficient to give the experiment a fair trial, and solve the great problem whether or not an Indian can be made a civilized man.[5]

The Sacred Heart Mission among the Coeur d'Alene tribe (Idaho).

The St. Ignatius Mission among the Pend d'Oreilles (Montana)

These appear to be copies, possibly by Hastings, of sketches by Gustavus Sohon printed in John Mullan's military road report (1863). (Jesuit Missouri Province Archives, Linton Album)

Charles P. Chouteau (1819–1901), director of the American Fur Company, 1850–65. (Scharf, *History of St. Louis*)

James Bridger (1804–81), partner in the Rocky Mountain Fur Company, 1830–33. (Jesuit Missouri Province Archives)

Joseph La Barge (1815–99), Missouri River steamboat pilot, 1831–85. (Missouri Historical Society, neg. Por-L-13)

John Mullan (1829–1909), author of "Report on Construction of a Military Road" (1863). (Haynes Foundation Collection, Montana Historical Society, Helena)

At the dedication in 1834, Bishop Joseph Rosati declared that his new St. Louis Cathedral had been "built for centuries." Today the renovated structure, along with the nearby restored St. Louis Courthouse, are important components of the Jefferson National Expansion Memorial. (Jesuit Missouri Province Archives)

The facade of Fusz Residence Hall, Saint Louis University, was utilized by sculptor Greg Dirkinsky to convey the message that De Smet's St. Louis–based missionary activities extended across the entire American West. Other outstanding memorials are in Salt Lake City; De Smet, South Dakota; and Dendermonde, Belgium. (Jesuit Missouri Province Archives)

The first Indian of the Great Plains to become a Jesuit was a Delaware, Watomika (Swift-footed One) (1823–89), who in 1848 became James Bouchard, S.J. (Jesuit Missouri Province Archives)

Watomika in a prayer offering at his father's bier (Linton Album, Jesuit Missouri Province Archives)

The opening pages of the Linton Album present Watomika's narrative, solicited by De Smet, of his early years on the Delaware reserve, then located slightly west of Leavenworth, Kansas. De Smet and his friend shared the wish in their correspondence through the 1850s that they would be able to work together among the Indians, but Catholic missionary activities then did not point to the development of a native clergy. In 1861 Bouchard was assigned to work among the California Jesuits, where his notable success was recorded in John McGloin's Eloquent Indian. *De Smet's farewell letter in 1872 stated, "I long to see you once more before I die."*

Bishop Henry B. Whipple (1822–1901), an ardent and trusting crusader for reform, said, "There is a great heart in the Saxon race which although slow to act, will redress wrongs." Like De Smet, Whipple was praised by Indian leaders as being "of one tongue." (Minnesota Historical Society, c.n.)

Ely Samuel Parker (1825–95), *left*, and William Medill (1802–65), *right*, were commissioners of Indian affairs, respectively, from 1869 to 1871 and from 1845 to 1849. Like George Manypenny, who was Indian commissioner from 1853 to 1857, they attempted to implement needed reforms in the Indian Office, where the evil consequences of the spoils system were particularly evident. (Library of Congress, US262-14456; Ohio Historical Society)

BL. PHILIPPINE DUCHESNE

St. Philippine Duchesne was supported by De Smet in her efforts to provide educational programs for Indian girls. (Photograph by John William Nagel of a mosaic in the south dome of St. Louis Cathedral)

On January 19, 1852, Commissioner Lea passed on to Secretary of the Interior Alexander Stuart all the papers submitted by Mitchell. Lea added only his recommendation that "the best interests of the government" — not those of the Native Americans whose interests he officially represented — required ratification. Despite the incalculable benefits that were being realized at tribal expense, the Senate found a stumbling block in Article 8 regarding the amount of the annuity that was to serve as an ongoing retribution to the tribes. By congressional action the matter was referred back to the Senate Committee on Indian Affairs.[6]

De Smet waited, with an impatience shared by others, for ratification. On May 24 the treaty was approved by Congress, but only consequent to the adoption of a major amendment. On a unilateral basis — this procedure would cause later problems — Congress determined upon a 70 percent reduction of the compensatory annuity. Washington politicians saw fit to substitute *fifteen* for the promised *fifty* years of annuity payments.

If De Smet began to have second thoughts about the Great Father's concern for his red children, Mitchell saw no problem. It had been only six months since Mitchell had insisted that for a fair trial, fifty years of the annuity award of $50,000 would be required. Within those six months, however, Mitchell's experiences and reflections had resulted in a pessimistic outlook regarding the Indians. In October 1852 Mitchell stated: "This modification of the treaty I think very proper, as the condition of these wandering hordes will be entirely changed during the next *fifteen* years."

Only a year earlier, as he repeatedly informed the tribes, Mitchell had been negotiating a treaty that was intended entirely for the Indians' benefit and future welfare. Already the superintendent had moved to a fatalistic view of the Indians' destiny, a grim negativism in which he seemed to readily find self-justification:

> Notwithstanding the vast number of emigrants passing and repassing through their country, but little change has been effected in their condition; but the change thus far has been, as it ever has been, against the "poor Indian." Vast quantities of their game (their only means of subsistence) have been destroyed. Their limited forests have been laid waste, and loathsome diseases (unknown in their primitive state) scattered among them. This is greatly to be deplored; but there is, at present, no remedy.[7]

Like Fitzpatrick and William Clark before him, Mitchell bemoaned the tragic lot of the Indian. However, as the officials responsible for altering and implementing Indian policy, these men expressed no personal regret that consequent to the very projects they initiated and in which they played key roles, the impoverishment of the Native Americans was being pushed forward. Although sharing in the responsibility, these policy leaders exercised a paternalism less than benign. Rather, like most of their ethnocentric contemporaries, they regarded white expansion as an incontestable good. With professions of righteousness, they declared that some sympathetic help should be offered "to save, if possible, some portion of these ill-fated tribes" who were being dispossessed by the emigrants. Like the Indian policy he helped to fashion and implement, Mitchell stated a regard for the rights of the Indians; in practice, however, that concern was always subordinated to that greater and supposedly divinely determined good—the Manifest Destiny of the United States.[8]

AGENT FITZPATRICK: Final Assignments and Reports
Fitzpatrick's treaty-related activities would continue until his death in February 1854. As treaty commissioners, Fitzpatrick and Mitchell shared the subsequent responsibility assigned by Congress to bring delegates from the western tribes to Washington. Mitchell's proposals in 1849 had included a budget allotment of $20,000 for this procedure. Mitchell had also precisely defined for Congress positive and negative objectives of such a supervised visitation: "To impress them with the greatness and power of the United States, and the ability of their Great Father to punish them for any violations of treaty stipulations."[9]

As historian Herman Viola points out in his study of Indian delegations to Washington, the entire program was directed by Indian Office officials to dominate and intimidate tribal leaders. By midcentury this established exercise of big-stick diplomacy had become integral to Indian policy. The widespread presumption in Washington, despite considerable evidence to the contrary, was that the program was remarkably effective, that it achieved the purpose that William Clark, applying Jefferson's directive, had enunciated in 1806: To convince the delegates and consequently their nations "of the futility of an attempt to oppose the Will of our government."[10]

Before the treaty council, Washington authorities had recommended that Mitchell and Fitzpatrick select some twenty Indians to serve as delegates representing the tribes. As reported by De Smet, however, the commissioners were able to gain the commitment of only twelve Indians: five representatives from the Sioux, three from the Arapahos, three from the Cheyennes, and one from the Crows. This group of Native Americans was put under the charge of the interpreters John S. Smith and J. Tesson Honoré; neither was able to interpret for the Crow. By October 19, even prior to the landing of the *Clara* at St. Louis, the journey of this Native American had ended in tragedy. In one of his letters at the close of 1851 De Smet described the disappearance and death of the Crow:

> There was a Crow brave in the delegation, unhappily without an interpreter, & who could only communicate with others by signs. He came as far as Brunswick, when, whilst the boat lay up for the night, he suddenly left, without giving notice to anyone, & no trace could be obtained of him. The supposition at first was that he had become homesick, & would attempt to return to his nation. . . . When he left the boat he borrowed the knife of one of the Sheyennes. Very diligent search was made for him that night & the next morning, but no trace of him was discovered. We learned eight days later that his body had been found in the woods in the neighborhood of the town, & there was every reason to believe that he had committed suicide.[11]

The somber mood of the Indian delegation following this sorry incident was to continue throughout their tour of the East. One of the Washington newspapers reported on the formal reception of the group on November 17 by President Millard Fillmore. The article noted that while waiting upon the president the delegates were obviously "under much mental solicitude and constraint lest in his august greatness the President might not be gracious to them." The reporter, however, may not have offered a sufficiently deep explanation of the depression manifested by the Indians. In late November Fitzpatrick commented: "One of this delegation has recently committed suicide, and from the apparent depression of spirits prevailing among others of them, it would not surprise me in the least to see others commit the same act."

On December 18 the delegates were to visit notable displays of white power. In the morning they would be conducted on a detailed tour of the Navy Yard, to be followed by an afternoon visit to the

Washington Arsenal. Many of the Indians, however, requested in the afternoon that they be returned to their quarters at Maher's Hotel, remarking that they were now "certain that nothing was impossible to the white people."[12]

On March 3, from his St. Louis office, De Smet reported that "the Indians with Major Fitzpatrick have returned from Washington." However, their return would meet with further delay. De Smet noted that about the end of April Fitzpatrick conducted the group to Fort Leavenworth; "shortly thereafter they headed to their country, escorted by a band of soldiers."[13]

In late summer Mitchell informed Washington that Fitzpatrick had again set out to distribute annuity goods and presents to the tribes of the Upper Platte Agency. On the Arkansas Fitzpatrick distributed about $6,000 worth of presents to Comanches, Kiowas, and Apaches, hoping to encourage these tribes to participate in the treaty planned for the following year. On the South Platte, Fitzpatrick contacted the Arapahos and Cheyennes; in October, the Sioux at Fort Laramie. To these groups the agent distributed goods worth a much larger amount, the first annuity payment due them in accordance with the 1851 treaty. On his return journey to St. Louis Fitzpatrick halted for a few days at the St. Mary's Indian Mission in Kansas. Even before the agent's November return to St. Louis, Mitchell composed a warning and a proposal for the Indian Office:

> The treaty, however [as amended by Congress], should have been sent back to the Indians, for the purpose of obtaining their sanction to the modification. . . .
>
> I would recommend (as I have already done on several occasions) that the Comanches, Kioways, and other wild tribes on the Arkansas, be made parties to the Fort Laramie treaty, or that one similar in its provisions be entered into with them.[14]

Despite his achievement in negotiating the Fort Laramie treaty, Mitchell was quickly relieved of office. When Franklin Pierce became president on March 4, 1853, it was the Democrats' turn to grab the benefits of the spoils system. Continuity and long-range planning were never marks of the Indian Office. Lea was replaced as commissioner of Indian affairs by George W. Manypenny; Alfred Cumming took over Mitchell's post as the St. Louis superintendent. In what may have been his final official act Mitchell directed Fitzpatrick at the start of 1853 to proceed to Washington to offer a direct report at the Indian Office on conditions affecting the tribes of his agency.[15]

On March 3, acting on a recommendation in which Mitchell had joined, Congress took action to obtain title to much of the land on which the border tribes had been settled. The new president was authorized to initiate negotiations for land-cession treaties with the tribes west of Missouri and Iowa. It would be August 18, however, before Secretary of Interior Robert McClelland directed Commissioner Manypenny to conduct the negotiations.

Congress also acted upon Mitchell's proposal regarding the tribes of the southern Plains. On May 5 agent Fitzpatrick was directed to negotiate treaties with the Comanches, Kiowas, and other tribes on the Arkansas River. He was also instructed to obtain the consent of the tribes regarding the amendment made by the Senate to the Fort Laramie treaty. Moreover, Fitzpatrick was informed that Congress had already moved to exercise the right acknowledged by the Fort Laramie treaty "to establish roads, military and other posts within the Indian territory." The sum of $65,000 had been allotted for the construction of a new military post, Fort Riley, on the Republican Fork of the Kansas River. There would also be 150 miles of road to connect this new military installation, well within the Indian country, to the army headquarters at Fort Leavenworth on the Missouri River.[16]

Having made his preparations throughout June, Fitzpatrick concluded the Fort Atkinson treaty on July 27, 1853. Following a delay in obtaining interpreters, Fitzpatrick had quickly completed treaty negotiations with the leaders of the Comanche, Kiowa, and Apache tribes. In his subsequent reports Fitzpatrick expressed his satisfaction with the concessions he had extracted from the Indians "in view of the fact that at no distant day the whole country over which those Indians now roam must be peopled by another and more enterprising race."[17]

However, like Mitchell's report on the Fort Laramie treaty, Fitzpatrick's announcement did not include the treaty stipulation that the tribal leaders had regarded as most important. Like Mitchell, Fitzpatrick failed to point up the promise of military protection against depredations by emigrants.

On August 2 Fitzpatrick departed Fort Atkinson. In the vicinity of St. Vrain's old fort on the banks of the South Platte he found a large encampment of Cheyennes and Arapahos "anxiously waiting for the distribution of their annuities." Reporting his meetings with these tribes in August and some of the Sioux leaders at Fort Laramie in September, Fitzpatrick noted that he had distributed the annuities only *after* he had provided an explanation for, and gained tribal approval of, the congressional modification to their treaty.

That task completed, Fitzpatrick hurried eastward from Fort Laramie. He had been shocked by what he saw and heard on this expedition, the sorry evidence of a tragic situation that he could no longer overlook. By the comments, attitudes, and critical needs related in his report, he would attempt at last to alert the Indian Office. His report would sound a general warning regarding the condition of these three major tribes of the central Great Plains. Further, he would insist that the growing complaints of the Sioux were an extremely serious matter.

In June of that year a Minneconjou had been accused of shooting a soldier. A military detachment under Lieutenant Hugh B. Fleming had marched into the Minneconjou camp demanding the surrender of the Indian reported to be the murderer. When a shot rang out, the soldiers fired, killing five of the Sioux. The detachment then retreated to the fort without apprehending the suspect. Fitzpatrick heard the Indian leaders demand a remedy for this depredation. They complained that "the soldiers of the great father are the first to make the ground bloody." Fitzpatrick appreciated that a portent may indeed have occurred, that the seeds of disaster might have been planted. Had Fitzpatrick lived, he would not have been surprised by the Grattan tragedy in August of the following year.[18]

The return to St. Louis would be Fitzpatrick's final journey along the Great Medicine Trail, the transcontinental thoroughfare for which he was especially responsible. At long last, and seemingly now for the first time, Fitzpatrick was facing that responsibility. He had come, quite abruptly, to an appreciation of the cost of the corridors splitting the Great Plains, to a realization of the tragic consequences for the Native Americans. As he moved eastward from the Forks of the Platte to Fort Kearney, Fitzpatrick became increasingly aware of the evidence: through the previous four months, the road had served some 23,000 people traveling west with 6,000 wagons, 150,000 cattle, and 50,000 sheep.[19]

On November 9 Fitzpatrick arrived in St. Louis. Through the following days the agent composed an extensive annual report, which must have proved a difficult task. On November 19 Fitzpatrick gave the report to Superintendent Cumming. For officials of the Indian Office, this report presented a serious message. Their best-known Indian agent, the most highly experienced and knowledgeable representative on the Great Plains, had publicly condemned the government's Indian policy; he had criticized their practice as "the legalized murder of a whole nation."

Although this year-end report for 1853 marked Fitzpatrick's completion of six years of official service, its conclusion manifested an entirely new outlook and concern. Only during his final visit through his assigned territory was he awakened to a sensitive awareness of the Indians' suffering. Only in his final review of the conditions among the tribes under his jurisdiction did Fitzpatrick call for an appreciation of the Indian tragedy to which he had been a major contributor:

> The Indians will perish before the land thrives. Indeed, examples of all their race who have preceded them on the continent, would point to a condition of poverty, of humiliation, of extinction, as the natural result of the foster policy of the government. The emaciated remains of great tribes, who hover in parties upon the borders of Missouri and Arkansas, are evidences that cannot be ignored. But must it always be thus? Must the same system, which has resulted so unfortunately heretofore, be pursued remorselessly to the end? Must the course of removals from place to place, and successive contractions of territory, and perpetual isolation, which has thus far been fraught with such enormous expense, be likewise applied to the nations of the interior?
>
> . . . The fact, startling as it may appear, was made manifest in my recent visit, that the Cheyennes and Arrapahoes, and many of the Sioux, are actually in a *starving state*. They are in abject want of food half the year, and their reliance for that scanty supply, in the rapid decrease of the buffalo, is fast disappearing.
>
> . . . Their women are pinched with want and their children constantly crying out with hunger.

Fitzpatrick now professed a new objective. To cause "the improvement of the Indians," he proposed that only "one course remains which promises any permanent relief to them, or any lasting benefit to the country in which they dwell." In his final judgment, the Trade and Intercourse legislation had worked only to negative ends. Further, Fitzpatrick now condemned the long-standing policy of tribal removals and segregated relocations:

> The custom of "extinguishing the Indian title," as it is called, has, in many instances heretofore, prevailed as

a preliminary step to any settlement by the white man; but I confess that I cannot even allude to it without offering some reasons which seem to me to render it an objectionable course. In the first place, it renders necessary that very system of removals, and of congregating tribes in small parcels of territory, that has eventuated so injuriously upon those who have been already subjected to it. It is the legalized murder of a whole nation. It is expensive, vicious, inhumane, and producing these consequences, and these alone. The custom, being judged by its fruits, should not be persisted in.[20]

At the close of 1853 Fitzpatrick headed to Washington. He believed that he might supply information to the Indian Office and Congress regarding the treaties he had helped to negotiate as well as the much-discussed organization of Nebraska as a territory. But following a brief illness Fitzpatrick died in Washington on February 7, 1854.[21]

It was in his final report that Fitzpatrick became identified, not as a theorist but as a pragmatist, with Jefferson. In his final directives of 1808 to Governor Meriwether Lewis, Jefferson had pointed to achieving domination over the Indians by "the engine of commerce." Fitzpatrick echoed that philosophy with his pronouncement of 1853: "Trade is the only civilizer of the Indian."[22]

NEW ORDER:
Great Plains—The Kansas and Nebraska Territories
At the close of January 1852 the Indian Office passed on to President Fillmore and Congress the two proposals of Superintendent Mitchell. Based upon his realistic distinction between the border tribes and the "wild Indians of the Prairies and Mountains," Mitchell had called for basic variations in Indian policy.

Regarding the relationship with the more remote tribes, Mitchell presented the stipulations that the Indian leadership had accepted at the Fort Laramie treaty council. A peaceful coexistence in separate Indian and white territories would be supervised by the Great Father. The single but substantial modification of the exclusive Indian country would be the government's acknowledged right to establish roads as well as military and other posts. Toward the close of its first session and subsequent to the compromise of a major amendment, the Senate offered its ratification of this treaty package.

As a concluding act of its second session, Congress took the preliminary step to implement Mitchell's proposal regarding the border tribes. Appropriating $50,000 on March 3, 1853, Congress directed the president to enter into negotiations "with the Indian tribes west of the States of Missouri and Iowa for the purpose of extinguishing the title of said Indians tribes in whole or in part to said lands." The "amalgamation" of these already transplanted tribes, as called for by Mitchell — and in short order to be strongly endorsed by his field agent, Fitzpatrick — was to be officially undertaken by the Indian Office.[23]

Congressmen Stephen A. Douglas of Illinois and David R. Atchison of Missouri had grown in political power and influence since their initial attempts in 1844 to introduce legislation for the establishment of a territory across the Great Plains. The first territorial bill introduced by Douglas had backed the proposal of William Wilkins, as secretary of war, controlling the Indian Office. Wilkins had recommended that the Indians be pushed to the north and south of the Platte so that an organized and settled central district might be developed across the Plains — a district through which would run the safeguarded passageways to Santa Fe and Oregon.

Twice more in 1848 Douglas, among others, introduced bills for the organization of Nebraska, or the Platte Territory. Douglas's proposals received the endorsement of Commissioner of Indian Affairs William Medill. In his annual report Medill stated that the Indian Office had already begun "the establishment of two colonies for the Indian tribes." Medill noted that with one colony located north of the Platte, and the other south of the Kansas, there would be between these two rivers "an ample outlet for our white population to spread and to pass towards and beyond the Rocky mountains."[24]

Prucha notes that it was a policy adopted enthusiastically and restated by Medill's successors Orlando Brown and Luke Lea in 1849 and 1850. Further, it was a policy whose implementation was at least initiated through the treaty negotiations of Commissioner Manypenny. Prucha insists, as did these commissioners of Indian affairs, that humanitarian concerns continued to influence the changed planning of the Indian Office. It is true, as Medill and his successors repeatedly noted, that it had become "necessary to consolidate the Indians in order to preserve them and to civilize them." However, it is also true that such consolidation had become necessary for preservation only because of the Indians' loss of tribal territories. The Indian Office had not safeguarded the exclusiveness of the Indian country;

serving the expansionists rather than the Indians, the Indian Office had become one of the main instruments for the realization of Manifest Destiny.[25]

Douglas, then, was voicing "the aspirations of many," including the directors of Indian policy, when he defined "the new order of things" envisioned for the Great Plains. As an explanation of his purpose in introducing his Kansas-Nebraska bill, Douglas stated at the close of 1853:

> How are we to develope, cherish and protect our immense interests and possessions on the Pacific, with a vast wilderness fifteen hundred miles in breadth, filled with hostile savages, and cutting off all direct communication. The Indian barrier must be removed. The tide of emigration and civilization must be permitted to roll onward until it rushes through the passes of the mountains, and spreads over the plains, and mingles with the waters of the Pacific. Continuous lines of settlement with civil, political and religious institutions all under the protection of law, are imperiously demanded by the highest national considerations. These are essential, but they are not sufficient. . . . We must therefore have Rail Roads and Telegraphs from the Atlantic to the Pacific, through our own territory.[26]

Pushed through Congress on May 25, 1854, Douglas's measure was signed on May 30 by President Pierce. The Great Plains—from the banks of the Missouri westward to the boundary of Utah and the summit of the Rockies; from the thirty-seventh parallel and the New Mexico boundary south of the Arkansas River northward to the boundaries of Minnesota and Canada—had been fashioned into two territories, Nebraska and Kansas, separated along the fortieth parallel.

Explicitly, Douglas's legislation declared that the rights of the Indians were "not to be impaired" and that the areas as assigned by treaty to the tribes were to be "excepted out of the territorial limits or jurisdiction" of Kansas and Nebraska. However, the potential for change was also noted. Such Indian rights and territorial titles would remain only "so long as unextinguished by treaty." Douglas and his associates had erected the political framework for "the removal of the Indian barrier" from the Missouri to the summit of the Rockies.[27]

Prucha states: "The Indian reserves were extraordinarily attractive to designing speculators; leaders of Indian factions made use of the uncertain times for their own benefit; and the federal government was powerless—or lacked the will to exert power—to fulfill its promises to protect the Indians."[28] Through the next dozen years, such drastic changes would take place that even the remote "prairie and mountain tribes" would be reduced to dependence. Even before the close of 1854 De Smet would comment on the speed and the extent of those changes:

> The Government has just organized, in the western
> desert, two new Territories—Kansas and Nebraska.
> They embrace an extent of neither more nor less
> than between 500,000 and 600,000 square miles.
> . . . Whites are already pouring in in thousands, all
> hastening to take possession of the best sites. The law
> has just passed; no steps are yet taken to protect the
> Indians, and already fifty new towns and villages are
> in progress. . . . I did not think that the moment of
> invasion was so near.[29]

In 1851 De Smet had entered the political arena as a novice. At the conclusion of the Fort Laramie treaty he had optimistically predicted "a new era for the Indians—an era of peace. In future . . . the Indian will have little to dread from the bad white man, for justice will be rendered to him." By 1854 De Smet's hopes for justice in the government's treatment of the tribes had been shattered. In sharp criticisms expressing charges that would be repeated by Bishop Whipple in the following decade, De Smet pointed out the injustices tolerated by government officials and "the disparity of the parties who make the treaty":

> They [the Indians] must either perish miserably, or
> sell their reserves, or go and rejoin the wandering
> bands of the plains, or cultivate the soil. . . . But,
> observe well, they are surrounded by whites who
> contemn them, hate them, and who will demoralize
> them in a very short time. If it be asked, to what must
> be attributed the improvidence of the tribes, which
> neglect to exchange their permanent annuities for
> sums to be paid at limited terms, but of greater length?
> The reason is found in the disparity of the parties who
> make the treaty. On one side stands a shrewd and,
> perhaps, unscrupulous Government officer, on the
> other, a few ignorant chiefs, accompanied by their

half-breed interpreters, whose integrity is far from being proverbial.

. . . Yet in all the treaties, the agents promise them, on the part of the President, whom they call their Great Father, protection and privileges that are never realized.[30]

In his history of U.S. Indian policy Prucha points out that by midcentury, "following a precedent already well established in the East," the treaty determinations "were not the result of negotiations between two sovereign and independent powers." Rather, the treaties were "a convenient and accepted vehicle for accomplishing what United States officials wanted to do under circumstances that were frequently difficult. By treaty the government could provide Indian segregation on small reservations, throwing open the rest of the territory to white settlement and exploitation."[31]

COMMISSIONER MANYPENNY'S CRITICISM OF INDIAN POLICY

George Manypenny, appointed commissioner of Indian affairs in the spring of 1853, manifested from the start a genuine concern for the Indians. In his initial reports the new commissioner expressed an optimistic outlook: "Objections may be urged to the organization of a civil government in the Indian country; but those that cannot be overcome are not to be compared to the advantages which will flow to the Indians from such a measure, with treaties to conform to the new order of things, and suitable laws for their protection."[32]

The Kansas-Nebraska Act had specified that "the rights of person or property now pertaining to the Indians in said Territories" were not to be impaired, that all the lands held by the Indians would "constitute no part of the Territories . . . until ceded by treaty or otherwise."

Within two years Manypenny reported how successfully he had fulfilled the congressional directive to negotiate such treaties: "Since the 4th of March, 1853, fifty-two treaties with various Indian tribes have been entered into. . . . The quantity of land acquired by these treaties . . . is about one hundred and seventy-four millions of acres. . . . In no former equal period of our history have so many treaties been made, or such vast accessions of land been obtained."[33]

In his treaty negotiations Manypenny was influenced by the strong criticisms Fitzpatrick had directed against Indian policy and its system of removals. Further, as a reformer, Manypenny noted Mitchell's proposal, repeated in previous years, that among the border tribes each family head should be assigned a section of land. Consequently, as part of his treaty negotiations, Manypenny pushed the program of land allotment in severalty.

Hurried in his extensive activities, however, Manypenny failed to note the two qualifications that Mitchell had made part of his proposal for the assignment of land titles to individual Indians. Mitchell had thoughtfully insisted that each grant be "secured to their descendants for *fifty years, without any right of transfer*"; further, that the individual Indian landholders be given "the privileges of citizenship." In the simplistic fashion of a crusader Manypenny failed to demand any inalienability of Indian lands or security of Indian ownership equal to that of ordinary landholders. The commissioner also failed sufficiently to consider and provide for other administrative problems connected with severalty.[34]

Manypenny quickly realized that his program of severalty, founded upon such high intentions, had failed to ensure justice for the Indians. In his 1855 annual report the commissioner complained about the condition of the border tribes in Kansas Territory: "Many of the emigrants to, and settlers in the Territory of Kansas, are engaged in bitter controversy and strife in relation to the institutions to be formed there, as applicable to the condition of the African race; yet the hostile factions seem to have no sympathy for the red man; but, on the contrary, many of both sides appear to disregard his interests and trespass upon his rights with impunity."[35]

Manypenny's criticisms went beyond his comments concerning the faulty plan for allotment of land. Throughout his entire term of office from 1853 through 1856 he continued to call the attention of Congress to the defects of Indian policy and its implementation. In his first report, after pointing up the failures of the field agents, the commissioner had stated: "I am satisfied that abuses of the most glaring character have existed in the Indian country, and that a radical reform is necessary there, in every department connected with the Indian service."[36]

Concerning the general disorder in "Bleeding Kansas," Manypenny stated in 1856 that the unsettled conditions had resulted in serious harm to the Indian tribes: "Trespasses and depredations of every conceivable kind have been committed on the Indians. They have been personally maltreated, their property stolen, their timber destroyed, their possession encroached upon, and diverse other wrongs and injuries done them. . . . Their rights and interests seem thus far to have been entirely lost sight of and disregarded by their new neighbors."[37]

As early as 1853 Manypenny called for the appointment of qualified individuals who would exercise a greater concern for the Indians' rights: "It is respectfully suggested, as a wise and prudent precaution, that commissioners — able, impartial, upright, and practical men — be appointed, as soon as possible . . . for the purpose of investigating the whole subject of our Indian relations there, and of negotiating and recommending such conventional and other arrangements as may be required to place them upon a safe, stable, and satisfactory footing."[38]

Calling for such a review of basic Indian policy, Manypenny also pointed out a major problem that had developed in the Indian Office. Repeating the complaint voiced by commissioners of previous years, Manypenny noted that the haphazard method of formulating treaties through the years had resulted in a "heterogenous mass . . . crude, inharmonious, and often contradictory."[39]

To these criticisms against the principles and practices that constituted Indian policy, Manypenny added a further complaint, pointing out the basic flaw that rendered Indian policy ineffective: the Indian Office was without enforcement power: "Occasions frequently arise in our intercourse with the Indians requiring the employment of force, although the whites may be, and often are, the aggressors. The Indian Bureau would be relieved from embarrassment, and rendered more efficient, if, in such cases, the department had the direct control of the means necessary to execute its own orders."[40]

The Indian Office, following its transfer to the newly created Department of the Interior in 1849, was no longer in direct contact with the War Department. On the reasoning that the duties of the commissioner of Indian affairs more appropriately pertain to peace, Indian affairs had been passed from military to civilian control. President Polk, even as he pressed for national expansion, had assured Congress that "a suitable number" of Indian agents would preserve peace with the Indians.[41]

On the troubled Great Plains, however, the civilian Indian Office quickly faced a serious internal problem: the Indian service lacked the means to execute its own orders. For the Indian agent, the completely nonmilitary phases of Indian management were few; the need for the cooperative support of the army as a police power was real and frequent. Yet as historian Robert Utley commented, "Competition and conflict between the two departments and their field officials complicated relations not only with the tribes but also with Congress on which both depended for appropriations." In his study of federal Indian policy, Loring B. Priest summarized the basic problem of shared jurisdiction as follows: "The Interior Department had no objection to granting the Army jurisdiction over warring tribes in accordance with previous practice. The problem was to decide when and where such control began, what constituted hostility, and who should have the final decision in questionable cases."[42]

The complaints of Fitzpatrick and Mitchell directed against the military have already been noted. As negotiators of the 1851 Fort Laramie treaty, they had been frustrated by what they condemned as minimal cooperation offered by the War Department. At the close of 1854, reporting the Grattan disaster, Manypenny criticized the military officials at Fort Laramie for their unauthorized activity in Indian affairs; two years later the commissioner turned completely against the military. Highly critical of Harney's tactics in the retaliatory military campaign against the Sioux in 1855, Manypenny became furious at the general's encroachment on Indian Office prerogatives in conducting a treaty council with the Sioux leaders at Fort Pierre in early March 1856. In his subsequent attacks on the military Manypenny was a dedicated fighter against the demand of the generals to transfer the Indian Office back to the War Department.

The power struggle over the control and administration of Indian affairs therefore began before the Civil War, and it was directly related to the Sioux troubles of the 1850s. The Indian Office obviously could not handle armed resistance by Native Americans. Yet the interracial conflicts of the 1850s and thereafter were caused by the demands and the unkept promises of the Fort Laramie treaty. The Indian Office had planned the stipulations of the 1851 treaty, but it had failed to plan for and consequently to implement the promises of the treaty.[43]

THE TRAGEDY OF SIOUX LEADERS—
CHIEF FRIGHTENING BEAR

In 1853 De Smet journeyed again to Europe, once more soliciting men and means for the apostolates of the Missouri Jesuits. It was not until the close of December that he returned to St. Louis. Through most of 1854 De Smet continued to be busy, working in the treasurer's office of the Jesuit Residence at St. Louis University. There were greater than normal distractions—the reported persecutions and the political discriminations caused by the anti-Catholic Know-Nothing agitators.[44]

A much more serious distraction, a grave crisis De Smet would live with for years, was connected with a news release carried by the *Missouri Republican* on September 11, 1854. Not many details were provided, but the article denounced a "Treacherous Slaughter of U. States Troops at Fort Laramie." The newspaper article stated:

> Following a period of mounting depredations by the Indians, a poor emigrant complained on August 18th that one of his oxen had been shot down by an Indian. The commandant had sent out a detachment of about thirty men, under Lieutenant Grattan, to apprehend the Indian offender. As head chief of the Sioux, the Bear "had expressed a willingness to give up the offender," and, along with the interpreter, accompanied the detail to the Indian encampment. The express indicated the need for reinforcements, for "the entire detachment had been massacred, and the head chief was reported among the Indians killed."

The newspaper account concluded with the judgment that the soldiers were "victims of a deliberately contrived plot on the part of the Indians." Within a few days the newspapers had moved to a bold proclamation: "A state of war now exists between the United States and the powerful, warlike nation of the Sioux." Other articles followed over subsequent months. It quickly became obvious that St. Louis had a special commercial interest in the situation. The newspaper proclaimed that "while the State of California is so dependent for stock of every description, we are dependent on them for a market—and this stock trade across the plains will now be suspended." Even the national press gave considerable publicity to the affair. Responsibility for the tragedy was in turn assigned to "the rebellious Indians," "the greedy traders on the scene," "the negligent Indian service," and "the incompetently-led military."[45]

From these reports and other sources De Smet composed the following account. Its sarcasm was somewhat exceptional and harsh, but so were the consequences that, as De Smet sadly predicted, would be the lot of the Indians:

> An unpardonable offense, it appears, has been committed in the eyes of our civilized people by the Indians. They had repaired, to the number of 2,000, to the appointed spot at the time fixed by the Government agent to receive their annuities and presents. They waited several days for the commissioner to arrive and

in the meantime they ran out of provisions. Then a
Mormon wagon-train, on its way to the Territory of
Utah, came peaceably by the Indian camp. One of the
party was dragging after him a lame cow hardly able to
walk. A famished savage, out of pity for his wife and
children, and perhaps, also, from compassion for the
suffering animal, killed the cow and offered the Mormon double value for it in a horse or a mule.

Such an act with such an offer under such circumstances passes for very honest, very fair and very
polite, in a wild country. Still the Mormon refused the
proferred exchange and went and filed a complaint
with the commandant of Fort Laramie, which is in
the neighborhood. . . . The illustrious commandant
straightway sent out a young officer with twenty
soldiers armed to the teeth and with a cannon loaded
with grapeshot. . . . The officer was inflexible, refused all offers; he must absolutely have his prisoner;
and when the latter did not appear, he fired his cannon
into the midst of the savages. The head chief, whom I
knew well, the noblest heart of his nation, fell mortal-
ly wounded and a number of his braves beside him. At
this unexpected massacre the Indians sprang to arms;
and letting fly hundreds of arrows from all sides, they
instantly annihilated the aggressors and provocators.
Will you, in Europe, believe this tale of a cow? And
yet such is the origin of a fresh war of extermination
upon the Indians which is to be carried out in the
course of the present year.[46]

Poorly informed regarding Indian leadership, the army officials,
except for Fleming himself, were not aware of the responsibilities
that government officials had conferred upon Frightening Bear by
appointing him head chief of the Sioux at the 1851 treaty negotiations. Even the Indian Office—with the spoils-system turnover of
personnel and unsatisfactory recording—had been at best poorly
informed of their obligation to deal with this formally recognized
authority. Chambers, whose earlier praise of Frightening Bear has
been noted, printed a final tribute to "this Logan of the West" in the
Missouri Republican:

We knew him well, and a better friend the white men
never had. He was brave, and gentle, and kind—a

wise ruler, a skillful warrior, and respected chieftain. Even in accepting his position, assigned to him some four years ago at the treaty of Laramie, he only consented after much persuasion; and then remarked when he did so, that he gave his life to the Great Spirit. So far from any charge of treachery attaching to his conduct, his own fate is a sufficient proof of his fidelity; in recording it, we feel like inscribing a worthy memorial of one of the most high-toned and chivalric of all the Indians we have known.

Senator Thomas Hart Benton, in one of his final congressional speeches, quoted Chambers's praise of Frightening Bear. Benton insisted that "such men as Fremont, Carson, Father De Smedt . . . could now go to every hostile tribe and arrange every difficulty with them in the very first interview."[47]

HARNEY'S REIGN:
"Galconda to the Whites, Golgatha to the Sioux"

In early February 1855 Secretary of War Jefferson Davis provided Congress military documents pertaining to the Grattan affair. All called for military action to achieve a single objective: "to punish the offenders, quickly." The lesson long preached by Fitzpatrick would be acted upon at last. On August 30 Fleming stated that if the Sioux were not punished immediately and in an effectual manner, "all the surrounding tribes, stimulated by neglect of this bloody massacre, will join hand in hand and rush on to the slaughter."[48]

As early as October 26, 1854, army officials contacted General William S. Harney, on leave in Paris. Returning to Washington, Harney received his appointment on March 22, 1855, with orders "to avoid, if possible, all partial operations until a sufficient number of troops has been collected to render the campaign short and decisive." By April 1 when Harney arrived in St. Louis, a number of infantry companies had already left Jefferson Barracks to reinforce the garrisons at Forts Leavenworth and Riley as well as Kearney and Laramie. In July Harney made his final preparations at Fort Leavenworth. On August 24, riding westward on the river trail from Fort Kearney at the head of six hundred men, Harney reportedly declared: "By God, I'm for battle—no peace."[49]

Even before his troops marched into Fort Laramie in mid-September, Harney had accomplished his military objective. Having surrounded the large encampment of the Brulé Sioux leader Little

Thunder at Blue Water Creek, just north of the Ash Hollow crossing from the South Fork to the North Platte, Harney had pressured the Sioux to violent resistance. In the military engagement of September 3 the Sioux were taught in drastic fashion the power of the United States. They were also taught that despite the coexistence promised in the 1851 treaty, the Great Medicine Trail from Fort Leavenworth to and beyond Fort Laramie was to be regarded as belonging exclusively to the white nation. At his peace council with the Sioux in March 1856 Harney issued an ultimatum: "The Indians must not obstruct or lurk in the vicinity of roads travelled by the whites."[50]

Moreover, Harney took further actions to make certain that the lesson of Indian subjugation would be remembered. Having destroyed all the equipment and provisions in Little Thunder's camp, Harney moved his forces up the North Platte to meet other bands of Sioux gathered west of Fort Laramie. Thomas S. Twiss, the new Indian agent for the Upper Platte, had summoned the leaders of all the Sioux who wanted peace. That peace, Harney forcefully informed the Indians, would be granted only after the surrender of the "murderers" who had attacked the Salt Lake mail-wagon train near the fort on November 13. Harney declared that these offenders would be sent down with the captives he had taken at Ash Hollow to be imprisoned at Fort Leavenworth.[51]

Harney then marched north toward the Cheyenne River. Unsuccessful in his attempt to contact other Sioux groups in the area, Harney turned east and reached Fort Pierre on October 20. At this post, purchased by the government from the American Fur Company, Harney set up winter quarters for his troops. On November 9 he sent word to the Sioux: a council would be held at Fort Pierre at the start of March; all groups wishing peace must participate; warfare against the tribe would be halted only if all demands of the government were accepted.[52]

On March 8, 1856, Harney forwarded to the secretary of war the minutes of the council he had concluded with Sioux leaders. Pressured by force, poverty, and fear, the Indians had capitulated, even agreeing to accept the "paper chiefs" Harney appointed for their tribal government. Harney had quickly conquered the Sioux; however, in his connected struggle with the Indian Office the general was less successful.

On the Upper Platte, agent Twiss had attempted to block the participation of the western Sioux in Harney's peace council. In February Harney ordered Twiss "to have nothing to do with the

Sioux." In March he issued a similar interdict on Twiss's relations with the Cheyennes and Arapahos. Agent Twiss hurried to Washington and readily obtained Commissioner Manypenny's backing in the power struggle between the two departments.[53]

Well aware of the parsimonious attitude of Congress regarding expenditures for the Indians, Manypenny was able to block congressional ratification of Harney's proposed treaty. Congressional reluctance to make funding allotments, however, did not extend to projects oriented to the needs of white emigrants in the recently established western territories. From 1854 to 1858 Congress appropriated almost $1.5 million for the construction of roads.[54]

The right "to establish roads through their respective territories" had been acknowledged by the western tribes in Article 2 of the Fort Laramie treaty. However, the road building initiated in 1855 across the new territories of Kansas and Nebraska was beyond all Indian anticipation.[55]

The Thirty-fourth Congress in 1856 established a new standard and a new agency for the construction of western roads. No longer would the exigencies for national defense be the motivating factor; rather, roads would be built through the territories purely as aids to their development and settlement. Further, since these would be emigrant wagon roads rather than military passageways, supervisory authority over them would be given to the Department of the Interior rather than, as previously, the Corps of Topographical Engineers of the War Department.[56]

Beginning in 1856, then, a new assignment had been given not only to the Indian Office but through that headquarters to all the field agents of the service: Indian agents were expected to use their influence with Indian leaders to eliminate any resistance to the road-building program. The Indian Office had been committed to territorial development.[57]

THE ENCIRCLING ENCROACHMENTS OF THE WHITE POPULATION

According to agent Whitfield's 1854 report, the historic separation of the Arapaho and Cheyenne tribes into northern and southern divisions had already taken place; neither tribe had come together since the 1851 treaty. Historians note that settlers and the overland roads along the South Platte and Smoky Hill rivers placed barriers between the northern and southern divisions of both tribes. At the peace council of 1856, however, General Harney gave all the Arapahos and

Cheyennes a stern warning: he would "sweep them from the face of the earth" if they did not stay clear of the emigrant roads.[58]

Even before Harney's threats these Indians had become scattered and uncertain about their relationship with the United States. Further, their impoverishment, first reported by Fitzpatrick in 1853 and by Whitfield the next year, had greatly increased. Whitfield noted in 1855 that "the time is not very far distant when the buffalo will cease to furnish a support for the immense number of Indians that now rely entirely on them for subsistence." Whitfield's successors, R. C. Miller in 1857 and 1858, and William Bent in 1859, documented the increasingly troubled living conditions of these tribes.[59]

Meeting with the Cheyennes at Bent's Fort late in June 1855, Whitfield reported that the Indians of the Upper Platte and Arkansas Agency had become so disturbed that he regarded "a destructive war on the plains" as inevitable. Throughout 1856 a half-dozen violent incidents took place along the eastern half of the Oregon Trail. However, on October 15 some forty-two Cheyenne leaders met with agent Twiss at Fort Laramie. Reporting that they had regained control of the retaliatory "war parties of angry young men," the chiefs took diplomatic steps for the reestablishment of peace.[60]

In one of his final official acts as secretary of war, Jefferson Davis declared that "at the springing of the grass" in 1857 a campaign would be directed against the Cheyennes, who must be "severely punished. . . . No trifling or partial punishment will suffice."[61] By early June Colonel Edwin Sumner directed a force of four hundred cavalry and infantry on the South Platte. On July 29, at the Solomon Fork of the Kansas River, Sumner's forces routed three hundred Cheyennes. The number of Cheyennes killed by Sumner's troops was less than the Sioux death count at Ash Hollow. But the destruction by Sumner of the Cheyenne village on the Solomon, with all the Indians' possessions in equipment and buffalo food supply, was as complete as that perpetrated by Harney on the Sioux.

On the Great Plains the horror of total war predated the reapplication by Sherman of that military technique he had used in vanquishing the South. Further, and most important, the psychological defeat was devastating for the Indians, who were already impoverished and struggling for survival. They had been pressured into revolt; their rebellion of force, however, had been abruptly and thoroughly smashed. They realized all too deeply that they were powerless, their medicine inadequate and ineffective against the military powers of the Great Father, now used to achieve white supremacy.[62]

The pessimism of the Cheyennes spread rapidly through the villages of the less belligerent Arapahos. Now the Arapahos were also terrified of the white soldiers, as Margaret Coel reports, for they knew that "whites could not distinguish one Plains Indian tribe from another." The tribes met with their agent, R. C. Miller, at Pawnee Fork on the Arkansas in the summer of 1858. They met again in 1859 with agent Bent at his fort on the Arkansas and with Twiss on the North Platte. For a people starving and broken in spirit, these leaders requested a new treaty; they would yield the Great Plains and the co-existence promised by the commissioners at the Fort Laramie treaty.[63]

In that council of 1851 these Cheyennes and Arapahos had been officially recognized as holding title to the land between the North Platte and Arkansas rivers. However, starting in 1854, their eastern border had been broken by the divided and turbulent settlers of Kansas Territory. Their total life source—the buffalo hunting grounds across the central and western country of northern Kansas and southern Nebraska—had been seriously disrupted by the emigrant trails. Finally their winter homelands along the eastern slope of the Rockies had been taken over by the white gold seekers. Regarding this headwater area of the South Platte, the prediction made only five years earlier by their first agent, Fitzpatrick, had been realized:

> The topography of this region—sheltered valleys, mild temperature, large growths of timber, and an immense water power, may be numbered amongst its advantages. These, together with an abundance of small game, render it the favorite resort of the Indians [the Cheyennes and Arapahos] during the winter months, and enable them to subsist their animals in the severest seasons. Indications of mineral wealth likewise abound in the sands of the water courses, and the gorges and canons from which they issue; and should public attention ever be strongly directed to this section of our territory, and free access be obtained, the inducements which it holds out will soon people it with thousands of citizens, and cause it to rise speedily into a flourishing mountain State.[64]

After but a few years public attention had indeed been strongly directed to this part of the Indian country. Billington reports: "News of the [gold] discoveries, carried to the Mississippi Valley by travelers, found its way into Missouri newspapers in exaggerated form, for understatement was never a weakness of frontier editors. . . . By the end of June more than 100,000 'fifty-niners' were in the Pike's Peak country."[65]

It was one of the most flagrant and serious violations of the guarantees made to the Plains tribes by the Fort Laramie treaty. Further, it was an invasion specifically outlawed by the Organic Act of Kansas Territory in 1854. However, although it was a major depredation far exceeding any Indian attack on emigrant wagon trains, it occasioned no government condemnation. The War Department fielded no expeditionary force to punish and remove the invaders and thus maintain the promised peaceful coexistence. The Indian Office, with direct responsibility, filed no official complaint; rather, William Bent simply noted in his 1859 report that the gold miners had already taken over this choice Indian territory and noted "the many causes of irritation" experienced by the Arapahos and Cheyennes. Bent reported that game was scarce, and stated in summary fashion:

> A smothered passion for revenge agitates these Indians, perpetually fomented by the failure of food, the encircling encroachments of the white population, and the exasperating sense of decay and impending extinction with which they are surrounded. . . .
>
> These numerous and warlike Indians, pressed upon all around by the Texans, by the settlers of the gold region, by the advancing people of Kansas, and from the Platte, are already compressed into a small circle of territory, destitute of food, and itself bisected athwart by a constantly marching line of emigrants.[66]

The days of freedom for the southern Arapahos and Cheyennes were at an end. Their way of life, independence, and buffalo culture were being terminated. These were the first groups of the Native Americans of the Great Plains to experience the tragedy. Their grim fate had been inflicted within a decade of the great promises of the Fort Laramie treaty.[67]

In 1859, on September 19—almost the anniversary of their signing the treaty of 1851—over seventy Indian leaders met with Twiss at his Deer Creek post on the Upper Platte. In 1851 Chambers had reported the area as "Indian Territory"; now it had become "Nebraska Territory." The Arapaho chief Medicine Man spoke for his people and the assembled Sioux and Cheyennes:

> Our country for hunting game has become very small.
> We see the white man everywhere; their Rifles kill

some of the game, & the smoke of their Camp fires
scares the rest away, & we are no longer able to find
any game; our little children are crying for food.
. . . It is but a few years ago . . . the Buffalo were
plenty, & made the Prairie look black all around us.
Now, none are to be seen. . . . We wish to live.[68]

Some eight years later the members of the Great Peace Commission would vainly attempt to gather the leaders of these tribes once again at Fort Laramie. Their report declared: "Here civilization made its contract and guaranteed the rights of the weaker party. It did not stand by the guarantee. The treaty was broken, but not by the savage."[69]

Chapter Eight

De Smet's Prediction

A *"Sombre and*
Melancholy Future" (1852–59)

> As early as 1848 government officials were agitating
> for a corridor through Indian country to permit set-
> tlers access to the Far West. . . . But it meant that
> Indian country in the traditional sense of a barrier
> state was finished. It meant additional removals. And
> it meant, finally, that the generations of undisturbed
> peace promised the tribes in exchange for their east-
> ern lands — generations in which to work out their own
> destiny at their own pace — would be, in truth, a
> precious few years.
> — Brian W. Dippie, *The Vanishing American*

DE SMET'S JESUIT ASSIGNMENTS, 1847–57

Following his return to St. Louis from Fort Laramie in 1851, De Smet
directed his activities throughout the next six years to his twofold
assignments connected with Jesuit administration. His travels were
many, but he did not again head westward until 1858. Throughout the
period, however, he continued to serve the Indian missions as fund-
raiser and general supplier, and through his extensive correspondence and personal contacts he was kept well informed of "the new
order of things" being established across the Great Plains.[1]

De Smet maintained close ties with his family in Belgium,
rejecting the negativism of "religious detachment" even though it
was emphasized by the asceticism of the times. He commented:
"Surely the rule of St. Ignatius does not forbid us to love our own."[2]
Yet De Smet did not restrict his affection to his family. He cared
deeply for the tragic American Indians because he cared about and
readily related to his fellow humans. Although in some of his
writings he disclosed some of the sectarian religious prejudices of
his day, in his actual contacts with individuals De Smet established
friendships spontaneously.

The personal touch abounds in De Smet's correspondence, in his
official and his private letters. Almost always he concluded his
letters with greetings to be passed on to the recipients' loved ones, to

individuals whose company De Smet readily declared his remembered joy. If any single trait marked De Smet's character, it was his open friendliness. Certainly his remarkable success as a fund-raiser was connected with the warmth of his personality; the genuineness of the interest he expressed in individuals was beyond question.

The main purpose that marked De Smet's life was his abiding dedication to the Native Americans. He would remain an activist. Through the period between the Fort Laramie treaties of 1851 and 1868, his attention would be directed primarily to the temporal welfare of the Indians then being dispossessed of their homelands. Yet he maintained a balanced and realistic outlook. Filling an assigned leadership role among the Missouri Jesuits, he appreciated the importance of the religious apostolates in which they became involved, for in the quarter century following their arrival in St. Louis the activities of his religious brethren had also been affected by the "new order of things."

In a letter of late 1854 addressed to a relative in Belgium De Smet discussed the twofold administrative responsibilities he had been assigned:

> I am now in Ohio, now in Kentucky, sometimes in the extreme western part of the State of Missouri. Our colleges, residences and missions are very far apart, and I have to go with the Father Provincial [as his assistant] in all his visits. Though I have my head and hands always full of business, it is not of a nature to overburden me and I am always happy among my brothers. . . . There is one thing, however, that gives me anxiety from time to time. I hold the general or common purse and have to supply all the needs; and this purse is never full; the greater part of the time it is flat; while I receive demands from all sides, especially from our poor Indian missions. These poor Indians are always present to my thoughts. I frequently receive letters and very pressing invitations from them to return among them.[3]

As the assistant to the superior of the Missouri Jesuits, De Smet was a policy adviser on the selection of apostolic activities and the annual assignments of Jesuit personnel. Despite his personal dedication to the Indians' cause, De Smet was not narrow-minded. He came to regard commitment to the Indians as his particular and unique apostolate.

In 1855 De Smet offered a defense of the Jesuits' parish residences. These had increased in number since Van Quickenborne's initial religious administrations in 1824 about St. Charles, Portage des Sioux, and the other settlements along the Lower Missouri. De Smet's pragmatic argument was twofold: there was a pressing need for such pastoral services among the white settlers developing these river towns following the pressured withdrawal of the Indians; further, certain Jesuits were better suited by their personal talents and character to such ministrations. Not all Jesuits proved to have the qualities required for the successful teacher, and as De Smet had seen in the 1840s, not all Jesuit volunteers were endowed with the strengths and qualities to labor happily and effectively in the Indian missions.[4]

By 1856 St. Louis University had an enrollment of over three hundred students; the university, however, was only the *collegium maximum* of the Missouri Jesuits. As Garraghan reports, "All through the fifties and sixties overtures continued to be made for the [educational] services of the St. Louis Jesuits." The expansion that had begun, even in the 1840s, continued.

In 1848 they had opened St. Joseph's College in Bardstown and St. Aloysius School in Louisville. As early as 1840, under Bishop Purcell, the Athenaeum in Cincinnati had become the Jesuits' St. Francis Xavier College. Under De Smet's encouragement, in 1855 the Missouri Jesuits took over St. Gall's Parish in Milwaukee. The academy connected with it was the beginning of Marquette College. In the following year De Smet also conducted negotiations that initiated the Jesuits' Holy Family Parish in Chicago, along with the antecedents of St. Ignatius College. Expressing in 1856 his basic conviction and his contributing role, De Smet commented that the colleges "are no doubt necessary and one would have to create them if they did not exist."[5]

De Smet continued to fulfill his twofold assignment until 1862. Responsibilities connected with the position of assistant to the Missouri Jesuit superior were then taken over by another. However, at the insistence of the Roman superior De Smet was "retained as procurator and consultor in view of what he had already done and might be expected to do in the future to advance the temporal interests of the province." In this function De Smet did more than act as the treasurer and a fund-raiser; he also served, effectively, as a vocation director. His was a solicitation not only for financial contributions but for manpower. It was not until the final quarter of the nineteenth century that the United States ceased to be a missionary country. De Smet's effectiveness was noted in a 1861 report of his superior Father William Murphy: "In my opinion the Vice-Province owes to him almost all it has. What an excellent number of young men he has brought to us! Moreover he collects the money with which more or less they are supported and in discharging the duties of his office administers it with the utmost prudence."[6]

Europe, especially Belgium and Holland, which De Smet knew well, was still the best source for any gathering of men and means. In April 1853, along with Bishop Miége, who would be reporting to Rome, De Smet set out for New York by way of Washington. Later De Smet reported: "We shook hands with President Pierce and were kindly entertained by his Excellency. I was made bearer of dispatches to various Ministers in several of the great European capitals, by recommendation of Colonel Benton. . . . May 9th embarked on Steamer Fulton—Crossed the Atlantic (eighth time) in eleven days—landed at Havre."[7]

Their return journey, with some twelve new recruits, was made at the close of 1853. De Smet proudly noted that the four Jesuit brothers among that number were destined for the Indian missions. He repeated such a solicitation expedition from September 1856 through May 1857 and returned from Belgium with seven new candidates.

With their manpower increased, however, the fund-raising required for the Jesuit apostolates became even more demanding. De Smet reported in 1854 that the Missouri Jesuits "may be called pennyless, for we have about 40 Novices to support as well as some 16 Scholastics, all in their studies." The situation soon became even more critical. In late 1857 the conditions in St. Louis mirrored the national financial depression. In his letters of October 1857 De Smet noted some of the serious results: "The financial crisis here in St. Louis is dreadful; no money can be had. Banks are tottering—six have already failed—and falling in all directions. Thousands of people must be ruined. Business is here almost stagnant; manufactories are closing; building is stopped; a hundred steamers lie idle in the river."[8]

With his outgoing personality and his reputation enhanced by his exceptional and widely publicized experiences, De Smet achieved a notable success in his quest for men and means. Moreover, in October 1855 at the Second Provincial Council of St. Louis the members of the American hierarchy nominated De Smet for the position of vicar-apostolic of the newly established Nebraska Territory. In 1866 he would be nominated again for a similar ecclesiastical post in the Idaho-Montana Territory. However, as with his nomination for that office in Oregon in 1842, by means of his direct appeal letters to his Roman superior, De Smet was able to avoid such appointments.[9]

Along with the personal satisfaction arising from his achievements as procurator, De Smet was encouraged by an honor bestowed upon him by Jesuit headquarters in Rome. Garraghan reports: "On August 15, 1855, Father De Smet pronounced his final vows as a Jesuit, which were the solemn vows of the professed members. His studies did not entitle him to this grade in the Society, which was assigned to him by Father Beckx [the Roman superior] in view of the distinguished services he had rendered."[10]

De Smet's public role as a priest continued, but on a somewhat restricted basis. On March 16, 1852, he had received an unusual request from Senator Benton for his priestly services. From his St. Louis home Benton asked De Smet to visit his son Randolph, who was seriously ill; he had recently enrolled as an extern student at St. Louis University. Benton remained lastingly grateful to De Smet for his spiritual ministration that evening to the dying young man. In 1854 De Smet ministered to the sick mother of D. D. Mitchell and in the same period to the mother of Colonel Benjamin Bonneville.

De Smet's official function as the financial director of the Missouri Jesuits resulted in internal criticism during this period. With the religious mentality of the time, such criticisms by some of De Smet's fellow Jesuits might have been anticipated. His demands for prompt and complete financial accountability were not appreciated by some of his brethren. Serving as a middleman to handle the missionaries' requests for government subsidies to cover basic operational costs at the Indian missions, De Smet especially realized the need for financial records and supportive statements regarding expenditures. Few of his fellow Jesuits had marketplace experience; few, if any, had fundamental training in financial record keeping.

Further, among his more secluded religious brethren a twisted interpretation of religious indifference had emphasized a disinterest in and disregard for worldly goods. A personal disdain approaching deliberate negligence was almost classified as virtuous. In addition, the high reputation De Smet enjoyed among externs, those outside the cloistered living quarters of the Jesuit communities, could be traced to his having spent considerable time in their company. Among the Missouri Jesuits by midcentury a quasi-monastic lifestyle had become inculcated to some degree, and by then De Smet "had become a name for always roaming with a hungry heart." In "the new order of things" for his Jesuit brethren, by midcentury De Smet was a somewhat disturbing connection to the freedom and social concerns of the original Jesuit missionaries both in Missouri and previously in the Orient.[11]

In his official capacity, De Smet had made two visits in 1854 to the Jesuit colleges in Kentucky and Ohio. These visits were repeated in 1855, along with a double round trip to Chicago and Milwaukee. In early 1856 after checking again on the financial situation at St. Francis Xavier College in Cincinnati, he had continued east for meetings in Philadelphia, Baltimore, New York, and Washington. Visiting the Indian Office in the capital, De Smet had conferences regarding the Jesuits' Indian missions in the Kansas Territory with Secretary of the Interior Robert McClelland and Commissioner Manypenny.

De Smet found working for but separated from the Indians less than satisfying; his personal eagerness for a return to the West was increasing. In 1855 De Smet had been disappointed by his inability to accept the invitation to participate in another treaty council. His help had been requested again by the St. Louis superintendent of Indian affairs with the plan of extending the agreements of the Fort Laramie treaty especially to the Blackfeet on the Upper Missouri. It had been a shared disappointment, as De Smet learned from Father Adrian Hoecken's report on the October meetings held near the mouth of the Judith River: "The grand council took place in the vicinity of Fort Benton. Our Indians who were in great expectation of seeing you with Majors Cumming and Culbertson, were very much disappointed at not finding you. The Blackfeet . . . are very anxious to see you again, and to have missionaries among them."

Upon his return to his St. Louis post treaty commissioner Cumming had given De Smet a firsthand report on the council. It had been attended by the leaders of the Blackfeet, Crows, and Flatheads. Hoecken's letter concluded with the remark that "all the tribes of the upper waters of the Missouri . . . are anxious to have the Blackrobes permanently among them." Commenting upon the Indians' request, De Smet piously noted that "religious should, before all else, be children of obedience. It is the affair of our superiors." Privately, however, even as a religious bound to obedience, De Smet continued to be an activist. He could and did consider it proper to contribute to the enlightenment of his superiors in their determinations in this regard. De Smet would repeatedly take such a course of action.[12]

MAJOR DE SMET OF THE UTAH EXPEDITION

In 1858 De Smet made two trips into the Kansas and Nebraska territories. During the summer, as Major De Smet of the Army of Utah, he marched up the highway of the Plains past the forks of the Platte River. Earlier, in the midst of ice and snow, he had headed out to St. Mary's, the Jesuits' Potawatomi mission on the Kansas River. This had been a difficult journey in many aspects, marked by personal loss and sorrow as well as growing depression over the Indians' "sombre and melancholy future."[13]

De Smet received the first news of his personal loss on December 14, 1857. Captain John Mullan, on his way back to Washington following brief military service at Fort Leavenworth, had stopped to visit De Smet at St. Louis University. From 1853 to 1854 Mullan had directed a railroad surveying party under Governor Isaac Stevens in the Northwest. From the Jesuits still working in De Smet's former reductions and the Indians of the area Mullan had heard the praises of De Smet. Understandably, he was eager to meet the Blackrobe who had gained legendary status.

More pressing, however, was the tragic news that Mullan had to report. At Westport he had heard that Father Duerinck, superior of St. Mary's Mission, was believed to have drowned in the Missouri on his way to St. Louis. De Smet dispatched a letter on the following day to Miége at Leavenworth recounting the circumstances.

Captain Mullan's report was confirmed in the following days. On December 21 De Smet wrote to Duerinck's parents in Belgium informing them of the tragedy and expressing his deep sympathy. De Smet had lost a dedicated coworker who for eight years "had devoted himself body and soul to the well being of the Potawatomies, to whom he had been both father and friend." Further, De Smet had lost his only blood relative among the Missouri Jesuits. De Smet's final letter to Duerinck, written on October 21, 1857, had carried the salutation "Reverend and Dear Coz." Duerinck's aunt had been the first wife of De Smet's father.[14]

Reaching St. Mary's, in his meetings with the Indians De Smet found only reinforcement for a gloomy realism: "They have great need, especially at present, for the whites have surrounded them on all sides. . . . [They] are at the present day in imminent danger of being totally dispossessed by another people."

De Smet was beginning to express publicly the complaints of a dedicated activist:

If the poor and unfortunate inhabitants of the Indian Territory were treated with more justice and good faith, they would cause little trouble. They complain, and doubtless, justly, of the dishonesty of the whites. These banish them from their native soil. . . . But they are scarcely at ease in their new abode when they are removed a second and third time. With each successive emigration, they find their grounds restricted, their hunts and fishing places less abundant. . . . Is it therefore astonishing that the savages give the whites the name of forked tongues, or liars?

They are styled savages, but we may boldly assert that, in all our great cities, and everywhere, thousands of whites are more deserving of this title.[15]

The dates of De Smet's round trip from St. Louis by way of Leavenworth to St. Mary's Mission are uncertain; conflicting evidence is found in the reports. Regarding De Smet's reaction to still another personal loss at this time, there are no records. De Smet's papers of the period provide no reference to the death of Thomas Hart Benton. Four years after publishing *Thirty Years' View,* his personal history of representing western interests in the Congress, Benton had died in Washington on April 10, 1858; on the sixteenth the funeral services were held in St. Louis.[16]

Benton's final tribute to De Smet, his praise of De Smet's special relationship with the Indians, an encomium expressed in one of Benton's final speeches in Congress, may have influenced De Smet's growing concern for more direct and ongoing contacts with the Indians. De Smet's recent trip to the Kansas plains may have whetted his desire to return to a more active role, to an apostolate of working not only for but among the tribes. De Smet had become freshly aware of the desperate situation certain Indian groups were already experiencing; it was increasingly important that he become more directly involved. In an earlier letter De Smet had written to his friend Edwin T. Denig the Indian trader, he had expressed his self-image of a lasting relationship: "Tell Crazy Bear, the Three Bears and others that the old Black-robe thinks frequently of them, and begs daily of the Great Spirit to bless and protect all his Indian friends." On January 13, 1858, De Smet informed Denig: "If I can possibly do it I will take another trip to the plains and visit the various Indian tribes in the spring. I received invitations from various quarters to that effect. . . . I have been strongly invited to commence an establishment either among the Crows or the Blackfeet; this would greatly strengthen our missions among the Flatheads and Pend d'Oreilles."[17]

At the close of May 1857 De Smet had received a pointed request from Alfred J. Vaughan, who for fifteen years had been an Indian agent on the Missouri. Reporting that he had been appointed agent for the Blackfeet, Vaughan stated:

> The object of this letter is to obtain your intercession with your superiors for the formation of a mission among the Blackfeet. . . .
>
> You know that the Government's treaty with these Indians on Judith river in the Blackfoot territory makes ample provision for the support of the establishment by yearly money payments.[18]

Vaughan's letter reminded De Smet of the report he had received from Superintendent Cumming following the treaty council on the Upper Missouri in 1855. Further, Vaughan's invitation was forcefully endorsed by Cumming in July 1857; the St. Louis superintendent passed on Vaughan's proposal to the commissioner of Indian affairs.[19]

De Smet also heard from Lieutenant Mullan. After visiting De Smet at the close of 1857 in St. Louis, Mullan had reported to Stevens, who was then in the national capital serving as a delegate from Washington Territory. On May 26, 1858, Mullan wrote optimistically to De Smet: "I have seen the chairman of the Indian Committee and he says that all the Indian treaties made by Governor Stevens are to be confirmed, and that in the treaties the most ample provision has been made for schools, farms, utensils, etc. All of which, in the mountains, will be under the eye of the Jesuits."[20]

De Smet could now build new dreams. With the new political leaders of the Buchanan administration and the Thirty-fifth Congress, the Great Father would apparently direct a benign concern toward the various bands of the Blackfeet. Perhaps a Jesuit program could be started without De Smet's efforts at fund-raising; further, with government subsidies, the poverty limitations that had handicapped De Smet's earlier programs among the northwestern tribes might be eliminated. Along the eastern slope of the northern Rockies De Smet could plan new missions where the transitional needs of the safeguarded tribes would be provided.

In the context of such dreams, apparently well founded on such specific proposals, De Smet's importunings of his Jesuit superiors in St. Louis and Rome can be appreciated. As early as mid-1857 De Smet was asking the Jesuits for such a commitment, including his personal assignment. However, by March 16, 1858, De Smet was considering a change in his plans. Apparently he had been approached by military authorities regarding the possibility of his serving as a Catholic chaplain with the Utah Expedition. Even before any official appointment was received, the eager De Smet had pushed for and obtained the approval of his Missouri Jesuit superior. By early May De Smet reported the news to Bishop Miége:

> General Harney is now in St. Louis with General Smith. I paid him a visit at the Planter's House. He seems really in earnest in asking for a Catholic chaplain for the Utah army. He assured me that I will receive my commission within two or three days. . . .
> I was just preparing for my journey among the tribes of the upper Missouri. Both ends may perhaps be accomplished in this and the following year, should obedience allow me. . . .
>
> It is probable that I shall proceed from Utah to the Flathead Mission to confer with the Fathers about a new establishment among the Blackfeet. There are fair prospects to bring it about. The Government appears favorably disposed.[21]

On May 13 De Smet received formal notification: an invitation from Secretary of War John Floyd "to attend the army for Utah to officiate as chaplain." As anything more than a concession to Harney's request, the purpose of the War Department in requesting De Smet's participation was not specified. It is also not clear what purpose Harney had in mind in making the request. The interpretation expressed by some historians that he was to function as an interracial conciliator would seem only conjecture.[22] Perhaps the only certainty is that the adventuresome De Smet was pleased to be again, though briefly, heading out to the Great Plains.

On June 28, 1857, General Harney had been placed in charge of the government's military operation against the Mormons. "Indecision, incompetence, and competition for lucrative contracts" reportedly surrounded the preparations conducted at Fort Leavenworth. The participation of civilian teamsters, wagon masters, and suppliers was so extensive that the entire operation was critically labeled "the Contractors' War." The swollen expeditionary force of about five thousand men started westward from the Missouri in late July and August. Harney, however, had been replaced by Colonel Albert S. Johnston.[23]

Delayed by numerous causes, the government's forces were compelled to halt for the winter near the charred ruins of Fort Bridger in southwestern Wyoming. Alfred Cumming had been appointed on July 11 as Young's replacement as governor of the Utah Territory. Along with the other civilians newly assigned to the federal posts in Utah, Cumming arrived at the military encampment on November 19. Throughout the winter attempts at a nonviolent settlement were initiated. Along with Governor Cumming, two presidential "commissioners of reconciliation" entered Salt Lake City in June 1858. They immediately met in conferences with Brigham Young and the other Mormon leaders.

In late May De Smet had been welcomed to Fort Leavenworth by General Harney, now in command of an auxiliary force. Assigned to the Seventh Regiment under the command of Colonel Morrison, De Smet headed west on June 1. After a brief stop at Fort Kearney the expedition passed encampments of the Pawnees and thereafter the Oglala Sioux and Cheyennes. Among these tribes De Smet enjoyed the opportunities to renew friendships he had made during his initial trips of 1840 and 1841 and the great council at Horse Creek. De Smet also found repeated cause for commenting on "the new order of things":

> You may often remark also on the various camping grounds, even as far as the Rocky Mountains, and beyond, the wrecks of wagons and the skeletons of oxen, but especially the remains of the wardrobe of the travelers. . . . These deserted camps are also marked by packs of cards strewed round among broken jars and bottles; here you see a gridiron, a coffee-pot or a tin bowl; there a cooking-stove and the fragments of a shaving-dish, all worn out and cast aside.
>
> The poor Indians regard these signs of encroaching civilization with an unquiet eye as they pass them on their way. These rags and refuse are to them the harbingers of the approach of a dismal future for themselves; they announce to them that the plains and forests over which they roam . . . are about to pass into the hands of the rapacious white man: and they, poor mortals . . . will be enclosed in narrow reserves . . . or driven back into the mountains.[24]

The negotiations in Salt Lake City having proved effective, Governor Cumming on June 14 proclaimed that peace had been restored and announced a general pardon. At Camp Floyd, some thirty miles west of the city, the army maintained a garrison of about three thousand men through 1859. Burns points out that "as late as March, 1859, and again in August, a real Mormon war was barely averted." Harney's forces had reached the forks of the Platte before they received their new orders. In late June they marched back to Fort Leavenworth.[25]

There had been a deeper lesson for De Smet in that summer of 1858. From his close contact with the military might of the United States and with his increased political awareness, De Smet's basic conviction had been notably reinforced: despite all provocations, the reactions of the Indians must be stopped short of armed rebellion. De Smet would continue as an activist, but this, in a realistic manner, was appreciative of the tribes' developing dependence upon the Great Father.

Fearful now that "the total destruction and ruin of the tribes" would be a swift consequence of any armed rebellion, De Smet would insist that all resistance be nonviolent. For the rest of his life the pragmatic De Smet would advise the Indians that survival was to be preferred to annihilation, for the cries of survival carried the potential for future justice. Hereafter De Smet's stand would repeat the counsel he had forwarded to his Indian friends of the Northwest in 1857:

> I know the case of the Indians is a hard one indeed. Many injustices and cruelties are committed against them; in many instances they are deprived of their just rights. But war, on their part can be no remedy in their favor, as the whole Indian history of this country fully shows. I daily beseech at the altar of God His holy protection over them — to guard them against bad counsellors and advisors who may drag them along in wars against the whites. For these will end, at last, in the total destruction and ruin of the unhappy warring tribes.[26]

BLACKROBE GATHERS THE CHIEFS OF THE NORTHWEST
In September 1858, to De Smet's surprise and great satisfaction, he was able to present that specific message in person to some of his favorite Indian tribes. With a ready justification, De Smet had delayed his return from the Plains to the drudgery of the official Jesuit assignments at his desk in St. Louis: "I made a little excursion of seventy miles to visit our dear fathers and brothers of the Mission of St. Mary among the Potawatomies."[27]

The letter that De Smet found on his desk at St. Louis University presented a providential proposal. Harney, ordered to report to the War Department in Washington, had paused in St. Louis long enough to formulate another invitation for De Smet. De Smet must have been thrilled to read the letter, a proposal to join the general in another even more distant and important campaign:

> From the announcement in the newspapers, the general is under the impression he is to be placed on service in Oregon, and in such an event, there is no one whose aid could be more valuable than your own, in the capacity of your profession.
>
> The general proposes, therefore, that you continue your commission with the army and accompany him to Oregon in case he is sent, due notice of which he will telegraph to you on his arrival in Washington.[28]

Both Harney and De Smet must have appreciated the distinctive reputations they had established in Indian affairs. Doubtless the general and his chaplain had exchanged recountings of their personal experiences, perhaps around the evening campfires on their recent journey along the Platte. Through the subsequent decade, either as an army chaplain or as a special Indian agent, De Smet would be closely associated with military leaders in the West. De Smet would grow in his realization of the pressures, the conflicting demands, and the personal moral dilemma experienced by these officers. In turn there would be the developing influence of the attitudes and loving convictions expressed by De Smet. That influence would vary. With Harney—and with Sully and Stanley, much more than with Sherman—De Smet's abiding concern for fair treatment of the Indians would be shared.

On September 7 De Smet received telegraphed orders from the secretary of war: report at once to Harney in New York "for the purpose of accompanying that officer to the department of the Pacific." De Smet's report, his enthusiasm only somewhat concealed, expressed his objective in taking on the assignment: "After ascertaining that it was agreeable to my superiors, I consented to retain my position of army chaplain in the new army. I hoped to be of some service in that capacity to the men, but above all to the Indian tribes of the mountains; I desired greatly also to be in touch with my missionary brethren in the difficulties which the war would doubtless bring upon them."[29]

In discussing the causes of the war in the Pacific Northwest, De

Smet pointed to the Indians' fears that the treaties negotiated by Governor Stevens would not protect their lands from the invasion of white settlers:

> Nine tribes . . . formerly so peaceable . . . had become very uneasy over the frequent incursions made by the whites upon the southern and western portions of the Territories of Washington and Oregon. From uneasiness, they had soon passed to displeasure and anger, when they saw these adventurers taking possession of the most advantageous sites and settling as owners upon the most fertile parts of the country, in total contempt of their rights and without the slightest preliminary agreement.
>
> The mountain tribes had become especially stirred up, and had resolved to drive back the whites, or at least to make resistance to their progressive encroachments. . . . Their first blow was a complete victory for them . . . for they had not only driven off the enemy [the forces of Colonel Steptoe, on May 17], but had besides captured his train and provisions. . . . Intoxicated with their first success, the Indians thought themselves invincible and able to meet the whole United States army.[30]

General Harney, accompanied by De Smet and other staff members, departed New York on the steamer *Star of the West* on September 20. On the twenty-ninth, by a three-hour railroad ride, they crossed the Isthmus of Panama. On October 2 they sailed from Panama escorted by 1,300 fellow passengers, most of whom were headed for the California gold fields. Arriving at San Francisco on the sixteenth, De Smet headquartered at the new Jesuit residence while he made a three-day tour of the rapidly growing city. More important, Harney, conferring there with General Newman Clarke whose northwestern command he was taking over, learned that the Indian rebellion had already been quelled.[31]

Having departed San Francisco on October 20, their ship turned into the mouth of the Columbia on the twenty-third. As they steamed inland for about a hundred miles, De Smet may have pointed out all the settlements that had developed along the banks of the river since his first voyage up the Columbia in August 1844. Landing at Fort Vancouver on the twenty-fourth, the general took command of the Department of the Pacific. De Smet reported at once upon his altered purpose:

The savages, formerly so numerous along the coast and the river, have almost entirely disappeared. Every approach of the whites thrusts them back, by force or otherwise; they go upon reservations, in a strange land, far removed from their hunting and fishing grounds, and where drink, misery and diseases of every sort mow them down by hundreds.

The news of the cessation of hostilities against the United States and the submission of the Indians had been received at Fort Vancouver. The savages, however, still retained their prejudices and an uneasiness and alarm which had to be dissipated, and there were false reports to be rectified. Otherwise the war might soon break out afresh.[32]

De Smet had been understandably eager to return to the Northwest. Over a decade had passed since his departure from the high country, the elevated areas of the western and eastern slopes of the Bitterroot Range. De Smet remembered that even in November the winter snows would restrict travel. He was anxious to live again not within the confines of Fort Vancouver but among the Coeur d'Alenes and the poor abandoned Flatheads.

The restless chaplain wasted little time proposing to Harney that he be allowed to spend the winter at the Coeur d'Alene mission. On October 28 Harney's permission was readily forthcoming, the general expecting that De Smet's presence among the mountain tribes would prove beneficial. As a missionary, De Smet had been forced to scrimp and beg to make his journeys; as a chaplain, he had all the material advantages of being sent on a military mission. Special Orders No. 4, issued by General Harney's adjutant, stated: "Officers commending posts and stations in route are directed to furnish the reverend father with every facility and means for prosecuting his journey securely, and in an expeditious manner. Orders will, therefore, be given to provide such guides, interpreters, escorts and animals to Father De Smet as will attain the object of this order."[33]

Within twenty-four hours the eager De Smet had set out. On November 1 he spent the evening visiting Catholic soldiers at the fort at Dalles City. The next day De Smet began the second leg of his journey in an army ambulance. Passing the mouths of the Deschutes, John Day, and Umatilla rivers, he turned away from the Columbia to ride eastward up the Walla Walla Valley. On the tenth he arrived at Fort Walla Walla:

I visited the Catholic soldiers at Fort Walla Walla. At this post I had the great consolation of meeting the Reverend Father Congiato [Jesuit superior] returning from his visit to the missions. . . . I also met here several Coeur d'Alène and Spokan families. They were prisoners, or rather hostages, from the war. . . . I learned with pleasure that all of them, and especially the Coeur d'Alènes, had managed during their capacity to gain the good will of the officers and soldiers of the fort, by exemplary and Christian-like conduct. . . . The commandant of the fort felt very kindly toward them. He accepted with much benevolence the proposition I made him, to take them with me into their own country. . . . He even issued orders to provide them abundantly with provisions for the journey. This condescension on his part will never be forgotten by the Indians. . . . Whatever their detractors may say, Indians know how to appreciate a kind act and to be grateful for a favor received.[34]

With the freed Indian hostages acting as his guides, De Smet headed north on the thirteenth. Having covered fifty miles, on the fifteenth they reached the Traverse, the crossing of the Snake River. There, near the small newly built Fort Taylor, they stayed in a large encampment of the Palouse tribe. Meeting that evening with a large group hungry for news, De Smet reported that though these Indians had "been the principal instigators of the warfare on the whites," they were "very attentive" to his advice and religious instruction.

For a few more days the good weather held, so that De Smet's party was able to make "three long days' journeys in the plains." On the evening of the eighteenth they arrived at another Indian encampment, a number of lodges of the Coeur d'Alene tribe, located on the western shore of the great Coeur d'Alene lake. It was a night of rejoicing. De Smet reported that he was received "with the liveliest cordiality"; further, "the unexpected return of the hostages heightened the universal joy."[35]

The weather, however, had turned to a mixture of snow and rain, De Smet reporting that his tent was partially under water. Even though another Jesuit missionary, Father Gazzoli, had come across the lake with a small party to escort De Smet on the final forty miles to Sacred Heart Mission, they were not to reach their destination until November 21. Thereafter De Smet recorded some forty-three days and nights of snow; the weather detained him at the mission until February 18, 1859. Meeting with the other Jesuit missionaries stationed at Sacred Heart—his old companions Father Joset, Father Vercruysse, and Brother Huysbrecht—De Smet received "a great deal of news, some consoling and some sad, concerning the country and the Indians." De Smet reported: "As the day of invasion by the whites approaches, the mind of the poor Indian becomes uneasy, gloomy and apprehensive. The idea of having presently to leave the place where repose the ashes of his fathers and of all those he has loved, and his hunting and fishing grounds, throws him into a state of entire hopelessness, which is the worse because it is irremediable and irresistible. The Indian sees nothing ahead of him but a dark and sombre future."[36]

Certainly it was less than the complete gospel that the returning De Smet was able to present to the Coeur d'Alenes in that winter of 1858–59. He could offer no guarantee of worldly justice to these Indians, no promise of beneficial returns to be gained from a reciprocal practice of the Second Commandment by the white newcomers. However, at this period of special holy-day celebrations De Smet could still be positive as a religious leader; he could focus the attention and the emotions of the Indians on the gift of faith that they had and would continue to receive, the self-gift of love from Father Above. Later De Smet reported: "On the day of the great feast of Christmas, I sang the midnight mass. All the Indians, men, women and children, intoned together the Vivat Jesus, the Gloria, the Credo and several canticles composed in their own tongue. . . . It recalled to me those meetings or *agapés* of the first times of Christianity, when, as says Saint Paul, the great apostle of the Gentiles, all had 'one heart and one soul.' "

Obviously it was for De Smet the thrilling reenactment of one of the most enriching experiences of his life—his 1844 Christmas celebration with the Pend d'Oreilles at the opening of St. Ignatius Reduction. De Smet had made the comparison to the shared celebrations of the primitive Christians even then as he tried to express "those pleasurable feelings, that overflowing of the heart." Again the 1858 ceremonies of divine worship shared by De Smet and the Coeur d'Alenes became two-dimensional: as participants in celebrating God's Fatherhood, professedly they were happily united as children.

De Smet admitted: "Such a scene is not forgotten, but remains among one's recollections as one of the happiest of his life." Moreover, "these happy results abundantly repay the Lord's workmen." Their shared ceremonies had served as emphatic declarations of essential human relationships, and these inspiring memories would serve as the natural support system to offset the missionaries' separation from their families and their native land.[37]

Before he departed from Fort Vancouver, De Smet had been instructed to "communicate freely" with headquarters. Obviously Harney was concerned about the tribes of the mountains and wished to be informed of their attitudes toward the whites and the government. Specific directions had been issued to the assistant quartermaster at Fort Walla Walla to cover the expenses of any express sent to that post by De Smet.

De Smet had dispatched his first field report in early December. Relayed through Walla Walla, the message reached the general at Fort Vancouver by the end of the month. Regarding the attitude of the tribes, De Smet merely confirmed the appraisal that Congiato and Ravalli had offered. However, his report did contain a new proposition—to bring a delegation of chiefs from the mountain tribes down to Vancouver to meet with Harney. The general readily approved the proposal, suggesting that the trip be made "as early in the spring as practicable."[38]

Waiting for Harney's reply, De Smet visited at the Indian camps along the Clark Fork trail. Down along the Bitterroot River and south of Flathead Lake the Blackrobe held conferences with groups of the Flathead Confederation. To all he had spread the same message: armed rebellion would lead only to ruin.

On April 16 De Smet set out from St. Ignatius Mission. Accompanying him on the journey to Fort Vancouver were nine chiefs, leaders of the mountain tribes: Gerry of the Spokanes; Kamiakin of the Yakimas; Andrew and Bonaventure of the Coeur d'Alenes; Dennis Thunder-Robe of the Kettles; Adolph Red Feather and Iroquois Francis of the Flatheads; Victor Happy-Man of the Kalispels; and Alexander of the Pend-d'Oreilles. The chiefs, working with De Smet, held a lengthy conference with General Harney. Later De Smet reported that the interview "produced most happy results on both sides." Following the meeting, De Smet escorted the chiefs to Salem for a visit with the Indian superintendent. At the directive of government officials De Smet then conducted the Indian leaders on an extended tour of the white establishments.[39]

Before directing the tour of the chiefs, De Smet had been requested by Harney to provide an official report on upper Washington

Territory. Perhaps the two men had already discussed the obvious problem connected with the system of small separated reserves then laid out in the Washington and Oregon territories. The Indian leaders believed, and De Smet concurred, that these scattered areas assigned to the various tribes, "surrounded and accessible on all sides by the whites," would soon lead to the destruction of the natives. Now De Smet recommended the establishment of a single northern Indian reservation. Harney promptly forwarded De Smet's recommendation to the general in chief with his endorsement: "The plan . . . places the Indians in a country abounding with game and fish, with sufficient arable land to encourage them in its gradual cultivation. . . . It would be well for us to . . . adopt the wise and humane suggestion of Father De Smet."[40]

THE RETURN TO ST. LOUIS BY THE UPPER MISSOURI

On June 15 De Smet departed Fort Vancouver with the chiefs on their return to their homelands. Convinced that he had presented his message—seeking justice by nonviolent means—as effectively as possible to the mountain tribes, De Smet felt that it was time to return to his duties in St. Louis. He pointed out to Harney that if he returned across the plains on horseback, he would be able to spread his message of nonviolence to the tribes of the interior. By Special Order No. 59, Harney authorized the return journey:

> On your arrival in St. Louis, the general desires you to report by letter to the adjutant-general at Washington, when your relations with the military service will cease. . . .
>
> By the campaign of last summer submission had been conquered, but the embittered feelings of the two races, excited by war, still existed, and it remained for you to supply that which was wanting to the sword. It was necessary to exercise the strong faith which the red man possessed in your purity and holiness of character. . . . This has been done; the victory is yours, and the general will take great pleasure in recording your services at the War Department.[41]

De Smet reached Sacred Heart Mission among the Coeur d'Alenes on July 7. Accompanied by Father Congiato, De Smet spent the next week riding across the Bitterroot Range so that he might spend a few days among the Flatheads at St. Ignatius Mission. On July 22, directed by Indian guides, the two Jesuits began the two-hundred-mile ride east to Fort Benton. On the twenty-sixth they crossed the continental divide and headed down the drainage of the Sun River to its mouth near the Great Falls of the Missouri; here they met their fellow Jesuits Father Hoecken and Brother Magri. On the twenty-ninth they arrived at Fort Benton. In the previous year, west of the fort, Hoecken had started a mission among the Blackfeet, St. Peter's, initially located on the Teton River. Thus Father Point's work among the Blackfeet had at last been revived.[42]

At Fort Benton De Smet had to change his plans. He had been provided with a string of six horses and had intended "to go all the way to St. Louis on horseback, in the hope of meeting a large number of Indian tribes." De Smet reported later to Harney that on his arrival at Fort Benton, his horses having given out, he had a small boat constructed and hired three young men to accompany him downriver. He visited the Assiniboines at Fort Union on August 16, the Hidatsas and Mandans at Fort Berthold on the twenty-second. At Fort Berthold De Smet was the guest of Henry A. Boller, a fellow passenger on the steamer *Twilight* during De Smet's 1858 voyage from St. Louis to Fort Leavenworth. Regarding De Smet's stay at Berthold, Boller reported:

> In the fall the Reverend Father De Smet, the celebrated Apostle of the Indians, arrived from the Blackfeet in a small boat. . . . Father De Smet is universally revered by all the Indian nations, and known far and wide. Among the rude mountaineers he commands the utmost respect. . . . The whole of a long life has been devoted to the welfare of the Indians, and they have no truer or abler advocate.
>
> Father De Smet remained with us over night and baptized five or six half-breeds, children of some of the retainers of the post, as well as a number of Indian children in the Four Bears' lodge.[43]

By August 24 De Smet had arrived at Fort Clarke, where he visited among the Arikaras. Arriving at Fort Pierre on September 1, he met with Sioux bands encamped in the area. On the ninth he stopped for a few hours at Fort Randall, taking lunch with the commandant, Colonel Munroe. Concluding his narrative, De Smet reported: "On the 16th I arrived in Omaha City, where I left my little skiff and went on board the steamer Thom. E. Tudd. We landed, at last, safe and sound, on the 23rd of September, in the harbor of St. Louis."[44]

As he had been directed, De Smet forwarded his letter of resignation to the secretary of war on September 29. On November 9 Lieutenant Pleasanton, Harney's adjutant, sent De Smet a final letter from Fort Vancouver:

> We all miss you so much; I have not met an officer of your acquaintance who has not expressed great regret at your departure, and we all feel indebted to you for the good understanding that exists between the poor Indians and the whites at this time. . . . The general desires me to express his warmest remembrances of the good offices you accomplished for his command and he assures you of his highest esteem and friendship always.[45]

Chapter Nine
"The Unhappy Indians . . . Driven to Desperation" (1861–65)

> The Indian, in truth, has no longer a country. His lands are everywhere pervaded by white men; his means of subsistence destroyed, and the homes of his tribe violently taken from him; himself and his family reduced to starvation, or to the necessity of warring to the death upon the white man, whose inevitable and destructive progress threatens the total extermination of his race.
>
> —General John Pope,
> *War of the Rebellion,* August 1, 1865

THE EARLY 1860s: A Nation Engaged in Civil War

In late September 1860 De Smet departed St. Louis on his sixth voyage to Europe. Again his purpose was to solicit men and means in the principal cities of Belgium and Holland. At the close of March 1861 he began his return journey "with rather a heavy heart," for he had learned of the national disunity proclaimed on February 8 at Montgomery, Alabama. Later he wrote:

> On the night of the 14th–15th April we arrived in New York—a dismal night, I shall never forget.
>
> A few hours previous to the arrival of the Fulton the great American Metropolis had been thrown in the greatest excitement and consternation, by the sad tidings, that Fort Sumter, in South Carolina, had been taken by the rebels & that . . . the Stars and Stripes . . . had been battered down by the enemy of the Union—once Union men themselves. . . . I am not a man for war & am averse to its horrors and bloodshed. . . . There is no Peace! I left New York on the 17th & reached St. Louis on the 19th. . . . On the long stretch of over a thousand miles, nothing but the clang of arms was heard & the war-cry repeated in every city, town & hamlet.[1]

Through the years of the Civil War De Smet found various reasons for visiting the national capital. After meeting with officials in the

Indian Office on July 21, 1861, De Smet reported that he could "hear distinctly the cannons from Bull's Run." In February 1862 he returned to Washington for a very practical purpose: the financial situation of the Jesuits' Indian missions in Kansas had become very serious. De Smet succeeded in obtaining some of the delinquent government subsidies. He reported: "I had the honor of being presented to our President, Lincoln, and I talked with him for over an hour."

In August 1862, following his return to St. Louis from Fort Benton, De Smet set off for another official tour of eastern cities. Once more attending conferences with Washington officials, De Smet reported that on September 17 "I heard the roar of the cannons at the battle of Antietam."[2]

By the close of 1863 De Smet had other reasons for repeated visits to Washington. From 1864 through 1869, under four consecutive commissioners of Indian affairs, De Smet served as a special agent for the Indian Office. In addition to reports filed from the Upper Missouri, De Smet personally presented his findings in Washington. Further, in view of his public recognition and his influence on political leaders at the national level as well as in the Midwest De Smet was repeatedly called upon by his pressured religious superiors to represent the Jesuit cause. In 1860 and again in 1864, 1868, and 1871 the Missouri superior assigned De Smet to undertake European journeys to recruit men and raise money. Before De Smet's assignment in the fall of 1868, Superior Coosemans reported to Rome: "After all, when there is question of recruiting for the novitiate, it is Father De Smet who has always succeeded best in obtaining good subjects and numbers of them, as also money for the Province and missions."[3]

Not only on such basics as manpower and funding but other practical matters the Missouri Jesuits found further cause to acknowledge an indebtedness to De Smet. At the close of the 1860s Coosemans openly stated that "many a disagreeable situation" during the Civil War had been avoided by the Missouri Jesuits, in large part because of De Smet's influence with the government.

For example, the Missouri military draft law was applicable to all male citizens, even clergymen, between the ages of eighteen and forty-five. In 1862, "owing, it would seem, to representations made by De Smet [that bearing arms was incompatible with their ecclesiastical status], the Jesuits resident in Missouri were granted exemption from the operation of the law." Superior Murphy later

informed the Roman authorities that "a single visit and petition on
the part of this excellent Father [De Smet] was enough to secure in
writing and by name the exemption."[4]

In 1865 De Smet's connections and influence were again called
upon. Under the leadership of political radicals a new Missouri
constitution had been adopted in June that required a test oath from
all voters, public officials, teachers, clergymen, lawyers, jurors, and
trustees of church property. The principal condition of this "Drake
Oath," a condition widely regarded as "a gross violation of religious
liberty," was that the individual had never sympathized with or aided
the South. De Smet inveighed against any implementation of the
legislation; however, the administration of the test oath proved a
prolonged problem. Not until January 1867 was De Smet able to
announce a victory: "Five judges out of nine pronounced against the
execrable test-oath; so to-day we can preach the Lord's gospel
without being exposed to fines or imprisonment."

Garraghan points out that all the Jesuit superiors under whom De
Smet lived expressed their gratitude for the services he rendered his
religious brethren. All acknowledged that by the early 1860s he had
gained a unique position of influence in secular, especially governmental, circles. Further, all the Jesuit authorities realized that the
cause for De Smet's influence in Washington was his unique status
and function as Blackrobe, the spiritual leader remarkably revered
by the tribes of the Great Plains.[5]

By the 1860s, then, De Smet had become a political activist. His
fellow Jesuits on the other hand had adjusted to a quasi monasticism;
they tended to exclude themselves from public affairs. De Smet's
Indian-related activities became exceptional. In the final quarter of
the century the Missouri Jesuits, preoccupied with the educational
apostolate, no longer conducted regular missions among the Native
Americans of the Great Plains.

From 1862 through 1864 De Smet spent most of the summer
months among the tribes of the Upper Missouri. Then in the fall of
1864, after a visit to Washington, he set off from New York on his
seventh business trip to Europe. He had returned from Rome to
Belgium before learning of the surrender of General Lee on April 12
at Appomattox. Arriving in New York on June 19, 1865, De Smet
expressed his wish for his adopted country:

> I learned with consolation that the sad and unhappy
> American War was drawing to a close . . . and that
> law and order . . . seemed to be returning . . . in the

States where secession had caused so many misfortunes and ruin. . . . Today, no one in the South seems to think any longer of undertakings hostile to the Government. The majority of the Southerners ask nothing but a fair change and the means of lifting themselves up once more. A true policy must tend to assure a solid peace and durable prosperity.[6]

THE TRAGEDY OF SIOUX LEADERS—CHIEF BEAR'S RIB

Returning from his January meetings with President Lincoln and the officials of the Indian Office, De Smet finalized his plans for the summer. On February 12 he wrote to his brother Francis: "In all probability I shall go and spend the summer among the numerous Indian tribes of the Great Desert east of the Rocky Mountains. They beg me urgently to come and see them."[7]

De Smet had obtained the approval of his Jesuit superior for the trip and had received some important practical contributions. General Harney had presented him with a tent. De Smet's former pupil Charles P. Chouteau, who had replaced his father as head of the American Fur Company, had offered him free passage on the *Spread Eagle*. In fact, a small chapel for De Smet's use was to be prepared aboard the side-wheeler for the run up to Fort Benton.

The year 1862 was marked by renewed competition for the fur trade and supplying transportation on the Upper Missouri. Captain Joseph La Barge, another of De Smet's friends, was attempting to break the power of Chouteau's organization by joining with associates in St. Louis to establish the firm of La Barge, Harkness and Company. As in previous years, however, the American Fur Company had obtained the contract to deliver the Indian annuity goods to the tribes along the river north of Council Bluffs.

In 1860 the Missouri had become the river road to Fort Benton, the eastern gateway to Montana, and as Chittenden states, the winter of 1861–62 marked the beginning of large-scale gold mining in Montana. In a letter of May 4, 1862, to the Belgian ambassador, De Smet reported: "A great number of passengers are going up on the same boat, and on several others, bound for Fort Benton on the Upper Missouri." De Smet predicted that the notorious racial injustices that had recently been perpetrated in California would be repeated in the northern Rockies.[8]

Although the number of passengers departing St. Louis for Fort Benton in the spring of 1862 did not reach De Smet's prediction, they were sufficient to load four steamers. La Barge's smaller boat, the light-draft *Shreveport*, departed on April 30, listing "seventy-five cabin and a 'goodly number' of deck passengers." On the firm's larger steamer, the *Emilie*, there were some eighty-five cabin passengers and fifty-three "deckers." The *Emilie*, fastest of the Missouri River steamers, did not set out from the St. Louis levee until May 14; among the passengers were the wives and children of the directors of La Barge, Harkness and Company.[9]

Two of the passengers aboard the *Spread Eagle* were responsible for exceptional amounts of freight. The recently appointed Indian agent for the Upper Missouri, Samuel N. Latta, had a large quantity of annuity goods. Following the loss of the *Chippewa* the previous June, the Assiniboines and Crows had not received their yearly payments as pledged by the Fort Laramie treaty. Moreover, De Smet, had presumed upon Chouteau's charity by requisitioning additional storage space. On May 6 De Smet had received a letter of request from the Jesuit missionaries serving the Blackfeet west of Fort Benton. With an immediate loan of $1,500 and Chouteau's promise of free transportation, De Smet was able to purchase the items.[10]

Among the passengers on the *Spread Eagle* at St. Joseph were the ethnologist Lewis Henry Morgan, and the newly assigned agent for the Blackfeet, Rev. Henry W. Reed. Reed had been directed by Secretary of the Interior Caleb B. Smith to take Morgan with him as a member of his party. In his journal of this voyage Morgan incorporated various comments on tribal practices as reported by De Smet. Striking up an immediate friendship, Morgan recorded a brief description of De Smet: "a noble looking man, about 61 years old, a most delightful gentleman."

The *Spread Eagle* passed the mouth of the Niobrara on May 22 and tied up at the Yankton Agency, where a large quantity of goods was unloaded for the Yankton Sioux. In some of his previous journal entries Morgan criticized various Indian agents for their malpractices, pointing out the injustices inflicted upon the Pawnees, the Iowas, and the Kickapoos. Morgan recorded criticisms against Walter A. Burleigh, appointed by the Lincoln administration as agent to the Yanktons. Historians agree with Morgan's criticism, describing Burleigh as "one of the most effective agents at enriching himself at the expense of the Indians."[11]

On May 23 the *Spread Eagle* tied up at Fort Randall to unload goods due the Ponca tribe. This was the last military post on the river, for all the other posts east of the mountains belonged to the fur companies. On May 27 the steamer halted a few miles north of the mouth of Bad River. Here, near the site of the old Fort Pierre, Chouteau directed the unloading of a considerable portion of the annuities. The boxes of Indian goods were stacked in seven separate piles, intended for distribution among the Sioux bands.

Several hundred Sioux arrived, and their chiefs, together with their "Frenchman" interpreter, approached Chouteau, whom they recognized from meetings in previous years. Seated alongside Chouteau was their new agent, Samuel Latta. The Indians had come not to receive presents but to air grievances. The chiefs accused Chouteau and his company of having cheated their people "for a long time" and refused to accept their annuities. They explained clearly and precisely that pressures from their tribe impelled them to cancel the peace pledges that had been made at Fort Laramie in 1851 and Fort Pierre in 1856. Condemning the Great Father's failure to keep his promises as expressed by Commissioner Mitchell and later by General Harney, they served formal notice that friendly relations with the government were being terminated.[12]

The memories of Harney's vindictive power and the fears caused by his strong threats in 1856 had faded. Further, the support Mitchell had promised to Frightening Bear in 1851 and the assistance Harney had pledged to Bear's Rib and the other "paper chiefs" he had designated at the start of 1856 had never materialized.

By the summer of 1862 these tensions had increased. Sioux discontent had grown as the power exercised for so many years on the Upper Missouri by the American Fur Company had weakened. In the presence of De Smet and all the other passengers aboard the *Spread Eagle* Chouteau heard his company publicly criticized by Indian leaders. Chouteau had lost the services of Charles Galpin, who with all his expertise and the influence of his Sioux connections was now working for "the opposition" headed by Captain La Barge. Further, Chouteau's long domination of the agents assigned by the Indian Office to the tribes of the Upper Missouri had lessened. Vaughan had been replaced by Latta, who before the end of this summer would file serious charges against the American Fur Company's illegal trade in whiskey. Moreover, these accusations would be emphatically repeated by two other new agents, Henry Reed and Mahlon Wilkinson.[13]

At the end of August Latta reported the angry speeches made at Fort Pierre by the disappointed chiefs:

> They requested me to bring no more goods under the
> Laramie treaty, nor would they receive those present.

> The same views were expressed by all the speakers, but after a long parley "Bear's Rib," a chief of the Sioux nation appointed by General Harney, a brave and good man, rose and said . . . that for years he had relied upon the promises made by General Harney and former agents to send him assistance, and yet none had come; that if he received those presents sent his people by his Great Father, he not only endangered his own life but the lives of all present; yet he loved his Great Father and would this once more receive for his people the goods present, but closed by requesting me to bring no more unless they could have assistance.

With small appreciation of the depth of the Indians' hostility, the white listeners readily dismissed the apprehensions voiced by Bear's Rib. Morgan flatly rejected the threat publicized by Bear's Rib as "mere pretence."[14]

By June 9 the *Spread Eagle* had tied up at Fort Union. However, the main camps of both the Assiniboines and the Crows had not yet come for their annual trading, and Latta faced the difficulties of storing the annuities until their arrival. Latta reminded the Indian Office that as long as the Indian agents were completely dependent on the American Fur Company for transportation, shelter, interpreters, and all other needs, "the agent cannot feel free to correct every wrong that he sees." That dependence was such that in distributing the annuities the Indian agent, and consequently the Great Father he represented, was all but identified with the American Fur Company, which Latta characterized as "the most corrupt institution ever tolerated in our country." He declared: "They have involved the government in their speculation and schemes; they have enslaved the Indians, kept them in ignorance; taken from them year after year their pitiful earnings, in robes and furs, without giving them an equivalent; discouraged them in agriculture by telling them that should the white man find that their country would produce they would come in and take their lands from them." The gravity of these charges can hardly be exaggerated. Morgan wrote that even if only one-quarter of the charges against the evils of the annuity system and the complicity of the American Fur Company in cheating the Indians was true, "it is time the whole system was overturned and reformed."[15]

In the afternoon of the twentieth the *Spread Eagle* arrived at Fort Benton. Morgan noted that there were "about 70 men, women, and children" living within the 250-feet-square quadrangle of the fort, while pitched around the outside were some sixty Blackfeet tents. On Sunday, June 22, De Smet conducted religious services at the fort.[16]

On June 21, two days after the departure of the *Emilie*, Chouteau's *Key West* also headed downriver. The following afternoon the *Spread Eagle* departed with "approximately 20 crewmen and some 30 passengers." Only the *Shreveport* remained at Fort Benton. In a most unusual omission, none of the written accounts record that De Smet jumped ship. Apparently Chouteau understood that his missionary guest could be expected to make at least a brief visit to the Jesuits' St. Peter's Blackfeet Mission, located a short distance to the west of the Great Falls. Seemingly, La Barge's generosity matched that of Chouteau, and room was to be made for De Smet on the *Shreveport*, which was not scheduled to leave Fort Benton until noon on Sunday, July 6.

On June 28, Harkness noted in his journal, the ceremonies marking the beginning of the construction of Fort La Barge took place. On the thirtieth Harkness reported that a party was made up to visit the Great Falls, led by De Smet and Mrs. Culbertson.[17]

Instead of returning to Fort Benton with the group, De Smet headed westward. It was about a dozen miles from the Great Falls to the mouth of the Sun River. Near that confluence Father Adrian Hoecken, De Smet's early coworker in the Northwest, had in 1858 renewed the Jesuits' missionary activities among the Blackfeet. De Smet later reported: "I offered the holy sacrifice of the Mass among them, by way of thanksgiving. An Indian choir, composed of men and women, young men and girls, chanted the litanies of the Holy Virgin and songs to the glory of God. Everything was sung in the language of the country."[18]

On Sunday, July 6, the *Shreveport* headed downriver. After a week of rapid travel down the Missouri the steamer tied up at Fort Pierre. De Smet had intended to spend three months with the Sioux but was forced to postpone his visit until the next spring because of the tragic news he received there: "On my arrival at Fort Pierre I learned that the Bear's-rib, the great chief appointed by General Harney over all the Sioux bands, had been murdered by his own people, because he had accepted the annual presents sent by the government."[19]

Two weeks before De Smet's arrival at Fort Pierre the *Spread Eagle* had tied up below the post. Two of its passengers also noted their reactions to the grim news. Agent Latta pointed out that Bear's Rib had been assaulted and killed "within the gates of Fort Pierre" by a Sioux band opposed to any intercourse with the government. Latta praised Bear's Rib: "This was a true man, the best friend the white man had in the Sioux nation," a tribute that echoed the praise of Frightening Bear, the Sioux chief slain in the Grattan affair of 1854. In his journal Morgan pointed out the mounting tragedy of the Plains Indians. A conflict of interest was developing among the Indians as a result of their increasing dependence on manufactured goods. "They [the Sioux], in common with the Assiniboins, Minnetares, Crows, and Blackfeet, hate the whites and say they would clear their country of them to a man if the white man had not become necessary to them. They want his guns, powder, and ball, coffee, blankets, and camp furniture, which have now become indispensable, and they therefore submit to his presence among them."[20]

Below Fort Pierre the downriver passages of the steamboats were uneventful. De Smet disembarked at Fort Leavenworth. Since his planned visit among the Sioux of the Upper Missouri had been canceled, he headed west for a brief visit with the Potawatomis at St. Mary's Mission. By August he had returned to St. Louis, and within the month his Jesuit responsibilities took him to several cities in the East. When De Smet arrived at the Indian Office in Washington, he was informed that Commissioner Dole was out of the city. On September 5 he met with Charles Mix, acting commissioner of Indian affairs, and following his directive wrote a brief statement regarding the situation on the Upper Missouri. After completing his business, De Smet returned to St. Louis.[21]

It had been a summer of greater personal achievements than De Smet may have realized. His unique status had been reaffirmed by the increasingly disturbed tribes of the Plains, and because of his publicized activities there was renewed appreciation of his exceptional power by the officials of the Indian Office. These administrators of government Indian policy had entered a highly critical period. From the beginning of the Lincoln administration, even in the context of the Civil War, they were aware that the problems of the Indian Office had multiplied.

Following the withdrawal of the southern constituents, Congress declared Kansas a "free state" at the close of January 1861. The Confederacy, however, had begun soliciting the Indian tribes along the lower Kansas border to supply armed troops for the rebellion. From the Northwest, William Rector, superintendent of Indian affairs in Oregon, filed criticisms of the Indian service. His report of June 1862 "read like a catalog of all the corrupt practices ever conceived by Indian Agents." In the Dakota Territory, accusations of fraud had been directed against the prominent Indian agent at

Yankton, Dr. Walter A. Burleigh, whose alleged crimes "involved high government officials." As Nichols comments, "Wherever Commissioner Dole looked, he found incredible examples of agent fraud." And in the newly admitted state of Minnesota, fraud in handling Indian affairs had finally resulted in armed rebellion. By mid-August the grim predictions expressed since the start of 1860 by Episcopal bishop Henry Whipple had been realized. On August 21 a telegram from Minnesota governor Alexander Ramsey informed the secretary of war: "The Sioux Indians on our western border have risen, and are murdering men, women, and children."[22]

TRAGEDY OF SIOUX LEADERS — CHIEF LITTLE CROW

By the treaties with the Minnesota Sioux in 1851—at Traverse des Sioux on July 25 and Mendota on August 5—the leaders of the four bands of the eastern Sioux, the Santees, were pressured into yielding over twenty million acres of "the finest land in the world." Through what has been characterized as "a monstrous conspiracy" the Santees had signed both the treaty documents and the claims papers of the traders. By such formalized agreements they were stripped of their homelands and the supposed monetary recompense. Regarding the government's representatives—treaty commissioners Luke Lea, commissioner of Indian affairs, and Alexander Ramsey, governor of Minnesota and ex-officio superintendent of Indian affairs—and the procedures utilized by these officials in conducting the negotiations, historian Roy Meyer comments: "It was a thoroughly sordid affair, equal in infamy to anything else in the long history of injustice perpetrated upon the Indians by the authorized representatives of the United States."[23]

It should be noted that Lea's attitudes and actions as treaty negotiator were in line with the prejudices he exhibited as commissioner of Indian affairs. One of the most important reforms initiated by his predecessor, William Medill, had been an updating of the 1834 Trade and Intercourse legislation. In 1847 Medill had secured regulations for distribution of the annuities that would eliminate the injustices perpetrated by the traders. Lea, however, in his general conduct as commissioner of Indian affairs and his dictatorial manner in negotiating these treaties, reversed the reform stand that Medill had taken. As historian Trennert reports, "The payment of annuity funds directly to traders crept back into general practice." This defeat of Medill's reforms was one of the most serious failures in the operation of the Indian Office. As Trennert concludes, "Private economic interests still controlled many aspects of national Indian policy, and the only reforms possible were those that did not threaten influential whites."[24]

Moreover, the 1851 treaties had proved a perpetual source of dissatisfaction. In June 1858 the Santee leaders were gathered in Washington, secluded from the disturbing pressures of their angry young men, to make a satisfactory "readjustment" of the 1851 treaties. All too readily trusting their benign Great Father, they signed this 1858 treaty as it had been prepared in Washington. In less than a year following their return to Minnesota the Indians learned that although they had yielded title to another million acres of land, the renewed claims of the traders had again canceled almost all the annuity payments to tribal members.[25]

Certainly other factors also influenced the fatal announcement voiced by the Santee chief Little Crow late on the night of August 17, 1862. Though the Santees had lost their entire corn crop in the summer of 1861, their agent, Thomas Galbraith, in mid-July 1862 ignored the demands for food of some five thousand hungry demonstrators. Galbraith designated Indian insolence and racial inferiority as the causes of the rebellion.

On August 17 a group of Indian leaders awakened the members of Chief Little Crow's household. The alarmed leaders wanted to discuss the report that four young Santees returning from Acton Township, a short distance to the northeast, had killed five white settlers there. As reported by Wowinapa, Little Crow's son, the chief's reaction was an angry denunciation of the actions of the irresponsible youths. Working as a farmer for some time, Little Crow had attempted to adapt to changing circumstances. That August morning he had participated in the Episcopal services at the agency chapel. But in their meeting late that evening Little Crow and most of the other leaders supposed that the entire tribe would be blamed for the slayings. Concluding that peace had already been irretrievably lost, the Santee leaders decided to attack the Lower Agency the following morning.

The armed rebellion, and slaughter of the Santee forces, was brief. By October 9 General Pope, appointed by President Lincoln to suppress the rebellion, reported: "The Sioux War may be considered at end." Over 300 Santee prisoners, many of whom had surrendered, were condemned by Henry H. Sibley's military court to be hanged. Through Lincoln's intervention the number was reduced to 39. Their execution was carried out on December 26. By congressional fiat on

February 16, 1863, the Santee Sioux were dispossessed of all land titles and treaty rights. On March 4 they were banished from Minnesota. On May 4 and 5 the last of the Santees, more than 1,300, were deported, shipped by steamboats and barges from Mankato.

The catastrophe of the Winnebagos, even more notable victims of the new settlers' prejudice and land hunger, followed almost immediately. Nichols reports that although the Winnebagos were not involved in the revolt, their lands adjacent to those of the Santees had proven attractive to the newcomers. Governor Ramsey applied the penalty of banishment to the Winnebagos of Minnesota. Ramsey's explanation to the Washington authorities highlighted the injustice: "It is enough to say the Winnebagoes are Indians."[26]

Despite his many travels De Smet had never visited the homelands of the Santees. But these eastern Sioux had not been neglected by religious leaders. In 1859 Henry B. Whipple was consecrated Episcopal bishop of Minnesota. From his headquarters at Faribault Bishop Whipple began an active crusade to right the wrongs suffered by the Indians of his territory. His missionary priests carried out over a quarter century of dedicated labors for the natives of Minnesota. But Whipple's greatest achievement was the publicity campaign that he directed for recognition of human rights. With candor and cynicism, Secretary of War Edwin Stanton had responded to Whipple: "What does Bishop Whipple want? If he has come here [the capital] to tell us of the corruption of our Indian system and the dishonesty of Indian agents, tell him that we know it. But the Government never reforms an evil until the people demand it. Tell him that when he reaches the heart of the American people, the Indians will be saved."[27]

As early as the fall of 1862 Whipple had begun to reach the hearts of some very prominent and powerful people. At the general convention of the Episcopal church in the United States, Whipple won endorsement for his call for basic reform in Indian affairs. On November 26 President Lincoln was presented with a formal petition signed by nineteen bishops and twenty other Episcopal leaders. Charging that "the history of our country's dealings with the Indians had been marked by gross acts of injustice and robbery," the paper attributed the Santee rebellion to the mismanagement through political corruption of a sadly defective Indian system.

A public stand had been taken, perhaps for the first time by a church group, criticizing the government's treatment of Indians. Moreover, this action was taken by the most influential religious group of the day. Whipple's voice had swelled into a chorus insisting upon three specific reforms: depoliticize the Indian service, thus eliminating the ill effects of the spoils system; establish procedures that would provide an alternative to the treaty process; and appoint a commission of "men of high character, who have no political ends to subserve, to . . . devise a more perfect system for the administration of Indian affairs."[28]

On December 12, 1862, De Smet forwarded to the Indian Office a recommendation concerning the condemned Santees awaiting execution in prison at Mankato. Having heard from Charles Galpin that an escaped party of six hundred Santee warriors with many white captives were camped one hundred miles north of Fort Pierre, De Smet presented a realistic proposal: "I fear that cruel and savage vengeance will be taken on the innocent and unhappy white people as yet under their [the Santees'] control. If I were allowed to express an opinion, I would say: Let the Sioux prisoners be kept as hostages; let it be known to the whole nation that, for every white man they kill, one of the prisoners will atone for the murder."[29]

Whipple had been encouraged by the determination expressed by the president's declaration: "If we get through this war, and I live, *this Indian system shall be reformed!*" In his annual messages at the close of 1862, 1863, and 1864 Lincoln reemphasized the urgency of legislation to remodel the system for the welfare of the Indians. The attention of Lewis Henry Morgan was called to Lincoln's declaration at the close of 1862. On the basis of his extensive field experiences Morgan notified the president: "I have no hesitation in saying that the present system is a total failure, a failure so complete as to be a disgrace to the government. Its defects are principally in the agency and annuity systems; and the remedy must be found in reorganizing both, and remodeling the Indian Bureau itself."[30]

THE DE SMET REDUCTIONS TWENTY YEARS LATER

At the start of 1863 De Smet was eager to depart St. Louis for the Upper Missouri. Jesuit officials had requested De Smet to assist two Jesuit brothers newly arrived in the United States from Italy. These Jesuits had been assigned to the St. Joseph Indian Mission serving the Blackfeet in their homelands west of Fort Benton. De Smet would serve as their guide, and he planned to visit the nomadic tribes of the plains during his return trip.[31]

Following the rebellion of the Santee Sioux, the situation along the central section of the Upper Missouri was highly unsettled. Indeed,

De Smet's travel plan seems to have been rather optimistic. At the start of 1863, however, even such realists as Charles Chouteau and Joseph La Barge were planning voyages up the Missouri to their posts at Fort Benton and Fort La Barge. These businessmen had good cause to agree with the prediction of agent Latta that a large number of emigrants would be heading in late spring for the gold fields of Washington Territory by way of the Upper Missouri.

Charles Chouteau provided De Smet and the Jesuit brothers with "the most commodious stateroom" and space for a chapel aboard the steamer *Alone*. In addition to their free passage, De Smet was permitted to bring aboard an exceptional amount of freight without transportation charge. On May 9 the *Alone* and the *Nellie Rogers*, the other steamboat chartered by the American Fur Company, departed St. Louis. Their difficult voyages to the Upper Missouri, as Sunder notes, were similar to "the trouble-filled trips of the *Shreveport* and *Robert Campbell*" (the steamboats used by Joseph La Barge). In contrast to the previous year 1863 proved to be a low-water year on the Missouri: none of the steamboats from St. Louis managed to reach Fort Benton.[32]

By June 29, because of reduced water depth in the river channel, Chouteau's steamboats were halted about 150 miles downstream from Cow Island. De Smet reported:

> The water was so low that the captain found himself under the hard necessity of putting all his ninety passengers and all his cargo (200 tons) ashore in the forest that covers the mouth of Milk river, 300 miles distant from his destination, Fort Benton. . . . Every passenger chose a spot for himself in the forest and bestowed himself as best he could. General Harney had made me a present of his big camp tent before I left St. Louis; I had my little chapel, my little kitchen, the necessary bedding and provisions, and in less than an hour, with the help of the two brothers, we were properly established, under the shade of some big cottonwoods.[33]

During the month's encampment on the bank of the Missouri only one serious incident took place. On "the 4th of July, as the camp was making ready to celebrate the great day of American Independence," a large party of hostile Sioux attacked. The attack, however, was halted almost before it began. The Sioux leader, the son of Chief Red Fish of the Oglalas, recognized De Smet as the "Blackgown" who had saved his sister. In De Smet's judgment it was a truly providential event; following an hour's conference, the Indian war party departed westward across the Plains.[34]

On July 30 a long train of wagons arrived at the camp. Finally the passengers and the freight from the steamboats could be hauled up to Fort Benton. Among the wagons was, as De Smet reported, "a comfortable conveyance for the journey," sent by "the good Fathers" of the Blackfeet Mission of St. Peter. After some sixteen days of rough travel the cavalcade arrived at Fort Benton. There De Smet happily presented the two Jesuit brothers to Father Imoda, who had come to the post from the mission located to the west of the Great Falls. The Jesuit group, De Smet wrote, "tarried here for several days." There was need for a rest, and De Smet wished to offer some religious instructions to groups of interested Crows encamped in the area. Moreover, De Smet needed time to review his plans.

In the foreseeable future the potential for a safe return down the Missouri was slight. Captain La Barge reported that the *Robert Campbell,* as it proceeded north from Fort Pierre, had been under constant attack from hostile Sioux bands. No southbound passage by steamboat could be anticipated until the following summer, and even then there was no guarantee. At Fort Benton De Smet reported his decision:

> I had thus far fulfilled the wishes of my superiors; I had brought the two Italian Brothers to the first Rocky Mountain Mission. My own principal object was a missionary visit to the wandering tribes of the plains; this I had accomplished only in part. . . . The contagion of this war had spread to the upper tribes of the Sioux, who had hitherto been at peace with the whites. The reports that reached us every day . . . caused me to take the resolution of returning to St. Louis by the Pacific Ocean. This is not only the safest route, but the most prompt . . . by way of the Isthmus of Panama and Aspinwall.[35]

It was also an occasion for De Smet to express his thoughts regarding the condition of the Indians, especially the Sioux. Even before his departure from St. Louis he had complained about the situation that had led in the previous year to the Santee revolt in Minnesota: "The unhappy Indians are often wronged, insulted and outraged beyond measure by the whites, and there is no recourse open to them for the obtaining of justice. Driven to desperation, they dig up the war hatchet and utter the cry of vengeance against the palefaces."[36]

St. Peter's, the Jesuit Blackfeet mission, was located off the north bank of the Missouri slightly upstream from the Great Falls and west of the mouth of Sun River, not far from the Blackfeet Agency. After a brief stay, De Smet headed west on August 25, traveling along the new military road connecting Fort Walla Walla with Fort Benton. This road was the work of Captain John Mullan, who spent seven years "exploring and opening a road of six hundred and twenty-four miles from the Columbia to the Missouri River." In the early pages of his report, printed in early 1863, Mullan expressed his appreciation of the Jesuit missions among the Coeur d'Alene, Pend d'Oreille, and Blackfeet, and added a specific tribute to De Smet: "The country and the Indians are mainly indebted to the zealous labors of the Reverend Father De Smet in establishing all these missions, for he truly is the great father of all Rocky Mountain missionaries. By his travels and labors, and the dedication of his years to this noble task, he has left a name in the mountains revered by all who knew him, and a household god with every Indian who respects the black gown."[37]

In 1841 the members of the original Jesuit missionary group had walked along the bank of the Hell Gate River. In 1863 De Smet camped once more near the opening through which the river tumbled into the beautiful valley and was joined by the Bitterroot River, flowing south to northwest. Here, near this natural landmark named Hell Gate (located near present Missoula, Montana), De Smet could contemplate the past and the present situation of the Jesuit missionary activities for the Indians of the area.[38]

Looking south up the river that in 1841 he had named St. Mary's, De Smet could recall the beginning of the first reduction, St. Mary's on the Bitterroot. Looking west and north, he could remember the rapid growth and development of his plan for a Native American Christian empire, an Indian republic to be based upon a fresh presentation of the gospel message — the gospel adapted and accommodated to the culture of the Native Americans rather than the European-style Christianity of the emigrants. Briefly De Smet had shared the vision of his models, earlier Jesuits from Spain and Portugal who had labored with and for the Indians of Paraguay.

Throughout the early 1840s De Smet's attempt to implement the reduction program among the bands of the Flathead confederacy had been a wonderful dream he had shared with the natives. Then this mountain country had been so remote and so secluded that without hesitation De Smet had assured his religious superiors in St. Louis and Europe that a record commitment of manpower and funds would be justified, that the investment would prove richly rewarding. The changes had been so abrupt, however, that by the mid-1840s De Smet realized that even in this high country the essential elements of privacy and seclusion no longer existed.

The harsh realities of 1863 demanded an adaptation not of the gospel message but the Indian recipients. As Burns starkly comments, time had run out in the Oregon country. Left with no other alternative to extermination, these people had to be hurried toward assimilation. Because Indians could continue to live only as non-Indians, the mission would have slight concern about fashioning an Indian Catholicism; rather, it would present the gospel according to the standardized Euro-American context. As in earlier periods of European colonization in the Western Hemisphere, efforts at Christianizing and civilizing once again merged. Once again the Cross would be a tool of the Crown.[39]

One day in early September De Smet's camp at Hell Gate was suddenly surrounded by a large number of visitors. Led by Father Giorda, the Jesuit superior, a large delegation of Flatheads and Pend d'Oreilles had come down from St. Ignatius Mission, south of Flathead Lake, en route to one of their final crossings of Mullan Pass, for they were "going 'to buffalo,' east of the mountains." For De Smet, it was a bittersweet reunion. All seemed to realize that the Indians' traditional way of life was quickly being terminated. Later De Smet reported his final celebration with these friends: "On the morrow I celebrated, *sub dio,* the most holy sacrifice of the mass, and addressed them some consoling words concerning religion and the joy with which this fortunate meeting inspired me. All the neophytes surrounded the humble altar, made of willows and poles, and chanted in chorus the praises of the Lord."[40]

With the breakup of the camp at Hell Gate, De Smet faced a short and easy journey north to St. Ignatius Mission. After spending three days there, De Smet departed on September 8, heading westward up to Sohon Pass "at the summit of the Coeur D'Alene Mountains." Recalling the spectacular view that he had enjoyed from this overlook in 1846, De Smet reported later:

> Toward sunset we reached the top, where we pitched
> our camp within a few paces of one of those immense
> snow masses that perpetually shroud this lofty chain.
> Here we enjoyed a most magnificent view — the hori-

zon for some hundred miles around presented a spec-
tacle of surpassing grandeur: as far as the eye could
reach, a long succession of mountains, towering cliffs
and lofty pinnacles, exhibited their dazzling snow-
capped summits to our astonished vision.[41]

On September 18 De Smet arrived for a five-day stay at Sacred
Heart Mission, the center of Jesuit activities for the Coeur d'Alene
tribe, who were gathered just to the northeast of beautiful Lake
Coeur d'Alene. Here De Smet reported recent evidence of the
Indians' most serious problem: "They are unceasingly threatened
with loss of their lovely fertile lands." In expressing his concern, De
Smet referred to the argument stated in Mullan's official report:
"When the whites take possession of the lands of the Indians, [they
either] push them farther back into the wilderness or . . . exterminate them."[42]

De Smet set out from Sacred Heart Mission on September 23,
heading southwest across the high plains. On October 1 he reached
the western terminus of the Mullan Road and reported the rapid
growth of the old army post: "Walla Walla City . . . barely a town of
yesterday, but already . . . over 2,000 inhabitants, with all the signs
of civilization in full swing." For at least two of the most recently
arrived inhabitants, De Smet's visit to Walla Walla must have
provided special satisfaction. It had been only in August that Captain
Mullan, recently married and retired from the army, had taken up
residence near Walla Walla. De Smet's reports fail to mention it, but
on the first Sunday of October 1863 "church services were held in the
small parlor of the Mullan's farmhouse, with De Smet officiating at
the Mass."[43]

By the evening of October 8 De Smet reached the old British post
of Fort Vancouver, which he had first visited in 1842. In Vancouver
and Portland, on the south bank of the Columbia, De Smet received a
special welcome.

On October 13 De Smet sailed from Portland. Arriving in San
Francisco on October 21, he was welcomed as a guest at the Jesuits'
St. Ignatius College. Here De Smet enjoyed a brief reunion with one
of his former coworkers in the Northwest reductions, Father Alois
Vercruysse. Vercruysse noted in a subsequent letter to a friend in
Belgium that De Smet's chin "was ornated with a gray venerable
beard." This is consistent with the dating ("circa 1863") on the
photos of De Smet with a beard taken by Gustavus Sohon during the
brief period he operated a gallery in San Francisco.[44]

De Smet departed San Francisco on November 3, the steamer landing at Panama on the seventeenth. After crossing the isthmus by rail, De Smet embarked from Aspinwall on the eighteenth aboard the *North Star.* The ship "reached the good harbor of New York, on the 26th of November, Thanksgiving Day by proclamation of the President of the United States." Within an hour De Smet was expressing his thanksgiving among his Jesuit brethren at St. Francis Xavier College.[45]

Learning that Father Coosemans, his Jesuit superior from Missouri, was expected for a brief official visit, De Smet decided to await his arrival and to make the return journey to St. Louis in his company. For the first time since 1848, De Smet was now informed by Coosemans, his administrative responsibilities would be limited to financial matters. Duties connected with the position of assistant to the Missouri provincial had been assigned to another. Their affairs in New York settled, Coosemans and De Smet set out on December 9, arriving in St. Louis on the seventeenth.[46]

THE 1864 ALTERNATIVES—DIPLOMACY OR WAR

Just one week before De Smet disembarked from the *North Star* in the New York harbor, President Lincoln had hurriedly returned to Washington from southern Pennsylvania where on November 19 he had delivered his dedication address at the Gettysburg cemetery. On this visit to the capital De Smet had a lengthy meeting with Commissioner William P. Dole, who requested him to serve in early 1864 on "a proposed mission of Peace and friendly offices to the disaffected Sioux of the Upper Missouri." Realistically, Dole recognized De Smet's exceptional influence on tribal leaders; as Athearn notes, "Dole felt that no western man was better qualified for the mission." De Smet's renown could enhance the reputation of the Indian Office, which was suffering mounting criticism.

With the start of 1864 General Pope, supported by General-in-Chief Halleck and others, was publicly denouncing Indian policy in general as "a woeful failure."[47] Pope was to continue his declared war on the Indian Office throughout the next twenty years. Other critics, like Bishop Whipple, continued to call for basic changes in government Indian policy. Pope, however, was not concerned with theoretical questions of rights and land titles; he insisted upon the solution of military domination.[48]

At the close of 1863, following an absence of some eight months, De Smet returned to his office at St. Louis University. As the province treasurer, he advised the Jesuit superior that he "found the ledger and day-book gaping and calling for a closing." As a weary traveler, he confided to his close friend and physician Moses Linton that any celebration of his sixty-third birthday on January 30 would have to be restricted. It was understandably difficult for De Smet, the rugged though part-time outdoorsman, to acknowledge his increasing physical limitations. It was equally difficult for De Smet the priest to be nonpriestly. In mid-March De Smet frankly reported: "Like a regular old man, I am full of infirmities. . . . I can seldom leave my room and go out of the house. For some time past my greatest privation is to be unable even to celebrate holy mass."[49]

Further, it was difficult for De Smet to predict how the Indians would react to the new role he was contemplating. His positive response to Dole's request had seemed quite proper in Washington. Having returned to the Midwest, however, he was having second thoughts. His correspondence through that late winter reveals uncertainty and worry, an anguishing over the possible negative reactions by the Indians. For years he had treasured his acceptance by the tribes, and he was eager not to compromise his reputation or jeopardize his credibility among them. In a report to his Jesuit superior at the close of March De Smet noted his concerns:

> I have been requested by the Commissioner of the Indian Department at Washington, to undertake the journey and to bring about, if possible, a peace among the hostile Sioux, acting in concert with the general of the troops and the appointed agents. . . . I fear I would lose all caste among the Indians. They have hitherto looked upon me as the bearer to them of the word of the Great Spirit and have universally been kind and attentive on all occasions and wherever I have met them. Should I present myself in their midst as the bearer of the word of the Big Chief of the Big Knives in Washington, no longer their Great Father but now their greatest and bitterest enemy, it would place me in rather an awkward situation. I have written to the Commissioner that if I can go, I will go on my own hook, without pay or remuneration; visit the friendly Sioux first, and in their company try to penetrate among their fighting brethren and do my utmost to preach peace and good will to them, and to make them come to a good understanding with the

general in command and the agents of the Government.[50]

The Indians' reaction to De Smet through the following four months was entirely positive, as it continued to be throughout the following four years of De Smet's heightened political activity. The tribes rejoiced in his visits to their encampments, attentively receiving and eagerly following his advice. A deeply religious people, they expected the Blackrobe to be concerned for their good and to offer them proper counsel regarding their future.

In his March 28 letter of acceptance to Commissioner Dole De Smet requested "a written Document which might serve me as a Passport," one that would provide him the assistance of all government agents in Indian country. Dole mailed such an endorsement to De Smet on April 2.[51]

Apparently Commissioner Dole also handled the paperwork integrating De Smet's mission with the activities of the Indian agents and the operations of the military. In his letter to De Smet on March 21 Dole repeated his wish for "the utmost harmony of action as far as possible" between the Indian Office and the War Department, and between special agent De Smet and the regular Indian agents. The following day Dole sent copies of his De Smet letter to General Sully and agent Samuel Latta, who had been reassigned as agent for the Upper Missouri Sioux bands. To both the military and civilian officials Dole stressed the importance of cooperation and unity.

There is no evidence, however, that Dole tried to inform the other Upper Missouri Indian agents, especially the novice field worker Mahlon Wilkinson, of De Smet's special assignment. This communication failure would shortly lead Wilkinson to report his criticisms of De Smet for "holding Indian councils along the river during the summer without notifying proper authorities." Wilkinson was also unaware that Dole had assigned De Smet to the supervision of Charles Chouteau. In addition to providing all transportation services, Chouteau had been authorized by the commissioner to furnish whatever funds De Smet might need for such expenses as interpreters and messengers. By the end of August the inexperienced and uninformed Wilkinson had filed yet another misconstruction to the Dakota superintendent of Indian affairs: "The Jesuit priest was a good simple minded old man but completely under his [Chouteau's] control." In fact, what appeared to be Chouteau's influence over De Smet reflected the power the American Fur Company had long exercised in activities supposedly directed by the Indian Office.[52]

One of the most serious problems affecting Indian-white relations on the Great Plains related to the distribution of annuities. It was a problem that abruptly arose as a tangled consequence of the land-acquisition treaties of the 1850s. Therein the government obtained title to vast areas of land; thereby the government assumed the obligation to provide compensation according to treaty specifications. By further agreement since living conditions would be drastically altered for the affected tribes, this compensation (generally specified to be made in "Indian goods") was to be distributed in annual payments. Following congressional ratification of such a treaty, distribution of the designated "annuities" became the responsibility, in justice, of the field officials of the Indian Office. Chittenden concluded that the tribes of the Upper Missouri received no more than half the annuity payments due to them. "The annuity system," he declared, "probably gave rise to more abuses than any other one thing in the conduct of Indian affairs." Reporting to General Pope, Sully noted that "this system of issuing annuities is one grand humbug."[53]

De Smet had spent previous summers visiting Indian encampments along the banks of the Missouri. Regarding the sufferings caused by the failures in annuity distribution, De Smet spoke out before his 1864 departure from St. Louis:

> The unhappy war which is now raging so fiercely over all the extent of the Great Desert, east of the Rocky Mountains, has, like so many other Indian wars, been provoked by numerous injustices and misdeeds on the part of the whites, and even of agents of the Government. For years and years they have deceived the Indians with impunity in the sale of their holdings of land, and afterward by the embezzlement, or rather the open theft, of immense sums paid them by the Government in exchange therefor.[54]

The sorry fact is that despite the ready promises given by negotiators Mitchell and Fitzpatrick in 1851; Manypenny in 1853–54; Cumming and Stevens in 1855; Carson, Bent, and agent Jesse Leavenworth in 1865, the Indian Office made no plans and took no steps to develop the capability of fulfilling such commitments. There continued to be general disregard for the 1834 directive specifying on-site residence for each tribal agent, who "shall not depart from the limits of his agency without permission." There continued to be no organized procedures for distribution of the annuities. Agents on the

Upper Missouri, for example, were without means of transportation, and no structures for the storage of their annuities and supplies had been provided, despite the 1847 legislation that specified, "Superintendents, Agents, and Sub-Agents shall be furnished with offices for the transaction of the public business, and the Agents and Sub-Agents with houses for their residence."[55]

That such basic failures in services continued throughout the 1860s can be documented from the comments of various travelers. The complaints of Lewis Henry Morgan in 1862 were repeated by De Smet in 1866 and again in 1867. Further, such complaints were expressed in the annual reports of the agents themselves. In 1853 Alfred Vaughan, serving on the Upper Missouri, requested that "an appropriation be made for erecting an agency building." Apparently Vaughan was not aware of the 1847 Trade and Intercourse legislation. In their annual reports for 1864 the agents on the Upper Missouri presented specific and distinct complaints. Recommending that the Upper Missouri Agency be located at the mouth of the Yellowstone, separate from any trading establishment, agent Wilkinson requested the construction of "a building suitable for an agent to live in." Calling for the establishment of agency quarters at Fort Berthold, special agent Reed complained, "There are insuperable difficulties thrown in his [the agent's] way, and will be, no doubt, till he is able to be independent of traders and all their influence." Agent Upson, assigned to the Blackfeet at Fort Benton, commented that "no agent should be left dependent on a 'trading post' for an office or storehouse for Indian goods."[56]

The distribution of annuities was a basic failure, prolonged and extensive. Officials of higher rank continued to disregard their responsibilities for such fundamental implementation of the law. The frequent excuse "beyond government control" cannot be applied here; the specific means to exercise control had been legislated by Congress. It was not the selfishness of the fur traders but the neglectful failure of Indian Office officials that perpetrated the most prolonged and serious violation of the Trade and Intercourse legislation. Further, such unjust practices were tolerated through a congressional lack of remedial supervision.

Leaving St. Louis by train on April 20, De Smet hoped to overtake the steamer *Yellowstone* at St. Joseph, Missouri. However, because of "a heavy rise of the river and a good moon," the new steamboat had passed north of that river town before De Smet's arrival. It required a hard ride by carriage from Fort Leavenworth to Omaha for De Smet to overtake the *Yellowstone*. Charles Chouteau welcomed his former teacher aboard on April 28, and once again De Smet was provided with a small chapel.

Although travel conditions were such that the *Yellowstone* had made good time during the initial portion of the voyage, the opposite was the case following the steamer's departure northward from Omaha. Throughout the next twenty days repeated and prolonged delays were caused by low water. These delays provided De Smet with opportunities to visit the Winnebagos. Following military removal from their Minnesota homelands in early 1863, they had been relocated on the Crow Creek Reservation on the Missouri about eighty miles north of Fort Randall. Having found that area unsuited for growing crops, the exiles had escaped downriver to the Omaha reservation in Nebraska. De Smet met them as squatters living on remote islands and secluded sections along the Missouri. His protests against "the barbarous conduct toward the Winnabagoes" were repeated by others. Even personnel of the Indian Office, field agents and higher officials, commented on the injustices inflicted on this tribe.[57]

DE SMET REPORTS: Indian Situation on the Upper Missouri

Since the Indian Office was under increasing criticism from military leaders, Commissioner Dole was pleased by De Smet's initial report.[58] De Smet gathered evidence from the contacts he made at various stops of the *Yellowstone* along the river, from Fort Sully northward. Moreover, when he disembarked on June 9 at Fort Berthold, he conducted a series of meetings with the leaders of the tribes camped in the area. De Smet noted that the other tribes were not about to join a rebellion led by the Sioux.

Nevertheless, these tribal leaders had two complaints: they were provoked by the harm to natural resources caused by the increased traffic of the whites, and they were disturbed by their agents' repeated failures to distribute their annuities. Further, they realized that the period of annuity payments and perhaps other provisions of the 1851 Fort Laramie treaty was ending. Their predecessors had made the promises at Fort Laramie. As spokesmen of the mid-1860s facing drastically changed conditions on the Great Plains, these chiefs wanted to share in shaping the new treaties. By and large, the tribes of the Upper Missouri, with the exception of the Sioux, had been pressured into the realistic admission that their days of freedom were at an end.

Two decades earlier De Smet had predicted that the Indian tribes of the upper Missouri would be drawn into final conflict with one another over the dwindling buffalo herds. But rather than a clash over the remaining buffalo, the struggle had been joined over the grazing areas where the last of the herds would wander. By 1864 the bands of the Teton Sioux, the most numerous and powerful of the tribes in this region, had begun to push back all competition, forcing other tribes to withdraw from the adjacent territories. Only the Sioux now resided in the secluded grazing grounds of the wandering herds. Thus, only the remote bands of Sioux could believe that the independence of their traditional way of life might be prolonged.

However, even the western Sioux, the Tetons, were not united in their assessment of their situation. Not all Sioux leaders believed that their people could resist the changes demanded by the invasions of the whites. Agent Latta generalized that of the thirteen thousand Missouri Sioux, ten thousand were hostile to the government. Offering another round figure, De Smet estimated that the combined military force of these hostiles would amount to five or six thousand warriors, all well mounted. De Smet also reported to Dole that the most hostile Sioux bands were the Blackfeet Sioux, the Oglalas, Hunkpapas, and Santees. Clearly the scattered Santees, already hounded by General Pope's military forces, were hostile to the government, but such a relationship did not extend to all the Sioux bands. A number of the tribal chiefs articulated the sharp division among their people about joining the armed rebellion.[59]

De Smet visited the scattered camps of some Sioux leaders as the *Yellowstone* worked its way up the Missouri. He sent Sioux messengers out from Fort Sully on May 31, and from Fort Berthold on June 9 and 29, attempting to get the remote camps to send delegations to the posts to discuss the issue. These messengers reported that the camps of many hostiles were moving farther northwest to the region of the upper Yellowstone. Finally, on July 8 a band of two to three hundred Sioux was seen approaching the west bank of the Missouri opposite Fort Berthold. De Smet's final messenger, dispatched with "a present of tobacco, as an invitation to come and smoke the pipe of peace," had proven successful. De Smet later informed Dole of his meeting with this group, principally Yanktonais but including representatives of various other bands, representing over 470 lodges encamped on the Heart River:

> The steamer Yellow Stone had then just returned from
> her trip to Benton. Mr. Charles Chouteau had the great

kindness to accompany me with his two yawls to meet the Sioux. The chiefs met us with tokens of kindness and of confidence. After the smoking of the calumet, at our request, they readily stepped into the yawls and accompanied us to the steamer. A council was held immediately. . . .

The Black-eyes and Red Dog [the principal chiefs] rose in turn, and in their speeches expressed their great desire of keeping at peace with the whites, and of preventing their young men from breaking it. It is to be hoped that they will keep their word and promises.[60]

Immediately after their meeting with these Sioux chiefs Chouteau headed the *Yellowstone* back downstream.

Late on July 9, as the *Yellowstone* approached the mouth of the Cannon Ball River, Chouteau and De Smet gazed upon the new encampment of General Sully, who from July 7 to July 18 directed the initial stages of the construction of Fort Rice. Busy with these matters and the final details of the punitive campaign ordered by General Pope, Sully had little time to listen to De Smet's report on his interviews with the Sioux bands. Noting that "the general was very busy at the time," De Smet reported:

He told me plainly that circumstances obliged him to punish by force of arms all the Sioux tribes that harbored in their camps any murderers of white men. "Unfortunately," he added, "all the Indian camps harbor some of these desperate ruffians, over whom the chiefs have little or no power."

In consequence of the general's declaration and the circumstances of the case, my errand of peace, though sanctioned by the Government, became bootless and could only serve to place me in a false position: namely, that of being face to face with the Indians without being able to do them the least service.[61]

Sunder notes that the *Yellowstone*, with a cargo of some 1,700 bales of fur and robes, landed at St. Louis on July 21. He also reports briefly on the July 28 defeat of the hostile Sioux at Killdeer Mountain. In the meantime De Smet had disembarked from the *Yellowstone* when it halted on its downriver voyage at Fort Leavenworth. After a brief meeting with Bishop Miége De Smet had headed west to his beloved St. Mary's Indian Mission. Returning to St. Louis University, De Smet posted another report to Dole on August 23, repeating his conviction that under existing circumstances his assigned objective could not be realized and promising to provide a fuller report in person to the commissioner in the near future. De Smet spent much of September in Washington. He had additional business in the Indian Office concerning the Osage and the Potawatomi schools conducted at the Jesuit Indian missions in Kansas. On September 23, following his conferences with Dole, De Smet wrote a final report concerning his contacts on the Upper Missouri.[62]

Perhaps the best summary on De Smet's efforts was presented by Dole in his annual report for 1864. Having noted the little evidence that military operations against the Sioux had been effective, Dole stated:

> It seems proper that allusion should be made here to the mission of Rev. Father De Smet to the Upper Missouri. . . . It will be seen that the confidence of this office in his disposition and ability to serve the government to advantage were not misplaced, his communications with the chiefs of various bands in the region north and east of Fort Berthold having resulted in finding many influential persons among the Sioux anxious for peace.[63]

THE VAST WORLD OF DE SMET'S EXPERIENCES

Following his September meetings in Washington De Smet was summoned back to St. Louis. His religious superiors wished him to prepare at once for another trip to Europe, again to solicit men and means. On October 12 he departed for New York, arriving in Belgium at the beginning of November. After conferring with Jesuit authorities there, he visited his relatives, then, traveling by way of Paris, Lyons, and Marseilles, arrived at Rome on November 19. There De Smet met with the top Jesuit figures, noting that he was especially pleased with "the honor, several times, to be presented to his Holiness Pope Pius IX." In the beginning of December De Smet returned to Belgium to visit friends and relatives.

During the first five months of 1865 De Smet delivered his solicitation talks in the principal cities of Belgium, Holland, and Luxembourg, and in London and Dublin. The total of the financial contributions he received was not recorded. However, in addition to money and material gifts for the Missouri Jesuit apostolates, he was granted public recognition and honor in his homeland, made Knight of the Order of Leopold by the king of Belgium.[64]

Before leaving Liverpool, De Smet was joined by fourteen young men, including one Jesuit priest, the recruits he had solicited to join the Missouri Province. These candidates were from England, Holland, and Belgium. De Smet, even at an advanced age, continued to be an effective promoter. On June 2, the afternoon of their departure from Ostende, De Smet revealed his personal feelings in a letter to a close friend: "I always miss something when I am not among my good Indians; notwithstanding the kindly welcome that I meet everywhere, for the sake of my apostolic mission, I am conscious of a certain void wherever I go, until I come again to my dear Rocky Mountains. Then calm comes over me; then only am I happy."[65]

It was not until the close of June that De Smet and the contingent of new Jesuits arrived at St. Louis University. The lateness of the season prevented him from visiting the Indians in 1865. However, with Sully leading another summer expedition to implement Pope's punitive policy along the Upper Missouri, De Smet must have realized that he had missed few opportunities that year to improve the lot of the Indians.

On another matter, one of considerable importance on the Upper Missouri, De Smet did comment, though briefly, at this time. His letter of August 6, 1865, presented some serious financial news to the Jesuits conducting the Blackfoot Mission west of Fort Benton—Chouteau's sale of most of the trading posts of the American Fur Company: "Mr. Charles Chouteau, the great benefactor of the missions, has sold out his whole concern in the trading posts on the Missouri river, except at Fort Benton. He may even sell that post before long. This would bring a great contrariety in regard to the upper missions, as freight on all the goods might be exacted, which would make a considerable amount." On November 11, 1866, De Smet summarized the debt of gratitude due the Chouteaus: "Until this year I have always had my passage with my effects *gratis* upon the steamers of the [American] Fur Company of St. Louis. This company is to-day dissolved and it is, consequently, very doubtful if I shall meet again with such a favor."[66]

Beyond transporting all of the supplies solicited by De Smet for the missions and granting free passage to mission personnel, the American Fur Company's hospitality at their remote outposts had repeatedly provided the life-sustaining supports that De Smet, struggling through the wilderness, needed. Such material assistance had been provided without charge or questioning. De Smet had good cause to declare his former student Charles Chouteau "the great benefactor of the Missions."[67]

The problem arises from what De Smet's writings failed to report—the absence of any and all criticism of Chouteau's firm. De Smet's extensive writings contain no reference to or even an indirect acknowledgment of the serious charges directed against the conduct of the American Fur Company on the Upper Missouri. In 1862, for example, De Smet maintained friendly relations with both Lewis Henry Morgan and Samuel Latta, at the same time continuing his uncritical friendship with and dependence on Charles Chouteau. Certainly De Smet was not less observant or less astute than his fellow passengers, who charged, as noted above, that Chouteau's firm was "the most corrupt institution ever tolerated in our country."[68]

De Smet's silence raises a question to which no completely satisfactory answer can be given. Perhaps a partial explanation can be found in the ready distinction accepted in the social thinking of the period. Morgan explicitly noted that Chouteau "adjusts all the business of the Company at the posts." Yet Morgan somehow distinguished between the Chouteau to whom he assigned responsibility for reprehensible company practices and Chouteau the prominent St. Louis Creole, aristocrat, and distinguished patron of the arts and sciences.[69]

A partial explanation is also to be found in a policy especially followed by the American Fur Company directors. The prominent travelers to the early West—artists, missionaries, and scientists— were given, as historian Sunder says, "company assistance to make their upriver visits memorable." These guests were thereby encouraged "to tell the world of the American Fur Company's virtues rather than its vices." Sunder notes that the poor conduct of the American Fur Company was masked, deliberately and effectively, by its leaders' concern for good public relations.

It should be noted that De Smet had no access to the records of the Chouteaus' firm. Moreover, De Smet was unable to review the files of pertinent information in the Office of Indian Affairs. As late as 1864 Commissioner Dole assigned De Smet, engaged in official government business, to operational dependence on Charles Chouteau and his firm. In making judgments, De Smet was affected by an additional handicap. His reasoning and statements were conditioned in part by the religious attitudes of his day. As a religious leader in a troubled context, De Smet was expected to be somewhat automatic in his public praise of all Catholic achievers. Not only the Chouteaus benefited from De Smet's religious prejudice. As prominent Catholics, Lewis V. Bogy and Thomas F. Meagher also received De Smet's unqualified praise.[70]

Still another personal relationship held De Smet's attention in the late summer of 1865. Throughout the trying period of the Civil War De Smet's loyalty to his adopted country had been beyond question. His sympathies, however, were tempered by "his wide and intimate acquaintance with persons of avowed southern sentiment." For the residents of Missouri, this was a period of division, a time of disunity among family members, friends, and members of religious groups.[71]

In 1861 Colonel Francis P. Blair had directly requested De Smet to serve as chaplain for the Union troops. Beyond personal friendship, Blair professedly sought the religious services of "one of the most beloved and honored priests in the entire country." Archbishop Kenrick, however, saw Blair's move as an inducement to Irish Catholics of the St. Louis area to join the Union ranks. Kenrick's sympathies were with the South, and the archbishop insisted that De Smet's Jesuit superior deny Blair's request.[72]

Still another prominent friend of De Smet's decided in 1861 to offer his services to the Confederacy. Daniel M. Frost, a resident of St. Louis who had recently directed the Missouri Militia, committed himself to serve as a military officer with the Confederate forces until 1863. Frost's wife and children were "banished from their plantation home outside of St. Louis." When De Smet returned from Rome, he wrote to the Frost family and recommended that they "make application to the President for pardon." Frost replied that he would initiate the request at once and that he placed full trust in De Smet's handling of the matter. De Smet's efforts to intercede—letters of appeal to various military leaders and petition signatures—proved effective. On October 23, 1865, President Andrew Johnson signed papers granting "a full pardon and amnesty to D. M. Frost of Missouri." Shortly before the Christmas holidays De Smet wrote to the Frost family, now happily relocated in their country home outside St. Louis: "I hope to be out, shortly, to say Mass at the intention of the Family, for the benefits received during this closing year."[73]

As Blackrobe, however, De Smet's special interest in the Indians continued. Shortly after his return from abroad De Smet indicated his awareness of the Sand Creek Massacre, the tragedy that had taken place in eastern Colorado at the end of March 1864. De Smet also expressed concern over the publicized reports of General Patrick E. Connor's insistence on a punitive policy in his Powder River campaign during the late summer of 1865:

The war against the Indians in the plains of the Missouri and its tributaries is being pushed to the utmost. Congress lately made an inquiry into the barbarous conduct of Colonel Chivington, accused of having ordered the massacre by his soldiers of 600 Cheyenne Indians. . . .

To-day's papers announce to us the circular of General Conner . . . in which he outlines the policy to be pursued toward the Indians. . . . "They must be severely punished to begin with," he says; "then we will see whether, by good behavior, they show themselves worthy to escape complete extermination." Always the same atrocious policy.[74]

Part Four

—

The Great Plains

—

The Buffalo People Removed

Chapter Ten
For Dependent Indians,
Very Limited Options (1865–66)

> But where to remove [the Indians]? In less than two
> decades Americans had scattered themselves over
> half a continent. Already, with the postwar westward
> surge yet to begin, there remained no blocks of
> territory large enough for the Indian to pursue his
> traditional way of life and still stay out of the white
> man's way. . . . Unless national expansion was to be
> arrested, the Indian would have to make do with less
> territory. This meant that he must yield his old way of
> life.
>
> —Robert M. Utley, *Frontiersmen in Blue*

CONGRESS HALTS MILITARY
CONTROL OF INDIAN AFFAIRS

"The policy of the federal government toward the American Indians," Paul Prucha points out, "cannot be understood as something
isolated from the main course of United States history." This integration of Indian affairs with other national concerns was clearly
manifested in governmental deliberations and decisions throughout
the second half of the 1860s.[1]

President Lincoln had shown himself in promises to Bishop
Whipple and De Smet a humanitarian in his approach to Indian
affairs. But preoccupation with the Civil War forced Lincoln to leave
Indian-related matters almost entirely to Congress and his commis-
sioner of Indian affairs, William P. Dole. Utley reports on the powers
Dole faced:

> In the Congress he [Dole] encountered Indian com-
> mittees dominated by westerners. In the West his
> agents found themselves powerless against military
> potentates. . . . Backed by regiments of warlike west-
> erners, supported by western public opinion, and
> unrestrained by a national authority preoccupied with
> saving the Union, the generals almost by default had
> made U.S. Indian policy overwhelmingly a military
> policy.[2]

In 1865, following Lee's surrender and Lincoln's assassination, the primary concern in Washington was the rebuilding of national unity. Indian affairs, it seemed, would continue to be directed by military leaders.

General John Pope, whose punitive policy had been directed against the openly rebellious Santee Sioux of Minnesota and all the Sioux of the Upper Missouri, had been given an increased command in the West. On November 30, 1864, General U. S. Grant, army commander in chief, appointed Pope to head the newly fashioned Division of the Missouri, in command of almost all the military forces across the Great Plains.[3]

On November 29, however, Colonel John M. Chivington had led his Colorado Volunteer Militia in the infamous assault on peaceable Cheyennes under Chief Black Kettle at Sand Creek. Thus, even before Pope had arrived at his new headquarters in St. Louis on February 4, 1865, his military powers had been indirectly circumscribed. The national repercussions of the Sand Creek Massacre quickly initiated a peace offensive based upon what Utley characterizes as a "wave of revulsion against the frontier army." After the Civil War, that army was hard hit by desertions, and orders were received from the beleaguered War Department to muster out many units. Further, the costly campaigns that Pope managed to field later in 1865—the expeditions led by General James H. Ford south of the Arkansas and by Generals Alfred Sully and Patrick E. Connor north of the Platte—ended in a failure, says Utley, "so complete that the generals could not gloss it over." Sully went on record repudiating the basic notion of such large-scale operations.[4]

For a variety of reasons, therefore, Pope's attitudes were changing. In place of the exterminationist views he stated in 1862 and 1863, Pope now expressed official concern for the future of the tribes. In his 1866 "Report on the West," Pope insisted that because of "solemn treaties with the Indians," the whites had no right to occupy "Montana and the larger part of Utah, Colorado, and Nebraska." Although Pope considered the traditional treaty system for dealing with the tribes anathema, on August 4 he ordered General John B. Sanborn to negotiate a peace treaty with the Indians.[5]

On July 6, 1865, Pope had been tactfully reminded by Secretary of the Interior James Harlan that the management of all Indian affairs, as specified by the Constitution, was restricted to Congress. Pope was well aware that before adjourning in the spring of 1865, Congress had enacted two measures by which military leaders would be forced to accept a secondary role in Indian matters.[6] Congress had created a Joint Special Committee, headed by Senator James R. Doolittle, "to investigate the condition of the Indian tribes and their treatment by civil and military authorities." Second, Congress had established the Northwestern Treaty Commission, headed by Newton Edmunds, governor of Dakota Territory, to approach the Sioux of the Upper Missouri regarding peace treaties. Congress thus had moved to an Indian policy formulated by diplomacy.[7]

With peace overtures mounting in 1865, Pope must have sensed the urgency for some display of his cooperation as the top military leader in the West. As Utley suggests, by a blanket refusal to participate Pope faced the unacceptable prospect of losing influence on the administration of Indian affairs throughout the Military Division of the Missouri. Further, active cooperation by ranking military leaders was made more acceptable by the diplomacy exercised by Secretary Harlan. In addition to Sanborn, General William S. Harney was appointed to head the peace commission on the southern Plains. Generals Samuel Curtis and Henry H. Sibley were assigned to the committee to deal with the Missouri River Sioux. Such invitations to participate could hardly be refused by military leaders, even though the generals were thereby joining in the search for nonmilitary solutions.[8]

Specific changes in Pope's thinking might be attributed, at least in part, to the influence of William Bent and Kit Carson. In meetings held October 14–18 at the mouth of the Little Arkansas, some of the southern Cheyennes and Arapahos joined with the leaders of the Kiowa Apaches, Comanches, and Kiowas in signing peace treaties. On October 27 Pope received the treaty papers, along with Bent and Carson's report. Believing that the recommendations of Bent and Carson could be used by his military superiors to influence the thinking of Washington politicians, Pope forwarded Bent and Carson's report to Sherman. In turn, Sherman was so impressed that he sent it on to Grant with the endorsement: "Probably no two men exist better acquainted with the Indians than Carson & Bent and their judgm[en]t is entitled to great weight."[9]

Like Fitzpatrick, Manypenny, and Whipple before them, Bent and Carson insisted upon acknowledgment of the government's fundamental responsibility to the tribes of the Great Plains: "Civilization now presses them on all sides—their ancient homes forcibly abandoned, their old hunting grounds destroyed by the requirements of industrious agricultural life. . . . By dispossessing them of their

After the Fetterman disaster of December 1866, President Andrew Johnson convened an Indian conference at the White House late in February 1867. The president, Interior Secretary Orville H. Browning, and acting Commissioner of Indian Affairs Lewis V. Bogy are on the lefthand balcony; De Smet is visible on the right balcony. Immediately below Johnson, wearing the full feathered headdress, is Lakota leader Saswe, great grandfather of Sioux spokesperson Vine Deloria, Jr. (Jesuit Missouri Province Archives)

Above left: Little Crow (Santee Sioux) (Minnesota Historical Society, 3510)

Above right: Little Thunder (Brule Sioux) (National Museum of the American Indian, Smithsonian Institution)

Left: Spotted Tail (1823–81; Brule Sioux) (South Dakota Historical Society)

Spotted Tail played no role in the Santee rebellion led by Little Crow, but this Brule chief was an exceptional leader. With Little Thunder, he was present in 1854 for the tragedy of Frightening Bear, and in 1855 he too endured defeat by General Harney. In the 1860s he met repeatedly with the peace commissioners on the plains, and in the 1870s with the authorities in Washington. A final confrontation took place in 1880 with Colonel Richard Pratt at the Carlisle Industrial School: disturbed by a curriculum that he condemned as faulty, Spotted Tail withdrew his descendants from the institution.

(Library of Congress, BH82-4569)

(Minnesota Historical Society, c.n.)

(National Archives, 111-SC-87714)

In this group photograph the peace commissioners at North Platte, Nebraska, November 6, 1867, display their frustration that their second proposal to parley at Fort Laramie was refused by Indian leaders. President Johnson had appointed eight commissioners: above left, John B. Henderson; above right, John B. Sanborn; below, from the left, Alfred H. Terry, William S. Harney, William T. Sherman; below, from the right, Christopher C. Augur, Samual F. Tappan, Nathaniel G. Taylor. The commission was authorized "to make and conclude such treaty stipulations as will most likely insure civilization for the Indians and peace and safety for the whites."

The southern Arapahos and Cheyennes accepted the stipulations of the peace commissioners on October 28, 1867, in the Medicine Lodge Treaty. In this sketch by James Taylor (printed in *Leslie's Illustrated Newspaper*), Margaret Fitzpatrick Wilmarth is seated in the center.

The northern Arapahos and Cheyennes signed their own version of the Fort Laramie Treaty on May 10, 1868. Here the signing is witnessed by several commissioners, including General Sherman. (Photograph by Alexander Gardner, Smithsonian Institution, 3686)

Eagle Woman (1820–88; Mrs. Matilda Galpin) continued to influence the policies of the Sioux on the upper Missouri even after her participation in the 1868 demonstration by the Indian Peace Riders. In 1872 she was a tribal delegate to Washington; in 1876 she effected the opening of the first Indian school on the Standing Rock Reservation. (Montana Historical Society)

The spokesmen for the Peace Riders were Running Antelope (Hunkpapa Sioux), above left, and Two Bears (Yanktonais Sioux), right. Both leaders stressed that the Buffalo People no longer enjoyed any option to live their traditional life-style (State Historical Society of North Dakota; Assumption Abbey Archives, Richardton, North Dakota)

country, we assume their stewardship, and the manner in which this duty is performed will add a glorious record to American history, or a damning blot and reproach for all times." As Bent and Carson noted in their report, the tribes located between the Platte and the Arkansas in 1865 were facing a serious crisis due to the invasion of the Kansas and Nebraska territories. If the Indians were to survive, they must be "amalgamated with the whites." Bent and Carson specifically advised Pope that the Indians be confined to reservations to develop "a capacity for industry and civilization" and thus become "capable of self subsistence by agricultural and mechanical pursuits."[10]

Identified with the Indians by marriage and offspring, Bent and Carson had cause to be more sensitive than Pope and his fellow officers to the lot of the tribes. Also, the motives of Bent and Carson could reasonably be interpreted as more sympathetic than those of ordinary traders and emigrants on the Great Plains. Yet they were not alone in their concern for the Indians' future. Trennert makes the point: "From all corners came the same general advice: the tribes had to be gathered at places where they would be out of the path of white expansion and where they could be kept from harming either whites or each other. Both the friends of the Indians and those who only wanted what they possessed favored this solution."[11]

For individuals like Bent, Carson, Whipple, and De Smet, recommendations were not based on an evaluation of Indian life and society in itself. Their proposals were not meant to offer any comparison, even implied, between two cultures. One must remember that like Carson and Bent, De Smet found his special joy and satisfaction in outdoor living beyond the pall of civilization. These were realistic leaders, and in the context of their special appreciation of the drastically changed conditions of the period across the Great Plains, they concluded that any possibility of tribal members continuing their traditional Indian way of life had already been terminated. Being Indian was not judged bad; rather, being Indian was no longer a viable option.

Thus, friends as well as foes held that the Indian in 1865 had to be removed. Furthermore, despite the violence called for by some groups of western extremists and the western press, the extinction of the tribes was not regarded as a desirable or even acceptable objective. Prucha points out that Commissioner N. G. Taylor and Colonel Ely S. Parker, expressing the views of highly divergent camps, publicly agreed in 1867 that "the sentiment of our people will not for a moment tolerate the idea of extermination."[12]

In general it was the hope of all self-styled humanitarians that military force would not be required for tribal removal. The treaties made with the southern Plains tribes at the mouth of the Little Arkansas had been duplicated (also in October) by treaties signed at Fort Sully with Sioux bands of the Upper Missouri. On October 28, 1865, the members of the Northwestern Treaty Commission offered an optimistic report: according to the leaders of the Minneconjous, the Sioux bands, the northern Cheyennes, and the Arapahos desired peace.

However, these treaties, as signed by the Minneconjou and representatives of eight other Sioux bands, failed to treat the central issue of tribal removal. Instead of complete withdrawal to designated reservations—a removal almost universally regarded by non-Indians as the primary matter of any peace negotiations at this time—the Sioux had been induced to promise only "to withdraw from the routes overland already established or hereafter to be established through their country." Furthermore, the task had not been completed. When three inches of snow fell on October 24, the commissioners had halted their negotiations. Declaring that various Indian groups had not yet been contacted, they recommended "a division of the present commission or the appointment of two new commissions to visit the Fort Laramie region and the Upper Missouri as early in the spring as practicable."[13]

The problem caused by the presence of white invaders—traditionally the problem is defined in the opposite terms—was not resolved in 1865. The military expeditions planned by General Pope had not removed the Indian threat from the Smoky Hill Road to Denver or the Bozeman Trail to the Montana mines. The diplomatic attempts on the Little Arkansas and the Upper Missouri also proved less than successful.[14]

Certain short-term benefits of these treaties should be noted. Despite the skepticism expressed by some military leaders, these pacts were regarded as diplomatic accomplishments by political leaders, and they were ratified by the Senate in the spring of 1866. In a sense, as Utley suggests, these treaties "assuaged a national conscience troubled by memories of Sand Creek." Further, the treaties offered the general public at least "the momentary illusion of peace," and in doing so they strengthened the widespread demand for an overall and permanent peace program with all the tribes of the Great Plains.[15]

At the same time, however, the feud between the military leaders and the Indian Office continued to mount. Sixteen years of divided responsibilities in the management of Indian affairs had not proven satisfactory to either branch of the government. Each now publicly claimed that the other was responsible for the tragic lot of the Indians and the critical situation on the great overland routes. Bitter charges were exchanged not only by the generals and the civilian officials of the Indian Office but by their prominent friends and political supporters. The battle regarding military versus civilian control over Indian affairs, as Utley notes, would "rock Washington for a decade after 1865."[16]

DE SMET'S FIELD REPORT OF 1866:
"Mounting Indian Grievances"

In 1865, for the first time in four consecutive years, De Smet had failed to visit the tribes of the Upper Missouri. In 1866, sandwiched between his official work as treasurer for the Missouri Jesuits, De Smet spent three full months in such visits. The initial portion of his journey, begun on April 9, was a voyage of fifty-seven days up the full navigable length of the Missouri River.

This 1866 voyage marked the termination of the American Fur Company's operation on the Upper Missouri. An era had ended. Late in July 1865 the company had sold its last steamer, the *Yellowstone*. Thus it was as passengers that Charles Chouteau and De Smet, as his guest, departed in 1866 from St. Louis aboard the *Ontario*. They would share their journey to Fort Benton.[17]

The departure of the *Ontario* from St. Louis could not have taken place much before noon on April 9. De Smet carried with him (or perhaps the papers were delivered to him aboard the steamer as it prepared to depart) two letters from General Sherman under that date. Calling attention to De Smet's rushed departure due to a change in plans, Sherman presented a short summary of his military plans for the West in 1866. In his concluding remarks Sherman stated: "The sooner the Indians can localize and get ready to raise food and horses without wandering in search of buffalo and Game, the better for them. You know as well as I do the difficulties attending this question, and may accomplish much good to both sides."[18]

Sherman also provided De Smet with a passport to ensure the success of his trip. In that document he stated that De Smet "has always been noted for his strict fidelity to the interests of our Government, for indefatigable industry and an enthusiastic love for the Indians under his charge."[19]

De Smet had initiated a friendship with Sherman and his family in 1865, calling at the general's military headquarters a few days after Sherman returned to St. Louis in mid-July. Since the general was engaged, De Smet departed after leaving some gifts—copies, certainly autographed, of his books on the West and some religious devotional objects for Mrs. Sherman. On the following day Sherman, and a few days later his wife, sent letters of gratitude. Over the years Mrs. Sherman was "a special benefactress of Father De Smet's Indian Missions, as well as his special advocate with General Sherman." The general's family—Mrs. Sherman, four daughters, and son Thomas—arrived in St. Louis to set up their new home in September 1865. Thomas was immediately enrolled at the Jesuits' school. The Shermans' younger son, Philemon Tecumseh, was born in St. Louis on January 9, 1867; at their request, De Smet acted as godfather at the baptismal ceremonies held shortly thereafter at St. Bridget's Church.[20]

De Smet's narratives of this 1866 voyage differ from his accounts of previous journeys. He took time to write a detailed account of the *Ontario,* its equipment, facilities, and staff. The golden age of steamboating on the Upper Missouri had begun. Before 1866 only four boats had managed to reach Fort Benton; before midsummer of that year the steamers had deposited thirty-one cargoes there. De Smet's narratives indicate that in 1866 the shipboard facilities and general living quarters provided for passengers had greatly improved. Reporting on the activities of his fellow passengers, whose needs were supplied by the *Ontario's* crew and staff of over fifty people, De Smet wrote:

> The long days are passed in social conversations, sometimes political, sometimes scientific or religious. Storytellers or jokers are never lacking in an assemblage of American travelers. . . . Evenings, we amuse ourselves by proposing charades—somebody imitates some animal or other, or suggests some word or question, and the audience guesses. But the principal amusement, in the main cabin, appears to be dancing to the sound of music, and on moonlight nights there are concerts out on deck, with mirth and refreshments.[21]

De Smet's baptismal record reports the baptism of a large number of Indian children at Fort Sully in early May while the *Ontario* was tied up briefly at that post. On May 25, while the steamer was halted at Fort Union, De Smet baptized a number of Assiniboine children. On June 7, the date of the arrival of the *Ontario* at Fort Benton, De Smet baptized "Joseph born in September 1863, legitimate son of Cyprian Mott and Meline his wife." This ceremony was a homecoming of sorts for De Smet; Joseph had been born in the month following De Smet's departure from Benton in 1863.[22]

Although there is no complete account of De Smet's stay in June 1866 at Fort Benton, we know that he was unable to contact the Jesuit missionaries at St. Peter's Blackfeet Mission to the west of Great Falls. Because of troubled relationships between the Indians and the invading miners, the missionaries had sought temporary refuge at St. Ignatius Mission, two hundred miles away on the west side of the Rockies.[23]

We have no direct statement that De Smet and Chouteau parted company at Fort Benton, but there is evidence that De Smet did not make the return journey aboard the *Ontario,* and we might presume that Chouteau hastened back to St. Louis aboard that steamer. But De Smet wanted more travel time; he wished to visit the two mission sites on the Missouri that General Sully had recommended.

Following his stay at Fort Benton, De Smet spent the second half of June at Fort Berthold. After performing a baptism "aboard the steamer, *Minor,* below Fort Rice," he spent much of July in the vicinity of Fort Randall at the Yankton Sioux Agency. Here, at long last, De Smet baptized the head chief, Man Struck by the Ree, and his wife. For over a quarter of a century this couple, to whom De Smet gave the names Peter and Anna, had been admirers and close friends of the Blackrobe.[24]

De Smet brought back from his trip the news that the "miseries, sufferings and griefs" of the tribes had gravely mounted, their complaints becoming increasingly strong.

> These Indians needed consolation — but good advice still more. In my quality of Black-robe I did my best to give them salutary counsels, as well as to console them. The grievances of the Indians against the whites are very numerous, and the vengeances which they on their side provoke are often most cruel and frightful. Nevertheless, one is compelled to admit that they are less guilty than the whites.
>
> The payment of their annuities, for the millions of acres of land that they have ceded to the Government, are often overlooked or deferred, though they are the

Indians's only means of support. . . . The terms of
the treaties are often transgressed, and the Indians
overwhelmed with injuries and insults. Woe to them,
if they resist the unjust and wicked aggressors, for
then they are driven out or massacred like wild beasts,
without pity, or the least remorse, or any thought that
the killing of a savage comes under the head of
murder.[25]

VESTED INTERESTS OF
THE WEST CONTRIBUTE TO RACIAL PROBLEMS

De Smet's writings concerning his 1866 journey contain no references to the activities of the Northwestern Treaty Commission. This
may be explained by the time factor. The Peace Commission had
been divided into two groups. Conferences with the western tribes
around Fort Laramie did not begin until June, at which time De Smet
was on the Upper Missouri. Meetings with the tribes of the Upper
Missouri did not commence until mid-July; by then De Smet had
concluded his travel on the Upper Missouri and was visiting the
Yankton Sioux near Fort Randall.

Commissioner of Indian Affairs Dennis N. Cooley issued his
annual report for 1866 on October 22. Regarding the diplomatic
activities conducted by the Northwestern Treaty Commission, Cooley reported that the group under Governor Edmunds and General
Curtis had negotiated three treaties: at Fort Berthold with the
Arikaras, Mandans, and Gros Ventres, and later with the Crows; and
at Fort Union with the Assiniboines. Regarding the Sioux, Cooley
stated that E. B. Taylor, head of the Northern Superintendency at
Omaha, and Colonel Henry E. Maynadier had concluded a peace
treaty with the Oglalas and Brulés on June 7 at Fort Laramie. Cooley
proudly stated that if this series of treaties were ratified, "peaceful
relations will have been established with powerful tribes . . . and uninterrupted use of routes of travel established through their country."[26]

Throughout the late summer and fall, however, Washington authorities received reports of growing unrest among the western
Sioux. The recently established Bozeman Trail, now bearing increasing traffic and supported by three newly erected army posts,
was the crux of the problem. Superintendent Taylor reassured the
Indian Office that peace would be maintained. As late as November
19 he reported that even the hostile bands of Sioux were prepared to
sign the treaty. Commissioner Cooley repeated this overoptimistic

assessment in his annual report, and President Johnson declared to Congress on December 5 that the Indians earnestly desired to establish friendly relations with the United States. Then on December 21 the tragic fate of eighty members of a Fort Philip Kearny patrol under the headstrong Colonel W. J. Fetterman—what Olson terms "the greatest disaster to befall the Army in the West up to that time"—indicated how false Taylor's promise of a lasting peace had been.[27]

Criticisms from various sources were directed against both groups of the Northwestern Treaty Commission. Military leaders charged that the Indian Office, by its policy of furnishing guns and ammunition to the tribes and Superintendent Taylor's inept diplomacy at Fort Laramie, had been responsible for the disaster. As was his custom, Sherman's initial reaction to the Fetterman massacre was a demand for extreme measures. Contacting General Grant, Sherman called for the extermination of the Sioux. Although the Indian Office, as might be expected, charged the military leaders with all blame for the Indian uprising, the publication of the report of a special Indian agent, E. B. Chandler, attributed full responsibility to the 1866 Fort Laramie treaty. Chandler stated that Taylor's promises had deceived the Indians and that the "so-called treaty was little better than a farce" and ought not be ratified.[28]

Perhaps the most serious of the criticisms against the Edmunds party was expressed by Captain Joseph La Barge, whose new steamboat, *Ben Johnson,* was chartered by the commissioners "to carry them up the river and back at three hundred dollars per day." La Barge pointedly criticized the imprudence and the lack of tact and experience of the commissioners; the absence of such qualities, in La Barge's thinking, disqualified the members for realistic achievements in dealing with the Indians. Although "the voyage seemed more like a pleasure excursion than a business enterprise," Captain La Barge concluded that the commission was looked upon as a mockery, its only productivity being to "aggravate an already serious situation."[29]

Charles Larpenteur, a long-term fur trader on the Upper Missouri, had received an appointment early in 1866 from Governor Newton Edmunds to serve as an interpreter for the peace commissioners. The succinct comment of Larpenteur was that "the great Peace Commission was a complete failure." An even more condemnatory judgment was expressed at the close of 1866 by Colonel William G. Rankin, who had been busy since mid-June with the erection of the new military post, Fort Buford, near the mouth of the Yellowstone. Rankin found his construction efforts seriously delayed and disturbed by "the energetic endeavors in the wrong direction" of the members of the Peace Commission. Further, in the judgment of Utley and other historians, Edmunds's activities as chairman of the Peace Commission of 1866 and director of the Sioux Land Commission of 1883 "rested on a large measure of self-interest."[30]

Edmunds, then, was the very personification of the problem facing the representatives of the federal government in the West. It is hardly an exaggeration that the whole western population, since it was so economically dependent upon federal expenditures, tended to act in all Indian-related matters as a vested interest. In a report presented to Grant's staff in late 1866, Sherman complained: "All the people west of the Missouri river look to the army as their legitimate field of profit and support." In turn, Grant expressed his displeasure to Sherman:

> I would advise that but little confidence be placed in
> the suggestions of citizens who have made their homes
> in the territories, in selecting points to be occupied by
> troops.
>   My experience is, and no doubt it is borne out by
> your own, that these people act entirely from selfish
> and interested motives.[31]

Such were the pressures exercised by the settlers, especially by the more recent arrivals on the Great Plains. Further, these pressures were due to the even stronger demands of manufacturers and producers, freighters and traders, who had come to depend upon federal expenditures for feeding or fighting Indians. Following his investigation of the causes of the Fetterman disaster, General Sanborn concluded: "The war policy is not urged by general public sentiment of the country, but furiously urged by ranchmen on the plains, army contractors, and some of the army officers who in this matter at the present time seem to be ruled and controlled by the ranchmen and contractors."[32]

Rumor seems to have been one of the pressure techniques used by the vested interests. In his annual report for 1867 Sherman pointed out his strong suspicion: "In the early part of the year there seemed to be a concerted and mischievous design to precipitate hostilities by a series of false reports almost without parallel." Sherman's charge was seconded by the commissioner of Indian affairs, who attributed the false reporting of a horrible massacre to "the rapacity and rascality of frontier settlers, whose interests are to bring on a war and supply our armies at exorbitant prices." Having served through the spring of 1867 as a member of the Fetterman Investigating Committee headquartered at Fort Laramie, General N. B. Buford reported: "Nine-tenths of all the business that is being done on the route is paid for by the government. At least two-thirds of the entire business of the Union Pacific railroad is for carrying troops and army supplies. Its employees are all for war."[33]

The Sand Creek atrocities indulged in by the Colorado Volunteers in 1864 had not purged Denverites of their bitter animosities toward Native Americans. Doolittle discovered in his 1865 visit to Denver that new residents were calling for the extermination of the Indians. As Utley writes, to Senator Doolittle even more than General Sherman, these blatantly prejudiced Denverites "dramatized the polarization of East and West in the dispute over peace pipe or rifle."[34]

SHERMAN'S UNANSWERED QUESTION:
Treaty Rights of the Indians

By the start of 1867 federal authorities had decided upon the removal of all Native Americans from the central section of the Great Plains. The War Department and the Indian Office were united in this objective, but they differed sharply on the means to effect removal.

In his 1866 annual report General Sherman had proposed to restrict all Teton Sioux to the area north of the Platte, limiting them to the country extending westward from the Missouri River to the Bozeman Trail. For the Arapahos and Cheyennes, as well as the tribes whose wanderings were limited to the southern Plains, Sherman proposed restriction to the land south of the Arkansas River. Sherman pointed out what he considered the major benefits that would be achieved for the expanding nation: "This would leave for our people exclusively the use of the wide belt, east and west, between the Platte and the Arkansas, in which lie the two great railroads, and over which passes the bulk of travel to the mountain Territories. . . . I beg you will submit this proposition to the honorable Secretary of the Interior, that we may know that we do not violate some one of the solemn treaties made with these Indians."

On January 18, 1867, Secretary of War Stanton forwarded a copy of Sherman's proposal to Interior Secretary Browning. Implying his approbation, Stanton noted that General Grant's express approval of the proposition had carried the specific qualification that Sherman had mentioned—"if it does not conflict with treaty obligations."

Within five days Browning had a formal reply from Acting Commissioner of Indian Affairs Bogy. Still eager to lay all blame for the recent Fetterman disaster on the army leaders—"the injudicious military interference has been the cause of most of our Indian wars"—Bogy manifested as simplistic a belief in Manifest Destiny as Sherman's:

> The fact that the railroads are now being built through this country, and that it is the highway for the thousands of emigrants going to our western Territories, imposes on the government the necessity of affording to them complete protection. To effect this object, the removal of the Indians from this strip of country is, therefore, an absolute necessity. . . . As already said, the time has come when these Indians must abandon this portion of country.

Although expressing such complete agreement with the military stand on the objective of total Indian removal, Bogy strongly insisted that the responsibility for that removal did not legally belong to, nor could it be properly and successfully implemented by, the War Department. He emphasized that "the country yet belongs to these Indians; it has not been ceded by them." Declaring that any attempt to wrest land title by military force would also be much too expensive, Bogy predicted that the officials of the Indian Office could and would achieve the removal of the Plains tribes by diplomatic negotiations.[35]

Quite properly, Bogy might have reported that in the key treaty regarding the major tribes of the Great Plains, the 1851 Fort Laramie treaty, the area between the Arkansas and Platte was officially declared "the territory of the Cheyennes and Arrapahoes" and that consequent to pointed insistence by the Sioux, their hunting and fishing rights across this section of the plains were specified.

However, Bogy presented no such chapter-and-verse response to Sherman's query about treaty promises; rather, he offered an indirect reply: "This country yet belongs to the Indians; it has not been ceded by them." Bogy's proposal for gaining that title was negotiations with the tribal chiefs. Bogy insisted that "without injudicious military interference," such negotiations be conducted by agents of the Indian Office and that the generosity of these agents in promising "means of subsistence" would be short-lived, for these gifts and annuities would cover only the "few years which, in all probability, they [the Indians] will yet exist."[36]

For Sherman, the realist, his theoretical question of land titles based upon treaty promises was of passing moment. Sherman had developed the pragmatic mind of the military achiever; he had cause to regard military might as the efficient and justified tool for resolving the Indian problem. As a professional soldier, Sherman's assignment was to ensure peaceful conditions for his countrymen, those traveling through and those settling on the Great Plains. Among these newcomers to the West, Utley notes, the common attitude following the Fetterman disaster had hardened into "undiscriminating hostility toward all Indians." Western journalists had reacted with that exaggeration in which Sherman had indulged when he first learned of the tragedy north of Fort Phil Kearny. The frontier press called for military action directed to Indian extermination; "some even scored the army for timidity." Sherman faced the demand of the West for action.[37]

At the start of 1867 Sherman completed his plans: three expeditions would implement a punitive policy against the tribes. General Alfred H. Terry would direct military operations in the Upper Missouri and the northern Plains; General Winfield S. Hancock, assisted by the flamboyant young Lieutenant Colonel George Armstrong Custer, would wage war against the Sioux and Cheyennes along the Smoky Hill route to Denver; and General Christopher C. Augur, Grant's replacement for Philip Cooke and Henry Carrington, would move to eliminate any Indian problem for the railroad builders south of the Platte and the miners heading up the Bozeman Trail into the newly created territory of Montana.[38]

A number of government reports published at the start of 1867 added fuel to the controversy between the War Department and the Indian Office. These statements even more sharply divided the proponents of "the rifle threat" and those who called for "the presenting of the peace pipe."

The report of special Indian agent E. B. Chandler publicly criticized Superintendent Taylor. In the verbal charges directed by military leaders against the Indian Office, Taylor's mismanagement and deception served as a classic repetition of the deplorable activities for which officials of the Indian Office had earlier been censured by General Pope.[39]

Chandler's report, however, offered support for the policy of diplomatic negotiations urged by the Indian Office and their increasing number of political supporters. His argument for recommending peaceful means had exercised a constant and major influence on the government's Indian policy from the very beginning: a course of action regarding Indians should be undertaken or rejected not on the basis of being judged right or wrong in itself, or helpful or disadvantageous to the tribes, but because it was regarded as either financially beneficial or harmful to the government. Chandler closed his report: "The alternative of feeding or fighting the Indians must soon be chosen; and economy, as well as justice, would dictate the adoption of the former policy."[40]

As noted above, the Doolittle report was not made public until January 26, 1867. Apparently Doolittle's reason for procrastinating was that the collected testimonials consisted mostly of unsubstantiated charges and serious criticisms lacking any documentation. The age of open criticisms of government figures, of their personal and perhaps selfish motivations and practices, an age that had moved forward during Lincoln's presidency and become widespread in the postwar context of the power struggle between Congress and President Johnson, had not yet developed the more reasonable procedure of presenting documentary proof with such accusations. The Doolittle report, even though it lacked such authentication, was used at once by the camp of the pacifists and those who called for a military solution in dealing with the Indians.[41]

Another important report was the statement prepared by Colonel Ely Parker (a Seneca Indian who served as General Grant's aide-de-camp), a "proposed plan for a permanent and perpetual peace" that called for the transfer of the Indian Office to the War Department. However, the main achievement of the Doolittle report and Colonel Parker's plan should not be overlooked. Although they disagreed on the means, Parker's and Doolittle's associates were closely united in calling for a basic reform in the management of Indian affairs.[42]

The seeds for such reform had been sown in 1853 by Commissioner Manypenny in his call for the appointment of "a commission of able, impartial, upright, and practical men" to formulate a more proper policy regarding Indian relations. Such a concern for reform had been cultivated by Bishop Whipple. In addition to his call for an end to the politicization of the Indian service, Whipple recommended the appointment of a commission "of men of inflexible integrity, of large heart, of clear head, of strong will, who fear God and love man." Both Manypenny and Whipple recognized the need for independent minds who would be better informed.[43]

The Doolittle report recommended that five commissions be established to function within a fivefold territorial division of the western tribes. Tribal diversity had at last been acknowledged.

Parker's proposal added still another dimension to the planned procedure for reform. Parker pointed out that such an Indian commission would serve more effectively as an integrated body: "The appointment of a permanent Indian commission, to be a mixed commission, composed of such white men as possessed in a large degree the confidence of their country, and a number of the most reputable educated Indians, selected from different tribes."[44]

Still another set of reports must have especially influenced the thinking of Interior Secretary Browning at this time. Commissioner Bogy, in his reports of January and February, pointed out that a properly qualified commission was "the one remedy for all the ills now existing in our Indian relations." From the Indian Office, then, Browning was hearing the same proposal—"a commission of first-rate men for an on-site study of the situation."[45]

SECRETARY BROWNING'S
FETTERMAN INVESTIGATION COMMISSION

By mid-February Browning had prevailed upon President Johnson and his cabinet for the appointment of a special Indian Commission to consist of "six persons, of whom two were selected by the General of the Army and four by the Secretary of the Interior." Since Browning was to direct the commission, providing all instruction and receiving all reports on activities and results, the secretary could afford to be conciliatory in his selection of members. On February 18 Browning sent the official papers and instructions to General Alfred Sully, who was honored as president of the commission; Generals J. B. Sanborn and N. B. Buford; Colonel Ely Parker; and two civilians, Judge J. F. Kinney and G. P. Beauvais.

Browning did more than use military manpower to carry the peace pipe. He informed the members that their commission was to assemble at Omaha on February 23 and "proceed on to Fort Laramie as soon as possible." Further, he explained and defined their purpose. The Fetterman affair was still being interpreted as the possible prelude to a major Indian uprising. Thus the commissioners were informed that the great object of their mission was "to prevent, if possible, a general Indian war." For this purpose they were to investigate the causes of the tragedy at Fort Phil Kearny and to attempt to segregate the nonhostile tribes from the belligerent Powder River Sioux. Although the commissioners were not to make any treaties, they were assigned "to win friends among the tribal leaders." By awarding presents to their leaders, the Indians were to be encouraged to consider peaceful solutions to their complaints. As a matter of practical importance, the commissioners were notified that the military commanders in the field had been instructed to cooperate with their diplomatic endeavors.[46]

Thus Sherman's plans to initiate a threefold attack in the spring had to be modified. The general, however, was determined to cooperate only as much as absolutely required. As the commission members headed at once to their field investigations well to the west of Omaha, Sherman had to postpone Augur's expedition against the Indians along the Platte River Road and the Bozeman Trail. However, after meeting on March 8 with Hancock regarding the expedition through the territory between the Arkansas and Smoky Hill rivers, Sherman endorsed Hancock's plan to eliminate the potential of any depredations by Indians. Utley offers a critical summary: "[Hancock] touched off a bloody and perhaps needless war, portrayed the army to the public even more sharply in the image of Colonel Chivington, and insured that the legacy of Sand Creek rather than of the Fetterman disaster would shape Indian policy in 1867."[47]

In late April, after his troops had been ordered to destroy an abandoned Cheyenne-Sioux village, Hancock notified Custer: "War is to be waged against the Sioux and Cheyenne Indians between the Arkansas and the Platte." However, on April 20, at the California Crossing of the South Platte, not more than two hundred miles to the north, the appointed Indian commissioners met with leaders of some four hundred Sioux lodges of the Brulé and Oglala bands. The commissioners expressed their approval of the plan proposed by these Indians: they would continue to live in their traditional nomadic lifestyle "anywhere in the section of country" between the Platte and the Smoky Hill Trail.[48]

Throughout the following months the government's military leaders and diplomats continued to take contradictory stands in their meetings and confrontations with the Plains tribes. Solid causes were provided for the editor of the *Army and Navy Journal* to be so bewildered as to publish a complaint: "We go to them Janus-faced. One of our hands hold the rifle and the other the peace-pipe, and we blaze away with both instruments at the same time. The chief consequence is a great *smoke*—and there it ends."[49]

Later in April the commissioners met with other tribal groups in the vicinity of Fort Sedgwick on the South Platte. Sully's reports to the Indian Office repeated the complaints of these worried Indians, complaints now seconded by the commissioners, regarding Hancock's punitive practices. Buford reported on June 6 that "but for General Hancock's expedition, we would have secured peace with all the tribes to whom we were sent." Sanborn stated on May 18 that Hancock's operations were "so disastrous to the public interests, and at the same time seem to be so inhuman," that he felt obliged to file a specific protest "with the sole view of subserving the public interest."[50]

It is not clear how well informed the commission members were regarding the general turmoil of Reconstruction politics in the nation's capital. The Senate, after a bitter power struggle against President Johnson for over a year, had passed the Tenure of Office Act. Morison points out that such a negation of executive powers was but the prelude to the attempted dismissal of Johnson, that consequently impeachment proceedings had become virtually inevitable. In this atmosphere of exceptional political infighting Bogy faced an added difficulty; charges of unethical practices had been directed against him. The Senate refused to confirm him as commissioner of Indian affairs. On March 29 Nathaniel G. Taylor was appointed to direct the Indian Bureau. Sully and the members of his commission were informed of their new director by a telegram from Taylor on April 16.[51]

In the reports that he had inherited Taylor found repeated cause for mounting a major peace offensive. Further, Buford and Sanborn returned to Washington in June and early July, their personal presentations directing sharp criticisms against the recent military procedures in the West. Sanborn, supported by his background of negotiating the 1865 Little Arkansas treaty with the Cheyennes, expressed such charges:

> We should easily have secured a general peace had it
> not been for the [Hancock] trouble with the Cheyenne.
> We may prevent general war still. Operations against
> the Cheyennes should immediately cease, and com-
> missioners be sent them; otherwise our mining inter-
> ests, our railroad interests of the plains, and all our
> interests in the mountains will suffer terribly, only to
> gratify the whims or caprice of some men and officers
> who have openly proclaimed that we must have a
> general Indian war and an extermination of the race.[52]

The work of the Sully Commission, however, was not completed by the end of spring or with the separation of the friendly from those hostile to the government, west of Fort Laramie. Taylor obtained

Browning's endorsement of a belated division of the commission, one part to visit the Indians around Fort Laramie, the other to investigate the attitudes of the tribes along the Missouri. Buford reported later that the commission separated at Fort Laramie on May 10, Generals Sully and Parker heading up the Missouri "to assure the tribes of protection and justice from the United States, if they remain peaceable." Reaching Fort Sully on June 6, Sully and Parker joined De Smet, whose assignment to visit the Upper Missouri tribes predated Commissioner Taylor's appointment.[53]

DE SMET'S EARLY 1867 ASSIGNMENT ON THE UPPER MISSOURI

De Smet's appointment had been worked out during his February visit to Washington. There, according to De Smet's records, he had refused any personal recompense but had accepted $2,500 to cover "the necessary travel expenses and the outlays for an interpreter, assistants, etc." Acting Commissioner Bogy, along with his head clerk, Charles Mix, had obtained the approval of Secretary Browning. De Smet's official assignment as special agent was outlined in a letter he received on March 2 from the Indian Bureau directing him to visit the Indians on the Upper Missouri, "endeavouring to prevent the hitherto neutral tribes, from joining the hostile bands."

De Smet had wisely declined personal remuneration from the Indian Office. This stand enabled him to continue to function as a religious leader and spiritual teacher to the Indians rather than a salaried social worker whose policies and practices were dictated by the government. During his travels in 1867 and 1868 with the peace commission there was no complaint that he continued his religious instructions and services. Nor was there any question from Indian leaders regarding his guidance; as Blackrobe, his advice in all matters was always regarded as trustworthy and beneficial.[54]

De Smet's original plans were to travel up the Missouri by steamboat as far as the Yankton Agency and thereafter, with Zephyr Rencontre as his interpreter, to continue upstream following the trails along the river. Traveling in such a manner, De Smet would have more time not only to visit the various Indian encampments scattered along the river banks but also to head inland to more secluded camps. After various delays De Smet arrived at Sioux City on April 22. Seemingly De Smet was still close to a schedule that he, Rencontre, and certain Indian friends had formulated while in Washington. De Smet reported in a later letter: "The good Chief Pananniapapi [Man

Struck by the Ree], with a band of twenty-eight Yanktons, had just arrived at Sioux City. We are hourly expecting a steamboat which is to take us all together to his country. He is on his way home from Washington where he has been to transact some business for his tribe."

On April 30 the *Guidon* reached Sioux City. De Smet reported that the steamer was "crowded with passengers and merchandise for the new Territories of Montana and Idaho. It was No. 15 of the immense fleet of steamboats that were going this year to Benton." Somehow De Smet and his associates, along with the entire Yankton tribal delegation, managed to find space aboard the crowded steamboat for the six-day voyage to the Yankton Agency. De Smet made no attempt to conceal his satisfaction in reporting the affectionate reception received there from the Yankton Sioux: "The head chief, Panan-niapapi, and his traveling companions were received with open arms by their families and friends after three months of absence. I too shared, in my capacity of Black-robe, in their friendly demonstrations. They were all delighted to see us again in such good health."[55]

That satisfaction, along with a deep sense of achievement and religious fulfillment, was to make the entire month of May a special time for De Smet. It was a unity with the members of these Sioux bands that must have reminded him of his earlier identification with the Indians of the Flathead Confederacy in the northern Rockies. In the relaxed days of waiting for the arrival of the *Big Horn* and the delivery of De Smet's equipment, Indian mothers presented over two hundred children to the Blackrobe " 'to dedicate them to the Great Spirit' by baptism."

With all preparations made for a friendly trail ride, the De Smet party joined the Yankton band and headed west from the agency on May 21. The nights were cold, so cold, De Smet reported, that "water froze in my tent." But as a man of high spirits once more on the trail, he also commented on the countless items of pleasing interest—the beauty of the land through which the company leisurely traveled: "The route lay across an elevated country, through lovely smiling prairies, slightly rolling. . . . The road crosses immense and beautiful plateaus . . . where, at this agreeable season of the year, the lovely little daisy abounds; it is really the queen of this country. It appears in all its splendor, in the most vivid and most varied colors; it ranges from snow white to purple, red, blue and the deepest yellow."[56]

Each morning, addressing an attentive congregation, De Smet

offered "the holy sacrifice of the mass." Each evening the party encamped with still another nomadic group of the Missouri Sioux. Before they arrived at Fort Thompson on the evening of May 26, De Smet had performed baptismal ceremonies for an additional hundred Indian children of various bands.

Upon their arrival at Fort Thompson, De Smet counted upward of one hundred Indian lodges in the immediate vicinity, "each lodge containing eight to ten inmates," some one thousand representatives of the Brulé, Two Kettles, and Yanktonais Sioux. Received with open warmth and confidence, De Smet called at once for a council. Some thirty-six chiefs and braves, he reported, eagerly responded and actively participated in the meeting. The conference opened with a solemn prayer to the Great Spirit, and De Smet then informed the Indians of the government's desire to learn of their problems and complaints. He repeated the promises of assistance and support that the government's representatives were instructed to make. De Smet later reported the Indians' reactions:

> I will quote their own words: "Commissioners and agents of the Government come to us every year; they are affable and prodigal of speeches and promises in behalf of our Great Father. What is the reason that so many fine words and pompous promises always come to nothing, nothing, nothing?" Then they entered into a series of details concerning the injustices and misdeeds of the whites, and closed by saying: "We continue to hope that our words will reach the ear of our Great Father, that they will enter his heart and that he will take pity on us. The presence of the Black-robe to-day increases our hope and our confidence."[57]

After two more days of travel along the Missouri the group made camp in the late afternoon of May 30 outside the remains of old Fort Pierre, a site that had subsequently served as the location of the initial Fort Sully. Here they joined a large camp of over two hundred lodges. Again De Smet was deeply pleased that he was received "with every demonstration of the warmest cordiality." Continuing his investigation, De Smet "convoked the chiefs and braves in a grand council" the following day.

> They complained bitterly of the bad faith of the whites, of the commissioners and agents of the Government, always so prodigal of promises and always so slow in fulfilling them, if they ever do so. . . . In

their speeches and in private conversation they declared themselves favorable to peace. . . . They expressed also a lively desire to settle on reservations
and cultivate the soil. But until such time as their
fields produce abundance, they choose to continue to
lead the nomadic life and to range the plains peaceably in search of animals, roots and fruits.[58]

Any search for the buffalo, however, would be long and hard.
Riding with the Yankton leaders, De Smet had shared their realization: "Formerly these fair plains supported numerous herds of
buffalo, elk and deer; today, since the military road had crossed
them, the large animals have disappeared." Yet having spent a month
among Indian groups of the area, De Smet had found some reasons to
be hopeful. Sending "several expresses into the interior of the
country to announce to the hostile bands my intention of visiting
them," he anticipated that when he returned downriver, these Indian
messengers would have made their way back to Fort Sully with a
positive response. Moreover, he had learned that Generals Sully and
Parker would arrive shortly. He was impressed that their mission was
to serve as "envoys extraordinary of the Government to take special
information in regard to the complaints of the Indians against the
whites, and the injustices of which they have continually been
victims."

Certainly De Smet must have been pleased that the General Sully
who in the recent past had been so preoccupied with the implementation of Pope's punitive policy in this area had now been delegated to
hear the complaints of the tribes. He must also have been pleased that
he had been requested to cooperate with Sully and Parker in soliciting
such information from the Indian leaders. He had been urged to
accompany the commissioners on their upriver voyage, with visits to
the various Indian camps around Fort Rice, Fort Berthold, and the
new Fort Buford located near the old fur-trading post of Fort Union at
the mouth of the Yellowstone.

In a general summary of the complaints he had already heard and
the impressions he had formulated, De Smet wrote:

Thus far, all that I have observed and been able to
learn among the different bands of Indians makes me
augur favorably of their good dispositions to live at
peace with the whites. . . . They ask, and have a
right to demand, to have justice done them; that the
annuities granted them by treaty should come to them;

that the practice of putting them off with fine words should cease once for all; that they be protected against the whites who come to sow iniquity and misery in their country; and in conclusion they humbly beg their Great Father the President to grant them agricultural implements, seeds, plows and oxen to till the soil. I repeat it, if our Indians become enraged against the whites, it is because the whites have made them suffer for a long time.[59]

DE SMET: Consultant to Commissioners Sully and Parker

On June 8, the day after the arrival of Generals Sully and Parker, another great meeting was held with the representatives of the bands. De Smet gave an introductory address, repeating the theme: "Their Great Father, the President, desired to know all their griefs, in order to apply, once for all, the proper remedy." The commissioners then promised the Indians that "all the speeches made in the council should be faithfully transmitted to Washington and submitted to the President." The responses of the chiefs were very frank. De Smet commented, "Each chief, in the name of his band, showed all his mind."

After formal religious services on Sunday morning, June 9, the commissioners and De Smet said their farewells and set out for a twenty-five mile horseback ride to the new Fort Sully. There they hastened to board the *Graham,* a steamboat preparing to continue upriver. After making arrangements to leave all their vehicles, animals, and baggage at the fort, Sully, Parker, and De Smet took their places aboard. De Smet noted that the *Graham* was transporting five companies of soldiers assigned to different upriver posts, reporting: "My quality of envoy extraordinary of the Government carries with it the title of Major, strangely mated, it must be owned, with that of Jesuit. Still, it must be said in its behalf that it gives me readier access among the soldiers, a great many of whom are Catholics. I gave them, not as a major but as a priest, all my spare moments."[60]

Sully's next report to the Indian Office was sent from Fort Rice, dated June 16. His hurried letter offered a reminder of the main limitation regarding postal services to and from such a frontier location: a boat about to depart on its downriver voyage was providing the commissioner an opportunity to send a field report. Sully noted excitedly that "over 500 lodges of Upper Sioux" were waiting for them in the vicinity of Fort Rice. These meetings would be especially important since representatives of the Hunkpapas, presumed among the most hostile of the Sioux, would be present. Their later conferences, as they continued upriver, would be with tribes other than the Sioux: at Fort Berthold with the combined Arikaras, Mandans, and Hidatsas (Gros Ventres); at Fort Buford with the Assiniboines and hopefully the Crows.

The meetings at Rice, conducted through the seventeenth and eighteenth, followed the pattern adopted at Fort Sully. De Smet made the opening speeches, Sully and Parker requesting expressions of the chiefs' complaints. Again, the government's failures to deliver annuities and other promises were repeated and emphasized. However, to the commissioners' surprise, the bands here seemed to be more peaceably disposed than any they had yet encountered. The tragic lot of the Indians, along with the twofold pressures under which they struggled, seemingly won Sully's sympathy. In his report to Taylor—a report that Sully noted he had read to Father De Smet, "who requested me to state that he concurs in all here written"—the general commented:

> It is as hard for an ignorant wild Indian as it is for an educated cultivated white man to remain quietly at home starving to death, having no means of hunting, being obliged to kill his horses to keep himself and children alive, and at the same time not allowed to purchase arms and ammunition to kill small game with, while he is visited daily by Indians from the hostile camp, trying to induce him to join them, and sees, by their warring with impunity on the whites, they have more horses and mules than they want, have plenty to eat, and possess all the arms and ammunition they want.[61]

Pleased with the understanding reached with the Sioux bands around Fort Rice, the commissioners and De Smet left on June 19. After four days of uneventful travel their steamboat put in at Fort Berthold near the mouth of the Little Missouri. De Smet reported the results of the conferences:

> At Fort Berthold . . . I met my old friends, the Aricaras, Mandans and Grosventres or Minnetarees, who form one large village nearly two miles in circumference. There are some 3,000 of them; they live in permanent earthen houses. All their children are

baptized; they are at peace with the whites; they cultivate a large field (1,200 acres), raising corn, potatoes, melons, and beans, with no tools but sharpened sticks, with a few spades and mattocks. They complained bitterly of the Government agents and the soldiers. The first deceive them and rob them in the distribution of their annuities, and the others demoralize them by their scandalous conduct.

Regarding these tribes, Sully offered this forceful comment: "Policy, as well as humanity, demands that the government make more strenuous efforts to ameliorate their condition." Here, as in the other conferences during their tour, De Smet later commented, the commissioners "kept a strict list of all the complaints made by the Indians, which has been transmitted to the Department of the Interior."[62]

On the twenty-fourth the steamboat began the last portion of the commissioners' voyage. De Smet reported that it was only when they had reached a remote area approaching the mouth of the Yellowstone that they spotted the first and only herd of buffalo on their journey. They arrived at Fort Buford on June 28.

It was not until July 7 that a goodly number of Assiniboine chiefs arrived at Fort Buford for a conference. The commissioners waited for still another week for representatives of the Crows to come in, at last receiving a report that the Crows were engaged in the all-important buffalo hunt and would not be able to answer the commissioners' call.[63]

Sully and Parker, having worked at their investigation since February and deciding that their task had been completed, departed on the *Lady Grace*, reaching Fort Rice on July 21. De Smet had decided to accompany them at least down to Fort Rice, then on to Fort Sully; his initial plan was to recover his equipment there, then set out for the interior to visit the hostile bands.

At Fort Rice the commissioners and De Smet received a double disappointment. From Fort Buford Colonel Rankin had sent word that shortly after their departure some sixty Crow leaders had arrived at that post. From Colonel Elwell S. Otis, commandant at Fort Rice, they learned that "over 100 warriors of the Hunkpapas" had just departed that post, having come in response to De Smet's invitation sent by Indian messengers. They had waited ten days for the commissioners but having run out of supplies, had decided to head west on a buffalo hunt. These Sioux leaders left word for the Blackrobe that they were anxious to meet with him and expressed their strong desire for peace.

Reboarding the *Lady Grace,* the commissioners continued their downriver voyage. At Fort Sully De Smet found his "wagon and animals in an unfit condition to stand a long trip," and considering the lateness of the season, De Smet continued downriver with Sully and Parker to Sioux City.

After he had returned to St. Louis, De Smet filed this final report with the Indian Office:

> It is my candid opinion, should due regard be paid to the just complaints of the Indians, should their annuities be delivered in due and proper time, and implements of agriculture be supplied to them, and should they be dealt with honestly and kindly by agents and other persons in the employ of the Government, the bands above mentioned will be kept friendly to the whites, and the warrior bands in the Upper Missouri plains will gradually and soon join the peaceable tribes.[64]

Chapter Eleven
Congressional Resolve
A Final Great Smoke (1867–68)

We know very well that you have been treated very badly for years past. You have been cheated by everybody, and everybody has told lies to you, but now we want to commence anew. . . . It is not the fault of your great father in Washington. He sends people out here that he thinks are honest, but they are people who cheat you and treat you badly. We will take care that you shall not be treated so any more.
—General William S. Harney, Fort Laramie Peace Council, April 28, 1868

CONGRESS AUTHORIZES A NEW "PEACE OR WAR" COMMISSION

"There is much talk just at present," De Smet reported in September 1867, "of placing all the Indian tribes on one or two large reservations." Many of these displays of interest must have been occasioned by the legislation that had been enacted by Congress on July 20: the Great Father had decreed the removal of the tribes from the Central Plains.[1]

Working from the reports of the Fetterman (Sully) Commission and De Smet, Commissioner Taylor on July 12 notified Acting Secretary of the Interior W. T. Otto: "We can have all we want from the Indians, and peace without war, if we so will." Taylor reported:

We have reached a point in our national history when, it seems to me, there are but two alternatives left us as to what shall be the future of the Indian, namely, swift extermination by the sword and famine, or preservation by gradual concentration on territorial reserves, and civilization. . . . I beg leave to recommend that the government take such steps as may be deemed proper to set apart a territory, somewhere north of the northern line of Nebraska, and west of the Missouri River, of liberal dimensions, for the exclusive occupation and ultimate home of all the Indians north of the Platte.[2]

On July 15 Senator J. B. Henderson, chairman of the Committee on Indian Affairs, introduced a bill that incorporated Taylor's proposal. As Utley reports, the debate was heated, and a considerable number of amendments were proposed. The political leaders who represented the West called for an immediate and forceful military solution. Sherman, who had crisscrossed the Central Plains in June and July, notified the secretary of war: "My opinion is, if fifty (50) Indians are allowed to remain between the Arkansas and Platte we will have to guard every stage station, every train, and all railroad working parties. In other words, fifty (50) hostile Indians will checkmate three thousand soldiers. Rather get them out as soon as possible, and it makes little difference whether they be coaxed out by Indian commissioners or killed."[3]

Reportedly, negative reaction to the above statement—Sherman's telegram to Stanton was read on the Senate floor during the congressional debate—helped to secure passage of the Taylor-Henderson proposal, and Congress voted to create the Indian Peace Commission. Four members were directly named by Congress: Taylor, Henderson, John B. Sanborn, and Samuel F. Tappan (the last two had served in the volunteer army during the Civil War). Congress called upon the president to appoint "three officers of the army, not below the rank of brigadier general," who would serve as the other members of this commission. Sherman's name headed the list of Johnson's appointees; also directed to serve were Generals William S. Harney and Alfred H. Terry.

In acting to resolve the problem of the Indian presence on the central Plains. Congress declared that the actual removal would be accomplished by civilian diplomatic maneuvers; in the event of their failure, withdrawal was to be achieved by the military under Sherman's command, that force augmented by raising up to four thousand volunteer troops. Utley points out that the volunteer amendment was "a concession to western belligerence," a realistic adjustment in Washington to the mounting influence of the West on national policy. Prucha notes that Congress had fashioned "an iron hand in this velvet glove." The commissioners were notified that the areas selected for the proposed reservations would have to gain congressional approval.[4]

Regarding the Peace Commission, certain historians refer to the strong reasons for anticipating a basic power struggle among the seven members appointed by the Congress and President Johnson. Athearn comments that the appointees were "quite a mixed crowd." The commission was indeed more than a highly bipartisan group;

within its membership were the central figures of the controversy over Indian management. The two most outstanding commissioners had become, even before their appointments, the principal proponents of contradictory policies regarding treatment of the Native Americans.

Taylor, as commissioner of Indian affairs, and with the support of Interior Secretary Browning, had gained congressional endorsement, at least for a trial period, of the new policy of endeavoring to conquer by kindness. General Sherman, although faulted as a "no good" fighter by the vociferous journalists and other vested interests in the West, had assumed the prominent position held until recently by General Pope. Sherman had become the spokesman for military domination and enforced subjugation of the tribes.

In Sherman's judgment any treaties the commissioners might make "could not last twenty-four hours." In the summer of 1867, however, as the military commander over the Great Plains, Sherman still needed time. The construction of the railroads would not be completed until the late 1860s. Until the railroads, partitioning the vast territory into specific areas, were capable of providing prompt troop transportation and rapid movement of supplies across the entire West, Sherman's limited forces remained incapable of safeguarding the railroad construction camps and the other thoroughfares. Although convinced that treaty negotiations with the Indians would not produce peace, Sherman realized that the promises and threats of such diplomatic conferences might preoccupy Indian leadership and forestall an outbreak of violence. "I agree with you that the chief use of the Peace Commission," Sherman wrote to Grant, "is to kill time which will do more to settle the Indians than anything we can do."[5]

The records of the Peace Commission show that it was Sherman, not one of the civilian members, who in the organizational meeting on August 6 at the Southern Hotel in St. Louis presented the motion that Taylor be named president of the commission. It was in response to Sherman's invitation that the group held the balance of their early meetings in his office, the headquarters of the Military Division of the Missouri. Further, the tentative operational schedule was proposed by Sherman, a schedule in line with Taylor's expressed thinking. Moreover, it was Sherman who in the absence of President Taylor from August 16 until September 12 presented the motion by which Sanborn rather than Sherman or one of the other military leaders "was declared Vice President of the Commission."

Through the first ten months of far-flung activities by the commission there is proof of ready cooperation by Sherman. Certain accounts are misleading in giving the impression that Sherman, because of his bluntness in expressing himself, was removed from the commission. Admittedly Sherman was outspoken, but his nature was such that he exercised little diplomacy at any time and before any audience. Further, all the commissioners spoke very frankly, though some with more patience, to their Indian listeners. Impressed with the gravity of their mission, they all gave the chiefs to understand that their only options were peaceful withdrawal or a war of Indian extermination. Repeatedly the various members declared that their commission was not only "a Peace Commission . . . it was also a War Commission."[6]

DEFECTIVE PROCEDURES OF THE PEACE COMMISSION

From the very start, the Peace Commission experienced serious problems. Difficulties both internal and operational, some attributed to the ineffective leadership of Taylor, plagued the commission. One serious handicap in conducting meetings was repeated absenteeism, especially the nonattendance of those who campaigned for the peace pipe. Taylor and especially Henderson were Washington-bound during much of 1868, the senator providing key support for President Johnson during his impeachment trial. As a consequence, Henderson missed all the meetings held outside Washington in 1868. The solitary functioning of Taylor as presiding officer was during the Chicago meetings, October 8–10.

Sherman also faced attendance difficulties, but any problem to ensure maximum input by military representatives had been resolved. On October 5, 1867, President Johnson had appointed General Christopher C. Augur to substitute for Sherman during the latter's absence. Augur's limited participation was officially recognized and agreed upon by the commissioners, as officially recorded in the minutes of the April 1, 1868, meeting in Omaha. Yet during the October debacle in Chicago, when the generals formed a strong majority to reject Taylor's philosophy "to conquer by kindness," Taylor permitted Augur to function as a full member of the commission, even with Sherman present.[7]

Following the initial meetings of the commission in August 1867, Taylor failed to call for the election of a vice president. That practical need was satisfied, in the rather immediate monthlong absence of Taylor, by a motion presented by Sherman to his fellow commissioners. Also, in those initial activities of the commission regarding its basic purpose — "to ascertain the alleged reasons for the Indians' acts of hostility" — Taylor failed to call for the standard preliminary procedure. Only belatedly was the practice introduced, so that "all evidence before the Commission be rendered under oath." Moreover, the controversial General Hancock was offered a double exemption. Despite the grave criticisms against Hancock for his recent military campaign against some of the very tribes who were of primary concern to the commissioners, the evidence offered by the general had not been so safeguarded. Further, within a month Taylor granted Hancock's request to revise the account he had presented, without a concluding statement as to how and under what supervision Hancock offered his amended version to the commission.[8]

Another matter handled by Taylor with delay, and then with sorry inconsistency, was the commission's treatment of newspaper correspondents. Since there had been widespread interest in the congressional appointment of the Peace Commission, there was good cause to anticipate detailed press coverage. Despite such widespread displays of interest and advanced publicity concerning their work, the commissioners had moved to Leavenworth before Taylor considered a motion regarding press coverage and set a policy regarding correspondents. Although the commissioners determined to limit the press corps to six reporters, Taylor never saw fit to enforce this regulation. In fact, some of the most serious defects of the commission centered on the relationships of the correspondents to the commission.

The failures in this matter are primarily to be attributed to the commission's secretary, A. S. H. White. At the initial meeting, White was "selected Secretary of the Commission with authority to call upon the President of the Commission for such clerical assistance from time to time as the business to be transacted and the labor performed may require." White, who had accompanied Taylor on the trip from Washington, was an employee of the Department of the Interior and served as "the Secretary of the Interior's man-on-the-scene." Shortly after White was installed as secretary, Henderson moved that "the President of the Commission have the authority to employ a Phonographer." Apparently White himself, exercising that authority, hired at least more than one supposedly qualified short-hand reporter.

As early as September 14 "the resignation of Mr. H. R. Kretzehman as Assistant Secretary of the Commission" was announced. John Howland, reporter for *Harper's Weekly*, "had signed on with the group in St. Louis as a shorthand stenographer." Still another assistant was George Willis, who "had been hired in St. Louis and like Howland was under the direct supervision of A. S. H. White." However, their work as recorders during the commissioners's initial westward trip from Omaha proved faulty. As described by White during the group's return, the problem was due to "the difficulty in transcribing Howland's shorthand."[9]

Thus White's activities to fill the recording functions resulted in a double failure: recording problems and a notable conflict of interests. Since Howland, the phonographer of the commission's transcripts, continued his commitment as a working member of the press corps, his maintaining of such records was not exclusive. And with such documents as ready material for Howland's newspaper, the other press representatives had cause to insist that *Harper's Weekly* not be granted special status in obtaining news releases.

One of the most difficult points treated in the negotiations at Medicine Lodge Creek was the right, insisted on by the southern Cheyennes and Arapahos, to continue to hunt buffalo along the Smoky Hill River between the Arkansas and Platte drainages. Commissioner Henderson informed the correspondents that "in order to obtain Cheyenne agreement to the treaty," the commissioners had yielded and acknowledged this right. This concession was reported by White and various correspondents. Later the commissioners justified this compromise as only temporary. In the actual treaty, however, as subsequently ratified by the Senate, the southern Cheyennes and Arapahos were allowed to hunt only south of the Arkansas. It is hardly believable, as Jones implies, that such a deletion was a deliberate restriction imposed later by deceptive senators. It seems more probable that there was little or no proofreading of the text of the treaty provided by the commissioners. One would think that Taylor, so committed in theory to the Indian cause, would have exercised closer supervision.[10]

Still another problem was caused by the defective reporting (or handling) of the records of the actions of the Peace Commission. This problem, however, did not affect the tribes who signed the 1867–68 treaties but the subsequent students of their history. It must be admitted that White's superiors presented him with a notable example of laxity regarding listing treaty dates and signatures of the broadly styled "participants." All the commissioners in attendance at the October 10 meeting made bold to sign the treaty documents, which although they had been executed earlier, had not yet been submitted to the Senate; these were the treaties dated April 29 (with the Sioux at Fort Laramie) and July 3 (with the eastern Shoshone and Bannock at Fort Bridger). Thus certain commissioners signed these treaty documents even though they had not participated in the preliminary negotiations and had not been present on the designated dates. If the justification was proposed that such signings were formally appropriate since both were official members of the commission though not actually present, consistency should have demanded that the papers be forwarded to Washington for Commissioner Henderson's signature. However, Henderson did not sign the late papers, and such an in absentia practice had not been followed in handling the earlier treaty documents of 1868.

Following such license, White manifested an unsatisfactory concern for correctness and accuracy in his conglomerate presentation of the names of chiefs and witnesses to the Sioux 1868 treaty. Further, the records now incorrectly list the signatures of some twenty Arapaho leaders as appended to this Sioux treaty rather than to the May 10 treaty concluded with the northern Cheyenne and northern Arapaho. The Sioux treaty of 1868, better known as the second Fort Laramie treaty, was accepted and dated at Laramie on April 29, May 25–26 and possibly 28, and November 6; in addition, there were major Sioux signings in early July at Fort Rice on the Upper Missouri. Although president of the commission, Taylor was present for none of these signings. And White was not on hand to supervise all the final reportings. In early July he was assisting General Augur in the negotiations at Fort Bridger with the eastern Shoshones and Bannocks.[11]

Still another failure in Taylor's reporting, one shared with other government negotiators, was his neglect to point out the difficulties experienced by the commissioners in their attempts to communicate with tribal representatives. Since their main function was to serve as investigators and negotiators, the commissioners, initially at least, must have regarded successful communication as highly important. Their experience all too often was an unsatisfactory dependence upon interpreters whose general competence was at best questionable.

Certainly it would be unfair to presume that Taylor and Henderson were less sensitive to the problems of translation than the members of the press corps. Henry Stanley, field reporter for the *Missouri Democrat,* publicly stated that the tribesmen had little comprehension of the significance of signing the treaties. There is reason to conclude that the humanitarians among the commissioners became so frustrated with the faulty communications that they decided to settle for a greater good. So utterly convinced of the righteousness and urgency of their purpose and predetermined procedures—the survival and betterment of the Indians to be achieved by their removal to secluded reservations—these reformers may have yielded to the pressures of their situation. Facing the double problem of gaining the subsequent endorsement of the treaties by Congress and achieving their acceptance by suspicious Indian leaders, the commissioners may have settled for gaining their long-term objective. Since they were committed to achieving what they considered essential for the Indians' survival, it became of lesser importance that the Indian leaders display an understanding acceptance and intellectual appreciation of what had been very thoughtfully determined by the consensus of the agents of the Great Father.[12]

DE SMET REPORTS TO
THE COMMISSIONERS AT FORT LEAVENWORTH

On its downriver voyage, the *Lady Grace* tied up at Fort Leavenworth on August 12. De Smet was immediately hurried off to present his testimony to the Peace Commission, whose late-morning meeting was being held at post headquarters. Who introduced De Smet is not recorded; since Henderson and Terry were still not in attendance, only Sanborn and Tappan were personally unacquainted with De Smet. The minutes provide the following report:

> Father De Smit, an influential missionary among the Indians being present and desirous to go to St. Louis as soon as possible, the Commission agreed that his testimony be first taken [prior to Hancock's], touching the feelings, disposition, and wants of the Indians he had recently visited in the Upper Missouri Country together with his views of the policy that should be adopted towards said Indians, looking to their improvement and civilization. He thereupon gave an exceedingly interesting narrative of this journey and visit to the tribes referred to.
>
> Many interrogatories propounded by the Commissioners and the answers thereto by Rev. Father De Smit are a part of this record. The thanks of the Commission were tendered to Father De Smit and he was invited to accompany the Board to the Upper

Missouri River which invitation he accepted on the
condition that he could make his arrangements to do so.

There is no record of how long De Smet addressed the commissioners, although his presentation apparently took longer than anticipated. By the time he returned to the landing, the *Lady Grace,* with
all his boxes and equipment, had departed for St. Louis. De Smet left
Leavenworth shortly thereafter on another steamer; when he arrived
in St. Louis on the following day, the inhabitants were suffering from
a severe heat wave. By the time he had recovered his baggage, he was
"exhausted and feverish, and incapable of moving about." After a
physical examination at the office of his physician, Dr. Moses
Linton, De Smet received in addition to medications the doctor's
orders to decline the invitation to accompany the Peace Commission.[13]

The official record of the testimony De Smet presented to the
commissioners has not survived. The statement of General Hancock,
who had been rescheduled to present his deposition immediately
after De Smet, is included (at considerable length) in the record.
After Hancock's talk ended, the commissioners took "a recess of one
hour and a half," then reassembled to hear a report from Governor
Samuel J. Crawford of Kansas. De Smet's and Crawford's depositions
are missing from the record.

Despite the lack of an official record, newspaper articles provide a
good account of De Smet's testimony.[14] In his opening remarks De
Smet repeated the information that he, Sully, and Parker had provided in their recent written reports regarding the tribes of the Upper
Missouri: a list of the conditions affecting the Indians, a record of the
complaints of tribal leaders, and the commissioners' assessment of
the situation. Having encouraged the chiefs to express their complaints, De Smet did not hesitate to restate their criticisms: misdeeds
perpetrated upon the Indians by the military at the posts in Indian
country, failures of their agents to deliver the entirety of their
annuities, and unfulfilled promises by various representatives of the
Great Father to provide agricultural equipment and other assistance.

It would have been unrealistic to expect De Smet to speak only
about the Indian groups he contacted during the previous months.
The Upper Missouri Sioux and other river tribes were but the latest
Indian nations to capture his special interest. In short order De Smet
told about the needs of the Potawatomis at St. Mary's Indian School
in Kansas and the Flatheads he had served in the northern Rockies.
Harney, remembering De Smet's reputation in the Northwest and

across the central Plains, interrupted the presentation to ask whether all the necessary equipment and supplies for these programs had been provided without government funding.

Tappan, with a personal interest developed by his study of Sand Creek, asked general questions about Indian hospitality. Other questions were asked regarding the character and customs of the Indians. For De Smet, it was a happy opportunity to express publicly his affectionate appraisal of the Native Americans.

There were also specific questions. It was Sanborn, perhaps, who because of his experiences earlier in the summer at Fort Laramie thought it important to ask De Smet's opinion on a difficult issue — the feasibility of attempting an integrated reservation to serve the Crows and the Sioux. Apparently De Smet's response, "that it would be very difficult if not impossible," seconded Sanborn's judgment. Perhaps a wider appreciation of that conviction led in the following year to the assignment of a reservation some distance west of Sioux territory for the Crows.

Taylor manifested his special interest by directing a pointed question to De Smet. Noting that a number of congressmen and others were inclined "to select as a last establishment for all these Indians a great accumulation of territory which would be appropriate both for agriculture, for pasture and for hunting," did De Smet agree that the territory west of the Upper Missouri "would be a suitable area, and would the immediate future serve as the most favorable moment for putting this system into practice"?

De Smet replied that "the buffalo were abandoning the lands where we have made trails" and were heading into the remote country west of the Upper Missouri and around the headwaters of the Yellowstone. He reminded the commissioners that the Indians would remain reluctant to move away from their home territories, but he agreed with Taylor that such an extensive Indian country "would be suited for their support as there would be enough fertile land for agricultural areas for all, and there would still remain a sufficient reserve for hunting."

De Smet indicated the pragmatic change in his thinking that had taken place across a quarter century. At the start of the 1840s his dream along the banks of the Bitterroot had been the formation of an Indian empire across the entire Great Plains. At the opening of the 1850s he had been persuaded that at least a temporary peaceful coexistence might be enjoyed because of the benign though powerful paternalism of the government. Finally, at the close of the 1860s, with circumstances so drastically changed—the economy of the Buffalo People in ruins, the Great Father promising remedial help— De Smet could dream of the formation of distinct Indian states to join the Union. De Smet insisted that it was a possible dream if "qualified agents" could be obtained:

> The best way would be to bring the reserves together, in a manner to form Indian States which could be, with time and if the Indians make themselves capable, incorporated into the American Union. Thus would come to disappear many of the difficulties we have already noted. However, the success of this project, of so great importance, will depend in great part on the choice of agents charged with its execution. We would consider the thing more than half done, if we were certain the government would use qualified agents.

ACHIEVEMENTS OF THE COMMISSION THROUGH 1867
Although he remained in St. Louis for the remainder of 1867, De Smet was able by a perusal of newspaper accounts to keep informed of the doings of the Peace Commission. Taylor's original plan had been to hold treaty meetings with the leaders of the northern Plains tribes at Fort Laramie in mid-September and with the southern Plains chiefs at Fort Larned in mid-October. Their initial determination had been to travel up the Missouri following their arrival at Omaha to sample the reactions of the tribes to the notion of a general Indian reservation. They had chartered the steamer *St. Johns* for a voyage to Fort Buford, but they were only able to reach Fort Sully, and their conferences were restricted to meetings with Sioux bands.

De Smet must have shaken his head in dismay at the published reports. Limited by time, the commissioners had traveled less than half the north-south length of the river within Dakota Territory. They had not reached Fort Rice; not contacted the leaders of the Sioux bands around the mouth of the Cannonball; not met with representatives of the Mandans, Gros Ventres, and Arikaras or the leaders of the Assiniboines or Crows.[15]

The commissioners returned to Omaha and prepared to head west on September 14. However, they were forced to alter their schedule. Word was received from Fort Laramie that the tribal representatives could not be present by mid-September. Either Sanborn or Sherman had proposed, quite readily but unrealistically, to reschedule the meetings for the beginning of November. With a more practical appreciation of the potential for severe winter weather and consequent travel problems for the Indians, correspondent Stanley remarked: "The Commission could not reasonably have expected the Northern hostile tribes to come [at that time] to Fort Laramie."[16]

When the commissioners arrived at North Platte on September 18, they were not greeted by an assembly of Indians. However, a preliminary meeting was arranged for the nineteenth with Chief Spotted Tail and other leaders of the Brulé Sioux. In preparation for that session, versions of a position statement were prepared by Taylor and by Sherman. On the following morning the members selected Sherman's presentation as "containing the views and determinations of the Commission."

Sherman stated that the construction of the railroads westward through Kansas and Nebraska was nondebatable: "We are building costly roads of iron with steam locomotives. You cannot stop these anymore than you can stop the sun or moon." However, the dispute over the Bozeman Trail would be a matter of negotiation at the Fort Laramie meeting in early November. Quite frankly, Sherman pointed out the limited option for the tribes: to accept the reservation assignment of the Peace Commission or to face a grave threat of extermination.[17]

In mid-October the commissioners gathered at Medicine Lodge Creek, about seventy miles south of Fort Larned. General Augur, following orders from Washington, filled in for the absent Sherman. On the nineteenth Henderson was appointed to prepare and present the commission's official statement to the Cheyennes, Comanches, Kiowas, Arapahos, and Kiowa Apaches. On October 21 and 28 the treaty papers were signed by the tribal leaders.

The commissioners returned at once to St. Louis. On November 2 Taylor telegraphed an overoptimistic summary to Browning: "Please congratulate the President and the country upon the entire success of the Indian Peace Commission thus far." Since the negotiations had assigned the five southern tribes to a very restricted territory located in the southwestern part of present Oklahoma, Athearn's criticism is valid: "The commissioners did little more than create an unworkable arrangement." Athearn, however, offers a historian's perspective. An on-site reporter, Stanley, declared: "Peace has been concluded with all the Southern tribes. Civilization is now on the move, and westward the Star of Empire will again resume its march, unimpeded in the great work of Progress."[18]

The commissioners soon departed for their second trip of 1867 to

Fort Laramie. Henderson, however, was called to Washington. Sherman had other meetings, but he was persuaded to go as far as North Platte. There the frustrations of the weary commissioners became all too apparent. They had anticipated a large gathering of Sioux leaders; only a small delegation under Brulé chief Swift Bear was on hand.

Arriving at Fort Laramie on November 11, the commissioners experienced another disappointment. Only a group of friendly Crows was encamped near the fort. Red Cloud had sent word that he would come in when the garrisons at Fort Phil Kearny and Fort C. F. Smith had been withdrawn. Even the Crows presented Taylor with a troubling question from the past: where was the Crow leader who had gone "to the States some sixteen years ago"? Had De Smet been present, he would have given a firsthand account of the disappearance of this Crow delegate following the 1851 Fort Laramie treaty. Disturbed further by their professed "hard feelings towards the Sioux," the Crow leaders decided to put off signing a treaty until the spring.

On their return journey the commissioners again got off the train at North Platte on the chance that more Indians had arrived; however, only a few were on hand, and their attitude was less than friendly. The commissioners headed back to Washington. On December 11 and 12 the final commission meetings of 1867 were conducted. As the first of two important items of business, "the subject of abandoning the Powder River Road was discussed but no decision reached." Sherman, Henderson, Sanborn, Terry, and Tappan all presented papers containing their views on matters they believed should be handled in the commission's forthcoming report. The actual report, however, would be mostly the work of President Taylor.[19]

On January 7, in a meeting in the Office of Indian Affairs, that report was again considered and further amended. On the following day the document was presented to the president. Utley offers this comment: "The Medicine Lodge treaties could be presented as corroborating the soundness of the peaceable approach. After all, they appeared to realize half the grand design of consolidating all the Plains Indians on two huge reservations out of the way of the principal travel routes."[20]

Further, the report pointed out: "But one thing remains to be done with honor to the nation." Congressional approval was sought for the specific districts the commissioners had unanimously selected to serve as the two Indian territories:

First, the territory bounded north by Kansas, east by Arkansas and Missouri, south by Texas, and west by the 100th or 101st meridian. . . . The second territory bounded north by the 46th parallel, east by the Missouri river, south by Nebraska, and west by the 104th meridian. If the hostile Sioux cannot be induced to remove from the Powder River, a hunting privilege may be extended to them for a time, while the nucleus of settlement may be forming on the Missouri, the White Earth, or Cheyenne River. To prevent war, if insisted on by the Sioux, the western boundary, might be extended to the 106th or even the 107th meridian for the present.[21]

The commissioners had come West convinced of their ability to achieve a challenging, important task: to obtain by diplomatic means the acceptance by Indian leaders of the removal of the tribes from the central Plains. Before the close of 1867 Taylor could claim that his commission had achieved much of its objective: hostilities had ceased across the Great Plains, and by negotiations almost all year-round Indian inhabitants, except for temporary concessions, had been removed, at least in theory, from the land between the North Platte and Arkansas rivers.

The commissioners were fully aware, however, that their achievement had been realized by stooping to a twofold compromise. The majority of the Indian leaders had not been made to understand thoroughly their new restricted status. The subsequent practice would prove the widespread failure of Indians to comprehend that they were bound to reservations. Further, the commissioners had too readily yielded to congressional attitudes expressive of the territorial greed of the new nation. The territory proposed for the great northern reservation had been reduced to one-third the area recommended earlier by the Sully Commission and De Smet.

EARLY 1868 POLICY COMPROMISES ON POWDER RIVER COUNTRY

De Smet made early plans for his 1868 activities on the Upper Missouri, requesting from the Indian Office another assignment with sufficient funds to cover expenses. In his usual thorough manner De Smet had obtained strong endorsements from Harney and Sherman. Harney's recommendation offers some insight into that general's feelings regarding his old friend:

It is well known that he [De Smet] has almost un-
bounded influence over the Indians, and his only
object in going among them is to prevent further
hostilities. . . . You know, I am sure, that he charges
nothing for his own individual services; priests never
do. I wish, my dear General that you would write to
him. His sole object is to do good. He is one of the
most modest and diffident men I ever knew; and he is
afraid of being misunderstood. He is universally beloved by all denominations where he is known; and I
think his presence and influence among the Indians
will insure all we want.

De Smet acknowledged Taylor's letters of appointment with sincere gratitude and informed Taylor of the reports he had received on
the situation of the Indian bands around Fort Rice and Fort Berthold.
At the latter post especially it had been "an unusually severe winter
of suffering and destitution." In addition, De Smet outlined his
general plan: "My intention is to proceed (at the opening of the
Missouri river, in the upper country toward the end of March or
beginning of April), to Forts Rice or Berthold, to which posts the
various tribes usually resort during the spring, and if practicable, or
in any way possible, I will hence proceed into the interior, to confer
with the hostile bands."[22]

De Smet had kept in contact with F. F. Gerard, licensed trader at
Fort Berthold. On February 25 De Smet wrote him that all the
complaints reported by the Indian leaders had been faithfully transmitted by Sully and Parker to the Washington authorities and that
important improvements had already been planned in the administration of Indian affairs.[23]

Throughout the winter of 1867–68 De Smet had also exchanged
letters with Charles Galpin, appointed by Sully as sutler at Fort Rice,
and Frank LaFramboise, the interpreter at that post. This correspondence centered on two possible projects: a trip into the interior to
visit the hostile Sioux (a trip that De Smet had been forced to
postpone the previous July) and a new proposition, one apparently
originated by the Galpins—an assembling of the Sioux at Fort Rice
to sign a treaty. On March 17 De Smet wrote:

You state in your letter: "Should the commission
come up here and give me timely warning, I think I
will have them all [the Sioux] here by the time you
come."

> I shall communicate your proposition to General
> Sherman or to the Honorable Mr. Taylor. . . . The
> telegraph from Washington (March 16th) . . . had the
> following "The Indian Peace Commission will meet at
> Omaha the 2nd of April." As soon as I receive inside
> news I will let you know. I intend to leave St. Louis for
> Fort Rice at the end of the present month.[24]

By March Grant had informed Sherman of the decision to abandon
the posts on the Bozeman Trail. The Peace Commission received
additional positive news from the Omaha office of the superintendent of Indian affairs, H. B. Denman. Special agent A. T. Chamblin,
at Fort Laramie, had reported that a gathering of about five thousand
Indians might be expected there at the start of April with Red Cloud
and other powerful Sioux leaders in the number. Taylor's reaction
was twofold: he scheduled a commission meeting for April 2 in
Omaha, and he directed his agents to notify tribal leaders that the
commissioners would be at Fort Laramie on the seventh.[25]

Receiving a last-minute invitation to travel with commissioners
passing through St. Louis, De Smet made a slight change in his
plans. In his careful manner, he requested and received from General
Sherman a special passport, anticipating that a goodly portion of his
journey would be made without military escort. Under date of March
28 Sherman wrote from his office at the headquarters of Military
Division of the Missouri:

> To the Commanding Officers of Posts: The bearer of
> this, Father De Smet, a Catholic priest, long con-
> nected with the Missions of the Mountain Indians and
> well known to you by reputation, is on the point of
> starting for Fort Rice and the Indian country there-
> abouts, by and with the sanction and approval of the
> War and Interior Departments. Whoever shall see this
> letter is hereby requested to exhibit to Father De Smet
> every courtesy due his excellent character and to
> furnish him protection and assistance in his mission to
> the extent of his wants and necessities.[26]

The commissioners, with General Philip Sheridan and De Smet as
invited guests "and several other envoys of the Government,"
departed St. Louis on March 30, traveling by rail by way of Chicago
to Omaha. As noted above, both Henderson and Taylor would miss
all meetings and negotiating sessions with the tribes during this
western expedition, the political situation in Washington demanding

their continued presence. During the Chicago train transfer Sherman received notice that his presence "was commanded in Washington." However, he continued with the group to Omaha. There, in the April 2 meeting, although he asked to be excused from his duties as a commissioner until the close of the month and officially secured Augur as his substitute, Sherman emphasized the principles and policy the members should attempt to implement:

> Inasmuch as two of the members of the Commission are absent, and my opinion may have some practical bearing upon your operations, I want to state . . . 1st, all the Indians east of the Rocky Mountains should be gradually assembled in the two territories that have been defined. . . . I do not believe it can be done in a single year but will take many years. Our actions, however, should all bear to that ultimate conclusion.

Thus Sherman himself in the spring of 1868 repeated the call for a highly realistic policy of gradualism. It was a repetition of Taylor's proposal of the previous July, with the announcement of a "gradual concentration on territorial reserves." Quite obviously, however, such a policy was open to a variety of interpretations. Certainly there would be marked differences regarding actions that were only indirect or somewhat related to reservation containment. Sherman might make a show of granting the Sioux the "privilege of hunting . . . west of their respective territories," but he would flatly demand that "all who voluntarily reside outside of those [reservation] limits for temporary purposes such as hunting should at once pass under the control of the military authorities."[27]

Sherman's views were readily accepted by the commissioners. By resolution he was delegated to solicit in Washington the support of both Henderson and Taylor. Further, he was appointed "to appear before the Committees of the two Houses of Congress to urge the immediate passage of legislation" concerning the organization of the two grand reservations and the necessary funding. As noted above, the boundaries of the northern reservation had already been defined by Taylor and other commissioners as the western half of present South Dakota. The territory west of this reservation as far as the Big Horn Mountains—the country between the 104th and 107th meridians from the 43rd parallel to the 46th—would be described by a new term. This Powder River region would be defined in the 1868 Fort Laramie Treaty as "unceded Indian territory," an area to be regarded as completely off-limits to any white person and for only temporary and restricted use by the Indians.

This new policy, therefore, would lead to another important diplomatic victory over the Indians. The policy was founded on what seemed a compromise; however, it was a compromise only in appearance. The Bozeman Trail would be closed, and as announced by Sanborn to Spotted Tail on April 4, the military posts would be abandoned. The government, however, would assume title to and exercise supervisory control over the entire Powder River country. With their signing of the 1868 treaty, the Sioux leaders relinquished their claims to any territory west of the 104th meridian. They yielded title to the land through which the Bozeman Trail passed and the land on which the forts were located. With the 1868 Fort Laramie treaty the Great Plains had legally become government property.[28]

Shortly after their April 2 meeting Sherman and the other commissioners went their separate ways. Official action had been taken to request Congress to legislate the organization and funding of the two grand reservations. Sherman hurried east to attend the impeachment trial. Sanborn and Tappan, with Generals Harney, Terry, and Augur, were joined by De Smet and the other members of the commission's party as they boarded the Union Pacific train westbound from Omaha.

De Smet must have been reminded of his many journeys across these Nebraska plains. Only one year earlier Nebraska had been admitted as the thirty-seventh state; only fourteen years earlier this buffalo-rich eastern region of Indian country had been proclaimed Nebraska Territory. At North Platte the commissioners lost little time turning to official business. Even before an eleven o'clock meeting on April 4 with Spotted Tail's delegation of Brulé Sioux, they attended to the special assignment proposed for De Smet. In addition to a formal military passport, the commissioners provided De Smet an official letter that stated his specific task:

> Revd. P. J. De Smet . . .
>
> The Indian Peace Commission have learned with pleasure that you are about visiting the Indian tribes, of the Upper Missouri, and fully appreciating the success that has ever attended your humane efforts amongst them, desired to embrace the opportunity, thus afforded, to convey to the Indians their intentions to hold councils with them at Fort Rice the coming season, and making arrangements, to be approved by

the Government, for their location in a region of country, to be selected, acceptable to their future wants as an agricultural and pastoral people, for the accomplishment of which objects the Commission are fully authorized and empowered to act.

We desire to be informed at as early a day as practicable what the feelings and intentions of the Indians of the Upper Missouri are and at what time and place they will be ready to meet the Commissioners.

You may explain to the Indians that it is not the design to curtail their hunting privileges, but to prepare a home and means of subsistence for them, when the game has become insufficient for them.[29]

Instead of returning at once to Omaha, De Smet accompanied the members of the commission as they rode the train west past Fort Sidney and beyond the western boundary of Nebraska. On April 6 they arrived at Fort Russell, just west of the new town of Cheyenne. De Smet later reported:

Together with the generals, we made an excursion of forty miles, for observation and pleasure, to the summit of the Black Hills, [Sherman Pass] which the railroad crosses on the way to San Francisco. We were assured that this is the highest point attained by a railroad hitherto, being 8,000 feet above sea-level. The Peace Commissioners then turned their faces toward Fort Laramie. According to the arrangement, I returned to Omaha, where I spent the Paschal period.[30]

At Fort Russell the commissioners received word of still another delay in meeting with the Sioux. Special Indian agent A. T. Chamblin reported from Fort Laramie that Red Cloud and other leaders would not be ready to meet the commissioners there until the end of the month. Still eager to initiate treaty negotiations, the commissioners headed north down the Chugwater drainage, on April 10 arriving at Fort Laramie at the junction of the Laramie and North Platte rivers. It was not until April 29 that a number of Brulé Sioux representatives rode up to the fort for a council. This group, the chiefs and head soldiers of the Brulé band, became the first Indian signers of the second Fort Laramie treaty. During preliminary negotiations Harney expressed the commissioners' promises and a warning:

I am afraid you do not understand why we want to make peace. Perhaps you think we are afraid. You can not be such fools as that, I hope. We do not want to go to war with you because you are a small nation, a handful only compared with us, and we want you to live. . . . We are kind to you here. You have true hearts and we want you to live. We have not been making war with you. You are at war with us. We have not commenced yet. I hope you will not drive us to war.

Although Harney manifested a sympathetic warmth and regret beyond Sherman's ken, he was also repeating the warning that Sherman had given the chiefs the previous year: the only choice for the Indian leaders was to capitulate and accept the removal and advantageous peace terms offered by the commissioners at this time or face the extermination of their tribes. It was an ultimatum that De Smet clearly recognized, for since the previous August he had heard it repeatedly. Henderson had warned the Yanktons: "He who among you now goes to war will soon die." Sanborn had stated the urgency of Indian acceptance of the offer, the final offer to be made by the government: "This is the last effort of the President to make peace with you and save for you a country and home." Like the other commissioners, Sanborn repeatedly told the Indians, "We are here as much to save you from impending destruction as to stop the war."[31]

De Smet had come to understand that the government had assigned these commissioners a determined purpose: "To secure, or to conquer, a peace." Confined to reservations, Indians were promised considerable assistance to implement the requisite change in lifestyle; by refusing to move to reservations, the Indians could expect only to be hunted down and exterminated. De Smet had repeatedly warned the people he loved: an armed rebellion would provide quasi justification for the policy of tribal extermination.

On May 8 the special treaty prepared for the Crows was interpreted to them and signed by eleven principal men. In line with the recommendation stressed by De Smet and Sanborn, the Crows were assigned a reservation in south-central Montana; further, by Augur's treaty at Fort Bridger on July 3, the eastern Shoshones were assigned a reservation off the eastern slope of the Wind River Range southeast of the Big Horns. With Taylor in Washington, his concept of a single northern reservation had been discarded.

On May 10 certain northern Cheyenne and Arapaho leaders signed a treaty specifically prepared for their tribes. Article 2 of the treaty gave them the choice of joining the Great Sioux Reservation or sharing in the area that had been assigned to their southern bands at the Medicine Lodge treaty of the previous October.[32]

Throughout April the commissioners had been repeating their promise that the forts on the Bozeman Trail would be removed, but May passed without the withdrawal of the army units. Red Cloud, the most prominent Sioux leader, reportedly sent notice: "When we see the soldiers moving away and the forts abandoned, then I will come down and talk." Not until the close of July were the posts abandoned following the military withdrawal.

Sherman did not join the commissioners at Fort Laramie until the end of April, after the treaty had been signed by the Brulé leaders. With Sanborn now acting as president pro tempore, the members (Sherman, Harney, Terry, Tappan), along with Augur, held their final western meeting as a group on May 9. They resolved to divide into four parts: Terry to go to Forts Randall and Sully on the Missouri to prepare for the arrival of Sioux groups there; Augur to proceed to Fort Bridger to negotiate a treaty with the Bannocks and Eastern Shoshones; Sherman and Tappan to head southwest to deal with the Navajos; Sanborn and Harney, following a hopefully productive stay at Fort Laramie throughout May, to join Terry on the Missouri. In addition, the proposal of Galpin and De Smet to visit the remote Sioux camps was accepted.

In late May Sanborn and Harney obtained the signatures of some leaders of two Sioux groups, the Oglalas and Minneconjous. Hoping that the leaders of other Sioux bands might come in, the commissioners left a copy of the treaty with General A. J. Slemmer, commander of the post, and Charles Geren, the commission's Sioux interpreter. On May 27 Sanborn and Harney left for the Upper Missouri by way of Omaha. On July 1 Geren forwarded to Taylor some later signings at Fort Laramie: Oglala and Bad Face leaders on May 28 and June 3, a large party of northern Arapahos on June 16. The final signings at Fort Laramie were reported by Slemmer's replacement, General William Dye, on November 20—the long-delayed acceptance of the treaty by Red Cloud and his associates on November 6.[33]

Following their arrival at Omaha, on June 4 Sanborn and Harney sent the Indian Office the following summary of the commission's policy and supposed accomplishments. The gradualism of removal, which Sherman had emphasized two months earlier, had now been interpreted, at least by commissioners on the scene, in a highly restricted manner; it proved an interpretation regarded as most unrealistic by the Indians. The signatures of only a minority of the Sioux bands had been obtained, yet the commissioners optimistically declared their success by setting a definite schedule for removal:

> We now believe that quiet and peace have been secured on the plains. The Commissioners have determined that the charities and the activities of the government to civilize the Indians should be made at a point as far removed as possible from the great lines of land travel across the plains. . . .
>
> Our treaty designates for the Sioux—the northern line of Nebraska and the 46th Parallel, and the Missouri River and the 104th Meridian. It is the purpose of the government to draw towards and into the above described country all the Indians of the above named tribes as fast as possible without producing wars. It is therefore determined that all business of the Interior Department with the Sioux and with the bands affiliated with them be moved to Fort Randall, or at such points near them as the Department should designate and provide with necessary buildings. Therefore the Commissioners directed that no regular issues and supplies from the Interior Department be issued at Fort Laramie after the 1st day of June.

Thus, though dealing with a people many of whom lived throughout the Black Hills or even west of the 104th meridian, the commissioners had decreed that the new supply center for all the Sioux would be located east of the 99th, in the extreme southeastern corner of the Great Sioux Reservation. This was about 250 miles east of Fort Laramie, the supply center that had so long served the Sioux. Certainly the commissioners' designation of Fort Randall was beneficial to the government: the cost of transporting treaty annuities would be reduced, and the power position of governmental manipulation and domination would be increased. It would also become clear rather quickly that only a minority of the Sioux, those living east of the Black Hills, would even try to adjust to such an inconvenient location. Utley bluntly comments that these stipulations "had been badly explained if not deliberately misrepresented" to Red Cloud and Spotted Tail, the leaders of distinct Sioux bands. Within five years the official agencies for both these groups were located

outside their reservation's southern boundary and much closer to
Fort Laramie than Fort Randall.[34]

THE SIOUX PEACE RIDE OF JUNE 1868

On April 21 De Smet left Omaha on the *Columbia,* heading for Fort
Rice. The captain and most of his staff happened to be Catholics, and
once again De Smet was provided a small chapel to conduct daily
religious services. However, hardly concealing his eagerness to
reach Fort Rice, he explained the reasons for the snail's pace at which
the *Columbia* ascended the Missouri: "The Missouri was at that time
very low, and our progress slow in consequence. . . . After thirty-
three days of constant struggle with the current, sandbars and snags,
I thanked and bade farewell to the worthy captain and all my old and
new acquaintances and was put ashore at Fort Rice."[35]

De Smet's baggage was taken to the lodge prepared for him while
he exchanged greetings with the Indian leaders. General Terry, the
first of the peace commissioners on the scene, did not arrive until
May 31. On the thirtieth De Smet posted a progress report to Taylor,
noting that a goodly crowd of Indians was already on hand and that
they manifested a well-developed interest in the peace council:

> At Fort Rice I found over four hundred lodges en-
> camped on both sides of the river. According to the
> promise I made them last fall & winter, they were
> anxiously expecting my arrival & [I] was warmly
> welcomed & received by them. On the 25th instant I
> held a Council with the Indians on the west side of the
> river composed of Chiefs & braves of various bands,
> Unckpapas, Blackfeet, Sans Arcs, Minikanjews &
> Upper Brulés—& on the 28th instant, [on the] east
> side of the river, with the Upper and Lower Yan[k]ton-
> nais, Sissitons, Cut-heads, Santees & Blackfeet. Each
> council occupied from three to four hours—in which I
> fully detailed the object of my mission. . . . They all
> expressed a sincere anxiety of my proceeding to the
> hostile bands, in the Interior of their country &
> promised to give me a powerful escort to assist me in
> my endeavours. They all feel sensible that a strong
> effort must be made to bring in the principal war
> chiefs, & with their assistance, bring about the de-
> sired peace. . . . At this very moment, an Indian
> warrior, from the hostile bands has come in, & brings

me the news that I am expected amongst them & that
they are willing to listen to words of peace.

By the first opportunity I shall let you know the
result of our visit to the hostile bands.

Additional details might be provided from De Smet's personal
letters and official reports and later accounts by the Galpins of the
advanced and final preparations for the planned visit. Such items as
the banner of peace, bearing the image of the Virgin, that the
Blackrobe would unfurl as he rode with the Galpins at the head of the
cavalcade, may have been made by some skilled seamstress back in
St. Louis. In a final planning meeting of the twenty-ninth, Hunkpapa
chief Running Antelope addressed the basic issue and offered his
endorsement of De Smet's proposal, declaring that the Indians were
no longer able to live "as our fathers taught us." His people "must
look to the Earth for subsistence."

In his May 30 letter to Taylor De Smet included a portion of the
speech by Running Antelope and forwarded a copy of the pledge that
Galpin had written out and presented to him: "I will herein most
respectfully tender you my services [as interpreter] for your trip to
the Interior to meet the Hostile Bands. My wife and relations will also
go with you." Mrs. Galpin (Eagle Woman) had voluntarily committed herself to the project some months before De Smet's arrival at
Fort Rice, and special acknowledgment seemed proper for her role in
organizing the expedition.[36]

This journey has been called an expedition for a number of
reasons. It covered some three hundred miles of Indian trails from
Fort Rice on the Missouri River in south-central North Dakota to the
remote encampment of Four Horns and Sitting Bull near the confluence of the Yellowstone and Powder rivers. Including the days spent
there in council, the activities occupied almost the entire month of
June. In reality this expedition was a "peace ride" whose participants
included over eighty Indians, male and female. When the group
returned to Fort Rice on June 30, they brought with them eight
delegates from the hostile camp, appointed to listen to the men sent
by the Great Father.

It is no longer possible—if it ever was—to list which Indian
leaders took part in the expedition according to what motivation.
Because of family background and her close identification with the
Hunkpapas and the Two Kettles, the urgings of Eagle Woman may
have proved effective among individuals of these bands. Some
Indian leaders may have joined because of special connections with

Charles Galpin, a long-term fur trader. Still others, like Running Antelope, through their experiences had apparently become convinced of the urgency of an all-out effort for peace. Realistically appreciative of their limited options, these Indians may have encouraged others to join. De Smet named nine leaders of various bands who served as his escort. Five individuals on his list were also named by Eagle Woman, who reported that she had invited seventy of the bravest men and ten women, the latter to demonstrate that the party came in peace.[37]

De Smet reported that he celebrated mass early on June 3 so that the expedition could head out from Fort Rice at sunrise. It proved a tedious and physically demanding ride, especially for De Smet. It was not until the sixteenth that contact was made with some far-ranging scouts of the Hunkpapas and not until the nineteenth that they rode into the Powder River encampment. By the estimates of Galpin and De Smet, the number of Indians involved totaled over four thousand. About one o'clock on the afternoon of the twentieth the great council was formally opened with the customary Indian ceremony of the peace pipe. De Smet and his company were then officially welcomed by Black Moon, the camp spokesman designated by Four Horns and Sitting Bull.

After the warrior societies had sung and danced, Black Moon said they were ready to hear the Blackrobe. In addition to keeping his journal, Galpin acted as De Smet's interpreter. Perhaps his twofold function explains why, although De Smet later stated that the council lasted three or four hours, the report of De Smet's speech consists of only two paragraphs. De Smet's summary affords the more satisfactory account:

> I spoke to them of the dangers with which they were surrounded, and of their weakness beside the great strength of the whites, if the "Great Father" were forced to use it against them. . . . Today his hand was ready to aid them, to give them agricultural implements, domestic animals, men to teach them fieldwork and teachers of both sexes to instruct their children, and all this offered without the least remuneration or cession of lands on their part.[38]

The subsequent speeches of Black Moon and Sitting Bull summarized the injustices inflicted by the whites. It is not possible to provide a verbatim report; the records differ. But all the versions are in accord in presenting Sitting Bull's determination: "Some of my people will return with you to meet the chiefs of our Great Father who are sent to make peace. I hope it will be accomplished, and whatever is done by them, I will accept and remain ever a friend to the whites."

As spokesman for the peace riders, Two Bears (Yanktonai) and Running Antelope (Hunkpapa) addressed the gathering. Boldly declaring that their party had not come "to beg of you any favor on the strength of our [Indian] relationship," Two Bears insisted: "I have come here with a few of our Chieftains and Braves of the Eastern Sioux who represent some 700 lodges, to tell you that our minds are made up and we will be guided by his [De Smet's] advice, and the great men, the Commissioners, sent by the President to accomplish something definite for our future welfare."

Running Antelope offered the concluding speech, speaking for himself and the entire party:

> I had made up my mind, on leaving the fort, to once more ask you to be at peace with the Whites & that is why you see me here today; but as the request is not necessary, you having with your own good seen the propriety of so doing, all now that remains now for me to say [is] I thank you in the name of the Great Spirit for your kind treatment and attention to the Black Gown & his party. . . . The men whom you will send to hear what the great men of the Great Father will say and do for our future good will be pleased.[39]

Following Running Antelope's speech, "the Council ended — & we returned to our Lodge, amidst shouts of songs & joy — the very earth seemed to shake with their dancing." One final gesture, an exchange of gratitude and confidence, was recorded by De Smet: the Black-robe gladly acceded to the wish expressed by the chiefs that his "great banner of Peace" be left in the camp "as a souvenir of the great day of the Council." As on the previous evening, De Smet and the Galpins were treated as special guests in the lodge of Sitting Bull. According to Galpin's account, the travelers made all their preparations to be able to leave early the following morning. Regarding their departure, De Smet reported: "June 21st . . . I said my Mass at an early hour, and before sunrise we commenced our return to Fort Rice, where the Government Commissioners were awaiting me. My escort of eighty-four men was on the spot. The eight Hunkpapa deputies were also on hand, and some thirty families of the hostile camp (numbering 160) chose to accompany me."

By the evening of June 24 the expedition had completed the first half of their return journey. De Smet had not been in contact with General Terry since June 16 when he had sent a messenger to report that a welcoming delegate had been received from Sitting Bull. On June 25, from "Box Elder Camp," De Smet and Galpin dispatched another messenger, All-Over-Black, to convey a brief report of the good news to the commissioners. By the evening of June 28 the messenger returned from the fort with congratulations from General Terry: "We are delighted to learn that your expedition had been so successful, and we feel that not only ourselves but the nation owes you a debt of gratitude for the extremely valuable service which you have rendered to it. Generals Harney and Sanborn arrived here on the twenty-first and they will remain until a treaty can be consummated."

FINAL NEGOTIATIONS AND
TREATY SIGNINGS AT FORT RICE

On June 30 the expedition made a "solemn entry into Fort Rice." De Smet noted that they were welcomed not only by the peace commissioners and Colonel Elwell Otis, commander of the fort, and his soldiers but by the "thousands of Indians who were there assembled." On July 2 the great peace council took place. De Smet reported later that "everything passed off favorably and the treaty of peace was signed by all the chiefs and principal warriors."[40]

The postsigning celebration—feasting and distribution of presents—was held July 3–4. De Smet and the Galpins found an additional (highly personal) reason for celebrating. On July 4 the Blackrobe joyfully responded to Eagle Woman's request by baptizing her. After bestowing the name Matilda, he hastened to bless the marriage of his two dear friends. With an appreciation of his indebtedness to the Galpins, De Smet must also have shared with them the grateful praise expressed by Terry, Sanborn, and Harney in their joint letter:

> We the undersigned, members of the Commission charged with concluding peace with the Indians were present at the council recently held at this post, and have a lively desire to express to you our high appreciation of the important services that you have rendered us and the country by your unceasing devotion and your efforts crowned with success to induce the hostile tribes to meet with us and to enter into treaty negotiations with the Government.[41]

The tribute expressed by the commissioners was based upon more than bringing Sitting Bull's delegates to Fort Rice. In long conferences throughout the morning and afternoon of July 2, Sanborn, Terry, and Harney met with Gall and the other Hunkpapa representatives as well as the leaders of other Sioux bands. The minutes of their meetings record statements made at that council by some twenty Indian leaders. Eight of those speakers from diverse bands emphasized the leadership status they accorded De Smet, a unique tribute. Expressing an affectionate trust in De Smet's singular dedication to their good, these Indians freely acknowledged his special influence in their lives.[42]

It must have pleased De Smet to hear their laudatory remarks and to note their willingness to negotiate with the representatives of the Great Father. Further, De Smet had reasons—the considerations he had proposed to Sitting Bull and his associates—for optimism regarding the outcome. The obviously benign paternalism expressed by Sanborn measured up to the high anticipations De Smet had formed and acted on. Having assured the Indian leaders that the hand of the Great Father "was ready to aid them," De Smet's high hopes were confirmed by Sanborn's statements:

> You must know well the purposes for which we are sent to you. You do know that great changes have taken place in your country during the last few years and are still taking place. Country that comprised your best hunting grounds when the older of you were young is now occupied by the whites. You see whites all around your country. You see from year to year your game diminishing. You blame the whites for these changes and go to war. This does not prevent the changes, but if the whites go to war too, hastens it. . . .
>
> You must know, as we know, that without the protection and aid of the President of the United States you must perish. There are two parties among the whites, a party who are your friends, and a party who are your enemies and who want to take your country and destroy your people. Now we have been sent out, as your friends, to meet you in council, talk with you, and hear your complaints and agree upon some plan whereby you can remain at peace with the whites and reserve to you and your children a country and home wherein you can always live.

Sanborn promised that all whites except the Indian agents and other government personnel would be excluded from the country between the Niobrara and Grand rivers and between the Missouri and the "Western base of the Black Hills." Further, the hated military posts along the Bozeman Trail would be removed, the entire Powder River country classified as unceded Indian land until the Indians saw fit to cede it by treaty. Sanborn then offered a choice to individual Indians:

> All Indians who have or hereafter shall abandon the chase and settle down permanently will do so in the country from which the whites are excluded West of the Missouri River and not elsewhere. All who wish to roam and hunt can do so whenever they please, while they remain at peace, and game lasts. To those who settle down and commence farming we agree to furnish food for four years, and cattle and horses, tools to work the ground, teachers, farmers, blacksmiths, mechanics and physicians, and to give a good suit of clothes each year to every Indian man, woman, and child, and such other things as shall enable them to live well for thirty years. To those who continue to hunt, we agree to give a good present of such things as they most want for the same time. The terms we propose are more liberal than you have ever had. . . .
> You should not think of rejecting them, for so liberal terms are not likely again to be offered.

De Smet was once again hearing expressions of understanding and generosity, attitudes expressed by the commission members who had in early April sent him from North Platte. He had been promised that such assistance was to be offered the Indians and specifically directed to tell them that the government's intention was not to curtail their hunting privileges but "to prepare a home and means of subsistence for them, when the game has become insufficient." De Smet must have been pleased with the commissioners' promises at the Fort Rice council.

In conclusion, Sanborn declared:

> We shut the whites out of a country which will be your own. And besides we give you the privilege of hunting wherever the game can be found. We quite understand you when you tell us that you don't want to receive any presents, that you don't wish to be thought as selling

your land. We are not going to give you these goods in
exchange for any lands. We give them to you to help
you along. You want land to hunt over, while we only
want it to raise stock; so that when the game will be
gone and you will not need it, then we shall require the
land. . . . If the treaty is satisfactory to you all, we
would like to have you come up and sign it now.[43]

Because of the language barrier, the exchange of communications
on highly critical matters was faulty at best. As is evident from his
presentation quoted above, Sanborn offered only a remote interpretation of the actual treaty text. For example, he substituted "the
Western base of the Black Hills," an expression extremely vague,
especially as then used, for the 104th meridian. Sanborn proposed
the boundaries of drainages rather than the parallels of cartogra-
phers.[44] Along with Harney, Sanborn attempted to be benign and
adaptable, but the Sioux version of this second Fort Laramie treaty
was already cast in stone. The one official Sioux document had been
prepared in late April for the signings by the Brulés and others at Fort
Laramie, and it was this document to which were appended the July
signings at Fort Rice.

In fairness, it might also be pointed out that Sanborn and Harney
had been preoccupied with the difficult matter of such negotiations
for almost a full year. By comparison, Mitchell and Fitzpatrick
opened the 1851 council on September 8 and marched away on
September 23. As peace commissioners, Sanborn and Harney had
been busy through most of 1868. They had journeyed to the southern
Plains, made two voyages up the Missouri, traveled to remote Fort
Laramie three times. It seems understandable that during that period
and in difficult circumstances Sanborn and Harney may have proved
less than consistent in their attempts to be sensitive and fair as well as
politically effective.

Certainly in the Fort Rice council Sanborn called for a much more
gradual Indian removal than the demands he had reported in previous
months. At this meeting Sanborn called for a Sioux reservation that
was less than one-half the extensive territory he and De Smet had
strongly recommended just one year earlier. In his final attempts at
Fort Rice to persuade these Sioux leaders to accept the treaty,
Sanborn repeatedly mentioned and seemed to promise that in the
near future there would be "additional reservations along the Missouri River."

There are good reasons to conclude that the Indian leaders received dissimilar messages. An indication of the Indians' uncertainty is evidenced by one of the concluding discussions at Fort Rice. The final stumbling block to widespread Sioux acceptance of the peace proposals was stated by Gall at the morning conference on July 2. It was the same Indian demand that De Smet had reported in 1866 and then repeated, along with his associates Sully and Parker, in 1867. It was one of the specific points made by Sitting Bull in the council at his Powder River camp. Gall told the commissioners: "There is one thing that I do not like. The whites ruin our country. If we make peace, the military posts on this [Missouri] river must be removed, and the steam boats stopped from coming up here."[45]

At least half the Indian leaders who rose to speak after Gall repeated the same demands: that the posts on the Missouri River, like those on the Powder River, be removed and that the Missouri River, like the Bozeman Trail, be closed to white traffic. These demands reveal the failure of the Indian leaders to understand the significance of the treaty. Four military posts—Sully, Rice, Stevenson, and Buford—were all north of the Grand River, which Sanborn had designated as the northern boundary of the Great Sioux Reservation. Further, the entire eastern bank of the Missouri was no longer to be classified as Indian territory. The Indian leaders failed to realize that they were signing away their lands and that they were not receiving any guarantee of their exclusive right to their homelands.

The fourfold purpose of the commissioners contained proposals that (1) a defined and limited area be acknowledged as assigned exclusively for perpetual residence of the Sioux; (2) the Powder River country be classified as an unceded area, to be used temporarily by the Sioux for hunting; (3) supplies and services necessary for the Indians' survival would be provided by the government; and (4) such supplies and services from the government be regarded as compensation by the Sioux who, as the treaty expressed it, would "relinquish all right to occupy permanently the territory outside their reservation."

The Indian leaders must have realized, in varying degrees, that they were powerless to press their unrealistic demands. The river forts were already situated outside the designated Sioux reservation. Furthermore, the leaders were aware, as Lone Dog openly reminded them, that their impoverished people "did not want to be dying from starvation and disease. . . . They said: 'we want the protection of the United States Government.'" Behind all the posturing of diplomatic procedures the Sioux leaders must have realized their dire poverty and dependence. With the buffalo rapidly disappearing from their territory, they were no longer negotiators but mendicants.

Throughout more than half a century the government had attempted to conduct an Indian policy based upon the treaty process. By midcentury, as Prucha points out, the treaty stipulations "were not the result of negotiations between two sovereign and independent powers." The treaty process had developed into "a convenient and accepted vehicle for accomplishing what United States officials wanted to do." Thus the treaties negotiated in 1867 and 1868 by the Great Peace Commission, a group controlled in the main by humanitarian concerns, had attempted to provide for Indian survival by tribal commitment to adjustment programs in restricted and exclusive areas.

Utterly limited in their options, the Indian leaders merely accepted the applications, to be supervised by government officials, of this objective. Indeed, these sessions on the southern and northern Plains might be regarded as the final Great Smoke. These meetings, with all the established protocol, were the last of the treaty process. On August 10 of the following year President Grant assigned a different tract of territory for the reservation of the southern Cheyennes and Arapahos by executive order. No longer was there cause to invoke the facade of formal negotiations. On March 3, 1871, Congress took steps to terminate the treaty system.[46]

Chapter Twelve

Western Echoes of
"They Must Necessarily Yield" (1868–78)

Established in the midst of another and a superior
race, and without appreciating the causes of their
inferiority or seeking to control them, they must
necessarily yield to the force of circumstances and ere
long disappear.
> —President Andrew Jackson, December 3, 1833

CONGRESS REAPPLIES JACKSON'S
POLICY OF TRIBAL REMOVAL

At the negotiation session held on the afternoon of July 2 at Fort
Rice, the Sioux accepted Sanborn's invitation to endorse the treaty.
De Smet signed six times as witness to the official signings by the
leaders of the Sioux bands. This was the only occasion on which De
Smet signed treaty papers.[1]

On the afternoon of July 4 De Smet joined Sanborn and Harney as
they boarded the steamboat *Agnes*. During the downriver voyage
Sanborn and Harney took depositions from four of the Sioux leaders
who were passengers on the steamboat: Santee chiefs Wapasha and
Big Eagle, Long Mandan of the Two Kettle band, and Grass of the
Blackfoot Sioux. The previous year Big Eagle and Long Mandan had
been members of the tribal delegations who had visited Washington.
Impressed now by their charges against the agents and policies of the
Indian Office, Sanborn declared: "I will look to these complaints
myself. I desire to have an end put to this dishonesty. The Indian
business may likely go to the military department. The Commissioners have requested a change in these things."[2] Although throughout the earlier meetings of the commission Sanborn had voted with
Taylor, Henderson, and Tappan for continued civilian control of the
Indian Office, his experiences in the field seem to have changed his
outlook. At the October meetings of the commission Sanborn would
back Sherman's resolution to transfer control of Indian affairs to the
War Department.

When the *Agnes* docked briefly at Fort Sully, De Smet exchanged
farewells with the commissioners and disembarked. Continuing
downriver, the commissioners reached Sioux City on July 9. From

the Western Union office Sanborn sent an optimistic report to Interior Secretary Browning: "That portion of the Indian Commission that went to Fort Rice held council there on the 2nd inst. Five thousand Indians were present, and 8,000 more Sioux were represented. The Hunkpapa—the most hostile Indians in the region—sent in a large delegation who made peace in behalf of their tribes. The council was eminently successful in all respects."[3]

At Fort Sully De Smet enjoyed the hospitality of his friend General David S. Stanley, commander of the post. The chiefs Long Mandan and Grass must have also disembarked at this landing, for their tribal encampments were in this general area. After visiting with their people for a few days, De Smet left by another steamboat on the eleventh. Following a stop at Omaha, De Smet continued downriver to Fort Leavenworth. There he headed west on his customary detour to St. Mary's Indian Mission. Kansas, however, was experiencing an extreme heat wave. De Smet hurried through a few more days of travel and reached St. Louis about the twenty-seventh. He had spent four busy months working with the Peace Commission.[4]

On August 4 De Smet wrote to the Galpins, but within a few days of sending this letter De Smet was surprised by the arrival in St. Louis of the Galpin family. Through the following two weeks of August the visits of Eagle Woman and her husband must have celebrated the shared achievement of "their long and interesting trip." In addition to reliving their adventure and parties there were shopping expeditions for the three Galpin girls and their mother. De Smet commented: "They enjoyed good health, but seemed to prefer Fort Rice."

There were important business matters to be handled, as De Smet mentioned in his letter of September 7 to Colonel Otis. De Smet introduced Major Galpin to General Sherman, "with whom he had long conversations." With the increased responsibility Sherman had received from Congress, the general must have been eager to learn Galpin's thinking regarding the Sioux. Galpin also met with General Harney. De Smet wrote: "I recommended the major in strong terms to both generals. . . . He might render great service to the Indians."

Harney had been appointed by Sherman in early August to oversee the Great Sioux Reservation. Harney had telegraphed Galpin in St. Louis from Omaha to report upriver immediately. By early September the Galpins joined Harney on the steamboat *Miner* and continued north on the Missouri to Fort Rice. In November the Galpins relocated their family to the newly established Grand River Agency about a hundred miles below Fort Rice; there the major set up his independent trading post and served under Harney as the agency interpreter. But after only one year Galpin took ill and died. A few months later De Smet received the following report from the Cheyenne Agency south of Grand River:

> The "Log," an Indian who accompanied you and Major Galpin to the hostile camps, speaks daily of you. He says he is in the same good road you put him in and he and a number of his people intend planting corn this spring. He is one of the most anxious to hear from you. He tells me to write to you that the death of Major Galpin has left him as an orphan, that the only hopes of the Indians were in Major Galpin and you; and one being dead their hopes are now solely in you. He says they know you are their friend and wish them all well and that you will do all in your power to help them.[5]

The termination of the impeachment proceedings against President Johnson at the close of May did not immediately restore harmony and unity in Washington. Pressures from the Indian Office finally gained congressional ratification of the Medicine Lodge treaties of the previous year. On July 27, however, Congress turned against the Indian Office and Taylor. Appropriating $500,000 to implement the treaties with the Plains tribes, Congress specified that the funds be spent under the direction of General Sherman. By thus bypassing the formal organization of administration of Indian affairs, "Congress in effect handed the Plains tribes over to the army."[6]

On August 10, from his St. Louis headquarters, Sherman's first power move was to issue General Order No. 4. The two recently established reservations located in the northern and southern areas of the Great Plains were redefined as military districts where Generals Harney and Hazen would have "the supervision and control of the Indians and of all issues and disbursements to them." They would report to Sherman, but "in matters affecting the United States troops stationed in the same districts" the Indians would be subject to Generals Terry and Sheridan.

Regarding the relocation of the tribes within these reservations, General Order No. 4 specified no means other than persuasion. In Sherman's thinking, however, *persuasion* was a general term. Diplomacy for such a military leader was quite restricted. Sherman utilized Big Stick diplomacy, with all the threats and pressures of covert force. No assistance would be granted to Indians off their reservation, and no traders would be permitted among them.[7]

In mid-August a group of some two hundred rebellious Cheyennes, joined by a few Sioux and Arapahos, went on a rampage in the Saline and Solomon drainages of the Smoky Hill Trail. Jumping to extreme conclusions, the general declared on August 21:

> No better time could possibly be chosen than the present for destroying or humbling those bands that have so outrageously violated their treaties and begun a desolating war without one particle of provocation; and, after a reasonable time given for the innocent to withdraw, I will solicit an order from the President declaring all Indians who remain outside of their lawful reservations to be declared "outlaws," and commanding all people—soldiers and citizens—to proceed against them as such.[8]

In March General Sheridan had taken command of the Military Division of the Missouri. By mid-September Sherman and Sheridan agreed on a winter offensive. As Utley notes "like Georgians and Virginians four years earlier, the Cheyennes and Arapahoes would suffer total war." Sherman expressed his hope "that by the time the new grass comes a very small reservation will suffice" for the survivors. On October 9 Sherman boldly authorized Sheridan to proceed: "Go ahead in your own way and I will back you with my whole authority. If it results in the utter annihilation of these Indians, it is but the result of what they have been warned again and again."[9]

Sherman's philosophy, expressed in his annual report for 1868, was presented to Congress by the secretary of war. The fate of the Plains Indians—"They must necessarily yield"—had been pronounced by a latter-day Andrew Jackson. By Sherman's determination, the coexistence called for in the 1851 Fort Laramie treaty had proved impossible.

Throughout the West there was general approval of Sherman's proposal. Journalist Samuel Bowles commented: "It will give us both peace and protection, and the Indians an easier path to the grave that lies before them now. General Sherman, now alive at last to the true nature of the question, expresses the new and necessary policy: 'Peace and protection to the Indians upon the reservation; war and extermination if found off from them.'"[10]

As already noted, neither Taylor nor Henderson had played an active role in the affairs of the Peace Commission since the close of 1867. Taylor, as a consequence of the negative publicity concerning the late-summer Indian outbreaks, must have anticipated serious problems at the October meetings of the commission; however, he may not have realized that the Indian Office had lost Sanborn's support.

Moreover, as Taylor attempted to call the October meeting to order, he faced another handicap: the presence of a distinguished guest, the Republican nominee for president, General Grant. Utley suggests the implications of his attendance: "Few doubted that Ulysses S. Grant would win the White House in the November election." Although Grant played no direct role in the commission's meetings, his opinions, expressed in published interviews, were strong disagreements with Taylor's peace program. All the commissioners were well aware of the attitude toward the Native Americans that Grant had professed: even if it meant the extermination of every Indian tribe, the Great Plains were to be secured for emigrants.[11]

As president of the commission, Taylor opened the initial meeting at noon October 7. Throughout the following two days, on issue after issue regarding Indian policy, the proposals of Sherman, Sanborn, Harney, Terry, and Augur were carried over the dissenting votes of Taylor and Tappan. Sherman's policy—"peace within the reservations, war without"—had been accepted by the majority. Before adjournment on October 9 Sherman concluded his power sweep. The commissioners resolved that Taylor, as spokesman for their group, should transmit the commission's resolutions to the president of the United States, among those proposals the recommendation that "the Bureau of Indian Affairs be transferred from the Interior Department to the War Department."

The session on the morning of the tenth was an empty formality. Some treaties were signed by those commissioners who had not been present for the actual negotiations. It was Sherman who offered the final motion: "That the Commission having discharged the duties imposed upon it by law do now adjourn, *sine die*."[12]

On November 23 Taylor forwarded the report of the commission to the secretary of the interior. He also sent his annual report as commissioner of Indian affairs, appending a statement, "The Question of the Transfer of the Indian Bureau to the War Department," in which he offered this searing criticism: "If you wish to exterminate the [Indian] race, pursue them with the ball and blade; if you please, massacre them wholesale, as we sometimes have done; or, to make it cheap, call them to a peaceful feast, and feed them on beef salted with wolf bane; but, for humanity's sake, save them from the lingering syphilitic poisons, so sure to be contracted about military posts."

In this final report to Washington authorities, and retort to military critics, Taylor went on to state emphatically the case of the dispossessed Native Americans of the Great Plains. He had lost the commissioners' endorsement, but he outclassed Sherman in rhetorical skills. More important, his presentation was more factual, for Taylor put the summer revolt of the Cheyennes in the proper context of the drastically changed conditions on the Great Plains:

> The passing through their [the Indians'] country of a continuous stream of emigration, dispersing or destroying the buffalo, is one of the causes of great discontent and suffering with them. Treated thus, and no adequate compensation being made to them for what they have yielded up or lost, their resources of subsistence and trade diminished, with starvation in the future staring them in the face, the wonder is that there prevails any degree of forbearance on their part, with such provocations to discontent and retaliation.[13]

Sherman, as might be expected, was not content with a victory in Chicago. Upon returning to his St. Louis headquarters, he directed Hazen to prepare the southern reservation for a great influx of Indians, for he had instructed Sheridan regarding off-reservation Indians to "prosecute the war with vindictive earnestness till they are obliterated or beg for mercy." Following such directions, Sheridan ordered Custer and the Seventh Cavalry to ride out of Camp Supply on November 23. On November 27, four years (almost to the day) after Sand Creek, Custer's forces wiped out Black Kettle's camp on the Washita River. In just four years Sherman had returned the army to power. His forces had captured the Great Plains.

Concerning the northern reservation, Sherman criticized Harney's kindly supervision of the Sioux. Manifesting more of De Smet's influence, Harney had failed to follow rigidly the directive of General Order No. 4. In late September he had reported to Sherman that acting out of sympathy for the Indians, he had given them more supplies than he was authorized to distribute. Even less pleasing was the empathy Harney manifested in the explanation offered to Sherman, Harney remarking that as fellow members of the Peace Commission, they were both working to put an "end to the perfidy and outrage which generally hitherto characterized the treatment of the Indians by the white men." Sherman complained to Augur in late November that Harney was too old to fill the assignment vigorously. By the end of January Sherman declared that he had decided to get rid of Harney altogether.[14]

Harney, however, continued to command the Great Sioux Reservation District for another half year. Sherman, newly appointed general of the army, was preoccupied with his problems in Washington, among these the visit to the Great Father of two prominent Sioux leaders, Red Cloud and Spotted Tail. It was a visit to which Sherman had expressed his opposition and presumably that of the president. Through the summer of 1869, however, Sherman was learning that President Grant was not General Grant. Sherman's victorious Army of the West had been stopped to some degree by Washington politicians. Eventually the post General Harney filled was simply terminated, and Governor John Burbank of the Dakota Territory abruptly inherited the supervisory responsibility for the Great Sioux Reservation.

It is not clear when De Smet learned that Harney was to be, or had been, removed. On November 14, 1868, De Smet wrote from St. Louis University to Harney at Fort Sully expressing his gratitude for Harney's "very kind letter and invitation." De Smet informed Harney that he would be leaving shortly for Europe and that he would be happy to convey any message the general might wish to send to his "two noble Daughters residing in Paris." De Smet asked his old friend to send on any news concerning the Indians of that area and promised he would be returning to the United States in the early spring; "if able shall proceed to meet you at your headquarters on the Upper Missouri." The *Missouri Republican* carried a notice on November 21 of De Smet's departure for New York and Europe, also reporting his intention "to return to the Indians of the Upper Missouri in March, to assist General Harney."[15]

INDIAN COMMISSIONER ELY PARKER
AND GRANT'S PEACE POLICY

De Smet was proud of his well-established reputation as a good traveler. During the June peace ride the aged De Smet had no longer been able to conceal his debility and exhaustion. His friends on the expedition and the commissioners at Fort Rice worried about his health. Returning from Europe at the start of July 1869, he found the late-summer heat of St. Louis so oppressive that he was without the strength to unpack "the four great trunks and five boxes, containing sacred vessels, pictures, and ornaments obtained for the poor Indian Mission churches." In early September, somewhat revived by the promise of cooler weather, De Smet informed the Shermans that before the close of the month he hoped "to make an endeavor to reach Fort Rice before the great cold sets in." To this end De Smet requested of the general "a letter or note to be used if necessary as a passport in the upper Missouri country."[16]

De Smet had also written in July to Ely Parker, the new commissioner of Indian affairs, stating his plan to make a delayed visit to the Sioux tribes of the Upper Missouri. In expressing congratulations to Parker on his recent appointment, De Smet indicated that he had managed to keep fairly well informed of the startling changes in policy and administrative personnel in the Indian Office since the close of 1868.

The origins of President Grant's Peace Policy lay in Ely Parker's attempts to resolve the Indian problem. Like De Smet, Parker was convinced that frontier tribes had more to lose by resisting than by accepting change. At the start of 1867 he presented to Grant a plan "for the establishment of a permanent and perpetual peace." One of the main recommendations was the formation of "a commission composed of some ten members" to assist the Indian Office in the management of Indian affairs. After Grant's election to the presidency, on April 10, 1869, Congress legislated such a board. Within the following month Parker contacted the members, individuals selected by Grant "for their intelligence and philanthropy," asking for their recommendations. Thus the Board of Indian Commissioners, one of the main components of Grant's Peace Policy, was established.

All too quickly, however, Parker and the board members were at loggerheads. Parker was unwilling to regard them as his equally empowered fellow commissioners. The board members held that "the real Commissioner of Indian Affairs, General Parker, is of slight importance as he is subordinate to the Board." In the troubled relationship of the Interior Department with the board that Parker had helped to establish, Grant's Peace Policy was not off to a good start.[17]

In his policy statement of June 12, 1869, Parker delineated precisely the status of Indian groups. As a consequence, Sherman had good cause to conclude that his call for military control of the Indians, at least any "troublesome Indians," had been granted. Waltmann points out the "perfect understanding" called for by the commissioner between his civilian Indian Office workers and the army officers who policed the districts identified with reservations: "This modus operandi — spelled out in a[n] . . . Indian office circular and parallel military orders — was simple and geographical in nature. It classified all Indians who confined themselves to reservations as 'friendly' subjects of the Interior Department, consigning all others to the army 'to be treated as friendly or hostile as circumstances might justify.' "[18]

In a letter of July 16 De Smet asked Parker two pointed questions. Having just returned from a seven-month tour of Europe, De Smet was nevertheless aware of the changes Grant's Peace Policy had introduced into the management of Indian affairs. First, he reminded the commissioner of his long-delayed plans to open a mission and manual labor school among the Sioux in the vicinity of Forts Sully and Rice, and requested approval for the project, "the situation of affairs in the upper country having somewhat changed in regard to missionary establishments." The second question concerned the Jesuits' longtime Potawatomi Mission at St. Mary's in Kansas. De Smet pointed out that the reservation agent, Dr. Palmer, whom the Jesuit missionaries had come to regard as exceptionally qualified, was reportedly to be replaced by Friends, or Quakers.[19]

Even before Grant's inauguration the Quakers had suggested to the president-elect that "the moral level of the Indian Service might be considerably improved by appointing religious men to the positions of Indian agent." Appreciative of the Friends' past and ongoing Indian ministries, especially the humanitarian aid they had provided his Seneca people, Parker offered his full endorsement and won Grant's acceptance of the proposal. The Quakers were requested to nominate members of their congregation for agency and superintendency offices.

Implementing the plan in the spring and summer of 1869, eighteen Quaker nominees were put in charge of tribes in the central and southern Great Plains. Determined to assign agents independent of the congressional patronage system, Parker also appointed sixty-eight "surplus" army officers to posts in the Indian service. Interior Secretary Jacob Cox endorsed Parker's action and in his 1869 annual report explained the reason for such remedial action:

> The tribes in Nebraska and Kansas, and some of those
> most recently placed upon reservations in the Indian
> territory, were placed under control of members of the

Society of Friends; the others were given in charge of
military officers, who were waiting orders under the
laws for the reduction of the army. . . . The selection
of the officers of the army was made partly for
economic reasons, as they were on pay though not on
duty. . . . The Friends were appointed not because
they were believed to have any monopoly of honesty
or of good will toward the Indians, but because their
selection would of itself be understood by the country
to indicate the policy adopted, namely, the sincere
cultivation of peaceful relations with the tribes.[20]

Parker wrote to De Smet on August 30 in reply to his questions.
Regarding the Potawatomi mission, Parker assured De Smet that the
Jesuits would have no cause to anticipate any problem from the
Quakers, for such agents were "positively and strictly prohibited
from interfering with any religious denomination." Regarding De
Smet's plan to open a mission among the Sioux, Parker expressed his
regrets that he could offer only encouragement without providing
material aid; however, he informed De Smet of his "sincere and
heartfelt wishes" for safety and success. In addition, Parker reported
that great obstacle he had already met in his attempts to implement
Grant's Peace Policy: "As a Christian people it is our duty to save the
Indian if possible—Congress, however, gives but little towards the
development of any settled policy to protect and save the Indian
race."[21]

Parker's complaint about Congress was an understatement. Since
the appointments of military and Quaker personnel struck at the
heart of the old Indian system, the patronage prerogatives of members of Congress, a strong reaction could have been expected.
Although it would have been politically unwise openly to oppose the
religious appointments, Congress boldly initiated legislation that
would restrict the directors of Grant's Peace Policy from assigning
military personnel to Indian service positions.

Such a stand was strongly supported by the bad publicity and
serious criticism of the military action conducted by Major Edward
Baker, under Sheridan's orders, in northeastern Montana on January
23, 1870. Humanitarians insisted that Baker's cavalry attack upon a
Piegan village was a deliberate and unprovoked massacre of women
and children. In spite of Sherman's defense—"Did we cease to throw
shells into Vicksburg or Atlanta because women and children were
there?"—the Army of the West and its leaders were convicted by

public opinion. In line with that reaction, Congress on July 15 readily pushed through a measure that prohibited the assignment of military officers to civil posts. Officers who had already been so assigned were forced to choose between retaining their appointments as Indian agents or relinquishing their commissions; as a consequence, some fifty agent posts were open.[22]

It was in this context that Grant was forced to make another important decision regarding his Peace Policy. Supported especially by Parker, along with Interior Secretary Cox and Vincent Colyer, secretary of the new Board of Indian Commissioners, the president decided to expand the church nomination plan; all the Indian agencies would be apportioned among the various church groups. "The plan is obviously a wise and humane one," Parker declared in his 1870 annual report; "the President wisely determined to invoke the coöperation of the entire religious element of the country." In his Second Annual Message to Congress at the close of 1870, President Grant explicitly offered an explanation for the changed procedure to all interested religious denominations:

> The experiment of making it [the management of Indian affairs] a missionary work was tried with a few agencies given to the denomination of Friends, and has been found to work most advantageously. All agencies and superintendencies not so disposed of were given to officers of the army. The act of Congress reducing the Army renders army officers ineligible for civil positions. Indian agencies being civil offices, I determined to give all the agencies to such religious denominations as had heretofore established missionaries among the Indians, and perhaps to some other denominations who would undertake the work on the same terms—i.e., as a missionary work.

Grant noted that the nominees presented by the selected societies would be subject to the approval and supervision of regular government officials, who would demand strict accountability. As Prucha points out, Grant and Parker were convinced that the Peace Policy must work; their decision to assign the agencies to the churches "appeared to be a wonderful solution, in tune with the idealistic, humanitarian sentiments of the day."[23]

In late 1869 De Smet expressed to Parker his gratitude for the explanation of "the Quaker System." Neither man realized that they were experiencing only the preliminary stage of the new system and that as an exceptionally controversial relationship between church and state, it would further contribute to the failure of Grant's Peace Policy. Parker, with his religious thinking conditioned by his Quaker background of all-too-exceptional religious tolerance, apparently failed to appreciate how widespread and strong were the religious prejudices and the sectarian divisions of the period. Loring Priest reports the cause for the failure: "All hope of success was dissipated and church nomination of Indian appointees failed miserably amid the clamor of disputing churchmen."[24]

DE SMET'S FINAL JOURNEYS AND REPORTS

De Smet's voyage of 1870 on the Upper Missouri was exceptional in many ways. It would prove to be his final excursion in this area and was perhaps the trip that covered the least territory. Although he had hoped to reach Fort Berthold to visit his Indian friends there, he failed to get as far north as Fort Rice. This was also his least recorded journey; his narratives were few and brief. De Smet openly admitted the obvious fact: his physical endurance was tried by "excessive heat and fatigues of our long journey."

There was another unusual feature about this voyage: De Smet traveled with a Jesuit companion. At the start of May De Smet was informed that Father Ignatius Panken had been assigned to accompany him. De Smet reported later that he and Panken had baptized some five hundred adults and children between Whetstone Agency, north of Fort Randall, and Grand River Agency, south of Fort Rice. Following their return to St. Louis, De Smet reported to Parker in mid-September, informing the commissioner that following the tour of inspection, he was in favor of establishing the proposed Sioux mission at the Grand River Agency.[25]

Such formal reports to the authorities, however, did not list all of De Smet's activities. The voyage enabled the aging Blackrobe to enjoy a final visit with a number of his dear friends.

Only a few months previously De Smet had written to the agent at Cheyenne River that he wished his best greetings relayed to a number of Indian leaders. On this trip, as he stopped just north of Fort Sully, De Smet was able to embrace once more some of the old companions with whom, along with the Galpins, he had shared the peace ride of 1868. Gratefully he recalled the names of some of these friends: The Log, Two Bears, Running Antelope, All-Over-Black, Ghost Spirit, Burning Cloud, and Sitting Crow.

At Grand River Agency, after disembarking from the steamer *Far*

West, there was an emotional reunion of De Smet with his special friend Eagle Woman and her daughters. Major Galpin, as noted, had died the previous winter. It was a time for the Blackrobe to attempt to console and encourage the widowed Eagle Woman and her girls, but it was also a time of celebration and rejoicing. De Smet was able on his return journey downriver to participate in the wedding ceremony of Lulu Galpin-Harmon in the Catholic church at Sioux City. Reporting on the marriage, the *Sioux City Times* stated on July 26: "After the ceremonies the party retired to the spacious dining room of the hotel; Father De Smet sat at the head of the table."[26]

By early August De Smet and Panken had returned to St. Louis University; there De Smet would continue to hope against hope that he would be among the Jesuits assigned to the new Sioux mission. He had grown accustomed to his growing physical weakness, though he remained intolerant of it. More difficult to bear now were the additional responsibilities being placed upon his shoulders, obligations that as he sadly realized, he was mentally and physically incapable of fulfilling properly.

At the start of 1871 De Smet was summoned to Washington by Secretary of the Interior Columbus Delano, Cox's successor, to participate in a joint meeting of the Board of Indian Commissioners with representatives of religious bodies interested in the government's program of apportioning agency positions. Supposedly Delano had checked with four archbishops—Bayley of Baltimore, McCloskey of New York, Purcell of Cincinnati, and Kenrick of St. Louis—that De Smet would be acceptable as their representative. The failure of Delano's office to check with the other Catholic authorities, such as the ecclesiastical officials in New Orleans, California, and the Northwest, was only one token of the unsatisfactory handling of the new program. Apparently Colyer's board had also failed to make the proper preliminary study of the extent and background of Indian-oriented programs conducted by Catholics.

De Smet complained that "the plan of civilizing & christianizing the Indian tribes had previously been formed by the President" and that the assembled church delegates were present only to be notified of determinations already made. He also complained—and government officials soon frankly admitted—that Catholic claims had been incompletely recognized. Of forty-three Indian agencies, De Smet noted, "only four are assigned to the Catholics." Furthermore, De Smet was not the sole critic of the apportionment. In his historical study Priest reports, "Not a single church seemed satisfied with the government's plan of distribution."[27]

De Smet realized, however, that his election to the post had been less than proper and that he was no longer the person to fulfill such a demanding and serious job. Shortly after his return to St. Louis De Smet sent the following letter of resignation to Delano:

> Allow me to observe upon this occasion, with regard to my appointment in December, 1871, to represent the Indian Catholic missions in the United States, with the consent of several Archbishops; that this appointment should with all propriety belong to those bishops in whose dioceses Indian Catholic missions exist, or some representative they may name, and who may be consulted when occasion requires. My health and age and want of competent knowledge of the various districts in which Catholic missions exist, render me altogether unable to fill the important office with the due attention it requires and I humbly send in my resignation.

On March 17, 1873, Archbishop Bayley, acting in the name of the Catholic bishops of the United States, invested Charles Ewing of Washington with full authority to represent Catholic interests regarding the Indians before the government. After a trial period, and since Ewing had come to recommend that an office be established, Bayley wrote to the secretary of the interior on January 2, 1874, that Ewing had been appointed to direct the Bureau of Catholic Indian Missions.[28]

De Smet faced another retrenchment in the spring of 1871. He learned that he would not be assigned to the new Sioux mission. In March De Smet wrote to the leaders of the Sioux bands in the Grand River area notifying them that "two Black-Gowns will soon arrive in your midst with the sole intention of devoting themselves to the welfare of all, particularly to the education of the dear children." This was De Smet's attempt to offer an introduction from a distance, his request that the Indians accept and support his substitutes. In another letter, dated April 29, De Smet asked for the special and thoughtful assistance of his good friend General Stanley, still serving as the commander at Fort Sully. It was almost as though with a sorry realism De Smet clearly sensed at their departure how unprepared his Jesuit associates would be for the situation on the Upper Missouri. De Smet disclosed the twofold problem to Stanley:

I hasten to inform you that Fathers Francis Kuppens and Peter De Meester left St. Louis yesterday for the Grand River Agency. They propose paying you a visit; allow me to recommend them to your kind attention. Being their first trip and visit to the Sioux Indians, they shall stand in need of counsel and advice, and shall be most grateful to receive it. . . . The Government assigned the Grand River Agency . . . to the care of the Catholics, but without assurance of pecuniary assistance in the establishment of said Mission. Our first expenses are already very heavy, and until means should be allowed I am not over sanguine as to the future of this undertaking.[29]

Kuppens and De Meester did not arrive at Grand River until mid-June; by early August, disillusioned and defeated, they had already returned to St. Louis. Although Kuppens had served briefly at the Jesuit stations among the Flatheads in the Northwest and the Potawatomis at St. Mary's in Kansas, he still embodied the ethnocentric spirit then so widespread. With little appreciation of the fading buffalo culture and the magnitude of the adjustment problems of the Sioux, Kuppens and De Meester apparently made little attempt to accommodate their message to a people abruptly dispossessed.

With the generous help of the Galpin family, however, Kuppens and De Meester had seen to building two log cabins on the river bluffs overlooking the Grand River Agency. Although intended to serve as a church and a school, the buildings were in short order offered for sale to the Indian Office. The would-be missionaries had also been received in the lodge of Two Bears, head chief of the Yanktonnais. Years previously in a solemn public ritual De Smet had been taken as an adopted brother by Two Bears. To Kuppens and De Meester the chief now extended an invitation to be the privileged spectators at "a solemn dance in honor of the Sun."

Kuppens's report of the ceremony they were permitted to witness is a startling narrative. His account clearly testifies to the failure of the missionary, well intentioned but misguided, to realize the basic religious dedication of these Indians. Kuppens manifested the outsiders' inability to evaluate properly the sacredness of an alien ceremony. Aware of the racial and the religious prejudices of the period, one might excuse the failure of these newcomers to appreciate the penitential prayer-offering danced by the Indians.[30]

Even before the return of Kuppens and De Meester to St. Louis De

Smet had made a hurried visit to the Jesuit Indian missions in Kansas. He had checked on the financial situation at the Osage Mission of St. Hieronimus and the Potawatomi Mission of St. Mary's. On his return to St. Louis he made plans for his final European trip. Obtaining testimonial letters regarding his proper ecclesiastical standing from Peter Richard Kenrick, archbishop of St. Louis, and his Jesuit superior, Father Coosemans, presented no difficulty. However, his request for an official passport was presented too late to proceed through normal channels. Near the close of June De Smet made an emergency request of his old friend B. Gratz Brown, now governor of Missouri. Graciously the governor provided a substitute, penning a testimonial letter regarding De Smet's character and standing, describing De Smet as "perhaps more esteemed than any other white man in the whole community."[31]

On July 1, 1871, De Smet sailed from New York; on the fourteenth he disembarked at Liverpool. This, his ninth and final European tour, was spread over eight months with visits to Belgium, France, Holland, Luxembourg, England, and Ireland. Once more his objective was to solicit men and means. By April 7, 1872, the departure date from Antwerp for his return journey, he had gained nine more recruits for the ranks of the Missouri Jesuits. However, while in Brussels during the previous month he had suffered a violent attack of nephritis. From this kidney trouble, a form of Bright's disease, De Smet would never completely recover. Having completed his twenty-first voyage on the Atlantic, he returned to St. Louis by the close of April 1872.

There was an opportunity in May for a final visit with a very special friend, Dr. Moses L. Linton. Although De Smet's scribbled entry was brief—he listed only a few statistics regarding wind and weather conditions of the ocean crossing—there must have been a shared awareness of this closing of the Linton Album. For fifteen years the annual addition of a brief narrative of De Smet's travels throughout the year had been awaited by his interested friend. For over a quarter of a century Linton had offered his professional services as the house doctor for the Jesuits and their boarding students at St. Louis University. In mid-May this Jesuit community received an affectionate letter from the doctor, a fond farewell by Linton, their respected associate. The doctor died at the start of June. The Linton Album would later be presented to the Jesuits.[32]

By his own admission De Smet had aged ten years since his return from Europe; he confessed now that "my cane has become my support and my constant companion." Toward the end of June he reported: "As regards my health, the machine is completely out of order. For two months I have been confined to my room by order of the doctor. . . . My mantlepiece looks like a drug-shop."

His last letters were written in the spring of 1873. His final messages to relatives in Europe still manifested his strong affection. His business letters — although he was replaced in 1871 as a Missouri Province consultor, he continued to serve as the Missouri Jesuits' treasurer — were still orderly and detailed. As an author, he hurried to gather pertinent information for his proposed history of the Jesuits in Missouri.

As Blackrobe, De Smet appreciated the special and ongoing need of the Indians for spiritual and temporal assistance. He realized all too well that the transition now demanded could become a prolonged tragedy for many individuals. His final prayer was that the memory of the unique relation he had shared with them would continue to serve as a comfort and support. For himself there was a ready declaration: "I consider amongst the happiest days of my life when in 1840 I was sent out" as the Jesuit answer to the request of the Flatheads. His gratitude and pride were simply expressed in the final tribute he paid his beloved Indians: "They exceeded all my expectations."[33]

DESTRUCTION OF THE BUFFALO
AND INDIAN INDEPENDENCE

Following his "Eight Expeditions Across the Great Western Prairies" in the 1830s, the Santa Fe trader Josiah Gregg reported that the buffalo supplied all the life needs of the Indians. For the prairie tribes, Gregg noted, the buffalo provided the necessities: food, raiment, and shelter. Gregg's listing, however, was incomplete. Even before midcentury the Plains Indians used the buffalo to barter for manufactured goods. As Mari Sandoz points out, "Not only were the herds their commissary but also their bank. They bought with robes as with money."

This was the tragic flaw that Catlin had noted during the 1830s on the Upper Missouri when he questioned the morality of the developing trade in buffalo robes: "It may be answered, perhaps, that the necessaries of life are given in exchange for these robes; but what are the necessaries in Indian life, where they have buffaloes in abundance to live on?" And like Catlin, Gregg offered a gloomy prediction on the increasing use of the buffalo as objects of barter. Gregg lamented that "the continual and wanton slaughter . . . not only for meat, but often for the skins and tongues alone (for which they find a ready market among their traders), are fast reducing their numbers, and must ultimately effect their total annihilation."[34]

De Smet repeated this grim prediction in 1849. Having gained firsthand knowledge of conditions across the Great Plains in the 1840s, he reported that the buffalo were diminishing yearly and that "the area of land that these animals frequent is becoming more and more circumscribed." Additional hunting pressures had been caused by the relocation of border tribes to the eastern edge of the Plains. Further, the greatly increased number of white travelers heading across the Plains had notable effects along the trails. Captain Howard Stansbury, reporting on his survey expedition of 1849, noted that the hunters of his party had failed to spot buffalo until the company had moved west of Fort Kearny. This condition, Stansbury stated, had surprised his guide, Auguste Archambault: "[He] told me that the last time he had passed this spot, the whole of the immense plain as far as the eye could reach, was black with herds of buffalo."[35]

By midcentury some buffalo were being slaughtered for their hides, the carcasses left for the wolves. Moreover, many animals were slain only for the tongue or such other choice sections as the hump ribs. Contrary to traditional Indian practice, the major portion of the meat was not used. As De Smet's companion on the Oregon Trail in 1841, Father Point reported on a practice that among the emigrants had become and would remain all too common: "Buffalo are so plentiful in this area [along the Sweetwater River] that a single member of the party killed eleven of them within a few hours, satisfying himself with bringing back only the tongues."

The marked emphasis on the slaughter of the cow seriously affected the future of the herds. De Smet reported on the widespread preference for the cow: "The meat of the buffalo cow is the most wholesome and the most common in the West. . . . It is more easily procured than any other, and it is good throughout." Stansbury's report provides an explanation for this choice: the flesh of the buffalo cow was wholly free from the rank flavor that marked the fat of the male. Only in necessity was the bull killed for food. Furthermore, in this early period of the robe trade the attacks were also directed specifically against the cow. Returning with Fitzpatrick from the rendezvous of 1834, William Marshall Anderson repeated a conversation around an early-evening campfire on the Plains: "Tho I have seen million and tens of millions at a view, I believe they are fast diminishing—And why should they not?—Mr. Fontenelle asserted this evening, to knowing ones, that the American Fur company at their posts on the Miss & Missouri rivers, traded with the Sioux alone, in one winter, for fifty thousand robes—For this trade, it is to be remembered the cows only are killed—The robes of the bulls are not saleable."[36]

The attack on the buffalo herds by fur traders had increased since the early 1830s. In 1839 De Smet reported from Council Bluffs that the American Fur Company shipped about 45,000 buffalo robes from the posts of the Upper Missouri; the following year the number increased to 67,000. The expansion thereafter was even more rapid. According to historian John E. Sunder, the trade "averaged 90,000 [robes] per year during the 1840s, and 100,000 during the fifties and the sixties."[37]

After midcentury, however, an indirect attack became even more devastating for the herds of the Great Plains. The right "to establish roads, military and other posts," acknowledged in the 1851 Fort Laramie treaty, was rapidly and widely exercised by the government. It was a land use far in excess of what any Indian had anticipated. By these roads and posts the previously unrestricted range lands that had been the habitat of the tremendous migrating herds were divided and reduced. The multiplication of posts, both military establishments and the expanding service centers for the coach and freight lines, and the increasing traffic on these roadways dealt a serious blow to the buffalo. The volume of that traffic is reported by historian Merrill J. Mattes: "Emigrant traffic along the Platte was a spasmodic trickle until 1843–48, when it swelled modestly with Oregon and Utah emigrants. Traffic reached epic proportions in 1849 and the early 1850's, dwindled in the middle fifties, zoomed briefly with the Colorado Gold Rush, dropped off during the early Civil War years, then crested again in the mid sixties."[38]

By 1856 a supplementary trail-road south of the Platte and north of the Arkansas had been discovered. A goodly number of the Fifty-Niners heading west from the Missouri traveled to the Denver mines by way of the Smoky Hill Trail. The Oregon and Santa Fe trails, as Utley points out, had disturbed only the northern and southern borders of the prime buffalo range; now "the Smoky Hill Trail pierced the heart of it."[39]

By the close of the 1860s more than thirty additional military posts had been erected across the Great Plains, and in general the thoroughfares had been made secure. In contrast to this multiplication of army facilities, the Indian Office in 1866 directed the affairs of over two hundred tribes across the continent. Serving under fourteen superintendents, only some seventy agents worked periodically among the Indians. Obviously the government considered military determinations on the future of the tribes more important than protective services that might be provided by the Indian Office.[40]

An annual supply caravan heading to the rendezvous on the Green had freighted the simple needs of the mountain men hunting beaver in the upland meadows. However, the emigrations to Oregon and California, the Mormon development in Utah, the mining operations established along the eastern slope of the Rockies, and the military posts scattered along the trails created a large and extensive market seeking an ongoing supply of manufactured goods. The trailheads along the Missouri had served as supply depots for the emigrants. Now Omaha, Nebraska City, Atchison, St. Joseph–Weston, Leavenworth, and Kansas City became competitive headquarters for the new commerce, the freight lines moving military and civilian supplies and equipment across the Great Plains.

Horace Greeley, in his "Overland Journey" of 1859, was impressed by all these developing towns along the Missouri. Greeley described the town and the fort named Leavenworth:

> Leavenworth is, of course, much the largest place in
> Kansas. . . . The Fort, three miles up the Missouri,
> is not included in this estimate; though that is a city of
> itself, with extensive barracks, capacious store-houses,
> many fine houses for officers, sutlers, etc. . . .
>
> But Russell, Majors & Waddell's transportation
> establishment, between the fort and the city, is the
> great feature of Leavenworth. Such acres of wagons!
> such pyramids of extra axletrees! such herds of oxen!
> such regiments of drivers and other employees!

After gaining almost a monopoly on transporting military goods west of the Missouri River in 1855, Russell, Majors & Waddell had started with 300 wagons. By 1858 the firm operated 3,500 covered wagons, employed 4,000 men, and owned 40,000 draft oxen. Additional stations were erected in April 1860 to provide the services demanded for the Pony Express. By 1865 the Russell firm had been replaced by the new transportation empire of Ben Holladay, reportedly with stations located every ten to fifteen miles along the routes.[41]

The traffic increase affecting the Great Plains in the late 1850s and

1860s was connected with a series of Congressional subsidies. These appropriations were not only for express transportation but for stagecoach lines, mail services to the West Coast by way of Denver and Salt Lake, installation of telegraph lines, and construction of transcontinental railroads. All of these activities seriously affected the natural habitat of the buffalo. Construction of the railroads in particular represented a double attack that proved especially fatal to the herds.

By the summer of 1866 the Union Pacific's new service connected Omaha with Fort Kearney. That August General Sherman took the train as he began an initial survey of his new army command. Had Sherman delayed his journey to the close of the year, he could have been transported to the new town of North Platte at the river forks some three hundred miles west of Omaha. Unlike Sherman, however, many of the passengers on the new train were not making a round trip. As historian William H. Goetzmann notes, "The railroad was the instrument for settling the vast Western interior."[42]

In his report of October 1, 1867, Sherman anticipated what would be created shortly by the "Omaha [Union] Pacific" and the "Kansas [Missouri] Pacific." These railroads would section off the Great Plains: "When these two great thoroughfares reach the base of the Rocky mountains, and when the Indian title to roam at will over the country lying between them is extinguished, then the solution of this most complicated question of Indian hostilities will be comparatively easy, for this belt of country will naturally fill up with our own people, who will permanently separate the hostile Indians of the north from those of the south."[43]

By 1870 a wide east-west strip of land between the Platte and the Arkansas rivers, a vast rectangular area stretching west from the Missouri River across the center of the Great Plains, had been enclosed. With the railroads reaching from Omaha to Cheyenne, Kansas City to Denver, and Denver to Cheyenne, the important first step of Sherman's strategy had been made. The Indians could now be restricted to reservations north and south of the transcontinental railroads.

The new railroads advertised "shooting forays" for ordinary passengers. Political and military leaders organized more elaborate excursions for prominent friends or guests from foreign lands. Professional hunters like "Buffalo Bill" Cody were hired to provision the railroad work crews with fresh supplies of buffalo meat. The importance of the herds to the tribes was disregarded.

Moreover, the railroads provided more than ready access from the Missouri River towns. Returning eastward from the Great Plains, the railroads offered cheap freighting services for the first product harvested in that region — buffalo hides. Two technological advances of the early 1870s greatly expedited the harvesting, expanded markets, and extended the harvest period through the entire year. Further, the harvesters, increased in number by the financial depression of 1873, were not handicapped by restrictive legislation.

Until 1870 the direct attacks on the herds had been threefold: the animal was killed for robes, meat, or sport. In 1871, however, tanneries in Europe and America devised new methods for processing buffalo hides as leather, creating an entirely new and extensive demand. Further, the slaughter of the animals was no longer restricted to a particular season. For robes, the most thickly furred hides had to be taken in fall or early winter; for leather, the uninterrupted harvest was a year-round slaughter that presaged rapid extermination.[44]

The second technological advance was in the harvesters' equipment. After the Civil War the army musket had replaced the muzzle-loading Hawken rifle long treasured by the mountain men. The hide hunters, however, demanded improvements in their single-shot breech-loading cartridge rifles. Sharps, Remington, and other eastern companies quickly made more accurate guns chambered for more powerful cartridges. One of the favorite new weapons, the "big fifty" Sharps rifle, fired a heavy lead bullet at low velocity providing a killing power ranging from three hundred to six hundred yards.

Above the long octagon-shaped barrel the hunters mounted their new telescope sights from ten- to thirty-power. With such heavy guns, about twelve pounds, and such powerful scopes, the hunter took "a stand." Firing from a kneeling position or seated on the ground, the hunter used a "rest stick" to support and steady the scoped gun barrel. From a single such stand, the skillful shooter was frequently able to complete his slaughter quota for the day. Hide hunter Frank Mayer reported later: "We never killed all the buff we could, but only as many as our skinners could handle. . . . My regular quota was twenty-five a day, but on days when my crew weren't tired, I sometimes would run this up to 50 or even 60. But there I stopped, no matter how plentiful the buff were. Killing more than we could use would waste buff, which wasn't important; it also would waste ammunition, which was."[45]

Billington notes that at the start of the 1870s probably 13 million buffalo roamed the Great Plains. From 1871 through 1873 the hide hunters concentrated their slaughter around western Kansas. Between 1872 and 1874 some 3 million hides were harvested annually.

In early 1871 and again in 1872 congressional attention was directed to "the indiscriminate slaughter and extermination" of the buffalo and other wild animals. However, as Dary reports, too many congressmen "favored the business interests that profited from the buffalo slaughter." In the spring of 1874 legislation was proposed that would restrict killing the buffalo cow to the Indian; finally this bill passed both the House and the Senate. The pocket veto then exercised by President Grant was in line with the general thinking of his administration. By 1878 the southern herds were eliminated, and the last of the herds, on the northern Plains, disappeared by 1883. As Dary comments, "The greatest slaughter of wild animals by human hands ever recorded in history" had been completed.[46]

Ever since the transfer of the Indian Office to the Interior Department, the War Department had attempted to regain control of Indian affairs. However, to one specific policy the leaders of both departments offered their united endorsement. As Prucha reports, "The slaughter [of buffalo] was applauded by both the civilian and the military officers of the government concerned with the Indians, for the disappearance of the Indians' means of subsistence would force them into the dependent condition."[47]

The success of that strategy has been noted by historians: with the extermination of the buffalo and the consequent collapse of the Native American economy on the Great Plains, the Indians' independence was destroyed. Mounting a major military campaign by Sherman and his generals had become unnecessary. The West had not been "won." Rather, conditions on the Great Plains had been so drastically changed since midcentury that the Indian was no longer a deterrent to Manifest Destiny.

Few historians manifest an appreciation of the tragedy imposed upon these Plains tribes. The removal of the southeastern tribes had been speeded by President Jackson with the justification "They must necessarily yield, or they shall disappear." For the natives of the West, however, more than yielding their homelands was demanded, more than the sufferings of removal imposed. Their buffalo culture had been destroyed, and now their way of life was to be ended.[48]

In 1878 General Sherman wrote, "Where in 1868 millions of buffalo could be found, not a single one is now seen."[49] The hide hunters of the 1870s had represented only the concluding chapter of fur trade history. Solely for material gain, conducting illegal operations, the mountain men and fur traders had eliminated first the beaver, then the buffalo. Ineffectively supervised by the Indian Office, which held full responsibility delegated by Congress, the fur trade had "won" the West. It had been an easy victory. After formally acknowledging the Indians' rights, the government's Indian policy failed to offer them more than token protection.

Epilogue
Where the Rivers Meet,
De Smet Ended (1873)

If you can talk with crowds, and keep your virtue;
Or walk with kings, nor lose the common touch.
— Rudyard Kipling, *If*

It was the thirteenth day of May of the year of our Lord, the one thousand eight hundred and seventy-third; of the independence of the United States, the ninety-seventh; of the acquisition of the Louisiana Territory, the sixty-ninth; of the statehood of Missouri in the Union, the fifty-second; of the incorporation of the city of St. Louis, the fiftieth. It was also fifty years, almost to the day, since De Smet first walked the St. Louis riverfront.

As late as the close of April De Smet had hoped that this would also be his departure date for another voyage on the Upper Missouri. Earlier he had reported to relatives and friends the generous offer of Captain La Barge to reserve a special cabin for De Smet's use. By the start of May, however, he had confessed that because of the poor state of his health, he would not be able to take the trip.[1]

La Barge, a devoted friend, had not only offered De Smet choice quarters but had presented him with another gift, an honor quite unique. Having decided to name his new steamboat *De Smet,* La Barge had persuaded his friend to conduct the christening ceremonies. It might become necessary thereafter for the captain, the military personnel, or the traders located at the various river posts to explain to the Indians the significance of the large-lettered name printed on the housing of La Barge's side-wheeler. That inscription would serve for years as a reminder of the dedicated Blackrobe.

On May 13 the La Barge family carriage, it may be supposed, provided transportation for De Smet from the Jesuits' residence at Ninth and Washington. As the carriage moved south along Broadway, De Smet's attention must have been drawn to the courthouse located on the Market Street corner; the impressive structure could have served as a reminder to De Smet of William Clark, Bryan Mullanphy, Thomas Hart Benton, and the many other political figures of St. Louis with whom he had been associated through the busy years.

As the carriage approached the intersection of Walnut and Third, De Smet may have requested a halt for a few minutes. He would have been especially eager to pay a prayerful visit to his favorite church. Since his arrival in St. Louis in 1823 De Smet had become identified with a number of Catholic churches in the area. In 1855 he had conducted religious ceremonies at the new St. John Nepomuck Church. The following year he had played a leading role in the dedication services at the new St. Ann's Church in Normandy just west of the city. At the close of 1866 he had been the celebrant at the rededication services of the renovated St. Joseph's Church a few blocks northwest of the St. Louis University campus. And in 1867 he had acted as Archbishop Kenrick's substitute in conducting the solemn blessing of the new Sacred Heart Church in Florissant. Commenting on the growth of his city, his church, and his religious society, a development he had witnessed during his half century of residence in St. Louis, De Smet had reported to a friend:

> When we first came to St. Louis the town boasted of 4,000 inhabitants and possessed but one church. To-day its population numbers 450,000, and next Sunday the Bishop will bless the thirty-sixth church. Our first [Jesuit] establishment in Missouri was composed of two Fathers, seven novices and three lay Brothers. We now number two hundred and seventy-five; we possess three large colleges and a dozen [parish] houses with prosperous missions.[2]

In his final visit to the St. Louis Cathedral De Smet's prayers must have been richly surrounded with memories. In 1831, as the first treasurer of St. Louis University, De Smet had participated in laying the cornerstone for the cathedral planned by Bishop Rosati. Beginning with his return to St. Louis in November 1837 and again with his departure only six months later for St. Joseph Indian Mission at Council Bluffs on the Missouri, De Smet had initiated a practice he followed throughout some thirty-five years—to begin and conclude each journey with a prayerful visit before the altar in this church. Certainly during this final visit he would have recalled his frenzied activities here on the night of May 17, 1849. With Archbishop Kenrick absent from the city, De Smet and his fellow Jesuits had ransacked the sanctuary, the sacristy, and the connected episcopal office, fearful that the building and all the contents would be destroyed in the giant conflagration that threatened to engulf the entire St. Louis riverfront.

De Smet would have returned to his seat in the La Barge carriage, but the ride was now quite brief. From the corner of Third Street, Walnut Street sloped eastward past two blocks of offices and warehouses to the riverbank. His host and De Smet must have shared a sense of pride in La Barge's new steamboat at the landing; freshly emblazoned along the side of the vessel was the name *De Smet*. Although so handicapped that he depended on his cane, De Smet must have enjoyed feelings of pleasure and gratitude as he performed the christening ceremonies.

Here at the riverfront De Smet must have been conscious of two major changes that differentiated the St. Louis levee of 1873 from the muddy riverbank along which he had first walked in 1823. One change was a startling addition. Glancing upstream some hundred yards, De Smet could see, despite his limited eyesight, the giant skeleton outline arching high above the river of the new Eads Bridge. "The first line of steel uniting the East and the West" had already been mounted upon the two great caissons grounded in the riverbed. Within a year this bridge, the first to span the Mississippi in the St. Louis area, would be opened for railroad traffic and all other forms of transportation. As two old river men especially committed to the Missouri River, La Barge and De Smet may not have realized what tremendous consequences would result for Missouri River navigation and the general economy of St. Louis from the erection of Eads Bridge.[3]

The initial growth of St. Louis, its development as the Gateway City, had been to a large extent founded upon its location—"Where the Rivers Meet." De Smet's arrival in 1823 had coincided with the city's establishment as the trailhead and capital of the western fur trade. From St. Louis the fur traders had initiated their invasion of the Indian country, primarily by way of the Missouri River. Also, from the warehouses located here the furs and hides harvested by the fur companies had been shipped east to world markets. By midcentury the westward traffic had increased, the vast majority of the new emigrants heading to or through the Great Plains—the settlers, the miners, and their freight-transporting suppliers. Most made use of the Missouri River highway.

Standing on the prow of La Barge's new steamboat, De Smet may have realized that in 1873 he was again a witness, this time to the closing of the gateway period of St. Louis history. Throughout the final quarter of the century the Eads Bridge would prove for commercial purposes much more advantageous to St. Louisans than their city's location near the mouth of the Missouri River. St. Louis would continue to develop—no longer as a river town but as a hub for railroad services.[4]

The second major change along the St. Louis riverfront was not an addition but an absence. By 1873 the canoes of visiting Indian bands were no longer drawn up along the west bank of the Mississippi. And in even more than a symbolic fashion, their absence was connected with the construction site of the new bridge.

Even at a distance De Smet and La Barge could see that a massive stone structure was being erected some distance westward and uphill from the riverbank. As the St. Louis terminus, this abutment would connect the upper and lower traffic levels of the bridge. Other than contemporaries of De Smet and La Barge, not too many St. Louisans would have remembered the original buildings supplanted by this new structure. Precisely here, at the corner of Vine and Market in old St. Louis, had stood the two-story brick home of General William Clark. For more than a dozen years before and after De Smet's arrival the city had been known among tribal representatives as Clark's Town. After setting up their camps along the riverbank, especially to the north of Vine Street, Indian leaders, some with their families, would march to Clark's "Council Chamber" for their conferences with their "red headed chief."

Even after Clark's death in 1838, with Joshua Pilcher his successor as superintendent of Indian affairs for the West, groups of migrating Indians frequently camped along the riverfront. Already demoralized by utter poverty and their culture loss, these groups had become dependent beggars. Pilcher described them as destitute in his official reports and complained about extraordinary expenditures to provide them with some assistance and the expense of transporting them from the St. Louis area.[5]

By 1873 Indians were no longer to be seen along the St. Louis landing. In 1863, when De Smet was seeking a passport to travel in the Indian country, it had been necessary to contact the superintendent of Indian affairs, whose office had been transferred from St. Louis to St. Joseph, Missouri. Not only the Indians but even the traces and memories of Indian presence had been removed from St. Louis by the time of building the new Eads Bridge.

There is no record of De Smet's reflections as he gazed for a final time upon the St. Louis riverfront. The changes here only mirrored the more drastic changes that he had witnessed across the Great Plains throughout the previous half century. De Smet had long predicted the tragic culture loss and resulting sufferings the Native Americans would have to endure. The Indian people, he realized, faced major and difficult adjustments, but he also knew, as did a number of Indian leaders by 1873, that there was no returning to the existence they had previously enjoyed.

However, because of the understanding and interest manifested by some of the government agents with whom he had worked during the peace negotiations of 1867 to 1868, De Smet had some cause for hope. The new supervised reservation programs were supposed to help achieve the basic assimilation now to be attempted by the tribes. The Indians had been given reason to anticipate a truly benign paternalism from the government, had been promised anew the enlightened and lasting support of the Great Father. Moreover, popular interest in the Indian cause, though it would prove at times misdirected, had increased considerably in eastern metropolitan centers. By the start of the 1870s the reformers were many and politically powerful.

The Indian policy that Jefferson and his associates had fashioned in 1774 and continued throughout the first decade of the nineteenth century had laid claim to such paternalism. As President Washington stated, "To enforce upon the Indians the observance of justice, it is indispensable that there shall be competent means of rendering justice to them." Jefferson also boasted of his concern for justice: "Not a foot of land shall be taken without the Indians' consent." Furthermore, Congress reserved for itself the control and management of Indian affairs. To the members of Congress, therefore, and to the people served by these elected political representatives must be charged the sorry and prolonged failure to safeguard the acknowledged rights of the Native Americans. Especially in the administration of the Indian policy it had fashioned, Congress failed completely to exercise the benign paternalism it repeatedly promised.[6]

Benjamin O'Fallon, Indian agent on the Upper Missouri, complained in 1822 about such congressional failure. By default, the restrictive legislation that to some degree would have safeguarded the exclusiveness of the western Indian country had not been enacted. O'Fallon's explanation—"What appears to be every bodies business is thought no bodies business"—provided only a rationalization for such neglect. However, Congress had promised concerned supervision and protective legislation. As early as 1787 the Continental Congress had boldly declared that "laws founded in justice and humanity shall from time to time be made, for preventing wrongs being done to them [the Indians], and for preserving peace and friendship with them."[7]

Perhaps in his final days De Smet reflected upon this rationalization and the other excuses he had heard repeatedly throughout the years. Some of the nation's leaders—political, military, and commercial—had presented a variety of excuses. Their statements in part may have been frank admissions of regretted failures. However, these leaders were convinced that the excuses they offered were to some degree valid. They also believed that De Smet, by his understanding and in all honesty, would appreciate that validity.

It may be noted that these same excuses are still found in current textbooks. They are excuses that cover the story; they offer only partial explanations for the tragedy that the Native Americans were forced to endure.

There was so little time. Burns reports in conjunction with the great and hurried influx of settlers in the Northwest: "Time ran out." DeVoto points out: "Perhaps the Indians might have been adapted to the nineteenth-century order and might have saved enough roots from their own order to grow in dignity and health in a changed world—if there had been time. There was no time at all."[8] Although there was no time to pass and implement updated Trade and Intercourse acts that would have restricted growth and expansion and to some degree safeguarded Indian rights, time was deliberately made for treaty negotiations and the subsequent legislation that would legally justify the invasion of Indian country.

There was so little manpower and funding. Prucha points out the reality of these two very serious limitations: "Protection of the rights and persons of the Indians remained more an ideal than a reality because the means applied had been out of all proportion to the magnitude of the problem. The expanse of the frontier and the multitudes of oncoming settlers were the basis of the problem." The United States, as Prucha notes, had neither a numerous nor a mobile police force. Moreover, another reason for the lack of success in carrying out the Indian program was "the continuing necessity for economizing under which the Indian department operated."[9]

Yet military forces proved sufficient, or quickly became sufficient, to subdue any threat from the Indians. On the other hand, such forces were all too rarely used to protect the Native Americans from invading whites. There was sufficient manpower—volunteer militiamen were quickly assembled, authorized, and salaried—to defend the miners who blatantly invaded the foothill territory around the

South Platte River, a country legally acknowledged as belonging to the Arapahos and Cheyennes. However, to defend the Black Hills, an area especially sacred to the Sioux, the federal forces from Fort Abraham Lincoln were ineffective, and Dakota territorial militiamen were not used.

Also, subsidies were legislated, or funds otherwise provided, to cover the expenses of the Corps of Engineers, survey expeditions, and other activities designed to benefit white expansion in the West. Funds were supplied the Indian Office for the indoctrination junkets of tribal delegates to Washington, D.C.; such expensive power displays were supposed to produce government domination over the Indians. The nation had grown wealthy with its vast land acquisitions, but the government had failed to provide qualified personnel or suitable funding to supply Indians with the services that had been pledged to them or safeguard the tribal rights that had been officially acknowledged.

There was so little control over the frontier. Sheehan notes that "humanitarians and politicians became increasingly intimidated by the frontier." The fears that had been expressed by President Washington would be too well realized: the injustices boldly perpetrated by whites on the frontier seemed beyond the control of federal authorities. A litany of factors, including faulty communication and lack of cooperation, contributed to this failure. Prucha points out some of the problems caused by the mentality of the new settlers and the miners: "To say that the territorial court system was rudimentary is to comment on only the beginning of the difficulty. The courts reflected the milieu in which they existed. The courts and juries were frontier-minded, opposed both to the Indian and to the federal army officers who were on hand to protect the red men. The Indians were a physical hindrance to the advance of white settlement."[10]

Still another group of causes for this lack of control related to the unsatisfactory relationships established with the Indians living along and beyond the frontier. The procedures followed by government officials in the implementation of Indian policy failed to achieve its basic objective, the preservation of peace and friendship with the tribes. Unscreened individuals had been appointed as Indian agents; they had not been provided with preparatory training nor operational directives; their official activities were not carefully scrutinized; and they lacked the prestige and support of any effective enforcement power. The main activity of the agent was to oversee annual annuity payments, yet there was never evidence of careful planning for goods or procedures to effect a fair and satisfactory distribution. Despite the obvious need, emphasized by complaints of the agents, officials in the Indian Office never initiated remedial actions to eliminate or even minimize the agents' dependence upon the fur traders for all aspects of the annuity payments.

De Smet had repeatedly called attention to this defective service, repeating criticisms he had heard from tribal leaders. Like other critics of his day, De Smet did not question the fundamental goodwill of the government; he criticized the failure of the Indian Office to provide proper field representatives with studied programs, legal procedures, and enforcement powers. Frustrated and underpaid, Indian agents were without the means to supervise the fur traders; they were also unable to conduct an effective campaign against the introduction of whiskey into the Indian country. In the early 1850s both agent Fitzpatrick and Commissioner Manypenny flatly declared that the Trade and Intercourse Act of 1834, "the ineffective mainstay of the Indian Policy," was completely outdated. Rather sarcastically, Secretary of War Stanton frankly confessed that "the Government never reforms an evil until the people demand it." Only with such an abiding tolerance of evil, within the Indian system and along the frontier over which the government had failed to maintain control, could federal officials continue to promise glibly corrective measures that they could not, or were reluctant to, enforce.[11]

There was so little unselfish concern. De Smet commented on the racial animosity that he found along the white frontier and in the camps of the Indians:

> Whence is it that the redman bends with such difficulty to the manners and customs of the European race? Whence is it again, that the European race refuses so obstinately to sympathize with the red race; and notwithstanding its philanthropy, or love of mankind, seems rather disposed to annihilate than to civilize these poor children, offspring of the same Father? Whence springs that insurmountable barrier between the two races?

Trennert insists that "American culture in the nineteenth century was impregnated with a strong ethnocentrism" and concludes that the frontier mentality regarded Indian ways as pagan and barbaric, consequently unacceptable. Moreover, Washington politicians, both humanitarians and pragmatists, had no appreciation or awareness that Indian culture had a value in itself. Prucha's explanation is

similar: "The tragedy is that white Americans—whether their phil-
anthropic impulse came from Christian sentiment or from social
science commitments—have never really been willing to accept a
pluralistic society. . . . The dominant sentiments of an age could not
make room for alternative or divergent patterns of life."[12]

Yet De Smet managed through that troubled half century to be a
relaxed citizen of two worlds. With some degree of ease and grace he
related to the different ethnic groups in the St. Louis area, and he
readily identified as Blackrobe with the equally diverse Indian
peoples of the Plains and mountains. Lacking the skills of a linguist,
De Smet was not able to communicate directly with any of the
Indians, but he was also unable to speak German or Bohemian. The
explanation for De Smet's ready identification, as DeVoto suggests,
eliminates the need to assign some extraordinary power or mystic
charisma as the cause for the almost universal, spontaneous, and
automatic acceptance he received. DeVoto held that De Smet asked
little and unselfishly gave his love. Somehow, yet quite naturally and
without heavy emotional demonstrations, De Smet managed to let
people know that he loved them.[13]

The christening of La Barge's steamboat was De Smet's final
public act. Chittenden and Richardson note that "upon returning
home in the evening he was taken quite ill and grew rapidly worse."
On the twentieth he requested the last rites as the sacramental
preparation for his death. On the twenty-first he was visited by
Bishop Ryan, coadjutor bishop of St. Louis, who reportedly found
him "full of courage and hope." De Smet died at a quarter past two,
the morning of Friday, May 23.[14]

The wake services, the body lying in state, began at seven o'clock
that Friday evening in the St. Francis Xavier Church on the grounds
of St. Louis University. Although unrecorded, it can be presumed
that his mourners joined in the recitation of the rosary, one of his
favorite prayers. On the morning of the twenty-fourth the St. Louis
Globe-Democrat reported: "The church was thronged last evening
with people anxious to take a last look at the familiar face." The
newspaper also predicted that "the funeral today will be one of the
largest ever witnessed in the city." On Saturday morning, prior to the
nine o'clock recitation of the Office of the Dead, there was a final
viewing of the remains. As editor of the Catholic weekly the *Western
Watchman,* Father David Phelan reported: "The church of the University was decorated in the style of subdued and sad magnificence.
The church was crowded to excess, and throngs of persons pressed

round the coffin, placed as it was in the center aisle in front of the altar, in order to take a last view of the familiar and benevolent countenance of the deceased."

The High Mass began at ten o'clock, with Father Judocus Van Assche, one of De Smet's classmates from Belgium, as the main celebrant. Archbishop Kenrick was present in the sanctuary, along with Bishop Ryan, who preached the sermon and pronounced the final absolution. In reporting on Bishop Ryan's sermon, the St. Louis *Missouri Republican* commented:

> The sermon was delivered in a very solemn tone. The speaker was himself deeply affected; in the death of the great missionary he had lost a personal friend. The entire audience, almost, was moved to tears. There was no relative to weep over his bier, but the subdued sobs throughout the church during the services showed how fully the people realized his virtues and how much they loved him. The audience was largely composed of old residents of St. Louis. The following persons were noticed among the hundreds present: Colonel Robert Campbell, General William Harney, General Daniel M. Frost, Colonel George Knapp, General A. J. Smith, Mr. Soulard, and Major Thomas.

The *St. Louis Times* pointed out how proper it was that two of De Smet's closest remaining friends happened to be present in St. Louis, able to attend the funeral services:

> Leading men of our country have held Father De Smet in the highest repute, and cherished his intimacy. The tender devotion of Colonel Benton to him was proverbial, while the friendship of General Harney for him is known to all. It is said that no living man so thoroughly knew the Indian character as General Harney and Father De Smet. . . . Colonel Robert Campbell, a staunch Scotch Presbyterian, loved and was beloved by Father De Smet, and often requested his presence at the table to meet persons of distinction.

The services at St. Francis Xavier Church concluded about noon. The funeral cortege, including many clergymen and a large number of friends, headed to St. Stanislaus Novitiate near Florissant, site of the Jesuit cemetery. Standing around the grave, the mourners joined in the Catholic burial services by responding to the prayers; in their number was John La Barge, brother of Captain Joseph La Barge.[15]

Directing the upriver voyage of the *De Smet,* Captain La Barge was notified, reportedly at Sioux City, of De Smet's death. With its flag at half-mast, the steamer continued on its long journey to Fort Benton. At all the stops—the forts, the trading posts, the new agencies, the tribal encampments where the boat refueled with wood cut by the Indians—La Barge spread the report, and the news was disseminated among the tribes. Jesuit Father Joseph Guidi, with missionary experience in western and eastern Montana, offered this summary at the close of the summer: "Not only the Christians but pagans as well wept over the loss of their beloved Father, and many Indians regard his loss as a calamity to their tribe, which, alas! is but too true."

In a final tribute to De Smet, the *Missouri Republican* offered this exceptional praise: "With an indomitable resolution he possessed a charming simplicity of character, that won the hearts of all with whom he came in contact. He not only adapted himself readily to the minds of children and Indians, and the low and humble, but he was able to hold instructive converse with kings and princes, and the accomplished and learned of all classes."[16]

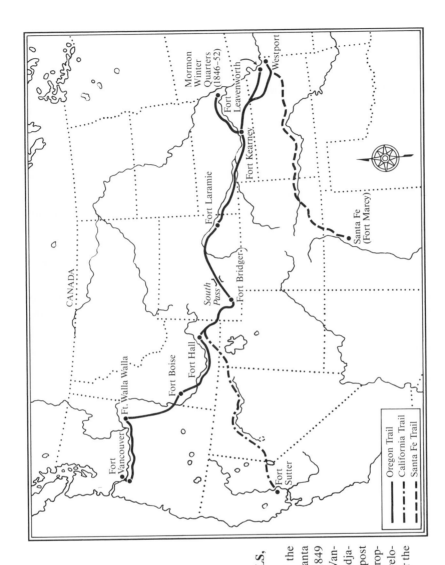

THE MAJOR WESTERN TRAILS, MILITARIZED BY 1850

Fort Sutter, at the western end of the California Trail, and Fort Marcy, in Santa Fe, were garrisoned in 1846. In 1849 army units were assigned to Fort Vancouver and to Cantonment Loring, adjacent to Fort Hall; to the old trading post purchased from the Chouteaus, now properly called Fort Laramie; and to the relocated Fort Kearney, now located near the Grand Island of the Platte.

Within map:

Mormon Winter Quarters (1846–52)

Fort Leavenworth

Westport

Fort Kearney

Fort Laramie

Santa Fe (Fort Marcy)

CANADA

Fort Bridger

South Pass

Fort Hall

Fort Boise

Ft. Walla Walla

Fort Vancouver

Fort Sutter

Oregon Trail
California Trail
Santa Fe Trail

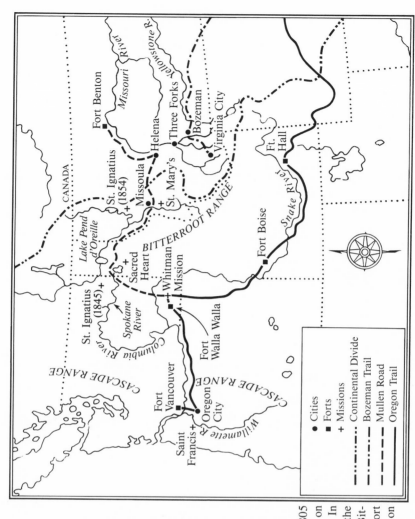

THE NORTHWEST

The Corps of Discovery had searched in 1805 for a brief portage, a passage from waters on the eastern slope to some Pacific drainage. In 1863 the Mullan Road, crossing not only the continental divide but also the connected Bitterroot Range, extended 624 miles from Fort Benton on the Missouri to Fort Walla Walla on the Columbia.

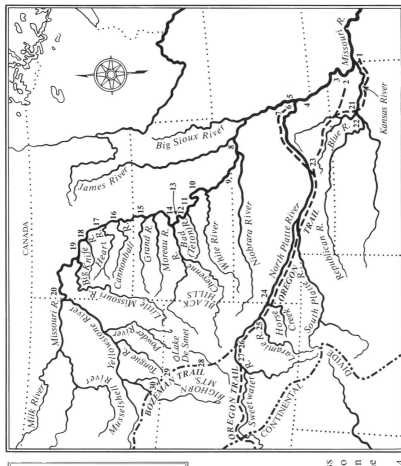

1. Westport	17. Fort Stevenson (1867)
2. Fort Leavenworth (1827)	18. Fort Mandan (1804)
3. Kickapoo Mission (1836)	19. Fort Berthold (1862)
4. Fort Kearney I (1846)	20. Fort Union (1828)
5. St. Joseph's (1838)	Fort Buford (1833)
6. Fort Omaha (1868)	Fort William (1833)
7. Fort Atkinson (1819)	21. St. Mary's (1848)
8. Yankton Treaty (1858)	22. Fort Riley (1853)
9. Fort Randall (1856)	23. Fort Kearney (1848)
10. Fort Thompson (1864)	24. Treaty Site (1851)
11. Fort Sully I (1863)	25. Fort Laramie (1834)
12. Fort Pierre (1831)	26. Fort Fetterman (1867)
13. Fort Sully II (1866)	27. Fort Caspar (1862)
14. Fort Bennett (1870)	28. Fort Reno (1865)
15. Arikara Blockade (1823)	29. Fort Phil Kearny (1866)
16. Fort Rice (1864)	30. Fort C.F. Smith (1866)

"MY BELOVED MISSOURI"

The prodigious length of the Missouri, the wildness and impetuosity of its current, induced the Sioux to call it "The Furious." The tributaries which have been given names number 123. From the mouth to the source of its three forks is 2,945 miles.

—De Smet, 1864

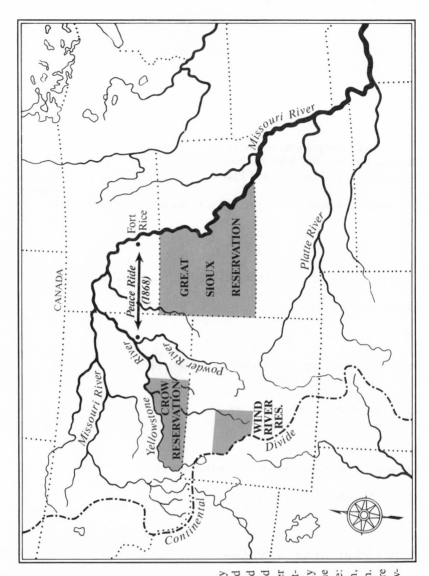

RESERVATIONS ASSIGNED BY FORT LARAMIE AND FORT BRIDGER TREATIES OF 1868

The abandonment of the military posts on the Bozeman Trail proved to be a hollow victory for Red Cloud. The 1868 Treaty limited Indian utilization of the Powder River Country to approved hunting expeditions. Their 1868 Treaty offered a residence option to the northern Arapaho and Cheyenne: to abide on the Sioux Reservation, or with their southern tribesmen. In 1877 the northern Arapaho were assigned to the Shoshoni Wind River Reservation.

Notes

PROLOGUE

1.   Pierre Jean De Smet was baptized on the day of his birth, January 30, 1801, in the Church of Our Lady in his hometown, Dendermonde, Belgium. De Smet's family life and educational background are presented in CR, 1:9–12, and Laveille, *De Smet*, pp. 1–40.

De Smet's companions in the 1821 voyage from Amsterdam had been Judocus Van Assche, John Anthony Elet, John B. Smedts, Peter J. Verhaegen, Felix L. Verreydt, and Francis de Maillet. These young men had been recruited by Father Charles Nerinckx, who advised them that the surest means of realizing their ambition to become Indian missionaries was to join the Jesuits. They applied at Georgetown College, were accepted as Jesuit candidates on October 5, 1821, and were sent at once to the novitiate at White Marsh. Bishop Du Bourg made the assignment of this group of Jesuits to his St. Louis diocese to establish his proposed Indian school.

On their 1823 journey to St. Louis the Jesuits stopped at Louisville for a brief visit with Father Nerinckx, who was then sending on a group of Loretto Sisters to Missouri. The Sisters of the Sacred Heart had arrived in St. Louis in 1818; moving their school from St. Charles to Florissant, they were generous neighbors to the Jesuits and hoped to offer similar educational training to young Indian girls. See Garraghan, *Jesuits*, 1:22; Hill, *Historical Sketch*, pp. 11–20; Faherty, *Dream*, pp. 26–29.

2.   In addition to Foley, *History of Missouri, 1673–1820*, McCandless, *History of Missouri, 1820–1860*, and Parrish, *History of Missouri, 1860–1875*, the standard histories of the state, other works offer a wealth of factual information about early St. Louis. See Scharf, *History of St. Louis*; Stevens, *Centennial History*; Billon, *Annals of St. Louis*; Houck, *History of Missouri*; Lionberger, *Annals of St. Louis*; Darby, *Personal Recollections*; Chittenden, *History of Steamboat Navigation* and *American Fur Trade*.

3.   By 1817 this ferry service demanded two landings. About this service Stevens wrote: "If it had not been so well conducted St. Louis would not have waited until 1874 for the first bridge" (*Centennial History*, 1:18).

4.   Scharf, *History of St. Louis*, 2:1097.

5.   Scharf, *History of St. Louis*, 1:311; Stevens, *Centennial History*, 1:114.

6.   Darby, *Personal Recollections*, p. 10; see also Flagg, *Far West*, 1:118.

7.   Scharf discusses the unusual activities of Pierre Chouteau, Sr., as Osage Indian agent; this position was terminated in 1818 (*History of St. Louis*, 1:182). Paul Wilhelm, duke of Württemberg, reported on the special status of the Osage Indians with the St. Louis merchants (*Travels*, p. 194). Both Stevens (*Centennial History*, 1:467) and Foley and Rice (*First Chouteaus*, pp. 58–59) note the unusual acceptance of these visitors.

8.   In 1808 Clark reported on the use of the council chamber in a letter to Secretary of War Henry Dearborn (Carter, *Territorial Papers*, 14:209). Clark's museum displayed some of the potraits of Indian leaders painted by

Charles Bird King in 1821, and following his 1832 visit George Catlin contributed some of his initial paintings of Plains Indians. These exhibits had a direct influence on Karl Bodmer, who visited the museum with Prince Maximilian prior to their 1833–34 voyage on the Upper Missouri. Another of Clark's guests in the mid-1830s, William D. Stewart, was much impressed by these paintings; when Stewart returned to the western plains in 1837, he brought with him the New Orleans artist Alfred Jacob Miller (DeVoto, *Wide Missouri*, pp. 391–415).

9. Wilhelm, *Travels*, pp. 190–94.

10. Garraghan, *Jesuits*, 1:82–107.

11. Stevens, *Centennial History*, 1:20; Scharf, *History of St. Louis*, 1:314.

12. Houck, *History of Missouri*, 2:48, 318–83; Foley and Rice, *First Chouteaus*, p. 189. Chambers indicates Benton's debt to Gratiot (*Bullion Benton*, p. 63). Darby reports that in 1804 Gratiot was one of the few persons in St. Louis who could speak English (*Personal Recollections*, p. 223).

13. The power of the Saint Louis junto is pointed up by Clokey, *Ashley*, pp. 46–49, and Foley, *History of Missouri*, p. 198.

14. Oglesby points out the importance to the fur trade of the example set by the Lisa expedition of 1807 (*Manuel Lisa*, pp. 40–67). The formation of the St. Louis Missouri Fur Company is treated by Chittenden (*American Fur Trade*, 1:125–50).

15. Scharf, *History of St. Louis*, 1:200.

16. Ibid., 1:198; Stevens, *Centennial History*, 3:433.

17. Franzwa, *Oregon Trail Revisited*, p. 77.

18. Stevens, *Centennial History*, 1:465; Scharf, *History of St. Louis*, 1:251–69; Houck, *History of Missouri*, 2:355–63; Chittenden, *American Fur Trade*, 1:104–5; Foley, *History of Missouri*, p. 74; DeVoto, *Journals of Lewis and Clark*, p. 477.

19. Hollon treats the questionable achievements of Pike's first expedition (*Lost Pathfinder*, pp. 10–110, 168–70).

20. Scharf, *History of St. Louis*, 1:190; Foley, *History of Missouri*, p. 123; Jackson, *Letters*, 2:444, 456, 458.

21. Lavender, *Fist*, pp. 112–77; Goetzmann, *Army Exploration*, p. 29, *Exploration and Empire*, pp. 30–35.

22. Chittenden, *American Fur Trade*, 2:561–62.

23. Billington, *Westward Expansion*, p. 452; DeVoto, *Wide Missouri*, p. 2; Chittenden, *American Fur Trade*, p. 570; Coues, *Expeditions of Pike*, 2:525; James, *Expedition from Pittsburg*, 2:361.

24. Franzwa, *Old Cathedral*, p. 47; Faherty, *Dream*, p. 27.

25. For references to Bishop Du Bourg's library, see Wilhelm, *Travels*, p. 169; Edwards and Hopewell, *Edward's Great West*, p. 34; Flagg, *Far West*, 1:169. Faherty notes that the bishop had a racially and religiously integrated cathedral choir and a religiously integrated St. Louis College (*Dream*, p. 23).

26. Garraghan, *Jesuits*, 1:91; Faherty, *Dream*, p. 27; Hill, *Historical Sketch*, p. 21; Billon, *Annals of St. Louis*, p. 422.

27. See Garraghan, *Jesuits,* 1:282, for a list of non-Indian students enrolled at St. Regis Indian Seminary.
28. Faherty, *Dream,* p. 15.
29. Garraghan, *Jesuits,* 1:74.
30. For extended treatment of the Indian school conducted by the Jesuits at Florissant, see Garraghan, *Jesuits,* 1:74, 92–170; Faherty, *Dream,* pp. 27–35.

1.   *JEFFERSONIAN CONFLICT OF INTERESTS*

1. Jefferson, "Observations on Demeunier's Manuscript," in Boyd, *Papers of Jefferson,* 10:44. Among the more complete studies of the development of early American Indian policy are Prucha, *Indian Policy in Formative Years* and *Great Father*; Horsman, *Expansion*; and Harmon, *Sixty Years.* Other works dealing with this subject include Sheehan, *Seeds of Extinction*; Dippie, *Vanishing Americans*; Rogin, *Andrew Jackson*; and Satz, *Indian Policy.*
2. Morison points out Jefferson's continued political power, especially noting the influence of his writings (*Oxford History,* pp. 207, 304–5). See also Fleming, *Man From Monticello,* p. 369; Horsman, *Expansion,* p. 108.
3. Speeches to a delegation of Indian leaders, Jan. 1809, quoted in Horsman, *Expansion,* p. 109.
4. Jackson, *Letters,* 1:153; Horsman, *Expansion,* p. 106.
5. *Journals of Continental Congress,* 25:602, 31:490–93; Prucha, *Documents of Indian Policy,* pp. 3, 9–10; see Prucha, *Indian Policy in Formative Years,* pp. 5, 13, 30.
6. Richardson, *Messages and Papers,* 1:117–56; Prucha, *Indian Policy in Formative Years,* p. 40.
7. Morison, *Oxford History,* pp. 333–34; Prucha, *Indian Policy in Formative Years,* p. 40.
8. *Journals of the Continental Congress,* 34:342–44; Richardson, *Messages and Papers,* 1:96; Prucha, *Documents of Indian Policy,* pp. 13–15; Fitzpatrick, *Writings of Washington,* 25:12.
9. Prucha, *Documents of Indian Policy,* p. 13; Morison, *Oxford History,* p. 318; Horsman, *Expansion,* pp. 54–59.
10. *American State Papers: Indian Affairs,* 1:61–62; see Prucha, *Indian Policy in Formative Years,* pp. 141–42.
11. Sanger, *U.S. Statutes,* 1:137–38; Prucha, *Documents of Indian Policy,* pp. 14–15.
12. Richardson, *Messages and Papers,* 1:80–81.
13. *Writings of Thomas Jefferson (memorial ed.),* 8:328–29, quoted in Prucha, *Indian Policy in Formative Years,* p. 141.
14. Prucha, *Indian Policy in Formative Years,* pp. 49–50; Fitzpatrick, *Writings of Washington,* 35:112.
15. Morison, *Oxford History,* p. 340.
16. Billington, *Westward Expansion,* p. 273; Horsman, *Expansion,* p. 105.
17. Bigelow, *Works of Franklin,* 2:336; Prucha, *Indian Policy in*

Formative Years, p. 86. Concerning the trade factory system, see Peake, *Factory System*; Wesley, *Guarding the Frontier*; Plaisance, "Factory System"; and Way, "Factory System."

18. Richardson, *Messages and Papers,* 1:340–41; Prucha, *Documents of Indian Policy,* pp. 21–22.

19. Jackson, *Letters,* 1:11.

20. Richardson, *Messages and Papers,* 1:371–72.

21. Carter, *Territorial Papers,* 7:68–70.

22. Ibid., 90–91.

23. Sheehan, *Seeds of Extinction,* p. 171; Richardson, *Messages and Papers,* 1:353, 375. Plaisance points out that "the custom of giving credits to the Indians was a usual practice at all the factories" ("Factory System," p. 72); obviously Jefferson was recommending a credit practice that went far beyond the ordinary extension of credit to Indian hunters.

24. Jackson, *Letters,* 2:444–45.

25. Lavender, *Fist,* pp. 108–10.

26. Jefferson to Lewis, Aug. 21, 1808 (Carter, *Territorial Papers,* 14:209).

27. Morison notes that the problem of U.S.-Indian relations had become localized (*Oxford History,* p. 445).

28. Sanger, *U.S. Statutes,* 2:402–4; Prucha, *Documents of Indian Policy,* p. 23.

29. Viola, *McKenney,* pp. 20, 110, 118; *American State Papers: Indian Affairs,* 2:62–79, 326–32. The tendency to dominate the Indians, and to do so in a very cost-conscious manner, was to be found in most of the political leaders of this period; it was notable in McKenney.

30. Benton, *Thirty Years' View,* pp. 20–21; see Chambers, *Bullion Benton.*

31. Chittenden, *American Fur Trade,* 1:17.

32. Crooks's lengthy arguments presented to Congress are reprinted in *American State Papers: Indian Affairs,* 2:329–32; see Lavender, *Fist,* chaps. 18–20.

33. Benton, *Thirty Years' View,* p. 21; Chambers, *Bullion Benton,* p. 111.

34. Sanger, *U.S. Statutes,* 3:682–83; Prucha, *Documents of Indian Policy,* pp. 34–35.

35. Lavender, *Fist,* p. 331; Wesley, *Guarding the Frontier,* p. 53; Harmon, *Sixty Years,* p. 131.

36. Carter, *Territorial Papers,* 15:682–83, 706; Morgan, *West of Ashley,* p. xxii.

37. Chittenden comments that throughout the decade of the 1820s Ashley "was the most influential man in Missouri, next to Senator Benton" (*American Fur Trade,* 1:248).

38. Morgan, *West of Ashley,* pp. 1–7, 227; Clokey, *Ashley,* pp. 67–68.

39. Nichols, *Atkinson,* pp. 82–84.

40. Morgan, *West of Ashley,* p. 1; Clokey, *Ashley,* p. 79.

41. Morgan, *West of Ashley,* pp. 1–3, 19; Clokey, *Ashley,* p. 80–88.

42. Sunder, *Pilcher,* p. 37.

43. Morgan, *Jedediah Smith,* pp. 374–75; Chittenden, *American Fur Trade,* 1:378.

44. Reprinted in the *Daily Intelligencer,* Sept. 17, 1822. See Lavender, *Fist,* p. 337; Morgan, *West of Ashley,* p. 19. The deeper objective of the fur traders' campaign (headed by Benton) was also obtained. The closing of the trade factories signaled an era of government disinterest in the fur trade; unless moved to achieve selfish benefits, Congress exercised no concern for the management of Indian affairs (Welsey, *Guarding the Frontier,* p. 53; Clokey, *Ashley,* p. 61; Harmon, *Sixty Years,* p. 131).

45. Carter, *Territorial Papers,* 14:109, 679; Foley, *History of Missouri,* p. 114; Steffen, *William Clark,* pp. 109–25.

46. Characterizing the government's policy of bringing delegations of Indian leaders to Washington, McKenney commented: "This mode of conquering these people is merciful, and it is cheap, in comparison to what a war with them would cost" (Viola, *McKenney,* p. 118). The treaties negotiated by Clark between 1815 and 1818 are printed in Kappler, *Indian Affairs,* 2:110–47. Steffen concludes that Clark exercised humanitarian concern for the Indians (*William Clark,* pp. 141–42); Clokey argues that Clark, like his fellow frontiersmen, viewed the Indians as an obstacle to be removed (*Ashley,* p. 81).

47. Carter, *Territorial Papers,* 15:712–15, 731–33.

48. *American State Papers: Indian Affairs,* 2:364–65; Steffen, *William Clark,* p. 129.

49. Despite his warning about possible problems with the Indians consequent to the invasion of their lands, agent O'Fallon consistently manifested a pro-trader attitude (Morgan, *West of Ashley,* p. 6).

50. Ibid., p. 17.

51. Ibid., pp. 18–19; Clokey, *Ashley,* p. 75.

52. Carter, *Territorial Papers,* 14:226.

53. Ibid., 291; Prucha, *Documents of Indian Policy,* pp. 17–21, 34–35.

54. Prucha, *Documents of Indian Policy,* pp. 17–21, 34–35; Prucha, *Indian Policy in Formative Years,* pp. 116–17. For historical treatment of the antiwhiskey crusade, see Chittenden, *American Fur Trade,* 1:22–31; Prucha, *Indian Policy in Formative Years,* pp. 66–93.

55. The treaties negotiated by Clark from 1824 to 1836 are printed in Kappler, *Indian Affairs,* 2:207–9, 217–25, 250–55, 262–64, 305–10, 365–67, 370–72, 376–77, 382–83, 468–70.

56. Steffen, *William Clark,* pp. 145–50; Clokey, *Ashley,* p. 81.

57. Morgan, *West of Ashley,* p. 23; Clokey, *Ashley,* p. 88, quoting from a letter written by Jesse Benton.

58. Morgan, *West of Ashley,* pp. 36–37, 44–45; Clokey, *Ashley,* p. 91–112.

59. Morgan, *West of Ashley,* p. xxix; Clokey, *Ashley,* p. 113. The character and life of the mountain men are detailed by DeVoto, *Wide Missouri,* pp. 42–163.

2. THE END OF THE BEGINNING

1. Clokey, *Ashley,* pp. 132–38; Morgan, *Jedediah Smith,* pp. 154–60.

2. Garraghan, *Jesuits,* 1:100, 147–69, 269–308.

3. Morgan, *West of Ashley,* p. 106; Clokey, *Ashley*, pp. 143–69; Morgan, *Jedediah Smith*, pp. 160–76.

4. Garraghan, *Jesuits*, 1:158–62.

5. Clokey, *Ashley,* pp. 169–80; Morgan, *Jedediah Smith,* p. 181–201. Clokey notes the resulting newspaper publicity concerning the ease of the transcontinental route.

6. Garraghan, *Jesuits*, 1:164.

7. Nichols, *Atkinson*, pp. 109–18.

8. Morgan, *West of Ashley,* p. 166, *Jedediah Smith*, p. 225; Sunder, *Sublette*, pp. 71–75; Clokey, *Ashley*, p. 179.

9. Garraghan, *Jesuits*, 1:164–65.

10. Faherty, *Dream*, pp. 34–43; Garraghan, *Jesuits*, 1:112, 136.

11. Morison, *Oxford History*, pp. 546–47; Billington, *Western Expansion*, pp. 531–33.

12. Morgan, *Jedediah Smith*, pp. 298–300, 318–20; *West of Ashley*, pp. 156–57.

13. Faherty, *Dream*, pp. 35–36; Barry, *Beginning of the West*, pp. 44–48; Garraghan, *Jesuits*, 1:282–83.

14. Hafen, *Broken Hand*, pp. 78–85; Russell, *Journal*, p. 51; Sunder, *Sublette*, pp. 78–84.

15. Faherty, *Dream*, p. 36; Garraghan, *Jesuits*, 1:61–64, 271–86, 376–85.

16. Morgan, *Jedediah Smith*, pp. 320–23; Barry, *Beginning of the West*, p. 175; Sunder, *Sublette*, pp. 84–89; Hafen, *Broken Hand*, pp. 86–88.

17. Garraghan, *Jesuits*, 1:166–67, 298.

18. Clokey, *Ashley,* pp. 181–91; Sunder, *Sublette*, pp. 93–101; Morgan, *Jedediah Smith*, pp. 325–30; Garraghan, *Jesuits*, 2:237–38. The Flatheads had been introduced to the Catholic religion by Catholic Iroquois from eastern Canada who had settled among them.

19. This Assiniboine chief has frequently been referred to as The Light. His actual name, *Ajaja* (Shiny), was apparently the Assiniboine designation for a type of large glass beads called by the traders "pigeon eggs." Catlin, *North American Indian*, 2:194–200; CR, 3:1176–81.

20. Garraghan, *Jesuits*, 2:236–44.

21. Irving, *Captain Bonneville*, pp. 13–79; Sunder, *Sublette*, pp. 101–13; Hafen, *Broken Hand*, pp. 105–26; Leonard, *Adventures*, pp. 28–29.

22. Chittenden, *Early Steamboat Navigation*, 1:136–38.

23. Irving, *Captain Bonneville*, pp. 154–56; Sunder, *Sublette*, pp. 114–33; Hafen, *Broken Hand*, pp. 121–37; DeVoto, *Wide Missouri*, pp. 48, 92–131; Lavender, *Westward Vision*, pp. 243–57; Sprague, *Gallery of Dudes*, pp. 7–15; Barry, *Beginning of the West*, pp. 231–32.

24. Thomas and Ronnefeldt, *First Man*.

25. Garraghan, *Jesuits*, 1:383–86.

26. Garraghan, *Jesuits*, 2:242–44; DeVoto, *Wide Missouri*, pp. 6–8; Franzwa, *Oregon Trail*, pp. 13–14.

27. CR, 1:13; Garraghan, *Jesuits*, 1:301–302, 351–52.

28. DeVoto, *Wide Missouri*, pp. 196–204; Sprague, *Gallery of Dudes*, pp. 15–17; Hafen, *Broken Hand*, pp. 138–45; Lavender, *Westward Visions,*

p. 250; Sunder, *Sublette,* pp. 134–43; Morgan, *Rocky Mountain Journal,* p. 188.

29.   Faherty, *Dream,* p. 48; Franzwa, *Old Cathedral,* pp. 49–60, pt. 2, chap. 2, n. 7; Garraghan, *Jesuits,* 1:355–57.

30.   Sanger, *U.S. Statutes,* 3:682–83; Prucha, *Documents of Indian Policy,* pp. 64–71, *Indian Policy in Formative Years,* pp. 250–73; Steffen, *William Clark,* p. 149.

31.   Larpenteur, *Forty Years,* p. 32; Sprague, *Gallery of Dudes,* pp. 18–21; Hafen, *Broken Hand,* pp. 146–51; Lavender, *Westward Vision,* pp. 270–80; DeVoto, *Wide Missouri,* pp. 217–38.

32.   Garraghan, *Jesuits,* 1:356–57; CR, 1:28–29.

33.   Garraghan, *Jesuits,* 1:392, 2:236–48.

34.   Drury, *Marcus Whitman,* 1:167; Jeffrey, *Converting the West,* pp. 66–67, 107; Barry, *Beginning of the West,* pp. 303–7; Sunder, *Sublette,* pp. 147–48; Sprague, *Gallery of Dudes,* p. 18; DeVoto, *Wide Missouri,* pp. 245–50.

35.   Russell, *Journal,* p. 41; Sunder, *Pilcher,* p. 110; Lavender, *Westward Vision,* pp. 291–305; Alter, *Jim Bridger,* pp. 162–68; Sprague, *Gallery of Dudes,* p. 21; DeVoto, *Wide Missouri,* pp. 260–65. Whitman's comment is quoted in Hafen and Young, *Fort Laramie,* p. 44.

36.   Hill, *Historical Sketch,* pp. 57–59; Garraghan, *Jesuits,* 1:350–59.

37.   Garraghan, *Jesuits,* 1:384–402.

38.   DeVoto, *Wide Missouri,* pp. 280–338; Hafen, *Broken Hand,* pp. 161–63; Sprague, *Gallery of Dudes,* pp. 22–25; Barry, *Beginning of the West,* p. 324.

39.   Garraghan, *Jesuits,* 2:236–48; DeVoto, *Wide Missouri,* pp. 330–38; Goetzmann, *Army Exploration,* p. 69; Lavender, *Westward Vision,* pp. 313–16.

40.   Garraghan, *Jesuits,* 1:359–60.

41.   Sprague, *Gallery of Dudes,* p. 25; DeVoto, *Wide Missouri,* pp. 4, 70–72.

42.   Goetzmann calls the corps "a central institution of Manifest Destiny" (*Army Exploration,* pp. 4, 70–72).

43.   Garraghan, *Jesuits,* 1:422–33; Steffen, *William Clark,* p. 151.

44.   Garraghan, *Jesuits,* 1:434, 2:81–82; CR, 1:136–46.

45.   Hafen, *Broken Hand,* pp. 166–68; DeVoto, *Wide Missouri,* pp. 378–84; Lavender, *Westward Vision,* pp. 335–37; Alter, *Jim Bridger,* p. 185; Sprague, *Gallery of Dudes,* p. 25.

46.   CR, 1:184, 3:930.

47.   CR, 1:178, 189–91.

48.   Ibid., pp. 29–30; Garraghan, *Jesuits,* 1:444, 2:248.

49.   Lavender, *Westward Vision,* p. 339.

50.   Garraghan, *Jesuits,* 2:251; Laveille, *De Smet,* p. 103, n. 12.

51.   Garraghan, *Jesuits,* 2:252–53. Stanley's letter, printed in CR, 4:1584–88, is misdated 1864; by internal evidence it has to have been composed in 1868.

52.   CR, 1:203–15; Alter, *Jim Bridger,* pp. 188–89; Lavender, *Westward Vision,* p. 340; Quaife, *Kit Carson,* p. 53 (mistakenly reporting a meeting with De Smet at the 1837 rendezvous rather than 1840).

53. Alter, *Jim Bridger*, p. 190; CR, 1:262. See Barry, *Beginning of the West*, pp. 392–409; Johansen, "Newell Memoranda," p. 39; Garraghan, *Jesuits*, 2:254

54. Garraghan, *Jesuits*, 2:254; CR, 1:216–20, 262.

55. Lavender, *Westward Vision*, pp. 340–42; Alter, *Jim Bridger*, p. 191.

56. CR, 1:221.

57. Laveille, *De Smet*, p. 108.

58. CR, 1:230.

59. Ibid., p. 231.

60. Ibid., pp. 233–34 (De Smet's preoccupation with baptism is understandable when viewed in the context of Catholic religious thought of his time).

61. Ibid., pp. 236–44, 268.

62. Ibid., pp. 245–58, 270.

63. Ibid., p. 258; Garraghan, *Jesuits*, 1:445.

64. CR, 1:258.

65. Billington, *Westward Expansion*, pp. 453–61.

66. Ibid., p. 465.

67. Prucha, *Indian Policy in Formative Years*, p. 258.

3.   1841—THE BEGINNING OF THE END

1. Garraghan, *Jesuits*, 1:170–75; Bangert, *History*, pp. 257–60, 350–54.

2. Burns, *Indian Wars*, p. 38; Graham, *Vanished Arcadia;* Caraman, *Lost Paradise;* Moore, *Indian and Jesuit;* Bangert, *History*, pp. 152–61.

3. Garraghan, *Jesuits*, 1:92–182, 376–438, 2:236–334.

4. In 1838 Fathers Francis N. Blanchet and Modeste Demers had been sent from Quebec to work in the Oregon country. On his 1840 journey De Smet exchanged correspondence with them; Blanchet had thereby been informed of De Smet's intention to return in the spring. Garraghan, *Jesuits*, 2:274; Mengarini, *Recollections*, p. 38; Schoenberg, *Paths to Northwest*, p. 24.

5. CR, 1:327–30.

6. De Smet appreciated the practical skills of the Jesuit brothers; through the following century they constituted over 40 percent of the Jesuit personnel engaged at the Indian missions (CR, 1:278). Garraghan comments: "In a Jesuit Indian mission the coadjutor-brothers lend services that one can only describe as indispensable" (*Jesuits*, 2:259, 428–30, 516).

7. Faherty, *Dream*, pp. 60–61; Garraghan, *Jesuits*, 1:490–96.

8. CR, 1:273.

9. Garraghan, *Jesuits*, 2:256.

10. In 1847 the Jesuits opened another mission not far south of Sugar Creek for the Osages; there the school for Indian girls was conducted by the Sisters of Loretto. In 1848 the Potawatomis were removed to the Kaw Reserve west of Topeka; the mission, with both schools, was transferred to form St. Mary's Mission. Faherty, *Dream*, p. 5; Garraghan, *Jesuits*, 2:175–235, 493–593; Barry, *Beginning of the West*, p. 433; Fitzgerald, *Beacon*, pp. 76–114.

11. Garraghan, *Jesuits,* 2:257.

12. CR, 1:276, 4:1552.

13. Garraghan, *Jesuits,* 2:258–59.

14. CR, 1:279; Donnelly, *Wilderness Kingdom,* p. 24; Laveille, *De Smet,* p. 121.

15. Garraghan, *Jesuits,* 2:260.

16. Donnelly, *Wilderness Kingdom,* p. 35; Williams, "A Tour to the Oregon Territory," in Hafen, *Mountain Man,* 3:220; Quaife, *Echoes,* pp. 23–26.

17. Donnelly, *Wilderness Kingdom,* p. 26.

18. Garraghan, *Jesuits,* 2:260. A listing of the published narratives is in Mattes, *Platte River,* pp. 39–44. According to Franzwa, some 30,000 people died on the Oregon Trail by 1859; the prime killer was not cholera but carelessness (*Oregon Trail,* p. 42).

19. Donnelly, *Wilderness Kingdom,* pp. 34–35.

20. Alter, *Jim Bridger,* p. 194; Mattes, *Platte River,* pp. 22–23; Quaife, *Echoes,* pp. 18–22.

21. Donnelly, *Wilderness Kingdom,* pp. 37–38; CR, 1:294, 310, 339, 4:1553.

22. CR, 1:304–307. It was in Ross's Hole, near the headwaters of the Bitterroot, that Lewis and Clark met the Flatheads (DeVoto, *Journals,* pp. 232–37).

23. CR, 1:316; Donnelly, *Wilderness Kingdom,* p. 39.

24. CR, 1:317.

25. Ibid., p. 327.

26. Ibid., pp. 330–31. Burns summarizes the programs and projects conducted in the reductions (*Indian Wars,* pp. 48–55); see also Donnelly, *Wilderness Kingdom,* pp. 43–45, 57–58.

27. CR, 1:329–38, 355, 381; for information on Prudhomme and Charles, see Fahey, *Flathead Indians,* pp. 67–68; Barry, *Beginning of the West,* pp. 181, 359; CR, 1:292, 2:575.

28. CR, 1:317–19.

29. Clothing too had become a need at the reduction; one of the Jesuit brothers was already dressed in buckskins, and among the priests Hudson's Bay blankets had been used as replacements for cassocks (CR, 1:342–58; Laveille, *De Smet,* p. 136).

30. CR, 1:342–57.

31. Ibid., pp. 337–38, 359.

32. Ibid., pp. 384–87.

33. The inter-Christian rivalry of the period, especially intense in the Oregon country, affected even De Smet, who had criticized the religious tenants and practice of Rev. Samuel Parker in 1836, characterizing him as "a modern Iconoclast" (CR, 1:380, 388). Burns offers this explanation: "The ghosts of Torquemada and Oliver Cromwell stalked the Oregon forests" (*Indian Wars,* p. 35).

34. CR, 2:449–51, 477; Schoenberg, *Paths to Northwest,* pp. 24–25; Burns, *Indian Wars,* p. 25; Garraghan, *Jesuits,* 2:278–86.

35. CR, 1:391.

36. Ibid., p. 392.

37. De Smet's report on his journey was dated at St. Louis University November 1 (CR, 1:393–402). The steamboat, present unusually late in the year on the Upper Missouri, was the *New Haven,* which belonged to the newly formed opposition to the American Fur Company (Chittenden, *American Fur Trade,* 1:367; Barry, *Beginning of the West,* p. 462).

38. Garraghan, *Jesuits,* 1:278.

39. Ibid., 2:290–91; Laveille, *De Smet,* p. 153.

40. Barry, *Beginning of the West,* pp. 473–74; Garraghan, *Jesuits,* 2:291.

41. Barry, *Beginning of the West,* pp. 472–73.

42. Father Mengarini, with Young Ignace as a guide, met the new missionaries and assisted them through the last section of their journey; they arrived at the reduction by September (Garraghan, *Jesuits,* 2:291).

43. Ibid., 3:101; CR, 4:1513–16, 1582.

44. Within three months, De Smet had collected "money and material to the value of 125,000 francs" (Garraghan, *Jesuits,* 2:292, 3:97).

45. Ibid., 2:282.

46. Laveille, *De Smet,* p. 156.

47. CR, 1:46–47, 2:408–49.

48. Schoenberg, *Paths to Northwest,* p. 36; Garraghan, *Jesuits,* 2:295–304.

49. CR, 2:466–71.

50. Ibid., p. 472.

51. Ibid., pp. 471, 478, 482.

52. Ibid., p. 475.

53. Schoenberg, *Paths to Northwest,* pp. 40, 597; Garraghan, *Jesuits,* 1:514, 2:358–59, 420–24.

54. CR, 2:475–76.

55. Ibid., pp. 484–552; Bischoff, *Old Oregon,* pp. 66–67.

56. Garraghan, *Jesuits,* 2:97, 352–55, 397.

57. CR, 2:485–86; Cline, *Peter Ogden,* pp. 159–75.

58. Within the first year the American population on the Oregon coast had doubled from 5,000 to 10,000 (Burns, *Indian Wars,* p. 20).

59. On his 1846 voyage down the Missouri at least half of the 150 baptisms De Smet administered were to mixed-blood children; he continued to offer such services through the rest of his life (CR, 2:600–612, 3:946–48).

60. In 1846 the Jesuits in Oregon faced the same issue of priorities as that debated by the Jesuits in Missouri a few years earlier (Garraghan, *Jesuits,* 2:394–431; Schoenberg, *Paths to Northwest,* pp. 54–55).

61. Garraghan, *Jesuits,* 2:299–300; Schoenberg, *Paths to Northwest,* p. 45.

62. In 1847, replying to a letter from St. Louis, De Vos commented, "Your letter did not find me among my dear Mountain Indians, but in the heart of an American settlement" (Garraghan, *Jesuits,* 2:298, 367–69, 424). Schoenberg states that Accolti became strongly prejudiced against

Oregon and the Rocky Mountain missions in favor of California (*Paths to Northwest*, p. 57).

63. Schoenberg, *Paths to Northwest*, pp. 29, 37, 595; Garraghan, *Jesuits*, 2:270, 272, 450–57. Although Roothaan wrote in February 1846 approving Point's request to be transferred, Point did not receive the letter until the following spring. Van de Velde reported that Point passed through St. Louis in early August 1847, heading to his new field of labor in Canada.

64. Jeffrey reports on bouts of depression and the exchange of sharp criticisms among the Whitmans, the Spaldings, and other Protestant missionaries in Old Oregon (*Converting the West*, pp. 154–61). Fahey, *Flathead Indians*, pp. 85–86; Palladino, *Indians and Whites*, p. 46; Schoenberg, *Paths to Northwest*, pp. 40–45.

65. Schoenberg, *Paths to Northwest*, p. 71.

66. CR, 2:533–612; Garraghan, *Jesuits*, 2:333–430.

67. With the sorry religious prejudices of the period, especially notable in Oregon, blame for the tragedy of the Whitmans was directed against the Catholic missionaries (Burns, *Indian Wars*, pp. 31–35, 62–63; Schoenberg, *Paths to Northwest*, pp. 43–44; Garraghan, *Jesuits*, 2:344).

68. CR, 2:570–72.

69. Ibid., pp. 591–93; Garraghan, *Jesuits*, 2:445–47.

70. CR, 2:600–612. There is a discrepancy in the records as to the means of transportation De Smet used from Westport; also as to the exact date of his arrival in St. Louis.

71. This journey to Europe was reported in part by the letters of Charles Lucas Hunt, who accompanied De Smet to Belgium; there Hunt accepted the appointment as the Belgium consul, and returned to St. Louis to fill that post (Laveille, *De Smet*, pp. 202–12; Hunt Family Papers, vol. 20, Missouri Historical Society; Garraghan, *Jesuits*, 1: 510–12, 2:452–53; Letter Book, 1847, JMPA; CR, 4:1561–63).

72. Although Roothaan disapproved of what he considered De Smet's excessive traveling, this was not the view of De Smet's American superiors, Van de Velde excepted. Further, Beckx, Roothaan's successor, authorized the superior of the Rocky Mountain Missions to secure De Smet's services as a resident missionary; Beckx commented that the unfavorable reports circulated about De Smet were exaggerated and without foundation. Garraghan, *Jesuits*, 2:333–430, 3:95.

73. Ligthart, *Return*, p. 146.

74. Garraghan, *Jesuits*, 2:377, 452.

75. Ibid., pp. 93–100.

76. Ibid., pp. 378, 383; Fahey, *Flathead Indians*, p. 88.

77. Garraghan, *Jesuits*, 2:438.

78. CR, 1:122.

79. DeVoto, *Wide Missouri*, p. 371.

80. Burns, *Indian Wars*, pp. 39–40.

81. The failure of some Catholic missionaries to respect Indian cultures has recently been noted, and lamented, by the U.S. Catholic Bishops in "Statement on American Indians," p. 1.

82. Washburn, *Indian in America*, pp. 123–25.

4. MOUNTING CONFRONTATIONS ON THE GREAT PLAINS

1. For general discussions of the complex social, economic, and religious relationship between the buffalo and the Plains Indians, see McHugh, *Time of the Buffalo*, pp. 50–140; Dary, *Buffalo Book*, pp. 20–68, and Mails, *Mystic Warriors*, pp. 187–216.

2. CR, 3:1126 n.9.

3. Branch, *Hunting Buffalo*, p. 26; McHugh, *Time of the Buffalo*, p. 17.

4. McHugh, *Time of the Buffalo*, p. 109; see Dodge, *Wild Indians*, p. 282.

5. McHugh, *Time of the Buffalo*, pp. 88–90.

6. Brown, *Wounded Knee*, p. xvii.

7. Billington, *Westward Expansion*, pp. 507–10; Gittinger, "Separation of Nebraska and Kansas," p. 445.

8. Hafen and Young, *Fort Laramie*, p. 137; Jackson and Spence, *Expeditions*, p. 47; Hafen, *Broken Hand*, p. 211. Goetzmann's assessment is that Frémont's 1842 expedition had "great significance for the American people and did more than all the ventures of the mountain men to point the way west" (*Exploration and Empire*, p. 243).

9. Richardson, *Messages and Papers*, 4:394–98. Polk "had pledged himself to secure the transcontinental boundaries needed to make the United States a world power" (Billington, *Westward Expansion*, p. 382); see Morison, *Oxford History*, p. 460; Unruh, *Plains Across*, p. 19.

10. Hafen, *Broken Hand*, pp. 229–41.

11. Hafen, *Broken Hand*, pp. 244–45; Fitzpatrick to Medill, Jan. 6, 1847 (OIA-LR, Upper Platte Agency); Trennert, *Alternative to Extinction*, pp. 163–67.

12. Utley, *Frontiersmen in Blue*, pp. 65–98.

13. Hafen and Young, *Fort Laramie*, pp. 26–28, 141–42; DeVoto, *Wide Missouri*, pp. 190–91.

14. Hafen and Young, *Fort Laramie*, p. 154; Utley, *Frontiersmen in Blue*, p. 68.

15. Billington, *Westward Expansion*, p. 590; Mattes, *Platte River*, pp. 480–500.

16. Harvey to Medill, Sept. 5, 1846 (AR-CIA 1846 [ser. 493], pp. 286–87).

17. Harvey to Medill, Oct. 29, 1847 (AR-CIA 1847 [ser. 503], p. 835).

18. Fitzpatrick to Harvey, Dec. 18, 1847 (OIA-LR, Upper Platte Agency).

19. Fitzpatrick to Harvey, Dec. 18, 1847 (OIA-LR, Upper Platte Agency).

20. Fitzpatrick to Harvey, Oct. 6, 1848 (AR-CIA 1848, pp. 471–72).

21. Fitzpatrick to Harvey, Oct. 19, 1847 (OIA-LR, Upper Platte Agency), Oct. 6, 1848 (AR-CIA 1848 [ser. 537], pp. 471–72).

22. Fitzpatrick to Medill, Aug. 11, 1848 (OIA-LR, Upper Platte Agency).

23. Fitzpatrick to Harvey, Oct. 6, 1848 (AR-CIA 1848 [ser. 537], p. 471).

24. Mitchell to Medill, June 1, 1849 (OIA-LR, St. Louis Superintendency).

25. Brown to Fitzpatrick, Aug. 16, 1849 (OIA-LS, vol. 42).

26. Mitchell to Brown, Aug. 27, 1849 (enclosing copy of Mitchell to Fitzpatrick, Aug. 21, 1849); Aug. 31, 1849 (OIA-LR, Upper Platte Agency). Because of the renewed power of the fur traders under Secretary of the Interior Thomas Ewing, Medill was removed from office on June 30, 1849. Brown was appointed commissioner but resigned within a year; he was replaced by Luke Lea July 1, 1850 (Kvasnicka and Viola, *Commissioners,* pp. 35–46).

27. Mitchell forwarded Fitzpatrick's letter of complaint to Brown; these blunt criticisms of the military leaders might well be connected with the subsequent refusal of the War Department to cooperate as requested in the Fort Laramie treaty. The quartermaster general offered a sharp reply to the Indian Office. Fitzpatrick to Mitchell, Sept. 8, 1849; Quartermaster General C. J. Jesup to Secretary of War, Sept. 27, 1849 (OIA-LR, Upper Platte Agency).

28. Mitchell to Brown, Oct. 13, 1849 (AR-CIA, 1849, p. 1070); Report of Committee on Indian Affairs, Mar. 18, 1850 (Senate Misc. Doc. 70, 31st Cong., 1st sess.). Regarding the interest and cooperation of Atchison and Douglas, Trennert notes that their concern "was more for clearing possible routes for a railroad than helping the Indians" (*Alternative to Extinction,* p. 50).

29. Brown's presentation of the Mitchell-Fitzpatrick proposal in his annual report of November 30, 1849, stressed the costly negative repercussions that might result from no action being taken: serious disturbance along the frontier, sorry consequences to the emigrants — all at an enormous expense to the government (AR-CIA 1849, pp. 942–43).

30. Mitchell to Lea, Sept. 14, 1850; Fitzpatrick to Mitchell, Sept. 24, 1850 (AR-CIA 1850, pp. 48, 55–56).

31. Summarized from De Smet, Letter Book, 1849, JMPA.

32. Scharf, *History of St. Louis,* 2:1089–1193; Barry, *Beginning of the West,* pp. 804, 850.

33. De Smet, Letter Book, 1849, JMPA; Mattes, *Platte River,* p. 84.

34. Barry, *Beginning of the West,* pp. 847, 850, 862.

35. Ibid., pp. 864–65, 878, 888; Barrow to Mitchell, Oct. 1, 1849 (AR-CIA 1849, pp. 1077–78).

36. U.S. Cong., Senate, Stansbury, "Exploration and Survey," pp. 43–46; Barry, *Beginning of the West,* p. 830; Lavender, *Bent's Fort,* pp. 336–38. Lavender points out that for Bent the tragic loss among the Southern Cheyenne was the end of an era; a few days after his return from the frontier Bent destroyed his fort. Garraghan reports that among the emigrants passing St. Mary's Indian Mission the wave of cholera lasted about six weeks (*Jesuits,* 2:613).

37. Coel, *Chief Left Hand,* p. 21.

38. Trennert, *Alternative to Extinction,* p. 185.

39. CR, 1:151, 2:612, 636.

40. Ibid., 3:1188.

41. De Smet's earlier comments on the "Indian Question," stated at various times in his letters, were gathered together in a formal statement on December 30, 1854, for publication in *Précis Historiques,* repr. CR, 3:1201–11.

42. Ibid., pp. 1186–89.

43. De Smet to Harvey, Dec. 4, 1848 (OIA-LR, Upper Platte Agency); CR, 3:1186; Trennert, *Alternative to Extinction,* p. 176.

44. Medill, AR-CIA, 1848, p. 390; Malin, *Westward Expansion,* pp. 39–83.

45. Trennert, "William Medill," "Luke Lea," in Kvasnicka and Viola, *Commissioners,* pp. 29–57; for Lea's role in the 1851 Minnesota Sioux treaties, see Meyer, *Santee Sioux,* pp. 77–84; Lea, AR-CIA 1852, pp. 344–53.

46. AR-CIA 1852, pp. 1–4. Lea also offered the false prediction that "all danger of future hostile collision between our citizens and one of the most numerous and powerful tribes of all that region has been happily removed"—this as a presumed consequence of Lea's negotiation of the 1851 treaties with the Santees.

47. Fitzpatrick to Harvey, Oct. 16, 1848 (AR-CIA 1848, pp. 471–72); CR, 3:856, 1209.

5. THE MOVE TO PATERNALISTIC CONTROL

1. Sanger, *U.S. Statutes,* 9:572.

2. Mitchell to Lea, Mar. 22, 1851 (OIA-LR, Upper Platte).

3. Lea's appointment letter also noted that about $50,000 of the appropriation was intended for the purchase of goods in New York (Lea to Mitchell, May 27, 1851, OIA-LS, vol. 42); Mitchell to Campbell, Apr. 1, 1851 (OIA-LR, St. Louis Superintendency); Campbell informed the commissioner that his St. Louis firm already had the contract (Campbell to Lea, May 25, 1851, OIA-LR, St. Louis Superintendency).

4. Mitchell to Brown, Oct. 13, 1849 (AR-CIA, 1849, p. 1070); Mitchell, "Circular to Indian Agents, Traders, &c.," Apr. 4, 1851 (Letter Book, 1851, JMPA).

5. Earlier and repeatedly Fitzpatrick commented on the essential need for good interpreters (Fitzpatrick to Mitchell, Sept. 24, 1850, AR-CIA 1850, p.50). Fitzpatrick stated: "The 'sign language,' that common to all the wild tribes of the west, while it might answer the purposes of barter, could not be relied upon in matters of so much importance and delicacy" (Fitzpatrick to Cumming, Nov. 19, 1853, AR-CIA 1853, p. 360).

6. In a letter to De Smet April 19, 1851, Mitchell stated that he was enclosing copies of the circular; a number of copies are preserved among De Smet's papers (Letter Book, 1851, JMPA).

7. Mitchell to Ewing, Mar. 29, 1849 (OIA-LR, St. Louis Superintendency).

8. Thomas and Ronnefeldt, *First Man,* p. 74.

9. Apparently Mitchell composed his letter while De Smet was present in the superintendent's office (CR, 4:1565).

10. Conrad to Mitchell, Apr. 7, 1851; Mitchell to Lea, Apr. 22, 1851

(OIA-LR, St. Louis Superintendency). Mitchell also insisted that whereas the funding had been reduced to $100,000, "the expenses of the military escort should fall upon the War Department."

11.   Lea to Mitchell, May 26, 1851 (OIA-LS, vol. 42).

12.   CR, 4:1473–74.

13.   Garraghan, *Jesuits,* 2:635–36.

14.   Ibid., p. 640.

15.   Ibid., 3:69 n.6; De Smet to Rev. Father, May 15, 1851 (Letter Book, 1851, JMPA).

16.   De Smet to Benton, May 11, 1851 (Letter Book, 1851, JMPA). For De Smet's 1851 "Journey to the Great Desert," see Garraghan, *Jesuits,* 2:611–30; CR, 2:638–92; De Smet, *Western Missions,* pp. 61–120. For Kurz's journal and sketches, see Hewitt, ed., *Journal of Rudolph Friederich Kurz . . . 1846 to 1852,* trans. Myrtis Jarrell, Bureau of American Ethnology Bulletin 115 (Washington, D.C.: GPO, 1937).

17.   CR, 2:640–52. After his return to St. Louis in late 1851 De Smet forwarded to Miége a record of the baptisms he had administered during this journey in Indian Country (Letter Book, 1851, JMPA). La Barge reported his later transfer of Hoecken's coffin to the Jesuit cemetery at Florissant (Chittenden, *Steamboat Navigation,* 1:193). Sunder's account of this voyage of the *St. Ange* includes reports on Kurz and Edwin Denig (*Fur Trade*, pp. 138–42).

18.   De Smet gratefully reported a recognition awarded him by his Indian companions before they left the Powder River drainage: "We arrived quite unexpectedly on the borders of a lovely little lake about six miles long, and my traveling companions gave it my name" (CR, 2:668); Bourke, *On the Border,* pp. 293–94.

19.   CR, 2:671–72.

20.   Ibid., pp. 2:672–73; Mattes, *Platte River,* pp. 15–16. On the basis of the trail of debris left behind, the emigrants of this period have been characterized as "the greatest 'litterbugs' of American history" (Unruh, *Plains Across,* p. 110).

21.   Barry offers a brief listing of the Overland Trail guide books (*Beginning of the West,* p. 1272); Unruh states that by 1849 "guides were clearly superfluous" (*Plains Across,* p. 76).

22.   Trennert reports the emigrants' hostile attitude towards the Indians and their lack of concern for the natural resources of the Platte valley: "Emigrants, cognizant only of their own well-being, destroyed most of the natural resources that came within reach. They fouled the water, used up the wood, ruined pastures, and drove off game animals" (*Alternative to Extinction,* pp. 138, 180).

23.   Harvey to Medill, May 6, 1846 (OIA-LR, Upper Missouri Agency); Medill to Harvey, June 4, 1846 (OIA-LS, vol. 30); Moore to Harvey, Sept. 21, 1846 (AR-CIA 1846, pp. 288–96).

24.   On May 30, 1850, the Democratic newspaper of St. Louis, *Daily Union,* had launched a campaign against Mitchell's treaty proposal; Mitchell replied in the *Missouri Republican* on June 2, 1850. Chambers's initial field report of July 31 was carried in the *Missouri Republican,* August 8, 1851.

25.   Barry, *Beginning of the West,* p. 1033; Trennert, *Alternative to Extinction,* p. 186. Campbell had discussed his plans with his field manager, John Dougherty (Campbell to Dougherty, Feb. 15, Apr. 28, 1851, John Dougherty Papers, Missouri Historical Society).

26.   *Missouri Republican,* Aug. 26, 1851. In his report of August 6 (*Missouri Republican,* Sept. 5, 1851), Chambers wrote: "A few miles from Westport we crossed the State line"; subsequent reports would be sent from "The Indian Territory." As this was Chambers's first visit to the plains, his first direct experiences with Indians, it seems fair to presume that many of his expressed judgments were secondhand presentations of the attitudes and reflections of his associates Mitchell, Fitzpatrick, and Campbell.

27.   On reaching Fort Laramie, Chambers expressed his "real gratification once more to be in the presence of something like civilization." His report contained a description of the post; further, he expressed his gratitude to the army officials (*Missouri Republican,* Sept. 26, 1851).

28.   Ibid.

29.   The Indian Office had been informed of the orders of the War Department with regard to the council. Reporting from the treaty grounds, Chambers stated: "There are about one thousand lodges encamped around us, and several delegations who are without lodges. The military consists of a fragment of a company of Dragoons, two companies of Mounted Riflemen, with a six-pound howitzer" (*Missouri Republican,* Oct. 1, 1851). Chambers reported the arrival of the Shoshone delegation; the subsequent turn of events, almost a catastrophic outbreak, was narrated by Percival Lowe, a member of B Troop Dragoons (*Five Years,* pp. 78–83); see also Alter, *Jim Bridger,* pp. 240–47.

30.   This demand of the southern tribes would be honored in the summer of 1853 by Fitzpatrick's treaty at Fort Atkinson (Kappler, *Laws and Treaties,* 2:600–602; Fitzpatrick to Lea, Nov. 24, 1851 [AR-CIA 1851 (ser. 636), p. 333]).

31.   *Missouri Republican,* Oct. 29, 1851. Sunder's statement that the Blackfeet were "represented at the council by Alexander Culbertson and Father De Smet" requires qualification; there is no evidence that they had been officially authorized by the Blackfeet. As with the nonparticipating tribes of the south, a separate treaty with the Blackfeet would be made later. Sunder, *Fur Trade,* p. 143; Kappler, *Laws and Treaties,* 2:595, 736.

32.   Trennert reports that Governor Brigham Young was eager for the Shoshone leaders to participate in the council, hoping for the opportunity of removing the tribe from Utah (*Alternative to Extinction,* pp. 186–87).

33.   Barry, *Beginning of the West,* pp. 1010, 1013. Agents of the American Fur Company located on the Upper Missouri reported on the cholera condition; an express was sent to Culbertson and Mitchell on the Platte, and notices were sent to the company's St. Louis offices (*Missouri Republican,* Oct. 14, 16, 1851; Sunder, *Fur Trade,* p. 137).

34.   *Missouri Republican,* Oct. 6, 1851.

35.   Barry, *Beginning of the West,* p. 1034.

36.   *Missouri Republican,* Sept. 21, 1851.

6. INITIAL GREAT SMOKE: The First Fort Laramie Treaty

1. Chambers's report of September 8, 1851 (*Missouri Republican,* Oct. 5, 1851). Chambers reported that all military forces at Horse Creek were under Major Robert Chilton. Among the military leaders, as Chambers had noted on September 1, was Colonel Samuel Cooper, the inspector general, whose factual reports "would remedy the lamentable ignorance in Washington of the real character of this frontier" (*Missouri Republican,* Sept. 26, 1851).

2. *Missouri Republican,* Oct. 6, 1851. Barry reports on the 1851 Independence–Salt Lake City mail service (*Beginning of the West,* pp. 1033, 1037).

3. *Missouri Republican,* Oct. 24, 1851.

4. Mitchell to Lea, Sept. 7, 1851 (OIA-LR, St. Louis Superintendency).

5. CR, 2:673–74; last paragraph, Letter Book, 1851, JMPA. There is good reason to presume that on this Sunday evening De Smet also visited Jim Bridger's camp. Although De Smet later recorded the date of his arrival at Horse Creek as September 11, this must be an error; Chambers specifically lists De Smet as "present in the arbor" for the opening ceremonies on Monday, September 8 (Linton Album, p. 43, JMPA; De Smet, *Western Missions,* p. 99; *Missouri Republican,* Oct. 24, 1851).

6. *Missouri Republican,* Oct. 24, 1851; CR, 2:681. Mitchell reported: "Some of the nations were present en masse, men, women and children; others were represented by delegations composed of their chiefs, headmen and warriors" (Mitchell to Lea, Oct. 25, 1851, AR-CIA 1851, p. 325).

7. *Missouri Republican,* Oct. 24, 1851.

8. *Missouri Republican,* Oct. 24, 1851.

9. The activities for September 8 are reported in the *Missouri Republican,* Oct. 26, 1851; Barry, *Beginning of the West,* pp. 874, 1045.

10. In De Smet's narratives frequent accounts are presented of "the peace pipe." Regarding the ceremony enacted on this occasion, De Smet stated: "Never did the calumet pass in peace through so many hands. To convey an idea of the importance of this action, I must observe that smoking the calumet together is equivalent to a treaty confirmed by oath, which no one can contravene without dishonoring himself in the eyes of all his tribe" (CR, 2:681).

11. *Missouri Republican,* Oct. 26, 1851.

12. Chambers presented in summary fashion the acceptance speeches by the three Indian leaders (*Missouri Republican,* Oct. 26, 1851).

13. CR, 2:676; De Smet, *Western Missions,* p. 102. Mitchell's profession of the government's benevolence was accepted without questioning by De Smet. After some twelve years of Indian-related activities, this gathering was in De Smet's experience the first manifestation of government concern for the cause of the Plains Indians.

14. *Missouri Republican,* Oct. 26, 1851. Within a year of concluding these negotiations, Mitchell presented a sorry summary regarding the lot of these Indians: "The change [in their condition] thus far has been, as it ever has been, against the 'poor Indian.' . . . This is greatly to be deplored; but

there is, at present, no remedy" (Mitchell to Lea, Oct. 17, 1852, AR-CIA 1852, p. 357).

15.　The activities of September 9 and 10 are reported in *Missouri Republican,* Nov. 2, 1851.

16.　CR, 2:680; *Missouri Republican,* Oct. 29, 1851. Both De Smet and Chambers provided a narrative on the ear piercing of the children and the Cheyenne-Shoshone gathering; this intertribal ceremony De Smet more accurately designated as "covering the dead."

17.　Chambers reported the speeches of leaders of the Cheyennes and Arapahos, which manifested the cooperative attitude of these tribes (*Missouri Republican,* Nov. 2, 1851).

18.　Mitchell's reference to the Santee Sioux was to the double treaties at Traverse des Sioux and Mendota that were being negotiated by Commissioner Luke Lea (Meyer, *Santee Sioux,* pp. 77–79; Kappler, *Laws and Treaties,* 2:588–93).

19.　The activities of September 11–14 were reported in *Missouri Republican,* Nov. 9, 1851.

20.　De Smet offered a tribute to this Crow chief in an 1852 letter to Archbishop Purcell in Cincinnati (Letter Book, 1852). De Smet also sketched "Big Robber"—a small picture decorating the top margin of the treaty map. Denig wrote a brief account of this Crow leader following the treaty council (*Five Tribes,* p. 194).

21.　*Missouri Republican,* Oct. 1, 1851.

22.　De Smet made brief mention of this occasion (CR, 2:677; De Smet, *Western Missions,* pp. 103–5).

23.　Letter Book, 1851 (JMPA); CR, 2:679. De Smet later forwarded to Bishop Miége, for recording in the journals of St. Mary's Mission, a list of the baptisms he had performed. On September 12 De Smet baptized Fitzpatrick's infant son Andrew Jackson. On the fourteenth Fitzpatrick acted as godfather during the baptism of Honoré, the infant son of the interpreter Joseph Tesson. On the return journey to Fort Kearney, as De Smet later recorded, he renewed the marriage vows of Bridger's partner, Louis Vasquez, and his wife, Narcissa; he also baptized their children, Louis, Mariana, and Sara Ellen; on September 25, at Fort Kearney, he baptized the "twin children of Sargeant Fox" (Letter Book, 1851, JMPA); see Hafen, *Broken Hand,* p. 298.

24.　Letter Book, 1851 (JMPA). The Sioux name is apparently *Wak ánt anka Wawókiya* (Helper of the Great Spirit).

25.　The activities for September 15 are reported in *Missouri Republican,* Nov. 23, 1851.

26.　The activities for September 17–20, including a summary of the treaty provisions, are reported in *Missouri Republican,* Nov. 30, 1851.

27.　It is interesting to note—no reason is provided—that De Smet did not sign as a witness to the 1851 Fort Laramie treaty.

28.　Fitzpatrick's Indian family had either accompanied him or the Arapaho delegation to the council; the John Pizelle who signed the treaty papers as a witness is supposed to be John Poisal, Fitzpatrick's father-in-law. Like Culbertson, his assistant in 1833 at Fort Mackenzie, Mitchell had taken an Indian wife (Thomas and Ronnefeldt, *First Man*). Later, when he submitted the proposition to the Indian Office, Mitchell testified that "a half-breed colony, properly located in the midst of the Indians, would form a semi-civilized nucleus around which the wild Indians would soon be drawn by necessity." Like De Smet, Mitchell regarded such a colony as a half-way establishment, to be located as far as possible from the transcontinental roads (Mitchell to Lea, Oct. 25, 1851, AR-CIA, 1851, p. 325). Fitzpatrick likewise endorsed the proposal, noting that "the half-breeds and white men married to Indian women . . . are becoming numerous, and in a few years will be formidable. They have of late years become very quiet and orderly" (Fitzpatrick to Lea, Nov. 24, 1851, AR-CIA 1851, p. 336).

29.   De Smet's correspondence for 1852 and 1853 indicates his concern for the half-breed children. His letters report on some of these children, who by his personal efforts were being educated in boarding schools in the St. Louis area. See Alter, *Jim Bridger,* p. 246.

30.   *Missouri Republican,* Nov. 30, 1851.

31.   Mitchell to Lea, Oct. 25, 1851 (AR-CIA 1851, p. 326); *Missouri Republican,* Nov. 30, 1851.

32.   CR, 2:682–84.

33.   Ibid., p. 683; Barry, *Beginning of the West,* pp. 1043–45.

34.   CR, 2:685; Barry, *Beginning of the West,* p. 1036.

35.   Barry, *Beginning of the West,* p. 1036; CR, 2:687–90; De Smet, *Western Missions,* pp. 117–18.

36.   CR, 2:691.

7.   *THE ATTEMPT AT PEACEFUL COEXISTENCE*

1.   Mitchell to Lea, Oct. 25, 1851 (AR-CIA 1851, pp. 322–23).

2.   CR, 2:662, 4:1497; Mitchell to Lea, Nov. 11, 1851 (AR-CIA 1851, p. 290). Mattes expressed high praise for De Smet as a cartographer ("Legend of Colter's Hell," p. 279 n.70).

3.   Mitchell to Lea, Nov. 11, 1851 (AR-CIA 1851, p. 290).

4.   Mitchell to Lea, Nov. 11, 1851 (AR-CIA 1851, pp. 289–90). The treaty text is printed in Kappler, *Laws and Treaties,* 2:594–96.

5.   Mitchell to Lea, Nov. 11, 1851 (AR-CIA 1851, pp. 289–90).

6.   "Articles of a Treaty," 32d Cong., 1st sess., Senate Confidential Document 11.

7.   Mitchell to Lea, Oct. 17, 1852 (AR-CIA 1852, p. 357).

8.   Mitchell had openly assigned to the white emigrants the responsibility for the sorry conditions found among the tribes: "The introduction of all these evils they [the Indians] charge, and I suppose justly, upon the whites" (Mitchell to Lea, Oct. 25, 1851, AR-CIA 1851, p. 324).

9.   Mitchell to Brown, Oct. 13, 1849 (AR-CIA 1849, p. 1071).

10.   Viola, *McKenney,* p. 118; Thwaites, *Western Travels,* 5:283. The effectiveness of the tribal delegation program was highly questionable; the program itself had been inherited from colonial times (see Viola, *Diplomats;* Turner, *Red Men*).

11.   Letter Book 1851 (JMPA). De Smet recorded the names of the delegates (CR, 2:688). Chambers reported on "The Affair of the Crow," on

Mitchell's subsequent problem concerning the discovery of the body and later additions of other delegates, from the Iowa and Oto tribes, in *Missouri Republican*, Oct. 31, Nov. 2, Nov. 9. As late as 1867 the Crows were asking about the missing delegate. As De Smet had predicted: "It will be difficult to reconcile the [Crow] nation to his death." De Smet also reported the incident to Robert Meldrum, with the request that his sympathy be expressed to the Crow people (De Smet, Letters Sent, 1851, 1852). See Stanley, *Early Adventures,* p. 268; POPC, pp. 85–88.

12.   Two unidentified newspaper clippings dated November 19 and December 19, 1851 (JMPA) provide accounts of the delegates' activities; Fitzpatrick to Lea, Nov. 24, 1851 (AR-CIA 1851, p. 325); Hafen, *Broken Hand,* pp. 305–7.

13.   De Smet to Miége, March 3, Apr. 2, 1852 (Letter Book, 1852, JMPA). It should be noted that westward travel was still dependent upon seasonal conditions.

14.   Mitchell reminded the Indian Office and Congress that because of congressional changes, the treaty Lea had made with the Minnesota Sioux had been returned to obtain "their sanction to the modification" (Mitchell to Lea, Oct. 17, 1852, AR-CIA 1852, p. 357). Meyer points out the reluctance of the Santees to accept the amendments (*Santee Sioux,* p. 85).

15.   Hafen, *Broken Hand,* p. 307.

16.   Malin's study points up the effects of such legislation upon Indian policy (*Westward Expansion,* pp. 52–95).

17.   Fitzpatrick to Cumming, Nov. 19, 1853 (AR-CIA 1853, p. 362); *Missouri Republican,* Aug. 9, 16, 1853; Lowe, *Five Years,* p. 134. The Fort Atkinson treaty was ratified on April 12, 1854, following certain minor amendments; agent Whitfield, Fitzpatrick's successor, obtained the approval of the tribal leaders to these changes on July 21, 1854 (Kappler, *Laws and Treaties,* 2:600–602).

18.   Fitzpatrick to Cumming, Nov. 19, 1853 (AR-CIA 1853, pp. 366–67); see Anderson, "Sioux Amendment." The incident in the Minniconjou camp is discussed in Bieber's introduction to Bandel, *Frontier Life,* pp. 23–24; also see *Missouri Republican,* Oct. 7, 1853.

19.   Barry, *Beginning of the West,* pp. 1158–59.

20.   Fitzpatrick to Cumming, Nov. 21, 1853 (AR-CIA 1853, pp. 367–71).

21.   Fitzpatrick to Cumming, Nov. 21, 1853 (OIA-LR, St. Louis Superintendency).

22.   Fitzpatrick to Cumming, Nov. 19, 1853 (AR-CIA 1853, p. 369).

23.   AR-CIA 1853, p. 387; Sanger, *U.S. Statutes,* 10:238.

24.   AR-CIA 1848, p. 388.

25.   Prucha, *Great Father,* 1:341–42. See Malin, *Westward Expansion,* pp. 77, 103.

26.   Quoted in Prucha, *Great Father,* 1:346.

27.   Sanger, *U.S. Statutes,* 10:277–85; Trennert, *Alternative to Extinction,* p. 50; Malin, *Westward Expansion,* pp. 64–67; Billington, *Westward Expansion,* pp. 595–616; Prucha, *Great Father,* 1:345–47; Gittinger, "Separation of Nebraska and Kansas," p. 443.

28. Prucha, *Great Father,* 1:349.
29. Olson, *History of Nebraska,* p. 128; CR, 3:1110–11.
30. CR, 2:684, 3:1207, 1209.
31. Prucha, *Great Father,* 1:318.
32. AR-CIA 1853, p. 251.
33. AR-CIA 1856, p. 571. As early as 1854, only a week after the signing of the Kansas-Nebraska Act, Manypenny had completed his personal negotiations of some nine treaties with the border tribes.
34. Mitchell to Lea, Oct. 25, 1851 (AR-CIA 1851, pp. 322–23). Prucha notes that "the great majority of the treaties concluded in 1853 and afterward contained provisions for the division of lands in severalty" (Prucha, *Indian Policy in Crisis,* p. 231).
35. AR-CIA 1855, p. 328.
36. AR-CIA 1853, p. 274.
37. AR-CIA 1856, pp. 483–84.
38. AR-CIA 1853, p. 260.
39. Ibid., p. 262.
40. AR-CIA 1854, p. 225.
41. Richardson, *Messages and Papers,* 4:645.
42. Utley, *Frontiersmen in Blue,* p. 11; Priest, *Uncle Sam's Stepchildren,* pp. 15–16.
43. Utley, *Frontiersmen in Blue,* p. 5.
44. De Smet continued: "Recent State elections have shown that Know-nothingism is not all-powerful" (CR, 4:1457–58).
45. A copy of Fleming's express report was among the testimonial papers submitted by Secretary of War Jefferson Davis to the House on February 9, 1855 (House Exec. Doc. 63, 33rd Cong., 2nd sess.); articles in the *Missouri Republican* from September to December 1854 continued to discuss the affair.
46. De Smet composed this letter on April 17, 1855. Two days later he stated: "Last year I had planned to resume my travels in the desert in the course of the present spring; but a war of extermination against the Sioux and several other tribes is soon to take place. . . . It matters not how great the provocations and wrongs of the whites against the Indians; the latter are always the dupes and victims" (CR, 4:1218–20, 1454). Reports on the Grattan affair by agent John Whitfield, Fitzpatrick's replacement, are printed in AR-CIA 1854, pp. 297–306.
47. *Congressional Globe,* 33d Cong., 2d sess., app., pp. 334–41.
48. House Exec. Doc. 63, 33rd Cong., 2d. sess.; Richardson, *Messages and Papers,* 5:286. Utley points out that consequent to the expansion and the migration, the federal government faced "new responsibilities." The most important of these obligations was "to police the West," to protect both peaceful Indians and peaceful travelers; "it was a large order, impossible of complete fulfillment given national attitudes that shaped policy" (*Frontiersmen in Blue,* p. 5).
49. Bandel, *Frontier Life,* pp. 29–31; Utley, *Frontiersmen in Blue,* p. 115.
50. Senate Ex. Doc. 94, 34th Cong., 1st sess., p. 2. Opinions differ on

Harney's conduct at Ash Hollow. Mattes suggests that what some historians have called the Harney massacre "was one of the most savage of all encounters between red and white men" (*Platte River,* pp. 311–38). See Hyde, *Spotted Tail's Folk,* pp. 71–73; McCann, "Grattan Massacre"; Utley, *Frontiersmen in Blue,* pp. 116–17; Bandel, *Frontier Life,* pp. 33–35, 82–88; Hafen and Young, *Fort Laramie,* pp. 240–44.

51. Harney reported the capture of some seventy women and children at Ash Hollow. Some of that number, along with the five "murderers" who surrendered to agent Twiss at Fort Laramie in late October, were escorted to a winter of detention at Fort Leavenworth (Reavis, *General Harney,* p. 256; Hyde, *Spotted Tail's Folk,* p. 75).

52. Sunder points out that Fort Pierre, "the American Fur Company's white elephant on the upper river," was purchased by the army for the exorbitant sum of $45,000 (*Fur Trade,* p. 169).

53. Hoopes, "Twiss, Indian Agent," p. 358. The report of Harney's treaty council appears as Senate Ex. Doc. 94, 34th Cong., 1st sess. See Case, "Golconda"; Anderson, "Harney vs. Twiss"; Hafen and Young, *Fort Laramie,* pp. 239–45.

54. The congressional determinations on funding for roads and military roads were made from July 17, 1854, to June 14, 1858 (Sanger, *U.S. Statutes,* 10:302–6, 581, 603–10, 641; 11:27, 163, 168, 203, 336–37).

55. Berthrong, *Southern Cheyennes,* pp. 123–31.

56. For studies of the federal road surveys and construction, along with discussion of the transfer of responsibility from the army's Corps of Topographical Engineers to the Department of the Interior, see Goetzmann, *Army Exploration,* pp. 341–74, 406–26; Jackson, *Wagon Roads West,* pp. 174–78.

57. Jackson points out that the secretary of the interior assigned supervision to the commissioner of Indian affairs, "presumably because the sponsors of the legislation in Congress had spoken of the aid that agents of the Indian Office could give the road builders" (*Wagon Roads West,* p. 174).

58. AR-CIA 1854, p. 300; Berthrong, *Southern Cheyennes,* p. 131.

59. AR-CIA 1854, p. 303; 1857, pp. 141–48; 1858, pp. 448–52; 1859, pp. 137–39.

60. Berthrong, *Southern Cheyennes,* p. 132.

61. Ibid., p. 137.

62. For the Sumner expedition, see Berthrong, *Southern Cheyennes,* pp. 127–48; Grinnell, *Fighting Cheyennes,* pp. 111–23; Lavender, *Bent's Fort,* pp. 354–67; Utley, *Frontiersmen in Blue,* pp. 120–25; Coel, *Chief Left Hand,* pp. 31–93; Hafen and Young, *Fort Laramie,* pp. 273–86; Hafen and Hafen, *Relations with Indians.*

63. Coel, *Chief Left Hand,* pp. 40–42; AR-CIA 1858, pp. 448–52.

64. Fitzpatrick to Cumming, Nov. 19, 1853 (AR-CIA 1853, p. 366).

65. Billington, *Westward Expansion,* pp. 619–21.

66. Bent to Superintendent of Indian Affairs, Oct. 5, 1859 (AR-CIA 1859, pp. 138–39).

67. Berthrong narrates the tragedy of the Southern Cheyennes and

Arapahos. Agent Albert G. Boone, Fitzpatrick's successor, had been directed by Commissioner A. B. Greenwood to push the treaty signing or "to make it over their heads." The treaty, however, was not ratified by the Senate until August 6, 1861. Thus prior to the formality of official acquisition of land title, the state of Kansas was admitted to the Union, and Colorado Territory was established—both actions taken in February 1861, "as soon as Congress had lost the Southern delegation." Berthrong, *Southern Cheyenne*, pp. 127–51; Coel, *Chief Left Hand*, p. 120; Morison, *Oxford History*, p. 669; Kappler, *Laws and Treaties*, 2:807–11.

68. Hafen and Hafen, *Relations with Indians*, pp. 177–78.

69. AR-CIA 1868, p. 492.

8. DE SMET'S PREDICTION: A "Sombre and Melancholy Future"

1. Commissioner of Indian Affairs George W. Manypenny optimistically predicted that organized civil government, as provided in the proposed new territories of Kansas and Nebraska, would enact suitable laws for the protection of the Indians (AR-CIA 1853, p. 251).

2. Letter Book, 1855 (JMPA), quoted in Laveille, *De Smet*, p. 286.

3. CR, 3:934, 4:1452.

4. Garraghan, *Jesuits*, 1:195–268, 2:5.

5. Ibid., 3:115.

6. Ibid., pp. 93, 100.

7. CR, 2:693.

8. Letter Book, 1854, to Rev. Congiato, S.J., Sept. 20, and 1847, to Bishop Miége, S.J., Oct. 2, 6, 28 (JMPA); Garraghan, *Jesuits*, 3:401.

9. Garraghan, *Jesuits*, 2:124–28; Laveille, *De Smet*, p. 266.

10. Garraghan comments on the earlier Vows of Devotion taken by De Smet. It may be that since De Smet had not fulfilled the canonical requirement of completing a full year of his second novitiate, his technical renewal of Jesuit membership did not formally commence until his Final Vows in 1855. Garraghan, *Jesuits*, 1:432 n.23, 3:99.

11. Burns, *Indian Wars*, pp. 35–51; Bangert, *History of the Society of Jesus*, pp. 279–84, 329–34.

12. CR, 4:1235–36; Burns, *Indian Wars*, pp. 121–23; Fahey, *Flathead Indians*, pp. 99–103; Kappler, *Laws and Treaties*, 2:736–40.

13. CR, 3:1198.

14. Howard, "Captain John Mullan," pp. 185–202; Jackson, *Wagon Roads West*, pp. 257–78; Burns, *Indian Wars*, p. 70; Letter Book, 1857, to Revd. & Dear Coz, Oct. 21 (JMPA); De Smet, *Western Missions*, pp. 521–32. De Smet's letter to Miége is printed in Garraghan, *Jesuits*, 2:675.

15. CR, 3:1195–96, 1209.

16. Scharf, *History of St. Louis*, p. 594; Chambers, *Bullion Benton*, pp. 443–44.

17. CR, 4:1493, 1499–1500.

18. Citing fifteen years of experience as an Indian agent, Vaughan declared: "The Catholic missionaries have always succeeded in gaining the Indians' hearts" (CR, 4:1316–17).

19. Garraghan, *Jesuits*, 2:454.

20.   De Smet wrote to Father Congiato, superior of the Jesuits' Rocky Mountain Indian missions, on April 1, 1858, repeating the proposal made by Mullan (CR, 4:1318–19).

21.   Ibid., 2:715–16. There is no evidence that De Smet initiated the request presented by Harney; however, he anticipated receiving the invitation with notable eagerness. Although Garraghan notes that "a friendship of many years' standing" existed between Harney and De Smet, there is no record of any association between these two prior to 1858; certainly they became close friends during this period, 1858–59, and remained so for the rest of De Smet's life. Garraghan, *Jesuits,* 3:71; Letter Book, 1858 (JMPA).

22.   CR, 2:728. See Burns, *Indian Wars,* pp. 329–32.

23.   Hafen and Hafen summarize the events connected with the Utah Expedition (*Utah Expedition*); the majority of the pertinent government documents were published in House Exec. Doc. 71, 35th Cong., 1st sess. Harney was reassigned to assist in controlling unrest in Kansas Territory; his outspoken threat to capture and execute Young and the Mormon leaders may have been a factor in his reassignment (Reavis, *General Harney,* p. 278; Arrington and Britton, *Mormon Experience,* pp. 53, 162–65; Arrington, *Great Basin Kingdom,* pp. 162–94).

24.   CR, 2:726.

25.   Burns, *Indian Wars,* p. 327.

26.   By means of a letter sent to Father Adrian Hoecken on August 7, 1857, De Smet forwarded his advice to the tribes of the Flathead Confederation (Letter Book, 1857, JMPA).

27.   CR, 2:729.

28.   Captain Alfred Pleasonton, Harney's adjutant, developed a close friendship with De Smet (CR, 1:73, 4:1570).

29.   Letter Book, 1858 (JMPA); CR, 2:732.

30.   CR, 2:731, 748.

31.   Ibid., p. 735; Burns, *Indian Wars,* pp. 327–55.

32.   CR, 2:740, 743.

33.   Ibid., 4:1573; Reavis, *General Harney,* p. 288; Burns, *Indian Wars,* p. 331. To his approval of De Smet's proposal, Harney added official instructions (House Exec. Doc. 2, vol. 2, 36th Cong., 1st sess., pp. 91–93).

34.   CR, 2:744–45.

35.   Ibid., p. 746.

36.   Ibid., p. 758.

37.   Ibid., p. 761.

38.   CR, 2:1572, 1574.

39.   Ibid., pp. 766–67; Burns, *Indian Wars,* pp. 341–45.

40.   CR, 4:1579–80.

41.   Letter Book, 1859 (JMPA); CR, 4:1577–78, 1581–82.

42.   Garraghan, *Jesuits,* 2:454.

43.   In addition to his report of October 5 to Harney, De Smet composed a second narrative of his return journey; this second account included a copy of the expense account De Smet forwarded to the War Department (CR, 2:769–776; Boller, *Among the Indians,* pp. 345–46).

44. Reavis, *General Harney,* pp. 313–14.
45. CR, 4:1580–81.

9. *"THE UNHAPPY INDIANS . . . DRIVEN TO DESPERATION"*
1. Linton Album, 1861, p. 57 (JMPA).
2. CR, 2:788, 3:839, 4:1505–7; Linton Album, 1861, pp. 57–78; Letter Book, 1861, 1862, JMPA; Garraghan, *Jesuits,* 3:100.
3. Garraghan, *Jesuits,* 2:159–60, 3:93.
4. Ibid., 2:160–61, 171.
5. Ibid., pp. 168–70; CR, 4:1444–46, 1462.
6. Garraghan, *Jesuits,* 2:147–72; CR, 1:134, 3:842–43, 4:1444–46, 1462.
7. CR, 4:1504.
8. Ibid., 3:783–88, 4:1504–11; Chittenden, *Steamboat Navigation,* pp. 266, 287–97; Sunder, *Fur Trade,* pp. 187–240. De Smet had the narrative of his round trip to Fort Benton copied in the Linton Album, pp. 58–60 (JMPA).
9. Chittenden, *Steamboat Navigation,* p. 288; White and Walton, *Indian Journals,* p. 220. Sunder notes that most of the "deckers" were gold hunters (*Fur Trade,* p. 235).
10. In 1860 De Smet had supplied St. Peter's Mission with a shipment of over 7,000 pounds (Garraghan, *Jesuits,* 2:361; Linton Album, p. 59, JMPA; CR, 3:836). Casper provides a short history of St. Peter's Mission; the missions on the eastern and western slopes of the Northern Rockies were no longer under the Missouri Jesuits (*History of Catholic Church,* 1:213–15).
11. White and Walton, *Indian Journals,* pp. 97, 135–48, 156; Ellis, *General Pope,* pp. 46–47; Nichols, *Lincoln,* pp. 21–22.
12. White and Walton, *Indian Journals,* pp. 151–54, 224; Sunder, "Delaney's 'Pocket Diary,' " p. 11; Sunder, *Fur Trade,* pp. 231–32; Vestal, *Sitting Bull,* p. 50; CR, 3:786, 831; Latta to Dole, Aug. 27, 1862, AR-CIA 1862, p. 336.
13. Sunder, *Fur Trade,* pp. 230–37; Harkness diary, p. 345, Montana Historical Society.
14. Latta to Dole, Aug. 27, 1862 (AR-CIA 1862, pp. 336–37); White and Walton, *Indian Journals,* p. 152.
15. Latta to Dole, Aug. 27, 1862 (AR-CIA 1862, pp. 340–41); White and Walton, *Indian Journals,* p. 97.
16. White and Walton, *Indian Journals,* p. 182; Sunder, "Delaney's 'Pocket Diary,' " p. 16.
17. Harkness, "Diary of James Harkness," p. 350; Garraghan, *Jesuits,* 2:480.
18. CR, 2:787. De Smet reported to Bishop O'Gorman that the Jesuits of St. Peter's Mission had created "a small and fervent congregation in and about Fort Benton" (Letter Book, 1862, JMPA); see Casper, *History of Catholic Church,* pp. 214, 236.
19. De Smet to Mix, Sept. 5, 1862 (AR-CIA 1862, p. 358). See CR, 2:786n.

20. Latta to Dole, Aug. 27, 1862 (AR-CIA 1862, p. 337); White and Walton, *Indian Journals,* pp. 197–98.

21. De Smet to Dole, Sept. 5, 1862 (AR-CIA 1862, p. 358).

22. Nichols, *Lincoln,* pp. 22.

23. Meyer, *Santee Sioux,* p. 87. See Prucha, *Indian Policy in Formative Years,* pp. 70–73; Sanger, *United States Statutes,* 9:556; Kane, "Sioux Treaty," p. 66.

24. Trennert, "Luke Lea" (p. 54), "William Medill" (p. 37), in Kvasnicka and Viola, *Commissioners.*

25. Meyer, *Santee Sioux,* pp. 103–5; Carley, *Sioux Uprising,* pp. 11–13.

26. Meyer, *Santee Sioux,* pp. 109–16; Ellis, *General Pope,* p. 7; Nichols, *Lincoln,* pp. 93–96; Sanger, *United States Statutes,* 12:652–54, 819–20; Prucha, *Great Father,* 1:441–47. See Oehler, *Great Sioux Uprising,* pp. 235–37; Carley, *Sioux Uprising,* pp. 11–17; Folwell, *History of Minnesota,* 2:230–35.

27. Meyer, *Santee Sioux,* p. 138; Prucha, *Great Father,* 1:473.

28. Whipple, *Lights and Shadows,* pp. 136–41.

29. CR, 4:1510–11.

30. Whipple, *Lights and Shadows,* p. 137; Richardson, *Messages and Papers,* 6:132, 187, 250; Kosok, "Unknown Letter," pp. 35–36.

31. De Smet Documents 1863 (JMPA); CR, 2:790, 794.

32. Latta to Dole, Aug. 27, 1863 (AR-CIA 1863, p. 289); CR, 2:783, 3:819; Sunder, *Fur Trade,* pp. 249.

33. CR, 2:791.

34. Ibid., pp. 630–32; De Smet, *Western Missions,* pp. 40–44.

35. CR, 2:792–93. While we might readily conclude that De Smet was eager to find an excuse for taking the long way home, Chittenden points out that the situation along the middle reaches of the Missouri River was much more serious than De Smet represented it to be.

36. CR, 3:785. Whipple and other critics would express similar charges concerning the "causes" of Indian warfare (Athearn, *Sherman,* p. 346; Utley, *Frontiersmen in Blue,* p. 348).

37. CR, 3:799; Linton Album, p. 67 (JMPA); Mullan, "Military Road," p. 58. See Jackson, *Wagon Roads West,* pp. 257–78, 369–72; Schoenberg, *Paths to Northwest,* pp. 58–59.

38. CR, 1:343.

39. Burns, *Indian Wars,* p. 40.

40. CR, 3:797–800, 1208–9. De Smet reported that he passed out among the Indians many small religious devotional objects, and as a practical man, he also distributed fishhooks to the young men, which they eagerly sought.

41. CR, 2:568, 3:798.

42. Ibid., 3:799.

43. Ibid., p. 304; Howard, "Captain John Mullan"; Jackson, *Wagon Roads West,* p. 277.

44. Ewers, "Gustavus Sohon's Portraits," p. 11.

45. Garraghan, *Jesuits,* 1:576–91; CR, 3:807–11.

46. CR, 3:808.

47.   Athearn, *Forts,* p. 130; Ellis, *General Pope,* p. 41.

48.   Utley, *Frontiersmen in Blue,* p. 310; Pope to Stanton, Feb. 6, 1864 (AR-CIA 1864, p. 428).

49.   CR, 3:814–15; Linton to De Smet, Mar. 2, 1864, quoted in De Smet to Dole, Mar. 28, 1864 (Letter Book, 1864, JMPA). In his letters of early 1864 to his family in Belgium De Smet commented on his poor health.

50.   CR, 3:816.

51.   De Smet preserved a copy of this letter in his papers (De Smet, Letters Received 1864, JMPA).

52.   Dole to De Smet, Mar. 21, 1864 (AR-CIA 1864, pp. 275–76). Sunder's presentation of Wilkinson's criticisms of De Smet is misleading; the testimonials Sunder notes as Wilkinson's sources had only to do with the handling of liquor by the American Fur Company (*Fur Trade,* p. 259).

53.   Chittenden, *Steamboat Navigation,* 1:359, 361.

54.   CR, 2:789.

55.   Sanger, *United States Statutes,* 4:735–38 (repr. Prucha, *Documents of Indian Policy,* pp. 68–71), 9:203.

56.   Vaughan to Superintendent Cumming, Sept. 20, 1853 (AR-CIA 1853, p. 358); Wilkinson to Governor Edmunds, Aug. 31, 1864, Reed to Dole, n.d. [1864], Upson to Dole, Sept. 1, 1864 (AR-CIA 1864, pp. 264, 270, 297).

57.   CR, 3:820–22; AR-CIA 1865, pp. 48, 400.

58.   De Smet, Document Files 1864 (JMPA).

59.   Latta to Dole, Oct. 1, 1864 (AR-CIA 1864), p. 274; CR, 3:827.

60.   CR, 3:828; AR-CIA 1864, p. 280; Sunder, *Fur Trade,* p. 255.

61.   AR-CIA 1864, p. 279; CR, 3:834.

62.   Sunder, *Fur Trade,* p. 255; AR-CIA 1864, pp. 282–83.

63.   AR-CIA 1864, p. 41.

64.   Linton Album, p. 78 (JMPA); CR, 1:87, 3:838–39; Laveille, *De Smet,* p. 333.

65.   CR, 3:838.

66.   Ibid., 3:836–37, 4:1327.

67.   Ibid., 2:783, 3:819; Linton Album, p. 69 (JMPA).

68.   Latta to Dole, Aug. 27, 1862 (AR-CIA 1862, p. 340).

69.   White and Walton, *Indian Journals,* p. 97; Morgan to De Smet, 1863 (JMPA).

70.   CR, 4:1526–28.

71.   Garraghan, *Jesuits,* 2:147; Faherty, *Dream,* p. 89.

72.   Garraghan, *Jesuits,* 2:151; Rothensteiner, *History of Archdiocese,* 2:213.

73.   Knapp, *Presence of Past,* pp. 10–11; Letter Book, 1865 (JMPA); CR, 4:1523; Frost, "Apologia," in Scharf, *History of St. Louis,* 1:501–4.

74.   CR, 3:844.

10.   *FOR DEPENDENT INDIANS, VERY LIMITED OPTIONS*

1.   Prucha, *Indian Policy in United States,* p. 20.

2.   Utley, *Indian Frontier,* p. 93.

3.   Ellis, *General Pope,* pp. 66–67.

4. Utley, *Frontiersmen in Blue,* p. 309; *Indian Frontier,* p. 95. See Hoig, *Sand Creek.*

5. Pope's 1866 Report on the West (39th Cong., 1st sess., House Ex. Doc. no. 76 [ser. 1263]); Ellis, *General Pope,* pp. 37–38; Schell, *History of South Dakota,* p. 87; Utley, *Frontiersmen in Blue,* p. 314; Berthrong, *Southern Cheyennes,* p. 239.

6. Harlan to Pope, July 6, 1865 (AR-CIA 1865, pp. 199–201); Utley, *Frontiersmen in Blue,* p. 309.

7. Sanger, *United States Statutes,* 13:572; Utley, *Indian Frontier,* p. 96; AR-CIA 1868, p. 489.

8. Utley, *Frontiersmen in Blue,* p. 337.

9. "Condition of the Indian Tribes" (39th Cong., 2d sess., Senate Rep. no. 156 [ser. 1299]), pp. 95–96; Ellis, "Bent, Carson," pp. 55–68; Kelsey, "Doolittle Report," pp. 107–20; Kappler, *Laws and Treaties,* 2:889; Athearn, *Sherman,* p. 26.

10. Ellis, "Bent, Carson," pp. 62–64.

11. Trennert, *Alternative to Extinction,* pp. 193–94.

12. Prucha, *Great Father,* 1:488.

13. Report of the Commission to Treat with the Sioux of the Upper Missouri, Oct. 28, 1865 (AR-Secretary of the Interior 1865, pp. 721–23); Athearn, *Forts,* p. 209. The treaties of October 1865 are printed in Kappler, *Laws and Treaties,* 2:883–907.

14. Olson, *Red Cloud,* p. 14. See Hyde, *Red Cloud's Folk,* pp. 134–67; Utley, *Indian Frontier,* p. 97.

15. Utley, *Frontiersmen in Blue,* p. 338; *Indian Frontier,* p. 97.

16. Utley, *Frontiersmen in Blue,* pp. 347; 39th Congress, 2d sess., Senate Rep. 156 (ser. 1279), pp. 7, 424–25; see Kelsey, "Doolittle Report."

17. CR, 4:1327.

18. Sherman to De Smet, April 4, 1866 (Letter Book, 1866, JMPA); see Athearn, *Sherman,* p. 42.

19. CR, 3:845, n. 4.

20. McAllister, *Ellen Ewing;* Sherman and Mrs. Sherman to De Smet, 1865 (JMPA).

21. CR, 3:847.

22. Garraghan, *Jesuits,* 2:482.

23. Linton Album, p. 94 (JMPA); CR, 4:1327.

24. CR, 4:1282–86; Linton Album, pp. 96–99. Garraghan indicates De Smet's move from the *Ontario* to the *Minor* for his return voyage down the Missouri (*Jesuits,* 2:482n.).

25. CR, 3:856, 1200–1201, 4:1323–25.

26. AR-CIA 1866, pp. 14–15; the reports of the Northwest Treaty Commission appear on pp. 168–76, 208–9. Congress ratified the 1865 treaties but not those of 1866.

27. Olson, *Red Cloud,* pp. 37–39, 51.

28. 39th Congress, 2d sess., Senate Ex. Docs. 15, 16 (ser. 1277).

29. Chittenden, *Steamboat Navigation,* 2:397–98.

30. Larpenteur, *Forty Years,* 2:379–82. See Athearn, *Sherman,* p. 121; Utley, *Indian Frontier,* p. 96.

31.   Utley, *Frontiersmen in Blue,* p. 348; Olson, *Red Cloud,* p. 72.

32.   40th Cong., 1st sess., Senate Ex. Doc. 13, pp. 3–6, 113.

33.   Athearn, *Sherman,* p. 125; Morison, *Oxford History,* p. 751; Buford to Stanton, June 6, 1867 (40th Cong., 1st sess., Senate Ex. Doc. 13, p. 113).

34.   39th Cong., 2d sess., House Ex. Doc. 20, p. 5; Utley, *Frontier Regulars,* p. 125 n.4; Utley, *Indian Frontier,* p. 102.

35.   Bogy to Browning, Jan. 23, 1867 (40th Cong., 1st sess., Senate Ex. Doc. 13, ser. 1308), pp. 18–19.

36.   Bogy to Browning, Jan. 23, 1867 (40th Cong., 1st sess., Senate Ex. Doc. 13, ser. 1308), pp. 18–20.

37.   Utley, *Frontier Regulars,* p. 111.

38.   Athearn, *Sherman,* pp. 47, 96, 101; Utley, *Frontier Regulars,* p. 118; Olson, *Red Cloud,* p. 53. By this time the Sioux country was surrounded by military posts: Terry had eleven forts north of the Nebraska border, and Augur supervised thirteen forts along the Platte, the railroad line heading westward below the North Platte and along the Bozeman Trail.

39.   Utley notes that the controversy between the Indian Office and the War Department was "focused on both personalities and policies" (*Frontiersmen in Blue,* p. 347).

40.   POPC, pp. 149–50; 39th Congress, 2d sess., Senate Ex. Docs. 15, 16 (ser. 1277).

41.   Kelsey, "Doolittle Report," pp. 118–19; Prucha, *Great Father,* 1:486–87.

42.   Grant received Parker's proposal on January 24, 1867 (40th Cong., 1st sess., Senate Ex. Doc. 13, pp. 42–49).

43.   AR-CIA 1853, p. 260; Prucha, *Great Father,* 1:467, 473; Whipple, *Lights and Shadows,* pp. 144, 513.

44.   40th Cong., 1st sess., Senate Ex. Doc. 13, p. 46. See Waltmann, "Ely Parker," pp. 123–33.

45.   Bogy to Browning, Jan. 23, Feb. 4, Feb. 11, 1867 (40th Cong., 1st sess., Senate Ex. Doc. 13, ser. 1308), pp. 9, 17, 39.

46.   40th Cong., 1st sess., Senate Ex. Doc. 13, pp. 55–56; Utley, *Frontier Regulars,* p. 113.

47.   Utley, *Frontier Regulars,* p. 114.

48.   Ibid., p. 118; 40th Cong., 1st sess., Senate Ex. Doc. 13, p. 11.

49.   Athearn, *Sherman,* p. 219.

50.   40th Cong., 1st sess., Senate Ex. Doc. 13, pp. 60, 111.

51.   Morison, *Oxford History,* pp. 720–25; see Unrau, "Bogy," "Taylor," in Kvasnicka and Viola, *Commissioners,* pp. 190–222.

52.   40th Cong., 1st sess., Senate Ex. Doc. 13, p. 113.

53.   40th Cong., 1st sess., Senate Ex. Doc. 13, p. 59.

54.   Linton Album, p. 115 (JMPA); CR, 4:1329.

55.   CR, 3:862–67. There is a discrepancy in De Smet's reports regarding the name of the steamboat he boarded at Sioux City.

56.   Ibid., pp. 870–72.

57.   Ibid., pp. 871–75, 884.

58.   Ibid., pp. 876–77.

59. Ibid., pp. 872, 877–79.

60. Ibid., pp. 878, 880–81, 884. De Smet characterized the *Graham* as a "floating palace" 249 feet long.

61. 40th Cong., 1st sess., Senate Ex. Doc. 13, p. 123. One of Sully's special complaints to Taylor, sent from Forts Rice, Berthold, and Buford, was the practice of naming "paper chiefs."

62. CR, 3:884–86.

63. Ibid., p. 885, 4:1528–29.

64. Ibid., 4:1330.

11. CONGRESSIONAL RESOLVE: A Final Great Smoke

1. CR, 3:886; Sanger, *United States Statutes*, 15:17 (Prucha, *Documents of Indian Policy*, pp. 105–6).

2. 40th Cong., 1st sess., Senate Ex. Doc. 13, p. 5.

3. Utley, *Frontier Regulars*, p. 131; Athearn, *Sherman*, pp. 161–62, 171; 40th Cong., 1st sess., Senate Ex. Doc. 13, p. 121. Reporting on his summer inspection trips across the Great Plains, Sherman admitted the failure of the military to distinguish between peaceful and hostile Indians.

4. Utley, *Frontier Regulars*, p. 131–32; Prucha, *Great Father*, 1:489.

5. Athearn, *Sherman*, pp. 171–72, 210–11. The characterization of Sherman as a "no good" fighter is from AR-CIA 1868, p. 29.

6. POPC, pp. 8, 31. Olson, *Red Cloud*, p. 59 n.4, corrects the error regarding the reported removal of Sherman from the commission.

7. A copy of the president's telegram to Augur appointing him to the commission in Sherman's place is in OIA-LR, Upper Platte Agency 1868 (M234, roll 893). POPC, p. 99. Congress manifested small confidence in the Indian Bureau by the decision of July 27 that all funding for treaty implementation would be distributed "under the direction of General Sherman" (Prucha, *Great Father*, 1:495; Utley, *Frontier Regulars*, pp. 102–9; Athearn, *Sherman*, p. 228).

8. POPC, pp. 29, 55. Although Taylor presented Hancock's request to revise his testimony, the motion for approbation was made by Sanborn, who had been so critical of Hancock's military campaigns.

9. POPC, pp. 8–9, 29, 56, 65; Jones, *The Treaty of Medicine Lodge*, pp. 20, 23–24, 103–4.

10. Jones, *Medicine Lodge*, pp. 181–82; Kappler, *Laws and Treaties*, 2:988; POPC, p. 84.

11. POPC, p. 172.

12. Jones, *Medicine Lodge*, pp. 104, 199–200. The question is not whether attempts were made at presenting reasonable and complete explanations of the treaty stipulations but whether (dependent upon the interpreters' knowledge and skills) the Indian leaders were made fully cognizant of the proposals.

13. *Missouri Republican*, Aug. 12, 1867; POPC, pp. 10–31; CR, 3:887, 889, 895, 4:1329; Letter Book, 1867 (JMPA).

14. Repeated searches in the National Archives have failed to locate any record of De Smet's testimony. Father J. Windey, S.J., however, kindly

provided copies of newspaper articles ("The Interesting Deposition of Father De Smet Before the Commission Meeting at Fort Leavenworth") from the Jesuit archives in Brussels that give a synopsis of De Smet's remarks.

15. POPC, pp. 40–41, 52. Henderson seems to have assumed the role of spokesman for the commission in Taylor's absence.

16. POPC, pp. 55–56; Stanley, *Early Adventures,* 1:290.

17. POPC, pp. 57, 61, 65. At North Platte Sherman had to invoke martial law to deal with the problems caused by the ready availability of liquor (Stanley, *Early Adventures,* 1:197; Athearn, *Sherman,* p. 179).

18. POPC, pp. 68, 74–76, 79–83; Olson, *Red Cloud,* p. 68; Athearn, *Sherman,* p. 183; Jones, *Medicine Lodge,* p. 185.

19. POPC, pp. 87, 91, 94.

20. Utley, *Indian Frontier,* p. 118. Prucha describes the report as "a jeremiad, a denunciatory tirade against the evils in the Indian system" (*Great Father,* 1:490–91).

21. The commission's initial report is printed in AR-CIA 1868, pp. 44–46.

22. Sherman to Taylor, Feb. 6, 1868, Harney to Taylor, Feb. 8, 1868 (OIA-LR M234, Upper Platte Agency 1868); CR, 2:892–97.

23. CR, 3:895–96.

24. Ibid., pp. 898–99. For De Smet's relation to the Galpin family, see Gray, "Mrs. Picotte-Galpin," and Holley, *Once Their Home,* pp. 284–89.

25. Olson, *Red Cloud,* p. 72; Denman to CIA, Mar. 5, 1868 (OIA-LR, Upper Platte 1868); POPC, p. 95.

26. Letter Book, 1868 (JMPA); De Smet's preserved this passport and another issued by Sherman in the following year in his letter books.

27. CR, 3:900; POPC, pp. 96–97.

28. POPC, p. 99; AR-CIA 1868, p. 46; Brown, *Fort Kearny,* p. 225; Olson, *Red Cloud,* p. 105.

29. POPC, p. 100.

30. CR, 3:901.

31. POPC, pp. 47, 102, 107, 116.

32. POPC, 112. The Cheyenne and Arapaho treaty is printed in Kappler, *Laws and Treaties,* 2:1012–15; the Arapaho signatures of a later date are mistakenly printed with the Sioux treaty on p. 1005.

33. POPC, p. 113, 118, 173–76; Olson, *Red Cloud,* p. 74–75; Geren to Taylor, July 1, 1868 (AR-CIA 1868, pp. 252–54).

34. Commission report, Sanborn and Harvey to Mix (OIA-LR, Upper Platte 1868); Utley, *Frontier Regulars,* p. 239.

35. CR, 3:901–2.

36. Ibid., p. 902; De Smet to Taylor, May 31, 1868 (OIA-LR, Upper Platte Agency); Pfaller, "Galpin Journal," p. 16.

37. Primary documents present five different versions of the Peace Ride. The biography of Eagle Woman reports on the expedition from the Indian point of view (Holley, *Once Their Home*, pp. 303–11). The narrative of Charles Galpin, appointed diarist by De Smet, was located and published by Garraghan in 1930 ("Father De Smet's Sioux Peace Mission").

The best-known version was composed by De Smet during his return journey from Fort Rice to St. Louis (CR, 3:899–920). The official version, titled "Presented to the Honorable Peace Commissioners," had been given by De Smet to Sanborn as the acting president at Fort Rice of the commission (John B. Sanborn Papers, Minnesota Historical Society). Still another version (seemingly copied, with slight differences, from the above) became part of the official records of the commission ("Statement by De Smet of reception by and Council with Uncpapa," POPC, pp. 130–35; *Papers Relating to Talks and Councils*, pp. 108–13).

38.   De Smet's report to Peace Commission for June 1868 (John B. Sanborn collection, Minnesota Historical Society); CR, 3:903, 915.

39.   CR, 3:917; De Smet's report to the Peace Commission for June 1868 (John B. Sanborn collection, Minnesota Historical Society).

40.   CR, 3:917–21.

41.   Ibid., p. 921; Harney, Sanborn, and Terry to De Smet, July 3, 1868 (copy in French) (Linton Album, JMPA), p. 147.

42.   POPC, pp. 135–44; *Papers Relating to Talks and Councils*, pp. 104–15.

43.   CR, 3:915; POPC, pp. 100, 136, 143.

44.   "Black Hills" was applied by some to include even Laramie Peak in the Medicine Bow Range west of Fort Laramie.

45.   POPC, pp. 136–37. Many writers on the 1868 treaty miss the fact that Gall (Man Who Goes in the Middle) attended the Fort Rice council as Sitting Bull's representative (Hyde, *Red Cloud's Folk*, p. 137; Utley, *Indian Frontier*, p. 120).

46.   POPC, pp. 137–38; Prucha, *Great Father*, pp. 318, 492–94, 531; Berthrong, *Southern Cheyennes*, p. 347.

12.   WESTERN ECHOES OF "THEY MUST NECESSARILY YIELD"

1.   Hyde had classified De Smet as a "bellwether," a specialist "in leading the Indians to a treaty signing" (*Red Cloud's Folk*, pp. 135, 163). To justify this charge Hyde proposed that following the signings at Fort Rice, De Smet was sent back to Fort Laramie to engage in "shameless attempts" at bribery of Red Cloud (pp. 166–67). This Hyde-professed "conjecture" has a quasifoundation in the defective recording of the 1868 Sioux Treaty. The Fort Laramie signings of November 6 were inserted in the middle of the earlier signatures at Fort Rice; thus De Smet seemingly is listed as a witness to that later signing by Red Cloud (40th Congress, 3d sess., Executive Z.A.A., and Executive A.A.; Sanger, *Statutes At Large*, 15:644–45; Kappler, *Laws and Treaties*, 2:998–1007).

The subsequent study by Olson introduced the Dye Report of Red Cloud's signing (*Red Cloud and the Sioux Problem*, p. 79). The Dye Report (not used by Hyde) makes no mention of De Smet in listing the witnesses who were on hand for Red Cloud's signing. Seemingly on the basis of the defective official recording, however, Olson provides an endorsement for the false criticism fashioned by Hyde (pp. 76–77). Apparently Utley was also influenced by Hyde and Olson; listing them as his sources, Utley implied that De Smet attempted similar bribery in his earlier dealing with Sitting Bull (*Indian Frontier*, pp. 120, 281–83).

2. POPC, pp. 144–48.

3. Sanborn to Browning, July 9, 1868 (OIA-LR, Upper Platte 1868). De Smet apparently sent a letter to Taylor from Fort Sully on July 10 (see De Smet to Mix, Sept. 21, 1868, in Letter Book, 1868, JMPA), but it has not been located. On the day following De Smet's departure from Fort Sully Stanley wrote a lengthy letter to Bishop Purcell expressing high praise for De Smet. Stanley's letter has been given an incorrect date in CR, 4:1584–88.

4. CR, 3:921, 4:1289.

5. De Smet to the Galpins, Aug. 4, 1868 (Letter Book, 1868, JMPA); Gray, "Mrs. Picotte-Galpin," pp. 2–4; CR, 4:1220–22, 1589–90.

6. Utley, *Frontier Regulars*, p. 137. See Prucha, *Great Father*, 1:488–95.

7. Athearn, *Sherman*, pp. 217–18. In his instructions to Hazen regarding Indian removal Sherman used the expression "by gradual process."

8. Ibid., p. 222; Utley, *Frontier Regulars*, p. 144; Sherman to Secretary of War John Schofield (AR-CIA 1868, pp. 536–37).

9. Utley, *Frontier Regulars*, pp. 144–47; Athearn, *Sherman*, p. 227.

10. Athearn, *Sherman*, p. 230; Bowles, *Our New West*, pp. 158–59.

11. Utley, *Indian Frontier*, p. 125; Athearn, *Sherman*, p. 228. It was Sanborn, as president pro tem, who called for the October meeting.

12. POPC, pp. 148, 171–73.

13. AR-CIA 1868, pp. 6, 11.

14. Athearn, *Sherman*, pp. 226–29, 275; Utley, *Frontier Regulars*, p. 151.

15. Athearn, *Sherman*, p. 287; De Smet to Harney, Nov. 14, 1868, Letter Book, 1868 (JMPA).

16. CR, 4:1460, 1535; Linton Album, p. 148 (JMPA); De Smet to Mrs. Sherman, July 1869, and to General and Mrs. Sherman, Sept. 1869 (Letter Book 1869, JMPA). The passport granted by Sherman was brief; it requested military officers on the Missouri "to extend to Father De Smet all the courtesy and facilities he may need."

17. Waltmann, "Parker," in Kvasnicka and Viola, *Commissioners*, p. 128; Sanger, *United States Statutes*, 16:40 (Prucha, *Documents of Indian Policy*, pp. 126–27); Utley, *Frontier Regulars*, pp. 157–58.

18. Utley, *Frontier Regulars*, p. 190; AR-CIA 1869, p. 452; Waltmann, "Parker," in Kvasnicka and Viola, *Commissioners*, p. 128.

19. CR, 4:1292–94.

20. Utley, "Celebrated Peace Policy," p. 125; *Indian Frontier*, pp. 129–33; AR-Secretary of the Interior, 1869, p. x; Prucha, *Great Father*, 1:512–19.

21. Letter Book 1869. Parker, a Native American of New York origin and experience, openly acknowledged De Smet's closer connection with and deeper knowledge of the Buffalo People of the Great Plains: "You, Reverend Sir, know more of the Indian character and their real wants than I do."

22. Utley, *Frontier Regulars*, p. 191; *Indian Frontier*, p. 133; Athearn, *Sherman*, pp. 278–79.

23. AR-CIA 1870, p. 474; Prucha, *Great Father*, 1:515–16; Israel, *State of the Union Messages*, 2:1216.

24. De Smet to Parker, Nov. 1869 (Letter Book, 1869); CR, 3:928; Priest, *Uncle Sam's Stepchildren*, p. 31.

25. Garraghan, *Jesuits*, 2:490; Linton Album, p. 152 (JMPA); Letter Book 1870 (JMPA); CR, 3:932, 4:1296, 1333.

26. Letter Book 1870 (JMPA); Gray, "Mrs. Picotte-Galpin," pt. 2, p. 8.

27. Linton Album, p. 154 (JMPA); CR, 4:1336; Priest, *Uncle Sam's Stepchildren*, pp. 31–34.

28. CR, 4:1335–37, 1542; Rahill, *Catholic Missions*, pp. 84–85.

29. CR, 4:1299–1304; Garraghan, *Jesuits*, 2:485; Letter Book 1871 (JMPA). Like the provider he had tried to be for the early missionaries in the Northwest, De Smet made bold to petition Stanley to allow the new missionaries to buy necessary provisions at the post quartermaster's store.

30. Garraghan, *Jesuits*, 2:485–86; Gray, "Mrs. Picotte-Galpin," pt. 2, p. 10; CR, 3:903–4. Mrs. Galpin was especially disappointed at the failure of Kuppens and De Meester.

31. Garraghan, *Jesuits*, 3:106, n. 85.

32. Hill, *Historical Sketch*, pp. 112–14; Killoren, "Doctor's Scrapbook."

33. Laveille, *De Smet*, pp. 381–83; Letter Book 1873; CR, 4:1341, 1548.

34. Gregg, *Commerce*, p. 369; Sandoz, *Buffalo Hunters*, p. 339; Catlin, *North American Indians*, 1:296–97. Reports on the destruction of the buffalo herds are also presented in Gard, *Great Buffalo Hunt*; Branch, *Hunting of Buffalo*; Martin, *Saga of Buffalo*; McHugh, *Time of the Buffalo*; Haley, *Buffalo War*; Cook, *Border and Buffalo*; Mayer and Roth, *Buffalo Harvest*.

35. CR, 3:1188–89; Stansbury, "Valley of Great Salt Lake," p. 29.

36. Donnelly, *Wilderness Kingdom*, p. 34; CR, 4:1397; Stansbury, "Valley of Great Salt Lake," p. 35; Morgan, *Rocky Mountain Journals*, pp. 179, 181.

37. CR, 1:179, 207; Sunder, *Fur Trade*, p. 172.

38. Mattes, *Platte River*, pp. 22–23.

39. Utley, *Frontiersmen in Blue*, p. 63.

40. Frazier, *Forts of the West*, p. xv; Utley, *Frontiersmen in Blue*, pp. 42, 109, 348.

41. Greeley, *Overland Journey*, pp. 47–48; Bowles, *Across the Continent*, pp. 51–55; Billington, *Westward Expansion*, pp. 638–41.

42. Goetzmann, *Exploration and Empire*, p. 301.

43. Athearn, *Sherman*, pp. 186, 251; AR-Secretary of War, 1867 (40th Cong., 2d sess., House Ex. Doc. 1 [ser. 1324]), p. 36.

44. Sandoz, *Buffalo Hunters*, pp. 128–69. Sandoz notes that the financial depression of 1873 contributed to the increased number of hide hunters.

45. Mayer and Roth, *Buffalo Harvest*, pp. 29–30; Dary, *Buffalo Book*, p. 103.

46. Billington, *Westward Expansion*, pp. 669–70; Dary, *Buffalo Book*, pp. 125, 133. Dary points out that there was no federal legislation protecting the buffalo until the Lacey Yellowstone Protection Bill, signed into law

on May 7, 1894, ten years after the slaughter on the plains had ended; the concern was that the buffalo be protected not for the Indians but for the sake of the white visitors to "nature's zoo—the Park of Yellowstone."

47.   Prucha, *Great Father,* 1:561.

48.   Richardson, *Messages and Papers,* 3:33.

49.   Sherman to Sheridan, Oct. 13, 1878 (Athearn, *Sherman,* p. 355).

EPILOGUE

1.   CR, 4:1545–47; Letter Book 1873 (JMPA).

2.   Laveille, *De Smet,* p. 383. For De Smet's role as a religious leader in the St. Louis area, see Garraghan, *Jesuits,* 2:35, 3:534; Jensen, "Historic St. Joseph's," pp. 273–76.

3.   Scharf, *History of St. Louis,* p. 1076.

4.   Chittenden, *Steamboat Navigation,* pp. 414–48.

5.   Sunder, *Pilcher,* pp. 141–52; Stevens, *Centennial History,* 1:467.

6.   Richardson, *Messages and Papers,* 1:185; Jefferson, "Observations on Demeunier's Manuscript," in Boyd, *Papers of Jefferson,* 10:44.

7.   O'Fallon to Crooks, July 10, 1822 (Chouteau Family Papers, Missouri Historical Society); Prucha, *Documents of Indian Policy,* p. 10.

8.   Burns, *Indian Wars,* p. 40; DeVoto, *Wide Missouri,* p. 371.

9.   Prucha, *Indian Policy in Formative Years,* pp. 275–76.

10.   Sheehan, *Seeds of Extinction,* p. 268; Prucha, *Indian Policy in Formative Years,* pp. 275–76.

11.   AR-CIA 1853, pp. 251, 369, 1854, p. 225; Whipple, *Lights and Shadows,* p. 144.

12.   CR, 4:1195; Trennert, *Alternative to Extinction,* p. 194; Prucha, *Indian Policy in United States,* p. 35.

13.   DeVoto, *Wide Missouri,* p. 373.

14.   CR, 1:107, 4:1598.

15.   Garraghan, *Jesuits,* 3:104–7; *Globe-Democrat,* May 24, 1873; *Missouri Republican,* May 24, 1873; *Western Watchman,* May 31, 1873; *St. Louis Times,* May 24, 1873.

16.   Garraghan, *Jesuits,* 3:106–7; Laveille, *De Smet,* p. 388; *Missouri Republican,* May 25, 1873.

Bibliography

ABBREVIATIONS

AR-CIA   *Annual Report of the Commissioner of Indian Affairs*

CR   Chittenden and Richardson, *Life, Letters and Travels of Father Pierre-Jean De Smet, S.J., 1803–1873*

JMPA   Jesuit Missouri Province Archives, St. Louis

OIA-LR Office of Indian Affairs, Letters Received (U.S. National Archives)

OIA-LS Office of Indian Affairs, Letters Sent (U.S. National Archives)

POPC   *Proceedings of the Great Peace Commission of 1867–1868*

ser.   U.S. serial set number

ACKNOWLEDGMENTS

A study of this scope could only be made through the assistance of capable and generous coworkers. By their important contributions, many have shared, directly or indirectly, in this presentation. I wish to acknowledge an exceptional debt of gratitude to all who participated in this reporting.

I would here express my gratitude to Raymond J. DeMallie, Professor and Director of the American Indian Studies Research Institute at Indiana University. Dr. DeMallie performed the key function of editor, and the Research Institute on the Bloomington campus supported that editing and manuscript preparation.

The Jesuits of the Missouri Province have provided a generous endorsement of the project; they have supported more than a dozen years of research and manuscript preparation. In addition to the encouragement and the assistance provided by numerous fellow Jesuits, the following have contributed as project consultants: Fathers William B. Faherty, James G. Knapp, and Robert F. Weiss.

A debt of gratitude must be acknowledged to Katherine Halverson, longtime Director of the Archives and Records Division, Cheyenne, Wyoming. Mrs. Halverson assisted with detailed reports on the histories of the Plains tribes under De Smet's influence. Andrea Paul, Archivist of the Nebraska State Historical Society, and Ron Mamot, of St. Stephens, Wyoming, were especially helpful in providing information on the eastern half of the Oregon Trail. Father Charles Brodersen, of Omaha, Nebraska, was highly supportive, and proved to be a great companion in gathering firsthand information on the western half of that passageway. With Father Brodersen, I also shared the satisfactions of tracing side trails that had been travelled by De Smet across western Montana and northern Idaho, and along the Columbia.

Dallas R. Lindgren, of the Minnesota State Historical Society, St. Paul, Minnesota, was very helpful regarding the De Smet Report of 1868 in the John B. Sanborn papers. Rebecca Kohn, Archivist with the Montana Historical Society, in Helena, Montana, provided important help with the collection of De Smet photographs. Beverly Boyd, Professor of English at the University of Kansas, contributed her special knowledge of De Smet memorabilia scattered across eastern Kansas. Mildred Goosman, former curator of the Western Collection in the Joslyn Art Museum in Omaha, Nebraska, was most helpful; so also were Eleanor Gehres, Director of the Western History Department of the Denver Public Library, and Professor Andrew D. Scrimgeour, Director of the Dayton Memorial Library at Regis University, in Denver, Colorado. Much appreciated advice was received from Robert T. Reilly, Professor Emeritus of Communications at the University of Nebraska at Omaha, and from Professor Vine Deloria, Jr., at the Center for Ethnicity and Race at the University of Colorado at Boulder.

Thanks also are due Margaret Coel and Virginia Trenholm; in connection with their published Indian studies, they graciously provided helpful information regarding De Smet's influence on the eastern Shoshoni, and on the Arapaho and Cheyenne. I am also grateful to "the People" of the Wind River Reservation in central Wyoming; members of both the Shoshoni and the Arapaho nations graciously shared their tribal legends regarding De Smet.

Throughout a 1982–88 residency in Kansas City, Missouri, I became greatly indebted to the following staff members of the main library of the University of Missouri at Kansas City: Marilyn Carbonell, Kathy Boutros, and Shirley Mickelson. While working at the Federal Archives and Records Center in Kansas City, I received generous help from Alan Perry, Archivist, in charge of the records of the Bureau of Indian Affairs; there, and at the Federal Records center in Denver, I learned to appreciate the courtesy of the staff personnel.

I would express my gratitude to my nephew, Robert A. Killoren, for important contributions consequent to his research work on the De Smet–related materials at the Elmer Ellis Library on the Columbia campus of the University of Missouri. At the Missouri Historical Society in St. Louis, Joseph Porter, Peter Michel, and Bryan Thomas were especially helpful; for a study centered on De Smet, the importance of the related manuscript collections of his contemporaries and associates, as now held in the archives of the Missouri Historical Society, cannot be overstated. An acknowledgment must also be made of the help offered by Robert L. Knecht, Manuscript Curator of the Kansas State Historical Society, in Topeka, regarding the special collection of William Clark's papers. Also, the Society in 1967 had microfilmed all the records of the St. Mary's Indian Mission, in which many items related to De Smet had been posted.

Father Anthony Short, S.J., has also made a significant scholarly contribution to this work. In the late 1970s Father Short studied the extensive materials compiled by William L. Davis, S.J.; these materials form the major part of the Desmetiana held in the Oregon Province Jesuit Archives. Professor J. Peterson-Swagerty, at Washington State University, has provided important help with the De Smet letters of the Chile Collection held in the Holland Library; this exceptional collection includes over two hundred letters written by De Smet.

Father Short also contributed by his research studies in the National Archives in Washington, D.C. One key report not located by Father Short in the early 1980s became the object of a second search—also gratefully acknowledged here—conducted in 1987 by Father Knapp with the assistance of Robert M. Kvasnicka, then Director of the Civil Archives Division; however, this search also failed to locate any official records of the testimony offered by De Smet on August 12, 1867, to the peace commissioners. A debt of gratitude is also acknowledged to Professor Vine Deloria, Jr., who provided confirmative information regarding the matter; Deloria stated, "In our 1975 search of the Archives' records, we were puzzled by our failure to discover anything resembling the De Smet interview."

As a related consequence, thanks are due to Father Joseph Windey, S.J., who for some years has conducted research on De Smet, especially in the archives of the Belgian Jesuits. Father Windey has graciously provided copies of the statements made by De Smet, including newspaper reports of question-answer interviews held during De Smet's 1868–69 European visit. These statements repeated, at least to some degree, the main points of the original testimony De Smet had given at the initial commission meeting. On other points of information regarding De Smet, Father Windey has also been very helpful.

Kathleen McGranaghan and Kay Fossey helped with their translations and their typing of the manuscript. Archivist John Waide, at the Pius XII Memorial Library at St. Louis University, repeatedly offered important help; so too did Martin Towey, Archivist of the St. Louis Archdiocese. Gratitude is offered to Father Faherty, Archivist of the Missouri Province Jesuits, and Director of the Museum of Western Jesuit Missions, at Florissant, Missouri; also to Father Faherty's assistants, Nancy Merz and Nini Harris. A grateful acknowledgment for financial support is offered to the members of the William-Julia Hadel family who have offered a memorial for their parents; such support has also been thankfully received as a Verona Vanderheiden Memorial, and from the St. Stanislaus Historical Museum Society.

DESMETIANA
De Smet's Published Works

Letters and Sketches: With a Narrative of a Year's Residence among the Indian Tribes of the Rocky Mountains. Philadelphia: M. Fithian, 1843. (In addition to this English edition, there were two French editions and editions in Dutch, German, and Italian.)

Oregon Missions and Travels over the Rocky Mountains, 1845–1846. New York: Edward Dunigan, 1847. (There were also two French editions and a Flemish edition.)

Western Missions and Missionaries: A Series of Letters. New York: James B. Kirker, 1863. (Besides the French editions of this work, William L. Davis wrote the introduction to an edition published by the Irish University Press, Shannon, 1972.)

New Indian Sketches. New York: D. and J. Sadlier, 1865.

Note: De Smet's *Letters and Sketches* were also extensively published in the *Annales de la Propagation de la Foi,* Lyons; in the *Précis Historiques,*

Brussels, edited by Ed. Terwecoren, a friend and correspondent of De Smet; and in several Catholic periodicals in the United States. Shortly before his death, De Smet authorized Francois Deynoodt of Belgium to publish a complete edition of his writings, together with a biographical account; this work was not completed.

Letters and Sketches (reporting on De Smet's trips of 1840 and 1841–42) and *Oregon Missions and Travels* (covering his journeys in the Northwest, 1845 to 1846), are reprinted in Reuben G. Thwaites, ed., *Early Western Travels,* 27:122–411, 29:108–409 (1906).

De Smet's Manuscripts

Letter Books and Letters Received. De Smet made a copy of almost all the letters he wrote; he also preserved a copy of most of the letters he received; these volumes, by year, are in the Jesuit Missouri Province Archives. Related De Smet notebooks and other pertinent materials are contained in the archives of the Pius XII Memorial Library at St. Louis University. These materials were utilized by Chittenden and Richardson for their *Life, Letters and Travels of Father De Smet.*

Linton Album. This scrapbook, gathered and edited by De Smet and his close friend Dr. Moses L. Linton, is in the Missouri Province Jesuit Archives.

Davis Collection. The William L. Davis Collection of Desmetiana is in the Oregon Province Jesuit Archives at the Crosby Library, Gonzaga University, Spokane, Washington.

Chile Collection. This extensive collection of De Smet's correspondence across a half century with his European relatives is in the Manuscripts and Archives Division, Holland Library, Washington State University, Pullman, Washington.

De Smet Papers. Various materials in the Manuscripts and Archives Collection, Missouri Historical Society, St. Louis.

Windey Collection. Collection of Belgian and Roman documents studies by Father J. E. Windey, S.J., used in his book *Machetakonia.* These materials are in the Collection Desmetiana, Jesuits Archief Noorbelgische Provincie.

BIOGRAPHIES OF DE SMET

Chittenden, Hiram Martin, and Alfred T. Richardson. *Life, Letters and Travels of Father Pierre-Jean De Smet, S.J., 1803–1873.* 4 vols. New York: Kraus, 1969; orig. ed., 1905, Francis P. Harper, New York.

Hopkins, J. G. *Black Robe — Peacemaker.* New York: Kenedy, 1958.

Laveille, E. *The Life of Father De Smet, S.J.* Translated by Marian Lindsay. Repr., Loyola University Press, 1981; orig. ed., 1915, Kenedy, 1915.

Magaret, Helene. *Father De Smet: Pioneer Priest of the Rockies.* Milwaukee: Bruce, 1940.

Pfaller, Louis. *Father De Smet in Dakota.* Richardton, N. Dak., 1962.

Terrell, John Upton. *Black Robe: The Life of Pierre-Jean De Smet, Missionary, Explorer and Pioneer.* New York: Doubleday, 1964.

THESES AND DISSERTATIONS

Bischoff, William N., S.J. "The Yakima Indian War: 1855–1856." Ph.D. diss., Loyola University of Chicago, 1950.

Brumback, David M. "Peter John De Smet, S.J.: Fundraiser and Promoter of Missions." Ph.D. diss., Washington State University, 1992.

Cain, Marvin. "Edward Bates: The Rise of a Western Politician, 1814–1850." Master's thesis, University of Missouri, 1957.

Donnelly, John J., S.J. "The Liquor Traffic Among the Aborigines of the Northwest, 1800–1860." Master's thesis, St. Louis University, 1978.

Donnelly, William P., S.J. "Father Pierre-Jean De Smet: United States Ambassador to the Indians." Master's thesis, St. Louis University, 1934.

Durateschek, Claudia. "The Beginning of Catholicism in South Dakota." Ph.D. diss., Catholic University, 1943.

Edwards, Lawrence E., S.J. "The Desmetiana of St. Louis University." Master's thesis, St. Louis University, 1937.

Glauert, Ralph Edward. "The Life and Activities of William Henry Ashley and Associates, 1822–1826." Master's thesis, Washington University, 1950.

Hoopes, Alban W. "Indian Affairs and their Administration, 1849–1860." Ph.D. diss., Philadelphia, 1932.

Huss, Stephen F. "Taking No Advantage: Biography of Robert Campbell." Ph.D. diss., St. Louis University, 1990.

Loehr, N. P., S.J. "Federal Relations with the Jesuit Osage Mission, 1847–1870." Master's thesis, St. Louis University, 1940.

Myers, Elinor Mary. "The Services Rendered by Pierre-Jean De Smet for the United States Government." Master's thesis, Colorado University, 1950.

Plaisance, Aloysius. "The United States Government Factory System, 1796–1822." Ph.D. diss., St. Louis University, 1954.

Waltmann, H. G. "The Interior Department, War Department, and Indian Policy." Ph.D. diss., University of Nebraska, 1962.

Young, L. Marie. "The Literary Aspects of the Letters, Sketches, and Journals of Father De Smet." Master's thesis, Notre Dame University, 1933.

OTHER ARCHIVAL MATERIALS

National Archives, Washington, D. C.
  RG 48: Records of Office of Secretary of Interior
  RG 75: Records of Bureau of Indian Affairs:
    Office of Indian Affairs, Letters Sent
    Office of Indian Affairs, Letters Received
    St. Louis Superintendency, Letters Received
    Upper Missouri Agency, Letters Received
    Upper Platte Agency, Letters Received
    Utah Agency, Letters Received.
  RG 94: Records of Adjutant General's Office
  RG 98: Records of United States Army Commands:

Military Division of the Missouri
Department of the Platte.
Diocese of Kansas City–St. Joseph, Chancery Office, Kansas City, Missouri. (Notes of Rev. William Dalton and others regarding De Smet.)
Kansas State Historical Society, Topeka, Kansas.
 William Clark Papers, 1807–55. (Correspondence of St. Louis Superintendency.) Records (Microfilm) of St. Mary's Potawatomie Mission and St. Mary's College.
Marquette University Archives, Milwaukee, Wisconsin. Records of Bureau of Catholic Indian Missions.
Minnesota Historical Society, St. Paul, Minnesota. Papers of John B. Sanborn.
Missouri Historical Society, St. Louis, Missouri. Papers and Collections: Ashley, William H.; Benton, Thomas Hart; Chouteau, Pierre; Clark, William; De Smet, Peter J.; Dougherty, George; Drips, Andrew; Gardner, Alexander (photos); Harney, General Wm. S.; Henry, Andrew; Hunt Family; Kennerly, James; St. Louis History; Sibley, George C.; Soulard, James; Sublette, William.
Nebraska State Historical Society, Lincoln, Nebraska:
 Ricker Manuscripts, Tablet 86-B-90: "Record of Meetings of Peace Commission with Certain Hostile Tribes in 1867."
 Sheldon, Addison E. "Red Cloud, Chief of the Sioux."
Wyoming State Archives and Historical Department, Cheyenne, Wyoming. Historical Records and Research Division.

GOVERNMENT DOCUMENTS
American State Papers: Indian Affairs. 2 vols. Washington, D.C.: Gales and Seaton, 1832–34.
American State Papers: Military Affairs. 7 vols. Washington, D.C.: Gales and Seaton, 1860.
Carter, Clarence E., and John P. Bloom, eds. *Territorial Papers of the United States.* 27 vols. Washington, D.C.: GPO, 1944–69.
Clark, William. "The Preservation and Civilization of the Indians." U. S. Department of War, Not. 124 (Report of Barbour to 19th Congress, March 9, 1826). Washington, D.C.: Gales and Seaton, 1826.
Cohen, Felix S., ed. *Federal Indian Law.* (Revision and updating of "Handbook of Federal Indian Law," 1840). Washington: GPO, 1958.
Goldman, Perry M., and James S. Young, eds. *United States Congressional Directories, 1789–1840.* New York: Columbia University Press, 1973.
Journals of the Continental Congress, 1774–1789. 34 vols. Washington, D.C.: GPO, 1904–37.
Kappler, Charles J., ed. *Indian Affairs: Laws and Treaties.* 5 vols. Washington, D.C.: GPO, 1903–41.
New American State Papers: Indian Affairs. 13 vols. Delaware: Scholarly Research, 1972.
Papers Relating to Talks and Council with Indians of Dakota and Montana Territories, 1866–1869. Washington, D.C.: GPO, 1910.

Proceedings of the Great Peace Commission of 1867–1868. Introduction by Vine Deloria, Jr., and Raymond DeMallie. Washington, D.C.: Institute for Development of Indian Law, 1975.

Prucha, Francis Paul, ed. *Documents of United States Indian Policy.* Lincoln: University of Nebraska Press, Bison Books, 1975.

Richardson, James D., ed. *Compilation of Messages and Papers of the Presidents, 1789–1897.* Washington, D.C.: GPO, 1899.

Sanger, George P., ed. *United States Statutes at Large,* vols. 11–17, 1855–1873. Boston: Little, Brown, 1855–73.

U.S. Commissioner of Indian Affairs. *Annual Reports,* 1846–73.

U.S. Congress: House of Representatives.

> 33rd Cong, 2d sess., House Ex. Doc. 63 (1855), ser. 788. Reports on the Grattan Affair.
>
> 34th Cong., 1st sess., House Ex. Doc. 130 (1856), ser. 859. "Council with the Sioux at Fort Pierre."
>
> 35th Cong., 1st sess., House Ex. Doc. 71 (1858), ser. 956. "The Utah Expedition."
>
> 36th Cong., 1st sess., House Ex. Doc. 2 (1859), ser. 1023. Harney and De Smet: Reports from the Northwest.
>
> 37th Cong., 3d sess., House Ex. Doc. 1 (1861), ser. 1157. Missouri River Highway to Northwestern Mines.
>
> 39th Cong., 2d sess., House Ex. Docs. 1, 20 (1866–67), sers. 1284, 1288. Military and Civilian Reactions to Fetterman Disaster.
>
> 40th Cong., 2d sess., House Ex. Doc. 97 (1868), ser. 1337. "Report of the Indian Peace Commission."
>
> 41st Cong., 2d sess., House Ex. Doc. 1 (1869), ser. 1414. "Reports of Disturbances Among the Indians."

U.S. Congress: Senate.

> 31st Cong., 1st sess., Senate Ex. Doc. 70 (1850), ser. 563. "Report of the Commissioner of Indian Affairs on the Indians."
>
> 32d Cong., Special sess., Senate Ex. Doc. 3 (1853), ser. 608. Stansbury, Howard. "Exploration and Survey of the Valley of the Great Salt Lake."
>
> 33rd Cong., 2d sess., Senate Ex. Doc. 22 (1855), ser. 751. Report on the Grattan Affair.
>
> 37th Cong., 3d sess., Senate Ex. Doc. 43 (1863), ser. 1149. Report on Mullan's Military Road.
>
> 39th Cong., 2d sess., Senate Ex. Docs. 15 and 16 (1867), sers. 1267–77. Reports on Massacre at Fort Phil Kearny and Fetterman Commission.
>
> 39th Cong., 2d sess., Senate Ex. Doc. 156 (1867), ser. 1279. The Doolittle Report on Tribal Conditions.
>
> 40th Cong., 1st sess., Senate Ex. Doc. 13 (1867), ser. 1308. Sully Commission Reports, and "New" Indian Bureau Proposal.
>
> 41st Cong., 3d sess., Senate Ex. Doc. 39 (1871), ser. 1440. "Report of the Indian Commissioners."

U.S. Secretary of Interior, Annual Reports, 1850–72.

U.S. Secretary of War, Annual Reports, 1824–72.

War of the Rebellion: A Compilation of the Official Records of the Union and Confederate Armies. Ser. 1, vols. 22, 34, 48.

Washburn, Wilcomb E. *The American Indian and the United States: A Documentary History.* 4 vols. New York: Random House, 1973.

NEWSPAPERS
Cheyenne Leader, Cheyenne, Wyoming.
Daily Intelligencer, St. Louis, Missouri.
Daily Reveille, St. Louis, Missouri.
Daily Times, New York, New York.
Gazette, St. Joseph, Missouri.
Globe-Democrat, St. Louis, Missouri.
Jefferson Inquirer, Jefferson City, Missouri.
Missouri Democrat, St. Louis, Missouri.
Missouri Gazette, St. Louis, Missouri.
Missouri Republican, St. Louis, Missouri.
New York Times, New York, New York.
Omaha World-Herald, Omaha, Nebraska.
Picayune, New Orleans, Louisiana.
Public Ledger, Kansas (City), Missouri.
Riverton Ranger, Riverton, Wyoming.
St. Louis Daily Union, St. Louis, Missouri.
St. Louis Enquirer, St. Louis, Missouri.
St. Louis Times, St. Louis, Missouri.
Statesman, Walla Walla, Washington.
Weekly Tribune, New York, New York.
Western Journal, St. Louis, Missouri.
Western Watchman, St. Louis, Missouri.
Wyoming Journal, Lander, Wyoming.

BOOKS
Abbott, Carl. *Colorado: A History of the Centennial State.* Boulder: Colorado Associated University Press, 1976.
Alter, J. Cecil. *Jim Bridger.* Norman: University of Oklahoma Press, 1962; orig. ed., 1925, Salt Lake City.
Anderson, Gary Clayton. *Kinsmen of Another Kind.* Lincoln: University of Nebraska Press, 1984.
Arrington, Leonard J. *Great Basin Kingdom: An Economic History of the Latter-Day Saints, 1830–1900.* Cambridge, Mass.: Harvard University Press, 1958.
Arrington, Leonard J., and Davis Britton. *The Mormon Experience: A History of Latter-Day Saints.* New York: Knopf, 1979.
Athearn, Robert G. *William Tecumseh Sherman and the Settlement of the West.* Norman: University of Oklahoma Press, 1956.
———. *Forts of the Upper Missouri.* Englewood Cliffs, N.J.: Prentice-Hall, 1967.
Bakeless, John. *Lewis and Clark: Partners in Discovery.* New York: William Morrow, 1947.
Bandel, Eugene. *Frontier Life in the Army, 1854–1861.* Edited by R. P. Biber. Glendale, Calif.: Arthur A. Clark, 1932.

Bangert, William V., S.J. *A History of the Society of Jesus.* St. Louis: Institute of Jesuit Sources, 1972.

Bannon, John Francis., S.J. *History of the Americas.* 2 vols. New York: McGraw-Hill, 1952.

Barry, Louise. *The Beginning of the West: Annals of the Kansas Gateway to the American West, 1540–1854.* Topeka: Kansas Historical Society, 1972.

Bartlett, Richard A. *Great Surveys of the American West.* Norman: University of Oklahoma Press, 1962.

Bennett, Richard F. *Mormons at the Missouri, 1846–1852.* Norman: University of Oklahoma Press, 1987.

Benton, Thomas Hart. *Thirty Years' View: History of Working of American Government, 1820–1850.* 2 vols. New York: Appleton, 1854.

Berthrong, Donald J. *The Southern Cheyennes.* Norman: University of Oklahoma Press, 1963.

Billington, Ray Allen. *The Protestant Crusade, 1800–1860.* New York: Macmillan, 1938.

———. *Westward Expansion: A History of the American Frontier.* New York: Macmillan, 1960.

Billon, Frederick Louis. *The Annals of St. Louis in its Earliest Days.* St. Louis, 1886.

Bischoff, William N., S.J. *The Jesuits in Old Oregon.* Caldwell, Idaho: Caxton, 1945.

Boller, Henry A. *Among the Indians: Eight Years in the Far West, 1858–1866.* Edited by Milo Milton Quaife. Chicago: Lakeside Press, 1959.

Bourke, John G. *On the Border with Crook.* Lincoln: University of Nebraska Press, Bison Books, 1971; orig. ed., 1891, Scribner, New York.

Bowden, Henry Warner. *American Indians and Christian Missions.* Chicago: University of Chicago Press, 1981.

Bowles, Samuel. *Across the Continent, 1865.* New York: Readex Microprint, 1966; orig. ed., 1865, Hurd and Houghton.

———. *Our New West.* New York: Arno Press, 1973; orig. ed., 1869, Hartford Publishing.

Brady, Cyrus Townsend. *Indian Fights and Fighters.* Lincoln: University of Nebraska Press, Bison Books, 1971; orig. ed., 1907, McClure, Philips.

Branch, E. Douglas. *The Hunting of the Buffalo.* Lincoln: University of Nebraska Press, Bison Books, 1962.

Brophy, William A., and Sophie D. Aberle. *The Indian: America's Unfinished Business.* Norman: University of Oklahoma Press, 1966.

Brown, Dee. *The Galvanized Yankees.* Urbana: University of Illinois Press, 1963.

———. *Bury My Heart at Wounded Knee.* New York: Holt, Rinehart and Winston, 1970.

———. *Fort Phil Kearny: An American Saga.* Lincoln: University of Nebraska Press, Bison Books, 1971; orig. ed., 1962, Putnam.

———. *The Westerners.* New York: Holt, Rinehart and Winston, 1974.

Buckley, Cornelius M., S.J. *Nicolas Point: His Life and Northwest Indian Chronicles.* Chicago: Loyola University Press, 1989.

Burns, Robert Ignatius, S.J. *The Jesuits and the Indian Wars of the Northwest.* New Haven, Conn.: Yale University Press, 1966.

Callan, Louise. *Life of Philippine Duchesne, 1769–1852.* Westminster: Newman Press, 1957.

Campbell, Thomas J., S.J. *The Jesuits, 1534–1921.* 2 vols. New York: Encyclopedia Press, 1921.

Caraman, Philip. *The Lost Paradise: The Jesuit Republic in South America.* New York: Seabury Press, 1976.

Carley, Kenneth. *The Sioux Uprising of 1862.* St. Paul: Minnesota Historical Society, 1961.

Casper, Henry W., S.J. *History of the Catholic Church in Nebraska.* Milwaukee: Bruce Press, 1960.

Catlin, George. *North American Indians: Being Letters and Notes on Their Manners, Customs, and Conditions.* 2 vols. Edinburgh: John Grant, 1926.

Chambers, William Nisbet. *Old Bullion Benton: Senator from the New West, Thomas Hart Benton 1782–1858.* Boston: Little, Brown, 1956.

Chittenden, Hiram Martin. *The American Fur Trade of the Far West.* 2 vols. Stanford, Calif.: Academic Reprints, 1954; orig. ed., 1902.

———. *History of Early Steamboat Navigation on the Missouri River: Life and Adventures of Joseph La Barge.* 2 vols. Minneapolis: Ross and Haines, 1962; orig. ed., 1903.

———. *The Yellowstone National Park.* Edited and introduction by Richard A. Bartlett. Norman: University of Oklahoma Press, 1964.

Clark, Ella Elizabeth. *Indian Legends from the Northern Rockies.* Norman: University of Oklahoma Press, 1966.

Cline, Gloria Griffen. *Peter Skene Ogden and the Hudson Bay Company.* Norman: University of Oklahoma Press, 1982.

Clokey, Richard M. *William H. Ashley: Enterprise and Politics in the Trans-Mississippi West.* Norman: University of Oklahoma Press, 1980.

Coel, Margaret. *Chief Left Hand: Southern Arapaho.* Norman: University of Oklahoma Press, 1982.

Cook, John R. *The Border and the Buffalo.* New York: Citadel Press, 1967.

Coutant, C. G. *The History of Wyoming.* 3 vols. Laramie: Chaplin, Spafford and Mathison, 1899.

Crawford, Lewis F. *Rekindling Old Campfires: An Authentic Narrative of Sixty Years in Old West.* Bismarck, N. Dak.: Capital Book, 1926.

Daniels, George G., ed. *The Chroniclers.* Chicago: Time-Life, 1976.

Dabry, John Fletcher. *Personal Recollections.* New York: Arno Press, 1975; orig. ed., 1880, St. Louis, G. I. Jones.

Dary, David A. *The Buffalo Book: The Full Saga of the American Animal.* Chicago: Swallow Press, 1974.

Deloria, Vine, Jr. *Custer Died for Your Sins: An Indian Manifesto.* New York: Macmillan, 1969.

———. *Of Utmost Good Faith.* San Francisco: Straight Arrow, 1971.

Denig, Edwin Thompson. *Five Indian Tribes of the Upper Missouri.* Edited and introduction by John C. Ewers. Norman: University of Oklahoma Press, 1961.

DeVoto, Bernard. *Across the Wide Missouri*. Boston: Houghton Mifflin, 1947.

————, ed. *The Journals of Lewis and Clark*. Boston: Houghton Mifflin, 1953.

Dippie, Brian W. *The Vanishing American: White Attitudes and U.S. Indian Policy*. Middletown, Conn.: Wesleyan University Press, 1982.

Dodge, Richard Irving. *The Plains of the Great West and Their Inhabitants*. New York: Putnam, 1877.

————. *Thirty-Three Years Among Our Wild Indians*. Introduction by General Sherman. Kansas City: Bailey and Kennedy, 1885.

Donnelly, Joseph P., S.J. *Wilderness Kingdom: The Journals and Paintings of Nicolas Point*. New York: Holt, Rinehart and Winston, 1967.

Drury, Clifford Merrill. *Marcus and Narcissa Whitman and the Opening of Old Oregon*. 2 vols. Glendale, Calif.: Arthur H. Clark, 1973.

Dunlay, Thomas W. *Wolves for the Blue Soldiers*. Lincoln: University of Nebraska Press, 1982.

Edwards, Richard, and Menra Hopewell. *Edward's Great West: Embracing a General View of the West and a Complete History of St. Louis*. 2 vols. St. Louis, 1860.

Egan, Ferol. *Frémont: Explorer for a Restless Nation*. New York: Doubleday, 1977.

Ellis, Richard N. *General Pope and United States Indian Policy*. Albuquerque: University of New Mexico Press, 1970.

————. *The Western American Indian: Case Studies in Tribal History*. Lincoln: University of Nebraska Press, Bison Books, 1972.

Evans, Lucylle H. *St. Mary's in the Rocky Mountains*. Missoula: University of Montana Press, 1976.

————. *Good Samaritan of the Northwest: Anthony Ravalli, S.J.* Missoula: University of Montana Press, 1981.

Ewers, John C. *Gustav Sohon's Portraits of Flathead and Pend d'Oreille Indians, 1854*. Washington: Smithsonian Institute, 1948 (Misc. Collections, vol. 110, no. 7).

————. *Blackfeet: Raiders of the Northwestern Plains*. Norman: University of Oklahoma Press, 1958.

Faherty, William Barnaby, S.J. *Dream by the River: Two Centuries of Saint Louis Catholicism*. St. Louis: River City, 1973.

————. *The St. Louis Portrait*. Tulsa, Okla.: Continental Heritage, 1978.

————. *St. Louis: A Concise History*. St. Louis: Print-Graphics, 1989.

Fahey, John. *The Flathead Indians*. Norman: University of Oklahoma Press, 1974.

Faragher, John Mack. *Women and Men on the Overland Trail*. New Haven, Conn.: Yale University Press, 1979.

Fitzgerald, Mary Paul. *Beacon on the Plains*. Leavenworth, Kans.: St. Mary's College, 1939.

Flagg, Edmund. *The Far West: A Tour Beyond the Mountains*. 2 vols. New York: Harper and Brothers, 1838; repr. Reuben Gold Thwaites, ed., *Early Western Travels*, vols. 26–27, Cleveland: Arthur H. Clark, 1906.

Foley, William E. *A History of Missouri 1673–1820*. Columbia: University of Missouri Press, 1971.

Foley, William E., and D. David Rice. *The First Chouteaus: River Barons of Early St. Louis*. Urbana: University of Illinois Press, 1983.

Folwell, William W. *A History of Minnesota*. 4 vols. St. Paul: Minnesota Historical Society, 1956.

Foreman, Grant. *The Five Civilized Tribes*. Norman: University of Oklahoma Press, 1934.

Fowler, Loretta. *Arapahoe Politics 1851–1978: Symbols in Crises of Authority*. Lincoln: University of Nebraska Press, 1982.

Franzwa, Gregory M. *The Old Cathedral of St. Louis*. St. Louis: St. Louis Archdiocese, 1965.

———. *The Oregon Trail Revisited*. St. Louis: Patrice Press, 1972.

Frazer, Robert Walter. *Forts of the West*. Norman: University of Oklahoma Press, 1965.

Fritz, Henry E. *The Movement for Indian Assimilation, 1860–1890*. Philadelphia: University of Pennsylvania Press, 1963.

Furniss, Norman F. *The Mormon Conflict, 1850–1859*. New Haven, Conn.: Yale University Press, 1960.

Gage, Jack R. *Wyoming Afoot and on Horseback*. Cheyenne, Wyo.: Flintlock, 1965.

Gard, Wayne. *The Great Buffalo Hunt*. Lincoln: University of Nebraska Press, Bison Books, 1968; orig. ed., 1959, Knopf.

Garraghan, Gilbert J., S.J. *The Jesuits of the Middle United States*. 3 vols. New York: America Press, 1938.

Gibson, A. M. *The Kickapoos: Lords of the Middle Border*. Norman: University of Oklahoma Press, 1963.

Gill, McCune. *The St. Louis Story*. St. Louis: Historical Record Association, 1952.

Gittinger, Roy. *The Formation of the State of Oklahoma, 1803–1906*. Berkeley: University of California Press, 1917.

Goetzmann, William H. *Army Exploration in the American West, 1803–1863*. Lincoln: University of Nebraska Press, Bison Books, 1979; orig. ed., 1959, Yale University Press.

———. *Exploration and Empire: The Explorer and the Scientist in the Winning of the American West*. New York: Knopf, 1966.

Graebner, Norman A., ed. *Manifest Destiny*. New York: Bobbs-Merrill, 1968.

Greeley, Horace. *An Overland Journey from New York to San Francisco, 1859*. New York: Readex Microprint, 1966; orig. ed., 1860, Saxton-Barker.

Gregg, Josiah. *Commerce on the Prairies*. Edited by Max L. Moorhead. Norman: University of Oklahoma Press, 1954.

Grinnell, George B. *The Fighting Cheyennes*. Norman: University of Oklahoma Press, 1956; orig. ed., 1915, Scribner.

Hafen, LeRoy R. *Broken Hand: The Life of Thomas Fitzpatrick, Mountain Man, Guide, Indian Agent*. Denver: Old West, 1973; orig. ed., 1931, Hafen and William J. Ghent.

———, ed. *Mountain Men and Fur Traders of the Far West*. 10 vols. Glendale, Calif.: Arthur H. Clark, 1965–72.

Hafen, LeRoy R., and Ann W. Hafen, eds. *Relations with Indians of the Plains 1857–1861*. Vol. 9, Far West and Rockies Historical Series. Glendale: Arthur H. Clark Co., 1954–61.

Hafen, LeRoy R., and Francis M. Young, eds. *Fort Laramie and the Pageant of the West, 1834–1890*. Glendale, Calif.: Arthur H. Clark, 1938.

———. *The Utah Expedition, 1857–1858*. Vol. 8. Far West and Rockies Historical Series. Glendale, Calif.: Arthur H. Clark, 1954–61.

Hagan, William T. *The Sac and Fox Indians*. Norman: University of Oklahoma Press, 1958.

Haley, James L. *The Buffalo War*. New York: Doubleday, 1976.

Harmon, George Dewey. *Sixty Years of Indian Affairs, 1789–1850*. Chapel Hill: University of North Carolina Press, 1941.

Hart, B. H. Liddell. *Sherman: Soldier, Realist, American*. New York: Dodd, Mead, 1929.

Hassrick, Royal B. *The Sioux: Life and Customs of a Warrior Society*. Norman: University of Oklahoma Press, 1964.

Herr, Pamela. *Jessie Benton Frémont*. Norman: University of Oklahoma Press, 1987.

Hill, Walter H., S.J. *Historical Sketch of St. Louis University, 1879*. St. Louis: Patrick Fox, 1879.

Hoig, Stan. *The Sand Creek Massacre*. Norman: University of Oklahoma Press, 1961.

———. *The Battle of the Washita*. Lincoln: University of Nebraska Press, Bison Books, 1979; orig. ed., 1976, Doubleday.

Holley, Frances C. *Once Their Home: Our Legacy from the Dahkotahs*. Chicago: Donohue and Henneberry, 1890.

Hollon, W. Eugene. *Lost Pathfinder, Zebulon Montgomery Pike*. Norman: University of Oklahoma Press, 1949.

———. *The Great American Desert: Then and Now*. New York: Oxford Press, 1966.

Horsman, Reginald. *Expansion and American Indian Policy, 1783–1812*. East Lansing: Michigan State University Press, 1967.

———. *The Origins of Indian Removal, 1815–1824*. East Lansing: Michigan State University Press, 1970.

———. *Frontier in Formative Years: 1783–1815*. New York: Holt, Rinehart and Winston, 1970.

Houck, Louis. *A History of Missouri*. 3 vols. Chicago: R. R. Donnelly, 1908.

Hughes, Thomas, S.J. *History of the Society of Jesus in North America*. 4 vols. New York: Longmans, Green, 1908.

Hyde, George E. *Spotted Tail's Folk: A History of the Brulé Sioux*. Norman: University of Oklahoma Press, 1961.

———. *Red Cloud's Folk: A History of the Oglala Sioux Indians*. Norman: University of Oklahoma Press, 1984; orig. ed., 1937.

Irving, Washington. *A Tour of the Prairies*. Edited and introduction by John F. McDermott. Norman: University of Oklahoma Press, 1956.

———. *The Adventures of Captain Bonneville*. Edited and introduction by Edgeley W. Todd. Norman: University of Oklahoma Press, 1961.

———. *Astoria: Anecdotes of an Enterprise Beyond the Rocky Mountains*.

Edited and introduction by Edgeley W. Todd. Norman: University of Oklahoma Press, 1964.

Jackson, Donald. *Custer's Gold: The U. S. Cavalry Expedition of 1874.* Lincoln: University of Nebraska Press, 1972; orig. ed., 1966, Yale University.

————, ed. *Letters of the Lewis and Clark Expedition with Related Documents.* Urbana: University of Illinois Press, 1962.

Jackson, Donald, and Mary Lee Spence, eds. *The Expeditions of John Charles Frémont.* Urbana: University of Illinois Press, 1970.

Jackson, W. Turrentine. *Wagon Roads West.* Lincoln: University of Nebraska Press, Bison Books, 1979; orig. ed., 1964, Yale University Press.

James, Edwin. *An Account of an Expedition from Pittsburg to the Rocky Mountains, 1819–1820.* 2 vols. Philadelphia: Carey and Lea, 1822–1823.

Jeffrey, Julie Roy. *Converting the West: A Biography of Narcissa Whitman.* Norman: University of Oklahoma Press, 1991.

Jones, Douglas C. *The Treaty of Medicine Lodge.* Norman: University of Oklahoma Press, 1966.

Josephy, Alvin M., Jr. *The Nez Perce Indians and the Opening of the Northwest.* New Haven: Yale University Press, 1965.

————. *The Indian Heritage of America.* New York: Knopf, 1968.

Kennerly, William Clark. *Persimmon Hill: Narrative of Old St. Louis and the Far West.* Norman: University of Oklahoma Press, 1948.

Knapp, Joseph G., S.J. *The Presence of the Past.* St. Louis: St. Louis University Press, 1948.

Kvasnicka, Robert M., and Herman J. Viola, eds. *The Commissioners of Indian Affairs.* Lincoln: University of Nebraska Press, 1979.

Larpenteur, Charles. *Forty Years a Fur Trader.* Edited by Milo Milton Quaife. Lincoln: University of Nebraska Press, 1978.

Larson, Taft Alfred. *History of Wyoming.* Lincoln: University of Nebraska Press, 1965.

Lavender, David. *Westward Vision: The Story of the Oregon Trail.* New York: McGraw-Hill, 1963.

————. *Bent's Fort.* Lincoln: University of Nebraska Press, Bison Books, 1972; orig. ed., 1954, Doubleday.

————. *Land of Giants: The Drive to the Pacific Northwest.* Lincoln: University of Nebraska Press, Bison Books, 1979; orig. ed., 1956, Doubleday.

————. *The Fist in the Wilderness.* Albuquerque: University of New Mexico Press, 1979; orig. ed., 1964, Doubleday.

Leonard, Zenas. *Narrative of the Adventures of Zenas Leonard.* Introduction by Milo Milton Quaife. Lincoln: University of Nebraska Press, 1978; orig. ed., Lakeside Press.

Ligthart, C. J. *The Return of the Jesuits: Life of Jan Philip Roothaan.* Translated by J. J. Slijkerman. London: T. Shand, 1983; orig. ed. in Dutch, Nijmegen, Netherlands: Dekker and Van de Begt, 1972.

Linford, Velma. *Wyoming, Frontier State.* Denver: Old West, 1947.

Lionberger, Isaac Henry. *The Annals of St. Louis.* St. Louis: Mound City Press, 1928.

Lowe, Percival G. *Five Years a Dragoon*. Kansas City: Hudson, 1906.

McAvoy, Thomas. *History of the Catholic Church in the United States*. South Bend, Ind.: University of Notre Dame Press, 1969.

McCandless, Perry. *A History of Missouri, 1820–1860*. Columbia: University of Missouri Press, 1972.

McColgan, Daniel T. *A Century of Charity: The St. Vincent De Paul Society in the United States*. Milwaukee: Bruce, 1951.

McCoy, Tim, and Ron McCoy. *Tim McCoy Remembers the West*. New York: Doubleday, 1977.

McCracken, Harold. *George Catlin and the Old Frontier*. New York: Dial Press, 1959.

McCulloch, Hugh. *Men and Measures of Half-a-Century*. New York: Scribner, 1889.

McGloin, John Bernard, S.J. *The Eloquent Indian: Life of James Bouchard*. Stanford, Calif.: Stanford University Press, 1949.

McHugh, Tom. *The Time of the Buffalo*. New York: Knopf, 1972.

McKenney, Thomas L. *Memoirs, Official and Personal*. Introduction by Herman J. Viola. Lincoln: University of Nebraska Press, Bison Books, 1973; orig. ed., 1849, Paine and Burgess.

McReynolds, Edwin C. *Missouri: A History of the Crossroads State*. Norman: University of Oklahoma Press, 1962.

Mails, Thomas E. *The Mystic Warriors of the Plains*. New York: Doubleday, 1972.

————. *Dog Soldiers, Bear Men, and Buffalo Women*. Englewood Cliffs, N.J.: Prentice-Hall, 1973.

Malin, James C. *Indian Policy and Westward Expansion*. Lawrence: University of Kansas, 1921.

Malone, Dumas. *Jefferson: Second Term as President*. Vol. 5 of *Jefferson and His Time*. Boston: Little, Brown, 1974.

Mardock, Robert W. *The Reformers and the American Indian*. Columbia: University of Missouri Press, 1971.

Martin, Cy. *The Saga of the Buffalo*. New York: Hart, 1973.

Mathews, John Joseph. *The Osages: Children of the Middle Waters*. Norman: University of Oklahoma Press, 1961.

Mattes, Merrill J. *The Great Platte River Road*. Lincoln: Nebraska State Historical Society, 1969.

Mayer, Frank H., and Charles B. Roth. *The Buffalo Harvest*. Denver: Sage, 1958.

Melville, Annabelle M. *Louis William Du Bourg, 1766–1833*. 2 vols. Chicago: Loyola University Press, 1986.

Mengarini, Gregory, S.J. *Recollections of the Flathead Mission*. Translated and edited by Gloria Ricci Lothrop. Glendale, Calif.: Arthur H. Clark, 1977.

Meyer, Roy W. *History of the Santee Sioux: United States Indian Policy on Trial*. Lincoln: University of Nebraska Press, 1967.

Miller, David Humphreys. *Ghost Dance*. Lincoln: University of Nebraska Press, 1985; orig. ed., New York: Duell, Sloan and Pearce, 1959.

Moore, James T. *Indian and Jesuit: A Seventeenth Century Encounter*. Chicago: Loyola University Press, 1982.

Morgan, Dale L. *Jedediah Smith and the Opening of the West.* Lincoln: University of Nebraska Press, Bison Books, 1964; orig. ed., 1953, Bobbs-Merrill.

———, ed. *Overland in 1846: Diaries and Letters of the California-Oregon Trail.* 2 vols. Georgetown, Calif.: Talisman Press, 1963.

———. *The West of William H. Ashley.* Denver: Old West, 1964.

Morgan, Dale L., and Eleanor T. Harris, eds. *The Rocky Mountain Journals of William Marshall Anderson: The West in 1834.* San Marino, Calif.: Huntington Library, 1967.

Morgan, Lewis Henry. *Houses and House-Life of American Aborigines.* Introduction by Paul Bohannan. Chicago: University of Chicago Press, 1965.

Morison, Samuel Eliot. *The Oxford History of the American People.* New York: Oxford University Press, 1965.

Murray, Robert A. *Fort Laramie: "Visions of a Grand Old Post."* Fort Collins, Colo.: Old Army Press, 1974.

Nevins, Allan. *Frémont: The West's Greatest Adventurer.* New York: Harper, 1928.

Nichols, David A. *Lincoln and the Indians: Civil War Policy and Politics.* Columbia: University of Missouri Press, 1978.

Nichols, Roger L. *General Henry Atkinson.* Norman: University of Oklahoma Press, 1965.

Oehler, Chester M. *The Great Sioux Uprising.* New York: Oxford University Press, 1959.

Oglesby, Richard E. *Manuel Lisa and the Opening of the Missouri Fur Trade.* Norman: University of Oklahoma Press, 1963.

Olson, James C. *History of Nebraska.* Lincoln: University of Nebraska Press, 1965.

———. *Red Cloud and the Sioux Problem.* Lincoln: University of Nebraska Press, 1965.

Palladino, Lawrence W. *Indians and Whites in the Northwest: A History of Catholicity in Montana, 1838–1891.* Baltimore: Murphy, 1894.

Parker, Samuel. *Journal of an Exploring Tour Beyond the Rocky Mountains.* Ithaca, N.Y.: Mark, Andrus and Woodruff, 1838.

Parkman, Francis. *The Oregon Trail.* New York: Garden City, 1948; orig. ed., *The California and Oregon Trail,* 1849.

Parrish, William E. *A History of Missouri, 1860–1875.* Columbia: University of Missouri Press, 1973.

Peake, Ora Brooks. *A History of the United States Indian Factory System, 1795–1822.* Denver: Sage, 1954.

Phillips, Paul Chrisler. *The Fur Trade.* 2 vols. Norman: University of Oklahoma Press, 1961.

Priest, Loring Benson. *Uncle Sam's Stepchildren: The Reformation of United States Indian Policy, 1865–1887.* Lincoln: University of Nebraska Press, Bison Books, 1975; orig. ed., 1942, Rutgers University.

Prucha, Francis Paul, S.J. *Broadax and Bayonet: Role of the United States Army in Development of the Northwest, 1815–1860.* Madison: Wisconsin Historical Society, 1953.

————. *American Indian Policy in the Formative Years, 1790–1834.* Lincoln: University of Nebraska Press, 1970; orig. ed., Cambridge: Harvard University Press, 1952.

————. *American Indian Policy in Crisis - Christian Reformers and the Indian, 1865–1900.* Norman: University of Oklahoma Press, 1976.

————. *Indian Policy in the United States.* Lincoln: University of Nebraska Press, 1981.

————. *The Great Father: The United States Government and the American Indians.* 2 vols. Lincoln: University of Nebraska Press, 1984.

————, ed. *A Bibliographical Guide to the History of Indian-White Relations in the United States.* Chicago: University of Chicago Press, 1977.

Quaife, Milo Milton, ed. *Echoes of the Past About California: Journal of General John Bidwell.* Chicago: Lakeside Press, 1928.

————. *Kit Carson's Autobiography.* Lincoln: University of Nebraska Press, Bison Books, 1972; orig. ed., 1935, Lakeside Press.

Rahill, Peter J. *The Catholic Indian Missions and Grant's Peace Policy, 1870–1884.* Washington, D.C.: Catholic University Press, 1953.

Reavis, L. U. *The Life and Military Services of General William Selby Harney.* St. Louis: Bryan, Brand, 1878.

Reinfeld, Fred. *Pony Express.* Lincoln: University of Nebraska Press, Bison Books, 1973; orig. ed., 1966, Macmillan.

Richmond, R. W., and R. W. Mardock, eds. *Readings in the History of the American Frontier.* Lincoln: University of Nebraska Press, 1966.

Riegel, Robert Edgar. *The Story of the Western Railroads.* Lincoln: University of Nebraska Press, Bison Books, 1964; orig. ed., New York: Macmillan, 1926.

Riegel, Robert Edgar, and Robert G. Athearn. *America Moves West.* 4th ed. New York: Holt, Rinehart and Winston, 1964.

Richardson, Albert Dean. *Beyond the Mississippi.* American Publishing, 1866.

Rogin, Michael Paul. *Fathers and Children: Andrew Jackson and the Subjugation of the American Indian.* New York: Random House, 1975.

Ross, Alexander. *The Fur Hunters of the Far West.* Edited by Kenneth A. Spaulding. Norman: University of Oklahoma Press, 1956.

Rothensteiner, John. *History of the Archdiocese of St. Louis.* 2 vols. St. Louis: Blackwell Wielandy, 1927.

Ruby, Robert H., and John A. Brown. *The Spokane Indians: Children of the Sun.* Norman: University of Oklahoma Press, 1970.

————. *Indians of the Pacific Northwest.* Norman: University of Oklahoma Press, 1981.

Russell, Osborne. *Journal of a Trapper.* Edited by Aubrey L. Haines. Lincoln: University of Nebraska Press, Bison Books, 1965; orig. ed., 1955, Oregon Historical Society.

Sandoz, Mari. *The Buffalo Hunters.* New York: Hastings House, 1954.

Satz, Ronald N. *American Indian Policy in the Jacksonian Era.* Lincoln: University of Nebraska Press, Bison Books, 1976.

Scharf, J. Thomas. *History of St. Louis, City and County.* 2 vols. Philadelphia: Louis H. Everts, 1883.

Schell, Herbert S. *History of South Dakota*. Lincoln: University of Nebraska Press, 1961.

Schmeckebier, Laurence F. *The Office of Indian Affairs*. Baltimore: Johns Hopkins University Press, 1927.

Schoenberg, Wilfred P., S.J. *Paths to the Northwest: A Jesuit History of the Oregon Province*. Chicago: Loyola University Press, 1982.

————. *A History of the Catholic Church in the Pacific Northwest, 1743–1983*. Washington D.C.: Pastoral Press, 1987.

Settle, Raymond W., and Mary L. Settle. *Empire on Wheels*. Stanford, Calif.: Stanford University Press, 1949.

————. *Saddles and Spurs: Saga of the Pony Express*. Harrisburg, Pa.: Stackpole, 1955.

Sheehan, Bernard W. *Seeds of Extinction: Jeffersonian Philanthrophy and the American Indian*. Chapel Hill: University of North Carolina Press, 1973.

Sprague, Marshall. *A Gallery of Dudes*. Lincoln: University of Nebraska Press, Bison Books, 1979; orig. ed., 1966, Little, Brown.

————. *The Great Gates: The Story of the Rocky Mountain Passes*. Lincoln: University of Nebraska Press, Bison Books, 1981; orig. ed., 1964, Little, Brown.

Stanley, Henry M. *My Early Adventures in America and Asia*. 2 vols. New York: Scribner, 1895.

Starkloff, Carl F., S.J. *The People of the Center: American Indian Religion*. New York: Seabury Press, 1974.

Steele, Thomas J., S.J., and Ronald S. Brockways, eds. *W. S. Howlett's Life of Bishop Machebauf*. Denver: Regis College, 1987; orig. ed., 1908, Pueblo, Franklin Press.

Steffen, Jerome O. *William Clark: Jeffersonian Man on the Frontier*. Norman: University of Oklahoma Press, 1977.

————. *The American West: New Perspectives, New Dimensions*. Norman: University of Oklahoma Press, 1979.

Stevens, Walter B. *Centennial History of Missouri*. 2 vols. St. Louis: Clarke, 1921.

Sully, Langdon. *No Tears for the General: The Life of Alfred Sully, 1821–1879*. Palo Alto, Calif.: American West, 1974.

Sunder, John E. *Bill Sublette: Mountain Man*. Norman: University of Oklahoma Press, 1959.

————. *The Fur Trade on the Upper Missouri, 1840–1865*. Norman: University of Oklahoma Press, 1965.

————. *Joshua Pilcher: Fur Trader and Indian Agent*. Norman: University of Oklahoma Press, 1968.

Swanton, John R. *The Indian Tribes of North America*. Bureau of American Ethnology Bulletin 145. Washington, D.C.: GPO, 1952.

Terrell, John Upton. *The Arrow and the Cross: A History of the American Indian and the Missionaries*. Santa Barbara, Calif.: Capra Press, 1979.

Terrell, John Upton, and Donna M. Terrell. *Indian Women of the Western Morning*. New York: Dial Press, 1974.

Thomas, Davis, and Karin Ronnefeldt, eds. *People of the First Man*. New York: Dutton, 1976.

Thompson, Robert L. *Wiring a Continent.* New York: Arno Press, 1972.

Thwaites, Reuben G., ed. *Early Western Travels, 1748–1846.* 32 vols. Cleveland: Arthur H. Clark, 1904–7.

Trenholm, Virginia Cole. *The Arapahoes: Our People.* Norman: University of Oklahoma Press, 1970.

Trenholm, Virginia Cole, and Maurine Carey. *The Shoshonis: Sentinels of the Rockies.* Norman: University of Oklahoma, 1964.

Trennert, Robert A. *Alternative to Extinction: Federal Indian Policy and Beginnings of the Reservation System, 1846–1851.* Philadelphia: Temple University Press, 1975.

Turner, Katharine C. *Red Men Calling on the Great White Father.* Norman: University of Oklahoma Press, 1951.

Unruh, John D., Jr. *The Plains Across: The Overland Emigrants and the Trans-Mississippi West, 1840–1860.* Urbana: University of Illinois Press, 1979.

Utley, Robert M. *The Last Days of the Sioux Nation.* New Haven, Conn.: Yale University Press, 1963.

———. *Frontiersmen in Blue: The United States Army and the Indian, 1848–1865.* Lincoln: University of Nebraska Press, Bison Books, 1981; orig. ed., New York: Macmillan, 1967.

———. *Frontier Regulars: The United States Army and the Indian, 1866–1891.* Lincoln: University of Nebraska Press, Bison Books, 1984; orig. ed., New York: Macmillan, 1973.

———. *The Indian Frontier of the American West, 1846–1890.* Albuquerque: University of New Mexico Press, 1984.

Utley, Robert M., and Wilcomb E. Washburn. *Indian Wars.* New York: American Heritage, 1987; orig. ed., 1977, American Heritage.

Vestal, Stanley. *Joe Meek: The Merry Mountain Man.* Lincoln: University of Nebraska Press, Bison Books, 1963; orig. ed., 1952, Caxton.

———. *Jim Bridger: Mountain Man.* Lincoln: University of Nebraska Press, Bison Books, 1970; orig. ed., 1946, Morrow.

———. *Sitting Bull, Champion of the Sioux.* Norman: University of Oklahoma Press, 1980; orig. ed., 1932, Houghton Mifflin.

Victor, Frances Fuller. *The River of the West: Adventures of Joe Meek.* Edited by Winfred Blevins. Missoula, Mont.: Mountain Press, 1983.

Viola, Herman J. *Thomas L. McKenney: Architect of United States Indian Policy.* Chicago: Sage, 1974.

———. *Diplomats in Buckskin: A History of Indian Delegations in Washington City.* Washington, D.C.: Smithsonian Institution, 1981.

Vogel, Virgil J. *This Country Was Ours: A Documentary History of the American Indians.* New York: Harper and Row, 1972.

Ware, Eugene F. *The Indian War of 1864.* Topeka, Kans.: Crane, 1911.

Washburn, Wilcomb E. *Red Man's Land, White Man's Law.* New York: Scribner, 1971.

———. *The Indian in America.* New York: Harper and Row, 1975.

Wesley, Edgar B. *Guarding the Frontier, 1815–1825.* Minneapolis: University of Minnesota Press, 1935.

Whipple, Henry Benjamin. *Lights and Shadows of a Long Episcopate*. New York: Macmillan, 1900.

White, Leslie A., and Clyde Walton, eds. *Lewis Henry Morgan: The Indian Journals, 1859–1862*. Ann Arbor: University of Michigan Press, 1959.

Wilhelm, Paul, Duke of Württemberg. *Travels in North America 1822–1824*. Translated by W. Robert Nitske, edited by Savoie Lottinville. Norman: University of Oklahoma Press, 1973.

Worcester, Donald E., ed. *Forked Tongues and Broken Treaties*. Caldwell, Idaho: Caxton, 1975.

ARTICLES

Abel, Annie H. "Indian Reservations in Kansas and the Extinguishment of Their Titles." *Kansas Historical Collections*, 8 (1903–4), pp. 72–109.

———. "History of Events Resulting in Indian Consolidation West of the Mississippi." *American Historical Association*, 1 (1906): 233–50.

———. "Proposals for an Indian State, 1778–1878." *American Historical Association*, 1 (1907): 87–104.

Altier, Keith. "Robert Meldrum and the Crow Peltry Trade." *Montana: The Magazine of Western History*, 36, no. 3 (1986): 36–47.

Anderson, Harry H. "The Controversial Sioux Amendment to the Fort Laramie Treaty of 1851." *Nebraska History*, 37 (1956): 201–20.

———. "Harney vs. Twiss: Nebraska Territory, 1856." *Westerners Brand Book* (Chicago), 20 (1963): 1–8.

Antrei, Albert. "Father Pierre De Smet." *Montana: The Magazine of Western History*, 13 (1963): 24–43.

Barry, Louise, ed. "William Clark's Diary 1826–1831." *Kansas Historical Quarterly*, 16 (1948): 1–40, 136–75, 274–306, 384–411.

Bidwell, John. "The First Emigrant Train to California." *Century Magazine*, 19 (1890–91): 106–30.

Bray, Kingsley M. "Lone Horn's Peace: A New View of Sioux-Crow Relations, 1852–1858." *Nebraska History*, 66 (1985): 24–43.

Brodman, Estelle. "The Great Eccentric: Dr. J. N. McDowell." *Washington University Magazine*, 51, no. 1 (1980).

Brooks, George R. "The Private Journal of Robert Campbell." *Missouri Historical Society Bulletin*, 20 (1963): 3–24; (1964): 107–18.

Burns, Robert I. "Roman Catholic Missions in the Northwest." In *Handbook of North American Indians*, vol. 4, *History of Indian-White Relations*, ed. Wilcomb E. Washburn, pp. 494–99. Washington: Smithsonian Institution Press, 1988.

Carley, Kenneth. "As Red Men Viewed It." *Minnesota History*, 38 (1962): 126–40.

Carter, Clarence E. "The Burr-Wilkinson Intrigue in St. Louis." *Missouri Historical Society Bulletin*, 10 (1954): 429–46.

Case, Ralph Hoyt. "Golconda to the Whites: Golgotha to the Sioux." *Laramie Treaty Centennial Program*, September 1951.

Cobb, Josephine. "Alexander Gardner." *Image*, 7, no. 6 (1958): 125–36.

Coe, H. C. "An Indian Agent's Experience in the War of 1866." *Oregon Historical Quarterly*, 14 (1913): 65–67.

Combs, Barry B. "The Union Pacific Railroad and the Early Settlement of Nebraska, 1868–1880." *Nebraska History,* 50 (1969): 1–21.

Corrigan, J. M., S.J. "Father De Smet." *Records of American Catholic Historical Society of Philadelphia,* 27 (1916): 95–112, 262–72.

Creel, George. "The Black Robe." *Collier's,* September 26, 1931, pp. 27–57.

Davis, William L., S.J. "Peter John De Smet: The Years of Preparation, 1801–1837." *Pacific Northwest Quarterly,* 32 (1941): 167–96.

———. "Peter John De Smet: Mission to the Potawatomie, 1837–1840." *Pacific Northwest Quarterly,* 33 (1942): 123–52.

———. "Peter John De Smet: The Journey of 1840." *Pacific Northwest Quarterly,* 35 (1944): 29–43, 121–52.

Donnelly, William P. (S.J.) "Nineteenth Century Jesuit Reductions in the United States." *Mid-America,* 17 (1935): 69–83.

Doyle, Susan Badger. "Journeys to the Land of Gold: Emigrants on the Bozeman Trail, 1863–1866." *Montana: The Magazine of Western History,* 41 (1991): 54–66.

Ellis, Richard N. "The Humanitarian Soldiers." *Journal of Arizona History,* 10 (1969): 53–66.

———. "Bent, Carson, and the Indians, 1865." *Colorado Magazine,* 46 (1969): 55–68.

———. "General Pope's Report on the West, 1866." *Kansas Historical Quarterly,* 35 (1969): 345–72.

———. "The Humanitarian Generals." *Western Historical Quarterly,* 3 (1972): 169–78.

Ellis, Richard N., and Charlie R. Steen, eds. "An Indian Delegation to France, 1725." *Illinois State Historical Society Journal,* 67 (1974): 385–405.

Ewers, John C. "The Indian Trade of the Upper Missouri Before Lewis and Clark." *Missouri Historical Society Bulletin,* 10 (1954): 429–46.

———. "Iroquois Indians in the Far West." *Montana: Magazine of Western History,* 13, no. 2 (1963): 2–10.

Faherty, William B., S.J. "Peter Verhaegen: Pioneer Missouri Educator and Church Administrator." *Missouri Historical Review,* 60 (1965–66): 407–15.

Farnham, Wallace D. "The Pacific Railroad Act of 1862." *Nebraska History,* 43 (1962): 141–68.

Forbis, Richard G. "The Flathead Apostasy, an Interpretation." *Montana: The Magazine of Western History,* 1, no. 4 (1951): 35–40.

Gailland, Maurice, S.J. "Early Years at St. Mary's Pottowatomie Mission: From the Diary of Father Maurice Gailland, S.J." Edited by James M. Burke. *Kansas Historical Quarterly,* 20 (1953):501–29.

Gallagher, Ruth. "The Indian Agent in the United States Before 1850," "The Indian Agent in the United States Since 1850." *Iowa Journal of History and Politics,* 14 (1916): 1–55, 173–238.

Garraghan, Gilbert J., S.J., ed. "Recollections of the Rocky Mountains," by Nicolas Point, S.J. *Woodstock Letters,* 11 (1882): 298–321; 12 (1883): 3–22, 133–53, 261–68; 13 (1884): 3–13.

――――. "Father De Smet: History Maker." *Illinois Catholic Historical Review,* 6, no. 3 (1924): 168–80.

――――. "Father De Smet's Sioux Peace Mission of 1868 and the Journal of Charles Galpin." *Mid-America,* 13 (1930): 141–63.

Gittinger, Roy. "The Separation of Nebraska and Kansas From the Indian Territory." *Mississippi Valley Historical Review,* 3 (1917): 442–61.

Gray, John S. "The Story of Mrs. Picotte-Galpin, a Sioux Heroine." *Montana Magazine of Western History,* 36, nos. 2, 3 (1986).

Greg, Kate L. "The War of 1812 on the Missouri Frontier." *Missouri Historical Review,* 33 (1938–39): 3–22, 184–202, 326–48.

――――. "Fort Osage." *Missouri Historical Review,* 24 (1940): 439–88.

Hafen, LeRoy R. "Etienne Provost." In LeRoy R. Hafen, ed., *Mountain Men and the Fur Trade,* 6:371–85.

Harkness, James. "The Diary of James Harkness of the Firm of La Barge, Harkness and Company." *Historical Society of Montana,* 2 (1896), pp. 343–61.

Holder, Preston. "The Fur Trade as Seen From the Indian Point of View." In John McDermott, *The Frontier Re-Examined,* pp. 111–27. Urbana: University of Illinois Press, 1967.

Hoopes, Alban W. "Thomas S. Twiss, Indian Agent on the Upper Platte, 1855–1861." *Mississippi Valley Historical Review,* 20 (1933): 353–64.

Horsman, Reginald. "Recent Trends and New Directions in Native American History." In Jerome O. Steffan, ed., *The American West,* 1979.

――――. "Well-Trodden Paths and Fresh Byways: Recent Writings On Native American History." *Reviews in American History* (1982): 234–44.

Howard, Allison. "Captain John Mullan." *Washington Historical Quarterly,* 25 (1934): 185–202.

Hughes, Thomas A., S.J. "The Journal of a Western Missionary." *Woodstock Letters,* 21, no. 2: 144–60.

Jacobs, Hubert, ed. "The Potawatomi Mission, 1854" (letter of Maurice Gailland). *Mid-America,* 36 (1954): 220–48.

Jensen, Dana O. "Historic St. Joseph's." *Missouri Historical Society Bulletin,* 19, no. 3 (1963): 272–77.

Kane, Lucile M. "The Sioux Treaty and the Traders." *Minnesota History,* 32, no. 2 (1951): 65–80.

Kelsey, Harry. "Background to Sand Creek." *Colorado Magazine,* 45, no. 4 (1968): 279–300.

――――. "William P. Dole and Mr. Lincoln's Indian Policy." *Journal of the West* (1971): 484–92.

――――. "The Doolittle Report of 1867: Its Preparation and Shortcomings." *Arizona and the West,* 17, no. 2 (1975): 107–20.

――――. "Charles E. Mix," "William P. Dole." In Kvasnicka and Viola, eds., *Commissioners of Indian Affairs,* pp. 77–98.

Killoren, John J., S.J. "Come to Us, Blackrobe," *The Wind River Rendezvous* (1973, no. 4); "The Indians of the 'Western Movies',", (1978, no. 2); "The Rendezvous on the Green," (1979, no. 4); "The Great Smoke at Fort Laramie," (1982, no. 1); "The Buffalo Culture of the Plains Indians," (1983, no. 2).

————. "The Doctor's Scrapbook: A Collaboration of Linton and De Smet." *Gateway Heritage*, 6, no. 3 (1985–86): 2–9.

Klein, Ada Paris, ed. "The Fur Trade." *Missouri Historical Review*, 44 (1949–50): 48–65.

Kosok, Paul. "An Unknown Letter from Lewis H. Morgan to Abraham Lincoln." *University of Rochester Library Bulletin*, 6 (1951): 34–40.

Kvasnicka, Robert M. "George W. Manypenny." In Kvasnicka and Viola, eds., *Commissioners of Indian Affairs*, pp. 57–67.

Lecompte, Janet. "John Poisal." In LeRoy R. Hafen, ed., *Mountain Men and the Fur Trade*, 6:353–58.

Lindley, Harlow. "William Clark: The Indian Agent." *Mississippi Valley Historical Association*, 2 (1910): 63–75.

Loos, John L. "William Clark: Indian Agent." *Kansas Historical Quarterly*, 3 (1971): 29–38.

Mattes, Merrill J. "Behind the Legend of Colter's Hell: Early Exploration of Yellowstone Park." *Mississippi Valley Historical Review*, 36, no. 2 (1949): 251–82.

Mattison, Ray H. "The Indian Frontier on the Upper Missouri to 1865." *Nebraska History*, 39 (1958): 241–66.

Mattison, Ray H., ed. "The Harney Expedition Against the Sioux: Journal of Capt. John B. S. Todd." *Nebraska History*, 42 (1962): 89–130.

McCann, Lloyd E. "The Grattan Massacre." *Nebraska History*, 37 (1956): 1–25.

McDermott, John F. "De Smet's Illustrator: Point." *Nebraska History*, 33 (1952): 34–45.

Minnesota Catholic Conference. "A New Beginning." *Bulletin, Catholic Conference of Minnesota*, April 1975.

Morgan, Dale L. "The Administration of Indian Affairs in Utah, 1851–1858." *Pacific Historical Review*, no. 17 (1948): 383–409.

Morgan, Lewis Henry. "The Indian Question in 1878." *The Nation*, 27 (Nov. 1873): 332–33.

————. "Hue and Cry Against the Indians," "Factory System For Indian Reservations." *The Nation*, 23 (July 1876): 40–41, 58–59.

Morris, Ralph C. "The Notion of a Great American Desert East of the Rockies." *Mississippi Valley Historical Review*, 13 (1926): 190–200.

Mullin, Frank Anthony. "Father De Smet and the Pottawatomie Indian Mission." *Iowa Journal of History and Politics*, 23 (1925): 192–216.

Neil, W. N. "The Territorial Governor as Indian Superintendent in the Trans-Mississippi West." *Mississippi Valley Historical Review*, 43 (1956–57): 213–37.

O'Connor, Thomas F. "De Smet, Frontier Missionary." *Mid-America*, 17 (1935): 191–96.

Oglesby, Richard E. "The Fur Trade as Business." In John F. McDermott, *The Frontier Re-Examined*, pp. 111–27. Urbana: University of Illinois Press, 1967.

O'Hara, Edwin V. "De Smet in Oregon." *Oregon Historical Quarterly*, 10 (1909): 239–62.

O'Malley, William J., S.J. "Peter De Smet: Friend of Sitting Bull." In W. J.

O'Malley, *The Fifth Week,* pp. 62–66. Chicago: Loyola University Press, 1976.

Pfaller, Louis L. "The Galpin Journal: Dramatic Record of an Odyssey of Peace." *Montana: The Magazine of Western History,* (1968): 2–23.

Prucha, Francis Paul, S.J. "Indian Removal and the Great American Desert." *Indiana Magazine of History,* 59 (1963):298–322.

Robinson, De Lorme W. "Editorial Notes on Historical Sketch: De Smet and Pizi, Gall." *South Dakota Historical Collections,* 1 (1902):130–54.

Schaeffer, Claude. "The First Jesuit Mission to the Flatheads, 1840–1850: A Study in Culture Conflicts." *Pacific Northwest Quarterly,* 28 (1937) 227–50.

Sherman, Thomas E., S.J. "Across the Continent." Memoir from 1877 diary. *Woodstock Letters,* 11 (1882): 141–63.

Shields, Lillian B. "Relations With the Cheyennes and Arapahoes in Colorado to 1861." *Colorado Magazine,* 4 (1927): 145–54.

Short, Anthony J., S.J. "The Centennial of St. Stephens Indian Mission." *Wind River Rendezvous* (1984, nos. 2, 3).

Sibley, Henry H. "Reminiscences: Historical and Personal." *Collections of Minnesota Historical Society,* 1, pp. 374–96.

Spiess, Lincoln B. "Mat Hastings, Artist: 1834–1919." *Missouri Historical Society Bulletin,* 36 (1980–81): 152–55.

Starkloff, Carl, S.J. "American Indian Religion and Christianity: Confrontation and Dialogue." *Journal of Ecumenical Studies,* 8, no. 2 (1971): 317–40.

———. "Mission Method and the American Indian." *Theological Studies,* 38, no. 4 (1977): 621–53.

Sunder, John E. "John O'Fallon Delaney's 'Pocket Diary of 1862.'" *Bulletin Missouri Historical Society,* 19 (1962): 3–22; 20 (1963): 127–49.

Swagerty, William R. "Marriage and Settlement Patterns of Rocky Mountain Trappers and Traders." *Western Historical Quarterly,* 11 (1980): 159–80.

Taff, Robert. "Additional Notes on the Gardner Photographs of Kansas." *Kansas Historical Quarterly,* 6, no. 2 (1937): 175–77.

Thompson, Larry. "Father Pierre Jean De Smet." *Montana, The Magazine of Western History* (1985): 52–61.

Trennert, Robert A. "William P. Medill," "Orlando Brown," "Luke Lea." In Kvasnicka and Viola, eds., *Commissioners of Indian Affairs,* pp. 29–56.

———. "William Medill's War with the Indian Traders, 1847." *Ohio History,* 82 (1973): 45–62.

Twiss, Thomas S. "Letter of Thomas S. Twiss, Indian Agent." *Annals of Wyoming,* 17 (1945): 148–52.

Unrau, William E. "Lewis V. Bogy," "Nathaniel Green Taylor." In Kvasnicka and Viola, eds., *Commissioners of Indian Affairs,* pp. 109–22.

U. S. Catholic Bishops. "Statement of U.S. Catholic Bishops on American Indians." *United States Catholic Conference,* May 1977.

Utley, Robert M. "The Celebrated Peace Policy of General Grant." *North Dakota History,* 20 (1953): 121–42.

————. "The Dash To Promontory." *Utah Historical Quarterly,* 29 (1961): 99–117.

————. "A Chained Dog, The Indian-Fighting Army: Military Strategy on the Western Frontier." *American West,* 6 (1969): 16–21.

Viles, Jonas. "Missouri in 1820." *Missouri Historical Review,* 15 (1920): 36–52.

Way, Royal B. "The United States Factory System For Trading With the Indians, 1795–1822." *Mississippi Valley Historical Review,* 6 (1919): 223–34.

Waltmann, Henry G. "Circumstantial Reformer: President Grant and the Indian Problem." *Arizona and the West,* 13, no. 4 (1971): 323–42.

————. "Ely Samuel Parker." In Kvasnicka and Viola, eds., *Commissioners of Indian Affairs,* pp. 123–34.

Wesley, Edgar B., ed. "Diary of Kennerly, 1823–1826." *Missouri Historical Society Collections,* 6 (1928): 41–97.

Wheeler, Douglas L. "Henry M. Stanley's Letters to the *Missouri Democrat.*" *Bulletin, Missouri Historical Society* (1980): 269–86.

Whipple, Henry B. "The Indian System." *North American Review,* 99 (Oct. 1864): 449–64.

Whitaker, Robert J. "The Early Explorations of Cheyenne Pass." *Annals of Wyoming,* 47, no. 2 (1975): 221–33.

Index